ILLICIT

Moisés Naím

ILLICIT

HOW SMUGGLERS, TRAFFICKERS, AND COPYCATS ARE
HIJACKING THE GLOBAL ECONOMY

Doubleday

New York London Toronto Sydney Auckland

PUBLISHED BY DOUBLEDAY
a division of Random House, Inc.

DOUBLEDAY and the portrayal of an anchor with a dolphin are
registered trademarks of Random House, Inc.

Library of Congress Cataloging-in-Publication Data

Naím, Moisés.
    Illicit : how smugglers, traffickers and copycats are hijacking
the global economy / Moisés Naím.— 1st ed.
      p.   cm.
    Includes bibliographical references and index.
    ISBN 0-385-51392-5
    1. Transnational crime. 2. Drug traffic. 3. Illegal arms transfers.
4. Intellectual property infringement. 5. Illegal aliens. 6. Money
laundering. 7. Globalization—Economic aspects. I. Title.

HV6252.N35 2005
364.1'35—dc22
2005045509

PRINTED IN THE UNITED STATES OF AMERICA

October 2005

First Edition

10 9 8 7 6 5 4 3 2 1

To Susana, Adriana, Claudia, and Andrés

CONTENTS

ILLICIT

THE WARS WE ARE LOSING

The famous former United States president, for eight years the most powerful man on earth, was born in a small country town blessed with "very good feng shui." As an adolescent struggling to excel in spite of his modest rural circumstances, he "admired the ambition of Gu Yanwu, who said we should walk 10,000 miles and read 10,000 books." Often during his political career he sought wisdom and guidance in the sayings of Chairman Mao. As for the starstruck young intern with whom he had an affair that nearly destroyed his presidency, he had this to say: "She was very fat."

The Chinese version of Bill Clinton's autobiography *My Life* that hit the streets in July 2004, months before the official, licensed translation, was obviously a grotesque forgery. Its appearance served as a welcome of sorts, introducing the former president to one of the more dubious honors of modern writerly fame. In Colombia, for instance, an entire cottage industry specializes in unlicensed copies of the works of the country's great novelist Gabriel García Márquez. In 2004 a master copy of the Nobel Prize winner's first novel in ten years vanished without a trace from the printing press. Days later, a pirate edition could be found on Bogotá sidewalks, its text accurate but for the final revisions that García Márquez, a perfectionist, had been waiting until the last moment to turn in.

Laughable as they may seem, little separates these scams from others with far more dire consequences. The same "knockoff markets" sell not only bootleg books and DVDs but pirated Microsoft and Adobe software; not only faux Gucci and Chanel accessories but bogus brand-name machinery made with substandard parts that can cause industrial accidents; not only placebo Viagra for gullible mail-order shoppers, but also expired or adulterated medicines that don't cure but kill. In defiance of regulations and taxes, treaties and laws, virtually anything of value is offered for sale in today's global marketplace—including illegal drugs, endangered species, human chattel for sex slavery and sweatshops, human cadavers and live organs for transplant, machine guns and rocket launchers, and centrifuges and precursor chemicals used in nuclear weapons development.

This trade is illicit trade. It is trade that breaks the rules—the laws, regulations, licenses, taxes, embargos, and all the procedures that nations employ to organize commerce, protect their citizens, raise revenues, and enforce moral codes. It includes purchases and sales that are strictly illegal everywhere and others that may be illegal in some countries and accepted in others. Illicit trade is highly disruptive, of course, to legitimate businesses—except when it isn't. For as we shall see, there is an enormous gray area between legal and illegal transactions, a gray area that the illicit traders have turned to great advantage.

The marketing and distribution channels that transport all this contraband—and the financial circuits that move the hundreds of billions of dollars that it generates every year—aren't exactly hidden from view. Some of the physical marketplaces can even be looked up in tourist guides to the world's great cities: Silk Alley in Beijing, Charoen Krung Road in Bangkok, Canal Street in New York City. Others, like the arms and drugs bazaar town of Dara Adam Khel in northwest Pakistan or the multiproduct trafficking and money-laundering center of Ciudad del Este in Paraguay, serving the Argentine and Brazilian markets, aren't exactly leisure spots but are no less widely known. Factories in the Philippines or China that produce licensed manufactured goods may run unauthorized second shifts with shoddy components. Shipments of methamphetamine and bootleg videos and night-vision military goggles often travel in the same containers and cargo holds as loads of semiconductors and frozen fish and grapefruit. The proceeds of illicit trade merge with the greatest of ease into the vast daily flow of interbank settlements and Western Union money transfers. And the Internet not only boosts the speed and efficiency of all of these trades but expands the possibilities by, for instance, hosting online markets for prostitutes from Moldova and Ukraine destined for shipment to markets in Britain, France, Germany, Japan, and the United States.

Neither are those who benefit from illicit trade always careful to hide in the shadows. Many exercise their trade in the open, daring authorities to crack down on them—or inviting them to collude. In Thailand, a massage parlor operator ran for public office in 2003 on a platform of criticizing the police—in effect, running to defend his own interests in the trade in human beings while tapping into broader public discontent. In neighboring Cambodia, the national police are partners with international watchdogs in cracking down on the traffic in children for sex, but the local units collect payment envelopes from known traffickers in full public view. Illicit traders may have forsaken grand, hubristic gestures—Pablo Escobar Gaviria, the famed drug kingpin, in his heyday offered to pay up Colombia's entire national debt—but they have grown sophisticated in forming front companies with complex financial structures spanning numerous countries, blurring their traces so well that they can safely operate in the open. Which means that not only is illicit trade on the rise, but its interplay with social crisis—conflict, corruption, exploitation—is more complex than it has been since the abolition of the Atlantic slave trade.

THREE ILLUSIONS

Yet in the face of all the evidence, at least three grand illusions persist in the way we—the public and the politicians in whom we place our trust—address global illicit trade.

First is the illusion that there is nothing new. Illicit trade is age-old, a continuous facet and side effect of market economies or of commerce in general. Illicit trade's ancestor, smuggling, traces back to ancient times, and many a "thieves' market" survives in the world's commercial hubs. Therefore, skeptics would argue that since smuggling has always been more a nuisance than a scourge, it is a threat we can learn to live with as we have always done.

But this skepticism ignores the important transformations of the 1990s. Changes in political and economic life, along with revolutionary technologies in the hands of civilians, have dissolved the sealants that governments traditionally relied on to secure their national borders. At the same time, the market-oriented economic reforms that swept the world in the 1990s boosted incentives to break through these sealants—legally or otherwise. Not only did the hold of governments on borders weaken, but the reforms amplified the rewards awaiting those who were prepared to break the rules.

Technology enlarged the market, not just geographically by lowering transport costs but also by making possible the trade in a whole range of goods that didn't exist before, such as pirated software or genetically modified marijuana. New technologies also made it possible to trade internationally products that in the past were hard or impossible to transport or hold in "inventory"—human kidneys, for instance. Markets, of course, were also enlarged when governments deregulated previously closed or tightly controlled economies and allowed foreigners to visit, trade, and invest more freely.

The massive transfer of goods and equipment once under the exclusive control of national armies into private hands released into the market products ranging from rocket launchers to SCUD missiles and nuclear designs and machinery. Moreover, governments also boosted illicit trade by criminalizing new activities. File sharing through the internet, for example, is a newly illegal activity that has added millions to the ranks of illicit traders.

A clue to the explosion of illicit trade is the relentless rise of money laundering. Eventually, every illicit line of business generates money that needs to be laundered. And there is ample evidence that despite all the precautions and enforcement measures now in place, there is more and more dirty money floating in the international financial system now than ever before.

Yet until now, with the exception of narcotics, illicit trade has simply not been a priority in international law and treaty making, or in international police work and cooperative law enforcement. The United Nations devised common language to describe it only in the year 2000, and most countries have a long way to go in adapting their laws to international standards, let alone enforcing them. It took the advent of software piracy and the birth of "intellectual property crime" to add a fillip to international efforts against counterfeiting. And trafficking in persons—the most morally outrageous of all the forms of illicit trade—was defined in the 1990s only by academics and activists, and made the subject of a specific, comprehensive law in the United States in 2000. (Only seventeen other countries have done the same.)

The second illusion is that illicit trade is just about crime. It is true that criminal activities surged and became global in the 1990s. But thinking about international illicit trade as just another manifestation of criminal behavior misses a larger, more consequential point. Global criminal activities are *transforming the international system,* upending the rules, creating new players, and reconfiguring power in international politics and economics. The United States attacked Iraq because it feared that Saddam Hussein had acquired weapons of mass destruction. But during the same time a stealthy network led by A. Q. Khan, a Pakistani engineer, was profiting by selling nuclear bomb–making technology to whoever could pay for it.

Throughout the twentieth century, to the extent that governments paid attention to illicit trade at all, they framed it—to their public, and to themselves—as the work of criminal organizations. Consciously or not, investigators around the world took the model of the American and Sicilian Mafia as their blueprint. Propelled by this mind-set, the search for traffickers—almost always in drugs—led to what investigators thought could be only corporate-like organizations: structured, disciplined, and hierarchical. The Colombian cartels, Chinese tongs, Hong Kong triads, Japanese yakuza, and eventually after 1989 the Russian mafiya were all approached this way: first as criminal organizations, only later as traders. In most countries, the laws employed to prosecute illicit traders remain those born of the fight against organized crime, like the racketeering and corrupt organizations (RICO) statutes in the United States.

Only recently has this mind-set began to shift. Thanks to al-Qaeda the world now knows what a network of highly motivated individuals owing allegiance to no nation and empowered by globalization can do. The problem is that the world still thinks of these networks mostly in terms of terrorism. Yet, as the pages ahead show, profit can be as powerful a motivator as God. Networks of stateless traders in illicit goods are changing the world as much as terrorists are—probably more. But a world obsessed with terrorists has not yet taken notice.

The third illusion is the idea that illicit trade is an "underground" phenomenon. Even accepting that trafficking has grown in volume and complexity, many—not least politicians—seek to relegate it to a different world than that of ordinary, honest citizens and constituents. The language we use to describe illicit trade and to frame our efforts to contain it betrays the enduring power of this illusion. The word *offshore*—as in *offshore finance*—vividly captures this sense that illicit trade takes place somewhere else. So does *black market,* or the supposedly clearly distinct *clean* and *dirty money.* All signify a clarity, an ability to draw moral and economic lines and patrol their boundaries that is confounded in practice. This is the most dangerous of all these illusions, because it treads on moral grounds and arguably lulls citizens—and hence public opinion—into a sense of heightened righteousness and false security.

This point is not about moral relativism. A thief is a thief. But how do you describe a woman who manages to provide some material well-being to her destitute family in Albania or Nigeria by entering another country illegally and working the streets as a prostitute or as a peddler of counterfeited goods? What about bankers in Manhattan or London who take home big year-end bonuses as a reward for having stocked their bank's vaults with the deposits of "high–net worth individuals" whose only known job has been with a government in another country? Many American high-schoolers can procure a joint of marijuana more easily than they can purchase a bottle of vodka or a pack of cigarettes, and they know they don't really run any major risk in doing so. Meanwhile honest Colombian judges or police officers are routinely gunned down in a war on drugs that the U.S. government funds to the tune of $40 billion a year. These are not just infuriating contradictions, unfair double standards, or interesting paradoxes. They are powerful clues about how age-old human mores have acquired new hues.

ELUSIVE AND POWERFUL

Since the early 1990s, global illicit trade has embarked on a great mutation. It is the same mutation as that of international terrorist organizations like al-Qaeda or Islamic Jihad—or for that matter, of activists for the global good like the environmental movement or the World Social Forum. All have moved away from fixed hierarchies and toward decentralized networks; away from controlling leaders and toward multiple, loosely linked, dispersed agents and cells; away from rigid lines of control and exchange and toward constantly shifting transactions as opportunities dictate. It is a mutation that governments in the 1990s barely recognized and could not, in any case, hope to emulate.

The world's first unmistakable glimpse of this transformation came on September 11, 2001. Politicians would later say that on that day "the world changed." It might be more apt to say that on that day something about the world was revealed—at the very least, the incredible power now residing in the hands of an entirely new kind of international entity, inherently stateless and deeply elusive. As subsequent events demonstrated, even experts disagreed as to what they were observing, and what it might have to do with specific states and regimes.

Left unchecked, illicit trade can only pursue its already well advanced mutation. There is ample evidence that it offers terrorists and other miscreants means of survival and methods of financial transfer and exchange. Its effect on geopolitics will go further. In developing countries and those in transition from communism, criminal networks often constitute the most powerful vested interests confronting the government. In some countries, their resources and capabilities even surpass those of their governments. These capabilities often translate into political clout. Traffickers and their associates control political parties, own significant media operations, or are the major philanthropists behind nongovernmental organizations. This is a natural outcome in countries where no economic activity can match illicit trade in size or profits and therefore traffickers become the nation's "big business." And once their business becomes large and stable, trafficking networks do as big businesses are prone to do everywhere else: diversify into other businesses and invest in politics. After all, gaining access and influence and seeking government protection has always been part and parcel of big business.

Therefore not only are illicit networks tightly intertwined with licit private sector activities, but they are also deeply embedded within the public sector and the political system. And once they have spread into licit private corporations, political parties, parliaments, local governments, media groups, the courts, the military, and the nonprofit sector, trafficking networks assume a powerful—and in some countries unrivalled—influence on matters of state.

Perversely, the awareness of the ravaging effects of illicit trade often sparks nationalistic impulses and insular responses. Ironically, these reactions end up working in favor of the traffickers—for the more states seek to raise barriers against the flow of illicit goods, services, and labor, the more the traffickers stand to profit from their trade. National borders are a boon to criminals and a block to law enforcement agencies. Borders create profit opportunities for smuggling networks and weaken nation-states by limiting their ability to curb the onslaughts of the global networks that hurt their economies, corrupt their politics, and undermine their institutions.

This story is no longer just about crime. It is also about a new form of politics in the twenty-first century. And about the new economic realities that have brought to the fore a whole new set of political actors whose values may collide with yours and mine, and whose intentions threaten us all.

BLIND SPOTS

My interest in illicit trade comes out of a decade of work on the surprises of globalization. As editor of *Foreign Policy* magazine, it has been my job to track and understand the unanticipated consequences of the new connections between world politics and economics. As I encountered these surprises, learned the stories, and often had the chance to meet their protagonists, this professional interest evolved into a personal fascination. I wrote about financial crashes on one continent that rock countries oceans away, and on the ways in which new standards of human rights developed in Europe ended up transforming politics in Latin America. I studied how corruption became a political lightning rod more or less simultaneously around the world—and not because corruption was born in the 1990s. What surprised me the most, however, was how often my research on a host of seemingly unrelated topics led me to the world of illicit trade and global crime.

My background is not in law enforcement or criminology. But as I investigated the effects of globalization on international economics, finance, and governance—in rich and poor countries alike—I was inexorably pushed toward this topic. Travels in Russia, China, Eastern Europe, and Latin America convinced me that there was much going on in those regions—and in the world—that we could never understand unless we paid more attention to the role of criminal activities in shaping decisions, institutions, and outcomes.

My work at *Foreign Policy* also gave me a privileged and panoramic window into the changes the world was experiencing and the chance to discuss with some of the world's more insightful analysts and practitioners how they were interpreting these changes.

I also made a habit, however, of devoting some time everywhere I went to seek out police officers, prosecutors, journalists, and academics who could give me a glimpse of the illicit trade situation in their country. It quickly became clear that even in countries as diverse as Thailand, Colombia, Greece, Mexico, and China, these conversations had an uncanny resemblance. Illicit trade was bigger, more pervasive, and less understood than most people realized, including me. Up close its political consequences were evident and frightening. Yet their discussion was at best marginal. The more I looked, the more I found specialists who knew a lot about one aspect of global crime and far less about the others or the ties that connect them. I began to assemble my own list of perplexities, anecdotes, data, sources, thinkers, practitioners, and surprises about the different illicit markets.

I soon discovered that it was impossible to read the newspaper on any day anywhere in the world without spotting news about illicit trade. Most of the time it was presented as different stories, but for me these news items had become manifestations of a single, unified global phenomenon driven by the same improbable combination of old human impulses, new technologies, and changed politics. It also became apparent to me that neither reporters nor academics were affording the political consequences of the events they were writing about the importance that those on the front line of these fights kept telling me they had. I was also intrigued by the scant attention specialists in international relations and world politics were paying to the consequences of illicit trade on their subjects of study. Most of all, I was baffled by how an inherently economic phenomenon was customarily treated with moral denunciations and law enforcement remedies.

In early 2002 the American Society of International Law invited me to deliver the Annual Grotius Lecture, which I centered on my views on illicit trade. I titled it "The Five Wars of Globalization"—referring to the illicit markets for arms, drugs, human beings, intellectual property, and money—and it was published in slightly different versions in the *American University International Law*

Review and the following year in *Foreign Policy.* The article was reprinted by many other publications and enjoyed a broad dissemination worldwide. The publication of "Five Wars" encouraged many scholars, magistrates, and prosecutors, law enforcement and intelligence officers, journalists, and even victims of trafficking from around the world to share their views and experiences with me. Again I encountered stories from different trades, different countries, different continents, and different contexts. Yet the stories' patterns and even details shared extraordinary similarities. More important, they illuminated even more sharply the prevailing blind spots, both in the analytical lenses we use to make sense of what is going on and in the public policies that governments have chosen to address this problem. These blind spots too were uncannily similar. Thus, the idea of this book was born.

A note about data: The volumes of the illicit trades and the profits derived from them remain at best gross estimates. All the numbers in this book come from the most reliable sources possible—usually international organizations and governments or nongovernmental organizations whose work is generally deemed to be serious and reliable. Each of the facts, figures, and events mentioned in the text is referenced at the end of the book. Most of the individuals I interviewed are also named in the references, except of course those who would speak only on the condition of anonymity.

Still, while the figures used here are the best available, it is important to remember that these are estimates of secret activities. They may therefore either underestimate or overestimate the reality. Nonetheless, all the available evidence supports the central empirical argument of the book: the volume of these trades is larger and their operations much more complex and sophisticated today than they were in 1990. And as the chapters ahead show, we are beginning to understand how they really work and what their effects are.

Chapter 2

GLOBAL SMUGGLERS ARE CHANGING YOUR WORLD

There is the story we know. And then there is the other story.

Here is what we know: The last decade of the twentieth century changed the world. A sudden, unexpected eruption of new ideas and new technologies in turn changed politics and economics everywhere. Billions of lives were transformed. The demise of the Soviet Union discredited communism and gave free politics and free markets unprecedented popularity. As a result, the 1990s will go down in history as an example of a period when the power of ideas became obvious to all.

Those years will also be remembered as another period when the pace of technological change took everyone by surprise. New technologies shrank the world and made distance and geography less important than ever. During the 1990s the only thing that seemed to drop faster than the cost of shipping cargo from Shanghai to Los Angeles was the cost of making a phone call across the world. Traveling to places once prohibitively expensive to reach or politically off-limits suddenly became a normal experience for millions. The political consequences were as enormous as the economic ones. Democracy soared and during the 1990s the number of countries where elections were held reached an all-time high. So did stock markets, international trade, international capital flows, and the number of movies, books, messages, and phone calls that crossed borders.

That is the part we know. It is a story in which we all participated and one that has been the subject of plenty of books and ample media coverage. But another story runs alongside it. That story is just as crucial but far less known.

That story is about smuggling and, more generally, about crime. During the 1990s smugglers became more international, wealthier, and more politically influential than ever before. Global crime has not just soared in volume but, thanks to its ability to amass colossal profits, has also become a powerful *political* force. And the lenses through which we interpret world politics and economics need to be adjusted to this change—urgently.

Behind this political ascendancy of global criminal networks is a dynamic of globalization that is powerful, yet usually overlooked. That dynamic is the theme of this chapter. It is how the changes of the 1990s did not just empower criminals but at the very same time weakened the agencies in charge of fighting them. Criminal networks thrive on international mobility and their ability to take advantage of the opportunities that flow from the separation of marketplaces into sovereign states with borders. For criminals, frontiers create business opportunities and convenient shields. But for the government officials chasing the criminals, borders are often insurmountable obstacles. The privileges of national sovereignty are turning into burdens and constraints on governments. Because of this asymmetry, in the global clash between governments and criminals, governments are systematically losing. Everywhere.

The signs are all around us: visible, recognizable, with tangible effects on our daily lives. Illicit trade today permeates rich and poor societies alike. Old smuggling and trafficking specialties are revitalized and whole new lines of business are sprouting. Forms of illicit commerce that we thought we had ended for good, just as medicine eradicated smallpox, are instead back in business.

Consider slavery. It was supposed to be dead. Instead it's thriving, in the form of coerced sex, domestic work, and farmwork by illegal migrants working off never-ending debts levied by traffickers. Yes, many foreign workers around us have voluntarily chosen their condition as illegal immigrants. But many others have been coerced into their current predicament, the exploited victims of criminals who profit from an illicit market worth billions. Slavery is just one facet of a global trade in human beings across borders that affects at least 4 million people every year, most of them women and children, for an estimated value of $7 to $10 billion. Whole new trade routes have opened up, joining the republics of the former Soviet Union, South and Southeast Asia, West Africa, Latin America, Western Europe, and the United States in baroque networks of recruiters, touts, extortionists, hired muscle, transporters, safe houses, and online dispatchers that can procure a "worker" of any desired age, nationality, or physical characteristics and deliver her or him across continents in as little as forty-eight hours.

Or take the drug trade. We still speak of drug "cartels," but the drug business today has largely dissolved the heavy organized crime–like operations of the past and works in more nimble, less traceable ways. And business is good. A ferocious new boom in opium poppies, the raw material for heroin, exploded in Afghanistan after the war that ousted the Taliban, and production has taken off in places where it was previously unknown, such as Colombia. Meanwhile methamphetamines and "party drugs" like ketamine and Ecstasy have surged onto the market. Global drug seizures nearly doubled in volume between 1990 and 2002, with no evidence of consumption coming down. In fact, Southeast Asia has seen a surge of party drugs, countries on the new trade routes such as Brazil, Nigeria, and Uzbekistan are wrestling with unprecedented levels of addiction, and in the United States heroin and methamphetamines are reaching the crisis proportions that crack cocaine assumed in the late 1980s. All this despite the declared war on drugs, the largest deployment of money, technology, and personnel that humankind has ever devoted to stopping drugs from moving across borders.

Meanwhile, the international weapons trade has mutated and gone largely underground, with ominous implications. During the cold war era, arms trading was associated with the efforts of powerful governments—together with a few big-name companies—to lock in the loyalty of client states with fighter jets, frigates, or munitions. That part of the arms business is still enormous, but it is joined today by a vibrant private trade in small arms and light weapons, such as shoulder-launched missiles, AK-47 assault rifles, and rocket-propelled grenades or RPGs. According to the United Nations, since 1990 the small-arms trade has fueled close to fifty wars around the world, especially (though not only) in Africa. Vast amounts of cold war–era overstock have flowed onto the market. Thousands of informal, often invisible merchants today ply the trade once reserved for large corporations that catered to governments. Now, private armies, informal militias, guerrilla groups, and all kinds of new organizations—including a private security business that is booming worldwide as a result of rising crime rates—fuel the boom in the small-arms business. Looming behind all this is something more worrying still: the international traffic in the knowledge, equipment, and materials used to produce nuclear weapons.

And although "loose nukes" might not turn up at every street corner, counterfeits—another immense growth area for illicit trade—increasingly do. Improperly copied clothes, cosmetics, compact discs, and even motorcyles and cars are produced and consumed at unprecedented rates around the world, often in full knowledge that the brand is fake. Music and film copied or downloaded under dubious conditions are a staple of countless homes around the world, to say nothing of college dorm rooms. Software manufacturers dread the "one-disc" effect, a phenomenon in which a single counterfeited copy can propagate until it has taken over an entire country, pushing the legitimate product out of that market. Yet even in countries with high intellectual property standards, such as the United States, or in the European Union, piracy rates of one-quarter or more for popular software and operating systems are common.

No product is safe. Counterfeit medicines range from lifesaving generics to life-ending hazards like the fake cough medicine that killed close to a hundred children in Haiti because it contained automobile antifreeze. In all these businesses the complicity of public officials and senior military officers is not only obvious but indispensable.

The financial industry, which exploded in the 1990s, has not been spared in the onslaught. Quite the contrary: money laundering and tax evasion have grown in proportion to the ballooning size of the international financial system, or faster. In 1998 the then director of the International Monetary Fund, Michel Camdessus, estimated the global flow of dirty money at 2 to 5 percent of the global economy, a figure he called "beyond imagination." Yet more recent estimates place the flows of laundered money at up to 10 percent of global GDP. It is clearly time to expand the reach of our imagination: dirty money is a fundamental part of the world economy. No longer the preserve of exotic "offshore" islands like the Caymans or the Isle of Man, money laundering has worked its way into the sinews of the financial system. The high speed, interconnectedness, and global reach of transactions have made common the practices of juggling accounts, establishing front companies, channeling funds through dizzying arrays of intermediaries, and blending legitimate and illicit uses. The island of Manhattan or the City, London's financial district, are as much the front line in the fight against money laundering as are Vanuatu or Curaçao.

The list of thriving contraband businesses goes on: Ivory from the tusks of elephants illegally culled in South Africa and Zimbabwe, openly sold in Guangzhou, China. Human kidneys from live sellers ferried from Brazil to South Africa and transplanted into German customers recruited online by Israeli brokers. Ancient Inca or Iranian antiquities spirited away from protected sites and sold in the art galleries of Paris and London. Exotic animals like pangolins and pythons. Chemicals that deplete the ozone layer. Long-lost Matisse and Renoir paintings. Junk computer parts saturated in mercury sent to dumping grounds in locales where environmental protection laws can be evaded. "Blood" or "conflict" diamonds illegally mined and smuggled from war zones. All of it for sale, in a thriving global marketplace that has been easy to overlook because it has merged so effectively and seamlessly into the legitimate market, using the same tools and often involving the same people—whether as suppliers, transporters, financiers, wholesalers, brokers, or final customers like you and me.

Illicit trade has broken the boundary and surged into our own lives. We can no longer ever be sure—not sure of whom our purchases benefit, not sure of what our investments support, not sure of what material or financial connections might tie our own labor and consumption to goals or practices we abhor. For traffickers, that spells triumph. A triumph that takes the form of unfathomable profits and unprecedented political influence.

GLOBALIZATION HAPPENED

How did this happen? Simply, globalization happened. That is not an explanation in itself, of course. Globalization is a loose and flexible concept invested with many meanings. But then, how else to describe the rapid integration of world economics, politics, and cultures that defines our time? And how to mark what is new about this time that makes the eighties feel so often like a distant antiquity?

One major change that this most recent wave of globalization often brings to mind is a revolution in politics as deep and transformational as the one in technology. That revolution represented the ascendancy of the Western political and economic system, or some version of it. It began with the fall of the Berlin Wall and the dissolution of the Soviet Empire, and it saw its application in a menu of economic reforms that countries around the world, rich and poor alike, implemented in full or in part. In policy circles, the "Washington consensus" sobriquet that came to designate this menu became a recognized "brand" of the 1990s. Its convenient use to summarize sweeping changes in economic policies glossed over the power politics that accompanied the new agenda, and it minimized the enormous variations in the way different countries actually executed these reforms.

Still, the reforms of the 1990s all pointed in a common general direction, toward what economists call an "open economy." In this view barriers to trade or investment should be as few and as low as possible; rules are known in advance, transparent, coherent, and uniformly enforced; and government interventions are bounded, meaning that few or no prices are set by the government and the economic weight of the state is reduced thanks to balanced budgets and the shedding of state-owned enterprises. Promoting exports and open trade is better than protecting local industry behind barriers that limit imports. During the 1990s these ideas provided the compass for economic policy makers around the world.

Globalization has given us new habits, new customs, new expectations, new possibilities, and new problems. That we know. What we know far less well is how richly globalization has translated for traffickers. The interconnected world has opened bright new horizons for illicit trade. What traffickers and their accomplices are finding on these horizons is not only money but also political power.

REFORM = OPPORTUNITY

Commerce of all kinds surged in the 1990s as country after country lowered its barriers to imports and exports and eliminated regulations that inhibited foreign investment. The change was dramatic. In 1980, the average tariff—or duty that governments levied on imports and exports—was 26.1 percent. By 2002, it had fallen to 10.4 percent. Crowning events in this trend included passage of the North American Free Trade Agreement (NAFTA) grouping the United States, Canada, and Mexico in 1994; the establishment of the World Trade Organization in 1995 and China's joining it, after long negotiations, in 2002; the enlargement of the European Union from fifteen to twenty-five member states in the spring of 2004; and a spate of trade facilitation treaties between countries or entire regions on every continent. With each of these measures participant countries agreed to accord their trade rules, always in the direction of lower tariffs, fewer obstacles, and simpler ways to resolve trade disputes should they occur.

The dramatic expansion of world trade during the decade—it grew on average at over 6 percent from 1990 to 2000—also created ample room for illicit trade. For there remained plenty of rules for legitimate trade to obey while markets and customer appetite for products that countries restricted kept growing. It was soon clear that the facilities that countries adopted to encourage legitimate trade in their success also benefited illicit traders in their own activities. One benefit was the reduction of border controls, either in number or in stringency; in some places, as among the so-called Schengen group of countries within the European Union, border controls were virtually abolished. And those that persisted tended to become swamped by the sheer flow of goods. Even after 9/11 and the ensuing crackdown on U.S. frontiers, the main border posts between Mexico and the United States can inspect only a small proportion of trucks—and for a few minutes at most—for fear of backing up traffic for miles. The situation at the world's cargo container ports is even more problematic. And everywhere increased traffic, express custom clearance schemes, the spread of free ports and export processing zones, the ubiquity of air cargo, and the impossibility of checking every FedEx or DHL package all offer smugglers new ways to traverse borders.

The crush of goods at congested border posts vividly illustrates that markets have integrated much faster than have political systems. Illicit traders have turned this reality into a crucial competitive advantage—one that strengthens their position both vis-à-vis legitimate competitors and in their cat-and-mouse game with authorities. As goods move more easily across borders, frontiers clearly still matter: on either side is a different jurisdiction with its own police, customs agents, laws, and regulations. Illicit traders can hop among these jurisdictions or spread their operations across them thanks to the many tools now available to commerce. With communication technologies that allow such tasks as warehouse management and shipment tracking to be done remotely, the trader and the goods need never be in the same place at the same time. This flexibility is a crucial advantage that illicit trade has over governments, and is a defining aspect of the problem. It gives traffickers an incentive to organize in ways that maximize the jurisdictional tangle.

Privatization and business deregulation have played their part as well. In the formerly closed or state-dominated economies, the sell-off or closure of state-owned companies ended a great many industrial monopolies, forcing factories to convert themselves in order to survive. For many, this meant supplying weapons and munitions with little attention to who might be buying, or playing fast and loose with patents and trademarks. Of course, state ownership is no insurance against illicit trading practices; quite the contrary, as shown by China, where firms controlled by the government or the military have been linked time and again to counterfeiting. Meanwhile, the tendency to lift regulations on businesses has not only spurred the desired forms of entrepreneurship and investment but also multiplied the avenues for illicit traders to establish legitimate fronts and launder funds, and generally reduced the cost of doing business.

Crucially, economic reforms have benefited illicit traders by weakening their enemy. Governments simply have less latitude to act, enforce, and spend as they please. Fiscal restraint has become the paramount value by which to judge a government's performance. Wedged into what the *New York Times* columnist Thomas Friedman famously called the "golden straitjacket" of the capital markets, few countries can afford to be blacklisted by global money managers turned off by large deficits. A large and unsustainable budget deficit, especially in poor countries or "emerging markets," is likely to spark massive capital outflows, resulting in high borrowing costs to finance government operations. This in turn can wreak havoc on a government's ability to deliver the public works and social programs its citizens expect. The answer in most emerging markets where taxes are hard to raise (or even collect) is to cut expenditures. And it is often easier to cut funding to law enforcement, jails, and the judiciary than to cut funds for politically sensitive social programs. This was the norm in many countries during the 1990s. So while traffickers saw their markets grow global and their revenues soar, funding for the agencies in charge of containing them either declined or stagnated.

In the most vulnerable settings, these effects went further. Fiscally constrained governments often have trouble compensating their civil servants adequately, or even paying them in full and on time—all of which almost guarantees corruption. They are limited in their attempts to change the incentives to traffic, for instance by supporting alternative cash crops to coca or opium poppies. And they are more likely to have to concede to traffickers the role of default social welfare provider, ensuring local support (or at least toleration) for the trade and blurring the situation's moral clarity. Few governments have the capacity to navigate all these perils without leaving some vulnerability unaddressed. The traffickers have enormous incentives to find these vulnerabilities. They almost always succeed.

TOOLS OF THE TRADES

It was not economic reform alone that stimulated the boom in world trade. New technologies have played a major part too: more efficient ships, roll-on/roll-off cargo container vessels, new loading and unloading tools, better port management, improved logistics, advances in refrigeration, new packing materials, just-in-time inventory management, satellite navigation and tracking, and more. To these—which serve all forms of trade, legitimate and otherwise—traffickers have added creative applications of their own. The generalization of high-quality latex condoms, for instance, reduces the risk of breakage (usually lethal) associated with the universally preferred container for drug packets smuggled in the digestive tract of "mules." Aggressive and inventive adoption of new technologies has helped traffickers to lower risk, increase productivity, and streamline their business. As Cesar Gaviria, the former president of Colombia, told me: "The Calí cartel was already using sophisticated encryption techniques in the early nineties. It was far ahead of the methods we had in the government."

Meanwhile, financial liberalization has expanded the flexibility of traffickers to invest the profits and the range of uses they can give to their capital, as well as generated many new instruments with which to move funds across the globe. The free movement of capital is a hallmark of globalization. In the pre-reform era most countries either banned or tightly limited foreign currency transactions. Foreign investment was closely screened and regulated, and "export of capital" was a crime. But in the 1990s, countries found themselves in need of the money, the technology, and the export marketing prowess of multinational corporations, and so they promoted foreign investment instead of constraining it. Mainstream economic thinking and research also confirmed that a country was better off with more foreign investment than with less of it—especially if investors could be persuaded to stay for the long haul. Opening the local stock market to foreign money made it boom, and listing local companies in stock markets abroad, in New York or London, became a symbol of success.

None of this, however, was easy—or even possible—if the country maintained controls on foreign exchange transactions. So the 1990s saw a major shift away from exchange controls. Free buying and selling of currencies became the new global standard. And the market boomed. In 1989 daily transactions in the global currency market totaled $590 billion. By 2004 daily trading had rocketed to $1.88 trillion. Technology fueled the fire. Once governments allowed foreign exchange transactions, computerized global banking networks let them occur at the speed of light, and from anywhere to anywhere.

Money launderers suddenly found themselves in paradise. Illicit traders gained opportunities and channels to conceal and launder their revenues. Legitimate banks, competing with one another for vast new flows of funds, had incentives to look the other way when dealing with "unusual" clients. To many bankers working on commission, luring wealthy individuals to park their holdings in their bank became more important than finding out where the wealth came from. Some countries ceded to the temptation to turn themselves into offshore havens, feeling that the new environment could accommodate competition to the established shelters such as Monaco and the Cayman Islands. Such obscure venues as Nauru, Niue, and the Cook Islands honed a specialty in no-questions-asked financial services, but so too did other more "reputable" countries. And even the most aggressive global efforts to impose and enforce uniform banking standards keep butting up against the competitive considerations of banks and national authorities.

Some of the financial technologies that have benefited illicit traders are quite ordinary and common. One is the humble ATM card, not long ago the preserve of a few developed nations but now employed almost everywhere. In December 2004 the U.S. Federal Reserve announced that for the first time in history electronic payments using debit and credit cards exceeded check payments. And this trend is visible everywhere. Unimaginable without a global financial communications backbone, the card is one of the most essential and taken-for-granted tools of daily life, including for traffickers. The rise of e-money and virtual money—for instance, smart cards that store value on a chip—offers both convenience and anonymity. Yet another thread of world financial integration useful to illicit traders is the expanding wire-transfer industry. Essential to daily life for emigrant diasporas, Western Union and its peers despite their best efforts almost inevitably circulate some degree of ill-gotten gains.

The realization that these were the tools that Mohammed Atta and his terrorist accomplices used to fund their murderous deeds on 9/11 led governments to launch a major effort to limit their ease of use for illegal purposes. But while the efforts have added costs, risks, and inconveniences for the criminals, the illicit money trade continues to be a large, ominous, and global reality.

Then there is the Internet. Its value to traffickers is immense, and its specific uses too many to enumerate. Those involved in illicit transactions communicate with one another from the privacy and anonymity of Web-based e-mail accounts, frequently changed and accessed from cybercafes and unobtrusive venues. They monitor shipments using the tracing services that FedEx and its peers provide. They offer goods for sale via online display cases. The modern-day slave auction is electronic, wherein local pimps can examine and purchase via e-mail women and girls from wholesalers in other countries, and where retail customers can order up the prostitute of their choice. The Internet recruits mercenaries, advertises unscrupulous transport companies, hosts professional-looking Web sites that are electronic fronts for bogus businesses. And Internet lotteries, sports books, and casinos—an immense and chaotic industry worth an estimated $5 billion in 2003—make a fine setting for shifting dirty money about. "The Internet has become an open medicine cabinet, a help-yourself pill bazaar to make you feel good," said Karin P. Tandy, the head of the DEA in 2005, when announcing the shut down of a drug ring that used two hundred Web sites based in the United States, Costa Rica, Canada, and Australia to sell amphetamines and other drugs manufactured in India and shipped illicitly anywhere in the world.

The convergence potential for trafficking and cyber crime, in the near and distant future, seems unlimited. The Internet allows traffickers to communicate privately and efficiently, to operate as many transactions as possible in virtual rather than geographic space, and creates new ways to move and conceal funds. All this without concern for physical location, freeing the traffickers to play across borders and cover their tracks without impeding the actual flow of goods.

NEW SOURCES, NEW ROUTES

The virtual world was not the only new territory that the 1990s opened up for illicit trade. With the end of the cold war, nations previously held outside the world trading system began to reenter, and ones that had regimented (or at least attempted to regiment) the flow of goods and money on their territory released their grip. Of course the systems that loosened or fell—the Soviet brand of communism and the Chinese one, the heavy "state capitalism" in vogue in India and elsewhere in the developing world, and even the highly directed economy in South Korea and Taiwan, and more—varied widely in their methods and results. But all had in common the principle that government knew best how to run the economy. And everywhere the rollback of central planning, price controls, import licenses, industrial subsidies, currency restrictions, and the like revealed markets-in-waiting, some of them already quite advanced, with entrepreneurs and moneylenders at the ready. So too were traders, legitimate and otherwise. When these markets-in-waiting joined up with the world market, the world economy became truly global. And so did illicit trade.

The opening produced a cascade of benefits for illicit trade. The most immediate was a supply shock. The fall of the Eastern Bloc and its overseas allies released onto the market whole new streams of supply of interest to illicit traders, some of them at bargain-basement prices. They included overstock weapons and military materials from the vastly oversize Warsaw Pact armies and the state-owned factories set up to supply them; nuclear materials and skills, set loose by the rapid and disorderly end of the Soviet Union; civilian and military aircraft and vehicles; ample natural resources, from nickel and copper to uranium and diamonds; but also migrant labor; babies for adoption; women for prostitution; and even human bodies, dead and alive, for organ sales. Political and economic reform also made available a vast infrastructure of industrial plants that governments had developed behind the protection of trade restrictions, now needing new activities to stay afloat—a perfect opportunity for manufacturers of goods for illicit trade.

As the Berlin Walls of the world came down, possibilities for traffickers multiplied and so did new national business specialties. Before long, countries like Ukraine and Serbia would be known for manufacturing contraband compact discs or ammunition. Moldova, wedged between Romania and Ukraine, suddenly sprang to the world's notice as a supply and trading hub for trafficked human beings, a bivouac for drugs and weapons shipments, and a go-to venue for fake aircraft registrations and more. Transdniester, a breakaway part of Moldova that pretends to be a country but really is a family-run criminal enterprise, became an important center for arms smuggling. Belarus developed as a hub for human trafficking. Romania, with its strong technical education system and high unemployment, became an early global leader in cyber crime and Internet fraud. The central Asian republics and the Balkans reassumed a central role in trade between Afghanistan and Europe—echoes of the old Silk Road, only this time in drugs and smuggled migrants. China's Yunnan province took on a similar role with respect to Myanmar. These transitions came easily, as much out of necessity as initiative.

All this happened fast—so fast that the world barely had time to register the trend before settling into the new assumptions it bred. Yet it was momentous, with parallels in places well outside the old Soviet orbit and profound consequences for the whole world order. And the dynamics were frustratingly hard to pin down. Jim Moody, a former top FBI agent who in the early 1990s pioneered the bureau's response to the onslaught of global crime, told me in frustration: "Even today we still don't know what happened to us in the 1990s. We will never know what [the criminals] did to us. Where did all that money go? I believe part of it is here in the United States and in many other developed countries, invested in legitimate business controlled by big-time crooks."

ALTERED STATES

Behind these changes another deeper political dynamic was lurking: the proliferation around the world of weak and failed states, ripe for traffickers to colonize. During the cold war, states took up residence in the "sphere of influence" of either superpower in exchange for military protection and economic assistance. When this protection collapsed, so did the safety net that prevented states with feeble or inept governments from losing control of their territory or their resources. Ever since the 1960s, political scientists had used terms like "strong states" and "weak states" to describe differences in a government's capacity to carry out basic functions. But the 1990s saw a new coinage, the "failed state"—a near-empty shell with a capital, a titular government, and the skeleton of some institutions but very little legitimate government control or effect on the economy and on real lives. Weak states in general and this extreme subset in particular have mushroomed since 1990.

In such countries, illicit trading networks can easily "capture" key government agencies—customs, courts, banks, ports, police. The recruitment of journalists, politicians, and business leaders is rarely far behind. Soon enough, they branch out toward legitimate businesses that implant them deeper into the communities: owning the local radio station or newspaper is often as necessary a cost of doing business as "owning" a judge or the chief of police. In the same way that al-Qaeda was able to "capture"—and for not a lot of money—the Taliban government of Afghanistan, the goals and needs of international traffickers have deeply permeated politics and economic life in many countries. This criminalization of the national interest has become an important characteristic of our time.

Take for example North Korea. Its involvement in the international trafficking of drugs, weapons, people, and endangered species and in all sorts of criminal activities is not some secondary project by groups of individuals who also happen to hold high-level government positions. Rather, according to most experts interviewed for this book, international crime is a core activity that defines in fundamental ways the nature of the North Korean state. Nauru, a tiny island nation in the Pacific, is well known as a haven for Russian laundered money. The small country of Suriname (population half a million) on South America's northern coast has become a transshipment haven for drug traffickers. No other economic activity in Suriname can compete in profits. It is hard to imagine that its government is immune to the seduction or the threats of the powerful foreign players that operate from there. Indeed, in 2004 the son and the half-brother of the former dictator Desi Bouterse were accused of belonging to one of the major drug organizations that used Suriname as a base to export cocaine to the Netherlands. Tajikistan's total economic output per year is about $7 billion. According to UN estimates, the street value in a European capital of just the drugs *seized* in Tajikistan in 2003 was equivalent to roughly half the value of all the goods and services produced in that country.

In Peru during the mid-to-late 1990s, Vladimiro Montesinos was the all-powerful head of the national intelligence services, a fundamental behind-the-scenes power broker who controlled members of Peru's Congress, top bankers, and media owners. At the same time he ran a large network that trafficked drugs and weapons and laundered money all over the world. As the former Peruvian prime minister Roberto Dañino told me: "Peru's national interest and important foreign policy decisions were often unilaterally defined or greatly shaped by Montesinos's interests." Those interests, we now know, were often criminal. A senior British intelligence officer confirmed that this is also the view many in his agency have of Alexander Lukashenko, the president of the former Soviet republic of Belarus, or of Transdniester's Igor Smirnov. For countries like these, trying to understand the "national interest" without reference to global illicit trade would miss a crucial driver of their policies and of the actions and omissions of the government.

The effect can be even sharper at the regional level, especially in remote regions or ones that span borders. In many countries local governments are easy prey for criminal networks who seek a pliant and convenient base of operation. When Colombia decentralized authority to local governments in the early 1990s, it proved to be a boon for the trafficking networks, which could now simply appoint their own mayors, governors, and judges. In Afghanistan the poppy boom benefits local warlords, and in Mexico the networks have taken over some of the most virulently criminal cities and states. The "Golden Triangle" of Thailand, Myanmar, and Laos and the no-man's-land between Pakistan and Afghanistan are notorious examples of cross-border regions where illicit trade has thrived. But in fact it is rare today to find a country without pockets of lawlessness that are well integrated into larger global networks. In its 2004 annual report to the U.S. Congress, the CIA announced that it had identified fifty regions around the world over which central governments exert little or no control and where terrorists, smugglers, and transnational criminals find a welcoming environment.

These places are perfect markets for arms smugglers and source or trans-shipment points for anything else. Rebels turn into traders: for instance, the FARC and AUC in Colombia's guerrilla organizations no longer merely sell protection to the drug trade but have turned themselves into cocaine brokers, trading with farmers, labs, transporters, and wholesalers in Mexico and the United States. The Colombian government estimates that the FARC alone earned $783 million in cocaine revenue in 2003. In West Africa in the late 1990s, the RUF rebels in Sierra Leone and Charles Taylor's faction in Liberia partnered with arms dealers to move diamonds and timber out of the region and cash, drugs, weapons, and other goods in. Even al-Qaeda got involved, according to the reporting of the journalist Doug Farah, transferring cash assets into Sierra Leone diamonds through deals in Liberia, all in the run up to September 11.

The trends are most extreme in failed states, yet any weak state is inherently vulnerable. Its borders are hard to patrol, and its officials are easily corrupted. In this way, for instance, Nigeria has turned into a major trading hub for heroin en route from the Middle East to Europe and North America. The route might not seem direct, and neither is Nigeria itself a major producer or consumer (so far) of the drug. But the vulnerabilities of the Nigerian state offer traffickers advantages that make the detour worthwhile. Similarly Haiti and other Caribbean nations became way stations for drug shipments into the United States when other routes got too hot. The precariousness of successive Haitian governments and the country's long-unpatrolled coastline made it an obvious pick.

Other weak states offer other specialties. "True-false" end-user certificates are prized in the smuggled arms business, for instance. Official certificates that guarantee that a cargo is going to a legitimate buyer, they are false because the weapons are going elsewhere but true because the letterhead and signature are authentic, purchased for a small fee. Chad, Panama, Bolivia, Ghana, Ivory Coast, and many more have cropped up as purveyors of such documentation. And in Romania, Albania, Slovakia, and Greece, where human traffickers corral women lured from around the region to "break them in" as prostitutes, border guards stamp passports they know are fake and look the other way as these modern-day chain gangs are convoyed to the West.

THE NEW ENTREPRENEURS

A powerful contribution of the former closed and state-dominated economies to the rise of global trafficking networks in the 1990s can be measured in human capital. The changes released into the marketplace an army of highly skilled, experienced, and ruthless operators who provided the backbone for the new criminal and semi-criminal businesses that soared thanks to the possibilities bred by open markets and freer politics.

After all, these economies had entrepreneurs—just not of the standard mold. Consider Russia's new capitalists. The typical post-Soviet tycoon did not train at Harvard Business School. He more likely spent his formative years in government, the military, or the KGB. He garnered his work experience not at some tony investment bank or multinational corporation but as a participant in the shady transactions that became a fact of life whenever rationing and government controls were the norm. Under Communism, smuggling was not an illegal international transaction undertaken by a few hardened criminals but a common survival strategy. Personal gain awaited just at the other side of the barriers government imposed on the exchange of goods and services, not abroad but inside one's own country. Prosperity, in relative terms of course, hinged on finding a way—never legal—to provide embattled factory managers with the raw materials they needed to reach their production quotas, or to "divert"—that is, steal—consumer goods from the government and sell them on the black market. It also meant gaining access to the stocks of foreign blue jeans that could be discreetly sold to the young, and to the vodka that their elders used as a lifeline.

For more than six decades, these were the incentives the system provided, and therefore entrepreneurial spirits had no other outlet than to find ways to break the law. Inevitably, the schemes required help and collaboration from someone inside the government. When straightforward partnerships or corruption did not work, the use of violence, threats, or blackmail was never beyond the means used to get cooperation. Decades of this environment produced an ample supply of experienced and clever organizations, ruthless gangs, talented operators, and reckless enforcers.

For the rest of the world *perestroika*, the restructuring of the Soviet economy, might have meant the victory of the free-market ethos. But for the entrepreneurs that the Soviet system bred, it meant more freedom to apply their experience undermining government efforts, breaking the law, and corrupting officials. They soon discovered that thanks to globalization they could now operate internationally and that the world at large also offered ample profit opportunities for organizations with their skills and proclivities. Once government controls were lifted, private ownership allowed, borders opened, factories privatized, rationing eliminated, and foreign bank accounts legalized, the market-oriented networks that used to operate illegally under the old system adapted faster to the new ways than almost any other group of society. Neither was this a Soviet phenomenon alone. Around the world, from China to Argentina and from Italy to India, talents honed by exploiting the labyrinth of official controls for private gain have found lucrative new outlets in global trafficking.

UNDERWORLD NO LONGER

Few industries could go through such explosive expansion without a major recomposition or restructuring of their own. Illicit trade is no exception. It no longer resembles either of the two dominant images that we still carry of it in our popular imagination: the freelance smuggler-frontiersman or the "organized crime" syndicate.

One reason is that these players no longer possess the ideal skills. The fast pace of world trade and the infinite combination of possibilities for supply, warehousing, transportation, banking, wire transfers, cell phone providers, Webmail accounts, encryption software, front company paperwork, and marketing to customers around the world stretch the capabilities of organized crime beyond the typical mafioso's comfort zone. Rigid hierarchies in which authority is centralized don't do well in a high-speed global marketplace where opportunities and risks change too fast. The more organized crime groups resemble corporations, the more their hierarchies and their routines prevent them from optimizing their activities. The new environment gives an advantage to organizations capable of responding and adapting rapidly to new opportunities and able to constantly shift locations, tactics, and ways and means to make the most money possible. As a result, "organized crime" itself is changing— becoming less organized in the traditional sense of command and control structures, and more decentralized. In this it is trying to catch up with the illicit trading networks that have forged ahead.

Just as obsolete is the assumption that different traffickers specialize in different types of merchandise. Of course, at any given time a particular ethnic group or local syndicate may appear to control the market for heroin, or child labor, or Kalashnikovs, or stolen cars, or cigarettes, particularly in a single city or region. But that is just the exposed part of the system. In fact, the economic and technical possibilities bred by globalization make it easier than ever for traders to combine their cargos or shift from one to another—and less of a competitive advantage to control, end to end, a given product's supply chain. They have mutated accordingly, focusing on skills instead of commodities. As the FBI's deputy director, Maureen Baginski, told me, "The specialization became the network itself, and its ability to procure, transport, and deliver illegal merchandise across countries. What the merchandise was became almost irrelevant."

Entire industries—finance, computing, entertainment, publishing, travel, pharmaceuticals, fashion—have been reconfigured by the rise of trafficking networks that cut through them and affect their operations and their bottom line. Citicorp and Deutsche Bank, Wal-Mart and Cartier, Microsoft and Phillips, Pfizer and Nestlé, Sony and Bertelsmann, General Motors and Nissan, Tommy Hilfiger and Armani—these are just a few of the well-known companies that can no longer ignore the challenges of global trafficking. Their marketing practices, distribution channels, procurement strategies, plant locations, human resource management, information systems, and financial practices have all been affected. Slipups in vigilance happen easily, even within large corporations. In 2003 Wal-Mart, the world's largest retail chain, was accused by the U.S. government of using illegal immigrants of eighteen different nationalities as cleaners in its stores.

Businesses are not the only ones affected. The surge of the global networks has also altered our surroundings. Milan, Barcelona, San Diego, and even orderly Zurich have seen their urban landscape transformed by improvised housing that has sprouted up to shelter the illegal immigrants massively "imported" by the people trade. From Rio de Janeiro to Detroit, the use of public spaces in neighborhoods ravaged by drug wars has been deeply altered by the unwritten but strongly enforced rules imposed by the traffickers and their retail associates. In American high schools—poor and affluent alike—drugs, pirated music, software, clothing, and, to a lesser extent, even small arms are as much a part of the experience as blackboards, books, and football games.

CHANGING THE WORLD

Ultimately, it is the fabric of society that is at stake. Global illicit trade is sinking entire industries while boosting others, ravaging countries and sparking booms, making and breaking political careers, destabilizing some governments and propping up others. At one extreme are countries where the smuggling routes, the hidden factories, the pilfered natural resources, the dirty-money transactions, can no longer be distinguished from the official economy and government. But comfortable middle-class lives in wealthy countries are far more connected to trafficking—and to its global effects—than most of us care to imagine.

This transformation has happened despite the fact that governments everywhere—particularly the United States and some European countries—are throwing vast resources into the project of containing global illicit trade. Despite massive financial appropriations, ever stricter laws, and better technology, the fact remains that no government can yet show any significant, durable progress in the fight against trafficking networks.

Complicating the fight is that these networks are simultaneously global and local. Their ability to exploit their international mobility at great speed and their deep entrenchment within local power structures give them a huge advantage over the national or local governments that try to contain them. The networks can evade governmental pursuit by moving to another jurisdiction or by using political influence to fend off their pursuers, or both. When a new opportunity comes up, it responds with incredible speed. Survival hinges on the networks' ability to recombine, form collaborations, and dissolve them with equal ease, forging new markets and always keeping a step ahead. Illicit traders are very creative, and their ingenuity is fueled by profits hard to find in any other business.

In coming decades, the activities of the global trafficking networks and their associates will have a far greater impact than is commonly imagined on international relations, development strategies, democracy promotion, business and finance, migration, global security, and war and peace. In too many nation-states, members of the political, military, and business elite will find it more important to defend the lucrative illicit trades from which they and their families and friends benefit than for their country to join the World Trade Organization, cooperate with the International Monetary Fund, or participate with the United States or the UN in whatever coalition is needed to fend off the crisis of the day. It is already a mistake to treat global illicit trade as mere "smuggling" and its participants simply as "criminals" and to reduce the solution to "law enforcement." Those words only begin to tell the story. It is all of this, but also much more. In coming years global illicit trade will become even larger and more complex, and these categories will become less and less adequate to convey the nature of a phenomenon that will be changing the world in myriad ways.

One of these effects is already with us. International terrorism as we are now coming to understand it follows in the footsteps of international illicit trade, employing the same tools and conveniences of the new global economy to melt into cities and countries, hiding in plain sight. Since 9/11 (and for that matter, even before), terrorist cells uncovered from Manila to Hamburg and London to New Jersey have had in common some use of illicit trade as a means to support themselves and fund their activities. It will be impossible to understand the tools, tactics, and possibilities of terrorists without also understanding those that the global trafficking networks have pioneered. Of course, seen separately, the prospect of a suicide attack using weapons of mass destruction in a crowded city and that of tons of cocaine or containers of illegally produced CDs flooding the market are of completely different degrees of alarm. But our tendency to look at them separately is part of the problem as well.

International terrorism, the spread of horrific weapons, the empowerment of "rogue regimes," the flare-up and persistence of regional wars and ethnic violence, the threat of environmental depredation, the stability of the world financial system, the fierce pressures and aspirations of international migration—all of these and more find their outlet, their manifestation, and often their sustenance in global illicit trade. The examples are everywhere once you start looking for them. The problems of West Africa, central Asia, or the Balkans—to name just a few—cannot be understood without considering the immense weight that traffickers have in their political and economic life. Can the behavior of China or Russia, two of the most important countries for the future of humankind, be properly understood without taking into account the enormous influence of global illicit trade on their governments' decision making? Can a legitimate business enterprise that operates internationally decide on a strategy without pondering the impact of traffickers? Can democracy be promoted in countries in which criminal networks are the most powerful political players? Of course not. The surprise is how easy it has been for politicians, military planners, journalists, and scholars to miss or ignore this reality.

SMUGGLER'S NIRVANA?

In its own raw and sordid way, illicit trade shows us some of the places globalization is going. We can learn from the innovations of illicit traders so that ultimately we may respond to them with the same creativity they have visited on us.

But that is getting ahead of the story, and ahead of today's reality. Right now it is the traffickers who are ascendant. Their work has grown easier to initiate, organize, and dissimulate, and they have adapted to take maximum advantage of these new possibilities. They are flexible, responsive, and rapid: no itinerary is too complex, no supply deadline too urgent. The trades in drugs, arms, human beings, counterfeits, money, or the other illicit markets discussed in the chapters ahead each has its own history and dynamics. But they all have in common this transformation, and they are coming together—ever harder to distinguish, both conceptually and in practice, from one another and from the legitimate economy.

So is the globalized world a smuggler's nirvana? For now, the evidence overwhelmingly says yes. After all, we have willed this: much of what makes illicit trade so successful today is the result of deliberate policies, ones aimed at global integration, open economies, and open societies. So it should really come as no surprise that legal trade and trafficking have grown hand in hand, or that the diffusion of power to individuals and groups has spurred innovation on both sides of the law.

But look a bit more closely: Why? Why has legal trade not

crowded out the illegal? Why have democratic values not ostracized the traffickers and educated their customers? Why has technological innovation not helped law enforcement crack down on the bad guys, once and for all? And where do we go from here?

The clues are in the stories.

Chapter 3

SMALL ARMS AND LOOSE NUKES

It was a delivery run gone bad that lifted the lid on the shadow world of the underground nuclear trade. One day in October 2003, German and Italian warships accosted a suspect cargo vessel in the eastern Mediterranean Sea. The ship, the BBC *China*, was steaming toward Libya, having loaded at the port of Dubai in the United Arab Emirates. Months of investigation by numerous intelligence agencies suggested that its hold contained something different from the "industrial equipment" that the bill of goods laconically cited. And indeed, when the Italians escorted the BBC *China* to the port of Taranto and inspected its cargo, they found just what they expected: specialized parts for building a centrifuge, specifically a nuclear centrifuge designed to enrich uranium to the isotope 235—the raw material of atom bombs.

The voyage of the BBC *China* (which despite its name was registered in Germany, to a shipping company in the port of Leer) was, the investigators knew, just one of a series of customer deliveries by an underground sales network centered in Islamabad, Pakistan, in the person of Abdul Qadeer Khan. Virtually unknown to the rest of the world, "Dr. A. Q." was a household name in his own country, nothing short of a folk hero. The dapper sixty-eight-year-old metallurgist was the revered architect of the country's indigenous nuclear weapons program, "father of the Islamic bomb," living symbol of national pride. But unbeknownst to the Pakistani public and completely outside the international limelight, Khan had long been a subject of interest for experts who monitor the spread of weapons of mass destruction. To this narrow professional community of analysts and spies, Khan was much more than a semiretired scientist resting on his patriotic laurels. Rather, it now appeared, he was something else, something more banal yet also more sinister: an import-export businessman with a highly exotic product line.

Between Khan and his clients stretched a complicated international commercial network. The centrifuge shipment to Libya, for instance, involved firms and individuals from at least a half dozen European and Asian countries. A Malaysian engineering firm called Scomi had produced the components, under the supervision of a Swiss engineer who monitored the manufacturing process while keeping a tight grip on the blueprints. The parts then found their way to Dubai in the custody of a firm called Gulf Technical Industries, which belonged in part to a British father-and-son tandem, Peter and Paul Griffin. A key intermediary, a Sri Lankan by the name of B.S.A. Tahir, divided his time between Dubai and Malaysia. In Dubai, he operated through a computer supplies and services company, SMB Computers, which he'd founded with his brother. In Malaysia, he was the close friend of two owners of the investment fund that controlled Scomi. He was even related to one of them by marriage, and both he and his Malaysian wife had recently belonged to the fund's board of directors. (The other fund owner, Kamaluddin Abdallah, was the son of Abdallah Badawi, Malaysia's new prime minister.) It was Tahir who had placed the centrifuge order on behalf of its ostensible buyer in Dubai.

Ties to Khan permeated the transaction. The designs for the centrifuges exactly matched one that Khan had produced in Pakistan. The elder Griffin had done business with Khan—official business—years before under the aegis of Pakistan's nuclear program. And the Swiss gentleman who carried the blueprints was himself the son of another engineer who shared with Khan a technical specialty and, it appeared, concurrent training in Europe in the 1970s. All these elements showed the signs of an intricate network, built on both business interests and close personal ties. And at the center of it, intelligence services were convinced that Tahir and Khan were intimate collaborators: Tahir the key commercial agent of the network and Khan not just its technical heart but the source of much of the entrepreneurial spirit and business acumen driving the process.

The centrifuge deal was no isolated incident. Intelligence investigations, assisted by Libya's new effort to "come in from the cold" by cooperating with Western services, were revealing a multiyear, multistranded pattern of deliveries of nuclear equipment and know-how—all the way to designs and assembly instructions for a nuclear bomb. The client list was worrisome: beyond Libya, it included Iran, by that country's own admission, and apparently North Korea too, despite Pyongyang's vehement denials. It was left to speculation whom other clients might have been. Moreover, the origins of the goods were barely concealed. Among the materials Libya handed over were some documents written in Chinese, leaving little doubt as to their original provenance. Industrial equipment was tagged with stickers marked "KRL," for Khan Research Laboratories. And the Libyans produced a sheaf of bomb blueprints in their original wrapping: plastic clothing bags labeled "Good Looks Tailors" with an Islamabad address. According to one senior U.S. official, Khan's role in destabilizing the twenty-first century will "loom up there" with Hitler and Stalin's impact in the twentieth.

After its discovery, A. Q. Khan's network may have become the most visible, but it was certainly not the only one privately plying the nuclear trade. The profit potential stemming from the global appetite for nuclear knowledge and bomb-making equipment was too alluring. Humayun Khan, another Pakistani national with the same name, also detected the same opportunity as his namesake—even though apparently the two are not related. "Humayun Khan is a black marketeer involved in the proliferation of nuclear weapons, and once this is all spelled out we're going to see the same scale of network that A. Q. Khan was involved in," said a U.S. Commerce Department official when it was announced that U.S. federal prosecutors were bringing charges against the second Mr. Khan in mid-2005. Once again, the pattern that emerged from the investigations was eerily similar: a global operation with multiple locations—Pakistan, South Africa, the United Arab Emirates, and the United States—led by a multinational team which in this case included Mr. Khan's Israeli partner Asher Karni. These clients had two things in common: they wanted nuclear technology and they were willing to pay illicit traders a lot of money for it. Again, profits not politics was the name of the game.

Dr. Khan's atomic supermarket may have grabbed the headlines, but the nuclear components trade is only one specialty segment in an expanding, and lucrative, international market for illicit weapons of all kinds: overstock mines and grenades, secondhand missile launchers, counterfeit AK-47 assault rifles, recycled helicopter gunships, not to mention billions of cartridges of ammunition and even human beings—pilots and trainers and fighters who move from conflict to conflict without regard to international law, embargoes, borders, politics, or ethics. All of these goods and services have proliferated as the end of the cold war dumped surplus capacity into the market, which responded eagerly with an explosion in intrastate conflicts, insurgencies, civil wars, and armed criminal enterprises of every kind. Of course the sudden appearance of these stockpiles did not on its own cause these wars. But the relatively unencumbered access to the large supplies of weapons of all kinds certainly sparked the imagination and the ambitions of governments and groups that would have been less prone to go to war without them. The newfound availability of weapons opened new possibilities for insurgents, guerrilla movements, criminal bands, and the governments they threatened. War became a cheaper, more attractive option as access to sophisticated weapons increased the probabilities of victory.

But what about this is *truly* new? The arms trade is very old, and smuggling has always been part and parcel of the weapons market. What has changed?

The short answer: everything.

Start with the composition of the market: a trade once domi-nated by governments making massive purchases from other gov-ernments or their state-owned companies is now driven and defined by far larger and more diverse networks of middlemen and thou-sands of new and independent producers. The links that tie produc-ers, financiers, brokers, and clients are fluid, global, and elusive. As always the brokers continue to be immensely creative, politically connected, and very wealthy. Now, however, they are no longer a small exclusive club of rogues but a large global community of traf-fickers. These myriad players produce, buy, trade, finance, and sell to and from companies and agencies that are no longer under the direct control of governments. Many of these new players don't even have a permanent nationality—or they have multiple ones to choose from. Most are, in effect, stateless.

As the illicit weapons business builds and recombines, it is melding with other illegal trades, sustaining the ambitions of com-mon criminals and terrorists alike. And as the death toll rises and more and more ominous threats become very real possibilities, gov-ernments are left playing catch-up in a game loaded against them.

STRICTLY BUSINESS

Why did he do it? What could possibly motivate A. Q. Khan—a national hero, his country's most decorated citizen—to jeopardize his reputation and court international opprobrium by running a smugglers' ring in the deadliest goods of all? To be sure, it wasn't just ideology. Yes, building an "Islamic bomb" that could tip the regional or even global balance of power was one of Khan's motives. But making enormous amounts of money for himself, his accomplices, and his enablers at senior levels in the Pakistani and other govern-ments was as powerful a motive as any of Khan's geopolitical or ide-ological justifications.

Indeed, Khan's client list—including the decidedly non-Islamic North Korea—and most of all his commercial methods suggested that Muslim pride was hardly his chief concern. A better clue to his motivation lay in his portfolio of properties built up over the years. He built villas across Pakistan and bought apartments in London. He owned an Islamabad restaurant, a bowling alley, and, no less incongruously, a luxury hotel in Timbuktu, Mali, which he named after his Dutch wife. (Ornate furnishings for the hotel were flown to Libya in a Pakistani air force jet and transported overland across the Sahara.) And Khan's habits were the signature behaviors of the successful corrupt businessman. He ran his state-sanctioned research facility, Khan Research Laboratories, with little distinction between the institution's and his own personal finances. He orchestrated preferential contracts for his relatives and friends. He set up a health and education charity. And he polished his image with donations, publicity events, a ubiquitous presence on the VIP social circuit, and even his personal motorcade.

In a word, Khan did it for the money. Real estate trumped ideology. Greed overrode geopolitics. Khan turned from engineer into entrepreneur by locating a niche. He took advantage of a rare, almost accidental opportunity—his role as gatekeeper to Pakistan's nuclear program—to develop a personal revenue stream. To do so, he deployed a businessman's assets and acumen, his relationships, drawing on ties forged decades earlier as a young engineer in Europe and connections in high places, easily mustered for a man of his public stature. He identified a rich source of demand: "rogue states," and maybe other groups as well, that were shut off from nuclear techniques by the rules of nonproliferation. He found willing partners for each crucial role: manufacture, transportation, finance. And, brilliantly, he submerged his transactions into the ordinary workings of global commerce, sourced from legal factories, piggybacking on ordinary cargo shipments, and delivered through a dizzying maze of intermediaries.

Nimbleness, opportunism: the Khan network made full use of the conveniences of the era, from the ease of establishing front companies in pliant jurisdictions to the flexibility of communications and travel and—crucially—the swiftness and anonymity of international financial transfers. (Old-fashioned craft came into play as well: investigators marveled at the skill of some Khan middlemen in covering up the trace.) And this consummate use of the marketplace distinguished the network's activities from those of a state—even a state like Pakistan, where Khan clearly had protectors, business partners, accomplices, and a measure of safe haven. His home country's government was simply a part of Khan's commercial environment: he knew, as any savvy businessman would, both the importance and the art of purchasing government approval by cutting deals with the key individuals within the system: judges, generals, ministers. Hampered by international law, by borders, and by its own bureaucracy, Pakistan was in no position to proliferate nuclear weapons as state policy. But free to operate in the global marketplace, a Pakistani scientist turned businessman could easily enlist official protectors in his network for a share of the proceeds. All it took, really, was an entrepreneur and an opportunity. Naturally, couching these activities in the language of geopolitics, ideology, national sovereignty, and Islam was the perfect "marketing platform" to justify the activities to those that wanted to know—or needed a cover.

And this combination of private and public roles—forged by the profit motive, not public policy—was a reality infinitely subtler than the rough lexicon of "allies in the war on terror" versus "rogue states" could ever describe. Pakistan, it turned out, was simultaneously both of these, or perhaps neither. Khan and his associates were neither a state nor a regime but a commercial network with far-flung offshoots that enmeshed more than any one country. And as for the infamous weapons of mass destruction, whether or not they were lurking in the vaults of an ill-intended state, one thing was certain: they were at large, hiding in plain sight, out there in the tumult of the global marketplace.

But A. Q. Khan's story is not simply one of commerce. It is also a tale of politics, in which the national interest of a sovereign state becomes inextricably intertwined with the criminal motives of a clique that captures and redirects important parts of the government to support a long-term illicit enterprise. It also illustrates how stealthy and resourceful criminal organizations can play larger geopolitical interests to their advantage. One member of the 9/11 Commission told me: "The U.S. government had for a long time a lot of information about A. Q. Khan." But, the commissioner said, "The government decided that clamping down on Khan would destabilize the Musharraf regime in Pakistan. The U.S. needed Pakistan's support first to help in the invasion of Afghanistan and then to capture Osama bin Laden. It was hard for the U.S. to ask for the deportation or the jailing of a popular national hero."

Khan and his accomplices in the Pakistani government knew this. Hussain Haqqani, who served as senior advisor to several Pakistani prime ministers, told me that Khan and his partners "felt that they could be Pakistani nationalists embedded within the state in the morning and rogue international businessmen in the afternoon—and that no one could touch them. They knew that the Americans knew and could do nothing about it."

UP FOR ANYTHING

Call it the fear factor: that special, sinister resonance that accompanies the concept of "weapons of mass destruction," with its images of rogue scientists in lab coats concocting fiendish formulas deep in underground bunkers. But the case of Dr. Abdul Qadeer Khan, arms vendor, was special only because his product line called for extra secrecy and, once exposed, attracted for good reasons the greatest alarm. In fact, Khan was only one of a fraternity of international arms dealers of a new kind: individual entrepreneurs, ruthless but talented, operating through complex and nimble networks that made use of all the possibilities of the day. In the rigid world order of the cold war era, it was massive corporations with power-state ties that earned the unflattering sobriquet "merchants of death": military-industrial behemoths with names like Lockheed, Dassault, Bofors, or Northrop Grunman. The brokers and middlemen existed on the edges of the picture, helping to grease a palm, smooth a deal, transfer a shipment to an obscure destination. But today's arms market looks nothing like this. The specialty plays—moving guns to rebels and renegades, across embargos and out of the law's reach—have multiplied. And with them, the opportunities for a new class of kingpins, deal makers who've renounced the heavy structures of states and corporations for the freedom and flexibility of the new global marketplace.

The lifestyle, of course, is not for everyone, though it has its vivid moments. When Leonid Minin, for example, was finally arrested in August 2000 in a suburb of Milan, it was in the private company of four young ladies, tucking into fifty-eight grams of cocaine. He also carried diamonds and large sums of currency from as far away as Mauritius. His passports, established under various names, included Israel, Russia, Germany, and Bolivia. And his criminal record, which included current investigations in five countries, stretched across Europe and back three decades, including racketeering, identity theft, drugs, money laundering, and even fraudulent arms deals.

But the fifty-two-year-old Minin's recent, lucrative trade of choice had been weapons—specifically two shipments of missiles, M93 grenade launchers and rockets and at least five million rounds of ammunition, destined for the Revolutionary United Front (RUF), the vicious rebel army in Sierra Leone, best known for systematically chopping off the arms of civilians with machetes. As a report by the International Consortium of Investigative Journalists (ICIJ) detailed, Minin placed orders with a firm called Aviatrend that belonged to a certain Valery Cherny; Cherny, in turn, purchased the weapons from manufacturers in Ukraine and shipped them from Bulgaria, once on a Ukrainian Antonov 124 chartered by a British transport company and once on Minin's own BAC-111. The official certificates that identify the final destination of an arms cargo—and without which manufacturers are not allowed to sell—listed Ivory Coast and Burkina Faso. But the cargos actually shipped to Liberia, which the RUF used as a rear base and through which it circumvented with the greatest of ease a UN embargo.

Minin organized the operation and concealed its finances by

masking it as the purchase of equipment for the timber industry—easy enough, as he conveniently owned a tropical logging firm in Liberia, where he'd grown close to the right people in the Charles Taylor regime, including the president's son. The Liberians were bankrolling RUF; Minin in turn moved the payment to Aviatrend via a simple wire order from his bank in Switzerland to Cherny's bank in Cyprus. As financial montages for illicit arms deals went, this one was relatively straightforward; it required no long trail of letters of credit, no secret "inner" and "outer" contracts outlining two completely different structures for the same deal. But it was typical enough in that it piggybacked on legal companies and transactions, crossed enough borders, and involved enough jurisdictions to make it difficult to unravel. Indeed, it wasn't these arms deals that brought Minin down but rather, more prosaically, his taste for a party. It took days before the sleazy businessman hauled in for drugs in a suburban Milan hotel and the international brigand pursued by numerous intelligence agencies were identified as being one and the same.

Minin's capture illustrated the hit-and-miss, uncoordinated quality of the law enforcement response to the rise of the new weapons kingpins. It also showed how the networked, decentralized structure of their transactions leaves any number of key players at large even when a major arrest is made. When another major dealer of the 1990s, the Belgian Jacques Monsieur, was arrested in Istanbul in 2002, he too left at large a range of accomplices, correspondents, and counterparts in France, Belgium, Iran, and both Congos, and no doubt elsewhere. Some were protected: Monsieur, who had helped Iran purchase weapons since not long after the 1979 revolution, had parlayed his strong Tehran ties into a lucrative business recycling Iranian weapons into embargoed conflicts in Africa. And in supplying the Lissouba regime in the Congo in 1997, Monsieur had dealt with the occult central African financing structures of the French state–owned oil company Elf. Elf arranged the financial back channel for Lissouba to purchase $61.3 million worth of light weapons from Iran and helicopters from Russia, accompanied by the services of forty Russian technicians. (Lissouba lost the civil war anyway, leaving Monsieur with a delicate accounts receivable problem that got him in hot water with his suppliers.) But other pieces of the puzzle remained a complete mystery—not least the identity of a certain "CH," listed as main beneficiary of client payments to Monsieur's network.

But if there is one iconic figure of the new illicit arms trade, that title goes by acclamation to Victor Bout, a man who has succeeded by himself in redefining what we call a "merchant of death." Born in 1967, Bout is a grizzled veteran of the new arms trade, having almost invented it himself at the fall of the Soviet Union, when as a young demobilized military pilot he saw novel, lucrative opportunities in private life. While in his early twenties, Bout began to buy up ancient Soviet cargo aircraft—Ilyushins and Antonovs, loud and rugged and adapted to rough conditions. And as his fleet grew to about sixty aircraft registered in a variety of permissive jurisdictions—Ukraine, Liberia, Swaziland, Central African Republic, Equatorial Guinea—Bout built around it a network of front companies, shells, and subsidiaries of almost delicious cleverness and complexity.

These entities provided the cover for an extraordinary sequence of assignments. Flying from second-tier airports like Ostend in Belgium, Burgas in Bulgaria, and Pietersburg in South Africa, Bout's operation shipped mortar bombs, assault rifles, rocket launchers, anti-tank and anti-aircraft missiles, and millions of rounds of ammunition to the UNITA rebel movement in Angola. He supplied the RUF and the Rwandan Hutu militias based in eastern Congo. Bout's Antonovs were spotted on airfields in such places as Khartoum, the capital of Sudan, being loaded with "green boxes"—the signature container for small arms—freshly disembarked from other airplanes, to continue to unknown destinations. On the return legs, Bout helped move diamonds from civil war zones—the infamous "conflict diamonds." He also transported more anodyne cargos, including fresh vegetables and frozen fish from Africa, and even ferried French soldiers in the Congo and United Nations peacekeepers into East Timor. As an air transporter, Bout was up for anything.

Trailed by the law in various places, Bout managed to keep a step ahead, folding and reopening his front companies, reregistering his aircraft, and moving his personal base of operations in ever-changing country combinations. By 1993, his planes were flying out of Sharjah in the United Arab Emirates. It was a convenient base from which to serve a particularly sensitive client, the Taliban. Bout's first encounter with the Afghan militia had not been a pleasant one: a plane he chartered delivering Israeli arms from Albania to the then Afghan government of Burhannudin Rabbani was intercepted and detained by the Taliban for an entire year in 1995–96. Negotiating with Mullah Omar for the release of the plane and crew, Bout discovered that there was value in keeping in touch; after the Taliban took power in 1998, Bout was put in charge of maintenance of the Afghan air fleet, and he helped run multiple weekly flights to Kandahar, the Taliban base, from his own base in the United Arab Emirates—conveniently one of the few countries to recognize the Taliban regime. The weapons he ferried—for an estimated $50 million profit—were destined in part for al-Qaeda.

By early 2002, Bout's network was finally under some stress, due to the growing mountain of investigations in different countries and accentuated by the new sense of urgency after the September 11, 2001, terrorist attacks. In February 2002, Bout's associate Sanjivan Ruprah, an Asian-Kenyan who represented him in many of his African dealings, was arrested in Belgium. Soon thereafter, the Belgians issued a warrant for Bout himself and launched a worldwide Interpol alert. But Bout, it turned out, was not to be perturbed. By this time, he was no longer in the Emirates but back at home in Moscow, where authorities declined to arrest him. On the same day that Russian police stated he was unlikely to be on national territory, Bout turned up impromptu at a Moscow radio station to claim his innocence live on the airwaves. A few Western journalists have tracked him down for interviews since then, always in Moscow under cloak-and-dagger conditions. He replies to every accusation with a flat denial. Bout, who has been called the Bill Gates or Donald Trump of modern gun running, prefers to describe himself as a simple airfreight operator, just another legitimate businessman looking for opportunity.

So far, the shrewd Bout has proven adept at finding ways to fit the reality to his self-description. By 2004, his companies and others with suspiciously close ties to him were turning up on Iraqi airfields, pressed into service as subcontractors and subsubcontractors to U.S. companies supplying logistics to the American military and the occupation authorities. The enormous transportation needs of the Iraq operation and its reliance on private contractors gave Bout an opportunity to profit off the military budget of the country that had blacklisted him. The head of a Bout-related firm recounted to a *Los Angeles Times* reporter how he had been awarded a card for free fuel refills out of U.S. military supplies. Complex times beget complex partnerships: "If you want it bad, you get it bad," one officer told reporters. If so, Bout may have found yet another way to come in from the cold.

A MIDDLEMAN'S DREAM

By combining the roles of broker and transporter, Victor Bout holds the catbird seat, the best position for making money in an arms market that has been drastically reconfigured since 1990. Sources of weapons have decentralized, even scattered. And so has the demand, as "rogue states" and rebel movements have destabilized whole regions, setting in motion local arms races and embargoes that do nothing to stop the trade, only raise prices and profits. In sum, a middleman's dream.

It's not that arms production has grown that much, at least in gross volume. The massive defense budgets of the cold war era shrunk in the 1990s and with them the landmark deals for fighter jets, missiles, and tanks. And despite their much more common everyday use—in law enforcement, security, recreation, or conflict—smaller weapons are produced in no greater numbers than ten years ago. By the best estimates (and it's a highly inexact science), production of small arms and light weapons—those designed for use by an individual or crew, from rifles and machine guns to grenades and shoulder-held missile launchers—is steady at about 8 million units per year. Seven-eighths of these are commercial firearms, the bulk of which are made and sold in the United States. The remaining million are military grade; at least 10 billion units of military-caliber ammunition are produced each year as well.

But aggregates are often misleading; these especially so. Weapons production may be stable, but it is far from stagnant. In fact, the industry is recomposing, with both consolidation and decentralization taking place at the same time. In 2003, Russia formed a state holding company called CAST to absorb all its small-arms producers. In 1998, Scandinavia's ammunition companies merged into Nammo AS. In 2002, Switzerland's RUAG and Germany's Dynamit Nobel became RUAG Ammotec. These newer names complete the list of major producers—Sturm Ruger, Remington, Smith & Wesson, Colt, Beretta, China's Norinco, and the Israeli IMI. Yet while there may be fewer large producers, there are now many more small producers than before. Officially, in 2004 small arms were manufactured by 1,249 formal corporations based in ninety countries. The most intense growth of activity has come in eastern Europe and in Asia, but the trend is global.

Technology and commercial concerns both help explain this proliferation. With small arms manufacturing techniques little changed in recent decades, it is relatively simple to establish production facilities where labor is cheaper and to transfer the necessary know-how. Commercial licensing is widespread and counterfeiting even more so, with a roster of the more industrialized developing countries taking part. The Turkish firm MKEK and the Pakistan Ordnance Factory (POF), for instance, manufacture assault rifles and submachine guns under license from Germany's Heckler & Koch. Among other win-win benefits, these Heckler-licensed guns can this way be sold to countries to which German law prevents direct exports. Illegal technology transfer is rife as well. A 2002 police raid in Sao Paulo, Brazil, shut down a technically advanced workshop that produced about fifty counterfeit submachine guns a month. Rebel and criminal organizations frequently manufacture at least part of their own arsenal. And although the term "craft production" evokes crude and unreliable equipment, sometimes imaginatively assembled, that image is increasingly obsolete. From the infamous and much-reported gun bazaar of Darra Adam Khel in northwest Pakistan to more surprising venues like Ghana—which despite its peaceful image has become a significant, if unofficial, gun supplier across volatile West Africa—artisanal production is fast catching up with the real thing. In Ghana there are now 2,500 small and medium manufacturers that offer perfectly functional copies of modern assault weapons, or cheap pistols for six dollars a piece.

Perhaps the single most important factor in galvanizing illicit weapons supply since the end of the cold war was the transformation of the former Soviet Bloc and its effect on arms producers there. Virtually every country in central and eastern Europe has a small-arms industry, with most firms established in the cold war heyday of the military industrial complex but others, like the Czech Republic's Ceska Zbrojovka and Sellier & Bellot, boasting a prestigious pre-Communist history. As with other industries, the 1990s found these companies oversize and often inefficient, and facing the drastic decline of defense budgets in their traditional customer base. Other classic problems—large employee rosters, important social welfare obligations in "company towns," and the like—further bedeviled the prospects for privatization or shutdown. As a result, these companies have turned to export markets, sometimes with official government policy support and sometimes of their own initiative. In 2001, 8 percent of handguns and 20 percent of rifles imported into the United States came from this region, including more than 40,000 firearms from the Czech Republic and Romania each. The same year saw the first firearms imports to the United States from Poland, Serbia, and Ukraine. But the drive to export also means that some eastern European firms are none too regarding when it comes to supplying more dubious customers—countries or movements under embargoes, or whomever else a broker might represent.

The same forces that drive exports from the former Soviet Bloc help fuel a vibrant secondhand market as well, for discarded and overstock equipment from the armies and air forces of the Communist era, now scattered across eastern Europe, as well as among the Soviet Union's onetime satellite states. In 2002 UN investigators documented that a series of six cargo flights into then embargoed Liberia carried 210 tons of Yugoslav army overstock, including 350 missile launchers, 4,500 automatic rifles, 6,500 grenades, and millions of rounds of ammunition. The Yugoslav army sold the equipment through a Belgrade company called TEMEX, and a series of brokers relayed it, all under the cover of a false certificate listing Nigeria as the final client.

Another important and more recent outpouring of small arms from a government arsenal into the marketplace took place in Iraq. After the fall of Saddam Hussein's regime it is estimated that seven to eight *million* small arms were scattered throughout Iraq and probably to neighboring countries. These include sophisticated weapons such as the ominous MANPADs, "man-portable air defense systems," which are missile-launching weapons that can be fired by one or two persons and can shoot down a low-flying airplane. The U.S. government estimates that four thousand such surface-to-air missiles once in Saddam Hussein's arsenal went missing in the chaos that followed the American invasion.

The global proliferation of MANPADs precedes the war in Iraq and is likely to continue well beyond it. In 2002 two MANPADs were fired at an Israeli passenger airliner taking off from Mombasa, Kenya. A tragedy was averted when the pilots were able to detect the missile and evade it. The U.S. State Department reckons that about forty aircraft have been struck by portable missiles since the 1970s. While 500,000 to 750,000 of these weapons were estimated to exist in the world's inventory in 2004 according to the authoritative *Small Arms Survey,* 100,000 fully operational units of this weapon are unaccounted for.

The *Survey* also claims that at least thirteen nonstate groups, including some terrorist organizations, are known to possess MAN-

PADs, and fourteen additional groups are reported to have them. Moreover, the report argues that the demand for this product is so strong that many new producers are now supplying it—and these are no longer the usual suspects in the high-tech arms industry. Companies in Egypt, North Korea, Pakistan, and Vietnam are now selling MANPADs. Together with the ample supply available in the secondhand market, the obstacles for a well-funded customer to get access to a shoulder-fired antiaircraft missile, or in fact any other such lethal weapon, have become far from insurmountable.

THE WEAPONS WAL-MART

The secondhand equipment market, of course, assists brokers in getting their operations going at low expense, as witnessed by Victor Bout's start-up investment in grounded Soviet air force planes. Around the world, workhorses like the Antonov An-12 and the Ilyushin Il-76 have been put to lucrative second careers in illegal and legal shipping alike. Personnel competent in operating these aircraft or training soldiers in the use of secondhand equipment are also in oversupply and have deployed around the world accordingly, swelling the ranks of the "private military contractors" once known by a simpler term: *mercenaries*. Indeed, one feature of the new illicit weapons supply is the blurring of lines—between vendors and combatants, brokers and suppliers, producers and subcontractors, and, sometimes, companies and states.

The blurring extends from the production and sales apparatus all the way to the client side, where government employees, military factions, rebel groups, legal companies, and criminal organizations can take part in arms procurement, often in interlinked ways. When the Taylor regime in Liberia, supplier to the embargoed RUF, itself came under a UN embargo, it turned to Burkina Faso and Ivory Coast as intermediate supply points. Togo served for many years as a transit point for shipments to Angola's UNITA movement. But most often it is corrupt individuals or groups within governments, not the state itself, that lend their services to the trade for profit, not policy. As discussed in Chapter 2, a Peruvian network led by Vladimiro Montesinos, the notorious security chief of then president Alberto Fujimori, organized the shipment of ten thousand AK-47 assault rifles from Jordan to the FARC rebels in Colombia. The most common case is the ordinary civil servant who is willing to issue, for a small consideration, an end-user certificate, that makes a false claim about the destination of a weapons shipment. Bearing the seal of Nigeria, Central African Republic, Chad, Venezuela, or any number of other countries, these certificates—still the only document universally required to authorize an arms sale—appear frequently in the market and underscore the ease with which illicit cargos transit from point to point.

It is a system symbiotically well adapted to the way modern conflict has evolved in the post–cold war world, where decentralized and sometimes stateless conflicts call for decentralized, sometimes stateless suppliers. In the rigid pre-1989 geopolitical order, the superpowers buttressed client states with enough basic efficiency to ward off much war between nations and, crucially, to keep the lid on domestic rebellion. Since 1990, however, separatist insurrections and small-to-medium-scale regional wars have become the norm. By and large, African conflicts lead the pack in number and duration. Consider the Congo conflict, which has lasted the better part of a decade and involves the armies of multiple neighboring states, along with their many rebel and criminal proxies; or the domino effect of civil wars in Liberia, Sierra Leone, and Ivory Coast. But Colombia, Bosnia, Kosovo, Sri Lanka, Chechnya, Nepal, and Afghanistan—along with more obscure but no less debilitating wars in places like the Solomon Islands—remind us that no continent has a monopoly on modern conflict.

What has made addressing these conflicts difficult is that they tend not to involve states, at least in the structured, organized sense of the word. Instead, entities at war in the world since 1990 have included quasi states like the Republika Srpska; separatist armies like the Tamil Tigers and the KLA; territorially entrenched militias such as Hezbollah; diversified political and criminal operations such as Colombia's FARC; paramilitary gangs that operate in government's shadow; and of course terrorist networks like al-Qaeda. Defying classification are numerous and varied others: Abu Sayaf, Lord's Resistance Army, Islamic Jihad, Interahamwe, and so on. When a government is involved, it may be through just one of its branches, beyond real executive control; or in loose, intermediary ways that fall short of officially sanctioned activities. And wars often occur in "failed states"—empty shells in which institutions no longer function at all or have been commandeered in the service of private, often illicit, interests.

All of these conditions make the principal method devised to restrict sales into these conflicts—the embargo—poorly adapted to its purpose and exceedingly easy to circumvent. But for an arms broker they simply describe a marketplace where customers are scattered and typically place small orders, require extra secrecy, and have bad credit or no credit. On the other hand, these customers are willing to pay premium prices and can afford to because they often control natural resources: coltan from Congo, used in cell phones; "conflict diamonds" from Sierra Leone or Angola, excluded from official marketing channels; concessions for mineral exploration; or marijuana, cocaine, or heroin. And the nontraditional destination and the need to violate an embargo, breaking the law in a supplier or transit country, and the doling out of bribes and side payments throughout the process serves to boost the price.

In his 1977 investigation *The Arms Bazaar,* the late British journalist Anthony Sampson concluded that "the ordinary citizen is right in thinking that the arms trade, like narcotics and slavery, is different from other trades." But in fact today's illicit weapons trade looks very much like an adaptation to the political conditions and commercial possibilities of globalization. When Sampson's book was published—subtitled *From Lebanon to Lockheed*—the vital center of the arms trade consisted of large government-sanctioned transactions tightly woven into geopolitics and diplomacy. Today, such deals are still important, but the dynamic segment of the arms business—if not the largest by volume—is the networked multinational supply system that Victor Bout and A. Q. Khan inhabit. In that respect, the bazaar, a place of ritualized commercial meeting, with its formalities, its ceremonies, and its underlying code of conduct, has given way to something much more like a Wal-Mart, or maybe even an eBay: a supermarket that knows no borders and in which virtually anything can be procured for virtually anyone, so long as the buyer is prepared to pay the price. Sadly, the evidence shows that too many clients are willing to pay the price and have the wherewithal to do so.

OWN YOUR OWN STATE

The new arms market still has hubs, but not in the way most people expect. States don't go into crime; criminals take over or even set up states. For instance, you may not have heard of the Transdniester Moldovan Republic. It's a rather obscure place. Yet weapons are to Transdniester what chocolate is to Switzerland or oil to Saudi Arabia. Some countries export oil and gas, others, cotton or computers. Transdniester exports weapons—illegally. What kinds of weapons? Vast quantities of Soviet shells and rockets. Newly manufactured machine guns, rocket launchers, RPGs, and more, produced in what are described as "at least six sprawling factories." Mines. Antiaircraft missiles. And Alazans—rockets that according to Joby Warrick, the *Washington Post* reporter who broke the story, are known to have been outfitted with warheads with radiological payloads, or "dirty bombs."

None of this is legal, but that is not really a concern for the government of Transdniester. For Transdniester is not, in fact, a country. Rather, it is a breakaway region of Moldova that has established its own government, army, and other trappings of sovereignty even though not a single other country has recognized it. Soon after the Soviet Union dissolved, Transdniester split from Moldova, the former Moldavian Soviet Socialist Republic. Transdniester is tiny, but it happened to contain the bulk of Moldova's industrial base. Because Moldova doesn't accept the secession, it refuses to patrol the border with the breakaway region. Allowing mysterious cargos to pass unhindered is a way for Moldovan officials to boost their slim civil service pay. Cargos also leave by air from Tiraspol, Transdniester's capital, and by road and rail to the port of Odessa in neighboring Ukraine.

Another thing about Transdniester: it is not your typical breakaway region with deep grievances or a popular liberation movement. It's a family-owned and operated criminal smuggling enterprise. A company called Sheriff runs the bulk of Transdniester's trade. Its head, Vladimir Smirnov, is helpfully in charge of the customs service as well. Even more conveniently, he is the president's son. In Transdniester politics, trade and finance are elegantly integrated into one single criminal undertaking that boils down, as a Moldovan scholar told the *Washington Post,* to "Father, Son, and Sheriff."

Transdniester is the epitome of illicit. The state is the criminal enterprise, and vice versa. Because no one recognizes it, there's no clear way to deal with it. Moldova, to which it officially belongs, has neither the capacity nor the political will to regain control of the situation. It's also an isolated place, the sort of location we still think of as a remote backwater. But that isn't quite true either. Isolated or not, Transdniester has achieved considerable international influence. Its weapons have spread into its neighborhood—a set of Alazans with radiological warheads has vanished, but all the clues point toward the Caucasus—and so has its capacity to weaken neighboring governments by producing rich opportunities for corruption and crime. Transdniester is in fact a global player, as weapons traced to it have appeared, for instance, in regional and civil wars across Africa. It offers goods that are sought; and nowadays, those who seek, find.

ARMED CIVIL SOCIETY

Easy shopping for weapons is a familiar concept in the United States, where a range of firearms are sold in actual Wal-Mart stores, as well as in thousands of other legal outlets, helping to fuel a vibrant licit and illicit secondhand trade. The United States is unusual for its political tradition of condoning, even celebrating, civilian gun possession. American civilians own an estimated 234 million small arms. Adding police and military equipment, there are nearly as many small arms in the United States as there are people, and more than one-third of the global stockpile. As a result, the United States is also distinct by the political power of the gun owners' lobby and its flagship organization, the National Rifle Association. The NRA's frequent stands against new restrictions on gun ownership or regulations on trade are nothing new to American public life. But these positions carry greater consequences at a time when the arms market is growing ever nimbler, more responsive to demand, and more adept at evading existing rules.

Yet if the United States remains, by a wide margin, the world's most armed nation, other countries are catching up. Larger numbers of weapons with greater lethal potential are finding their way out of the hands of the military, law enforcement, and sportsmen and into those of security guards, vigilantes, militias, criminals, and ordinary civilians. TV images display the prevalence of arms in places like the West Bank, where they are fired at political funerals, or Iraq, where civilians marked the capture of Saddam Hussein with celebratory shooting in the streets. But if the world's second-most armed country is another "trouble spot," Yemen, third place goes to tranquil Finland, with Norway, Germany, and France not far behind. Little reported, as well, is Europe's spectacular rise in gun crime. A string of tragic events from Sweden to Italy has shattered the European presumption that random shootings by unbalanced individuals in schools, offices, restaurants, and public spaces are an American specialty. In England, where as recently as 2000 the police did not even carry firearms, gun crime rose by 34 percent between 2000 and 2003. Arms seizures by European authorities are turning up heavier weapons, as well—fewer revolvers and rifles and more automatic pistols and submachine guns. Germans, for example, are buying almost as many firearms as are Americans. European citizens are far more heavily armed than is commonly acknowledged. The fifteen European Union countries together export more small arms than the United States; the pertinent detail, however, is that a significant percentage of these guns are sold inside Europe.

The toll is heavier elsewhere. A study in Uganda's capital, Kampala, found small arms accounting for a rising share of injury deaths, from 11 percent in 1998 to 23 percent in 2001. Another study, on the Philippine island of Mindanao, attributed 85 percent of external deaths to small arms, and more than three-quarters of deaths and injuries from criminal violence were caused by handguns and automatic weapons. Surveys in Latin America in 1996 placed gun crime at the top of the list of social and economic problems in the region. The *Small Arms Survey* calls the effects of the illicit trade and use of these weapons "development denied": not just the direct damage in injury and loss of life, but the destruction of roads and railways, diversion of investment, closure of schools and clinics under threat, induction of children into armies and gangs, and a host of other costs that drain public resources and the social potential of communities.

In the immediate, the steady seepage of overstock, low-cost, and secondhand weapons by means of a flexible, entrepreneurial global supply chain is exhausting the control capacity of states. And where states are losing grasp—which is in many places—rising to fill the void is a form of armed civil society made up of insurgent groups, private companies, bands of individuals, and even free agents, all with access to weapons and often accountable to none but themselves. Armed civil society runs not on ideals or on religion, but on fear and the illusion of protection created by having a gun handy. These instincts, fears, and illusions create a surging demand for weapons that the brokers of power, profit, and greed are happy to fuel and satisfy.

The mainstream industry most emblematic of the rise of armed civil society is private security, which is enjoying a boom of historic proportions. The global security business is estimated to be growing from $100 billion in 2001 to $400 billion by 2010. In many countries businesses and individuals spend more on private security than the government spends on police. From Mexico City to Manila and São Paulo to Moscow, security guards have flooded business districts and well-off neighborhoods, in some places easily identifiable in a signature uniform color but less organized elsewhere. Major beneficiaries of the turn to private services have been large international firms such as Wackenhut, Securicor, and ADT, some of which operate in up to a hundred countries.

But security is a local growth business too, and one with few barriers to entry and little oversight: Cameroon, for instance, counts over 180 private security firms. And a form of arms race leads those without professional protection to look to less established and shadier alternatives, creating a lucrative niche for vigilantes. A 2001 survey in Kaduna, Nigeria, found twenty security companies serving 295 customers—three times more customers than in 1997. At the same time, something called the "Vigilante Groups of Nigeria (Kaduna Chapter)" provided 4,300 households with protection for a fee.

Private security effectively fills in for the state and helps push it out at the same time, establishing a gray area of opportunity for large global corporations and unproven local freelancers alike—as well as a commercial destination pool for weapons that can leave the distinction between "legal" and "illegal" guns heavily blurred. By now a hallmark of globalization in its own right, the growth of private security reflects and reinforces the spread of weapons, underscoring not only the dynamism of the weapons market but its intimate connection to the failures of states and to the instability of those that, while not failed, are increasingly difficult to govern.

But these statistics also show a larger truth: the demand for weapons of all kinds is boundless and growing. And the attempts of governments to limit this demand or control the international trade in weapons are not succeeding. No insurgent group, criminal organization, or rogue army anywhere in the world seems to have any trouble getting the weapons it needs.

GHOSTS AND BORDERS

The new weapons market leaves states in the position of endlessly playing catch-up, with less and less success. In a marketplace defined less by a few large suppliers and more by a constellation of smaller producers and intermediaries, the proliferation of brokers involved in some aspect of the trade—thousands in Europe alone by some estimates—makes regulation an immense challenge and effective crackdowns exceedingly rare. Licensing and reporting rules governing brokers vary from country to country. A European Union code of conduct for arms deals, approved in 1998, remains nonbinding on the member states. From time to time, manufacturer countries impose restrictions on arms exports to certain destinations, but the diversity of supply and fluidity of the market mean that these have little effect.

The underlying dilemma, of course, is that states are ill equipped to put the lid on a problem that has outpaced them to the point that even defining it—and producing reliable numbers for weapons in circulation, purchased, or sold—is a matter of constant controversy. In fact, states are disadvantaged by their very nature, requiring complicated interagency coordination within countries and, even worse, across borders just to keep track of the movements and doings of highly autonomous businessmen who hop constantly across frontiers. Borders benefit dealers: in a classic illicit arms deal, the buyer, seller, broker, banker, and transporter are all in different countries. In the run-up to the Rwanda genocide of 1994, a French dealer delivered Polish and Israeli weapons to Rwanda by means of a Turks and Caicos company with a Geneva address, an eastern African cargo airline, and an Afghan intermediary representing the Rwandans from his base in Italy. In 1997, a German broker supplied combat helicopters from Kyrgyzstan to the Congo through a Belgian intermediary with a South African bank account.

The dealers move from jurisdiction to jurisdiction in an endless game of cat and mouse. Their preferred transport methods operate by the same principle, with aircraft registered under flags of convenience—just like ships—and chartered and crewed by various nationalities. A 707 freighter that ferried Slovakian weapons to Sudan in 1999 (courtesy of a Syrian trading company, with an end-user certificate from Chad) made up, on its own, the entire fleet of a Cyprus airline that belonged to a Swiss businessman. The plane itself was registered in Ghana—only the last of its many incarnations. An Antonov 12 that crashed in 2000 while on an arms delivery into Monrovia, Liberia, was registered and deregistered in Moldova on the same day, a "ghost" plane with no official home. Chartered by a fictitious Congolese company, it had two different sets of flight plans filed for it. A British businessman offered from his suburban London office a service to legally reregister an aircraft in a lenient country of convenience in a matter of minutes. The tricks of the trade go on—all of them based on the confusion created by dispersing the pieces of a transaction across as many jurisdictions as possible.

Efforts to curb the trade read like a litany of frustration. Deployed only twice before 1989 (against then-Rhodesia and South Africa), the United Nations Security Council embargo has become a common resort, used since 1990 against Haiti, Iraq, Liberia, Libya, Rwanda and its neighbors, Sierra Leone, Somalia, Yugoslavia (twice) along with the Bosnian Serbs, and the UNITA movement in Angola—the first nonstate actor to be sanctioned this way, in 1993. Yet none of these targets lacked weapons as a result; the chief effect of the embargo was simply to drive prices up. In West Africa, the regional organization ECOWAS launched a supposedly binding small-arms moratorium to much fanfare in 1998. The first-of-its-kind experiment is by any measure an utter failure, with small arms delivered into the region, circulating within it, and even locally produced, all in complete disregard of the policy.

A similar fate befell the long-awaited (and splendidly titled) United Nations Conference on the Illicit Trade in Small Arms and Light Weapons in All Its Aspects, held in July 2001. It aimed—as such grand gatherings do—to establish at least a minimal framework and guidelines for tackling the issue, which activist groups and concerned governments had spent many months helping to prepare. But instead, the conference was lethally sidetracked. The United States categorically rejected language concerning sales to nonstate actors, on the grounds that it violated the U.S. Constitution. The then undersecretary of state John Bolton, who would go on to become the U.S. ambassador to the United Nations in the second Bush administration, announced that Washington would not accept a document contrary to the United States' "constitutional right to keep and bear arms." The president of the U.S. National Rifle Association, Wayne LaPierre, accused the conference of placing "a global standard ahead of an individual country's freedom." The United Nations had to clarify that the conference had no purview over the domestic laws of member countries—but to no avail. The recriminations hopelessly diluted the conference findings and in effect scuttled the event.

And yet. Even a successful conference would have meant no more than a baby step, a tentative agreement by states to take on, in some form or fashion, a problem that seems on the verge of forever eluding them. In contrast, the adaptive capacity of the market seems finely honed, and the spread of weapons continues unchecked. The fundamental market signal—price—suggests that the transformation of weapons from a sensitive specialty to a common commodity is well under way, if not complete. In 1986, in the rural Kenyan town of Kolowa, it took fifteen cows to buy an AK-47. Now it costs just five. Armed civil society, it seems, is here to stay.

Chapter 4

NO BUSINESS LIKE DRUG BUSINESS

Every business has its stock characters, the drug business perhaps more than most: the dealer, the courier, the drug lord, the kingpin, as we are used to seeing them in the movies. The man I met one afternoon in an elegant restaurant in a Mexican border town fit none of these descriptions. Yet people like him play a crucial role in the drug trade today. They are hard to identify because they hide in plain sight. They are hard to take out, because their involvement in the trade is just one aspect of their business, lost in the stream of legitimate commerce. They are traffickers nearly by accident—the accident, that is, of running into a line of business too juicy to refuse.

Don Alfonzo (not his real name) is an exuberant man in his sixties and a proud father. He began our lunchtime conversation by telling me that his two children had graduated—with honors, he specified—from top U.S. universities and were now pursuing successful careers in art and medicine in Mexico City. He explained that his family had long owned a medium-size construction company. It was in the mid-1990s that Don Alfonzo found himself—almost inadvertently, but not quite—venturing into the "transportation" business.

He first learned about the details and mechanics of drug smuggling when he decided to find out the real cause of the high turnover rate among his company's truck drivers. He discovered that with just one border crossing carrying a relatively small shipment of drugs, his drivers made the equivalent of one year's salary. Naturally, after making such a killing their truck-driving job was no longer appealing or needed. Through his inquiry, Alfonzo also found out that the funders who put up the money for the drivers to purchase the drugs were upstart members of the local business community and well-known politicians, who made a huge profit on their loans. The loans bore little risk because the drivers were rarely caught. Besides, in the prevailing honor code repayment was very important. "Finally," Don Alfonzo said, "one day, and almost out of boredom and curiosity, I told one of my trusted employees who I knew was using our trucks for smuggling that it was only fair that he share some of the profits with the company. He immediately accepted and, as they say, the rest is history."

He continued: "Since then, I got involved more frequently, mostly as a financier, and while we did it only about once a month the profits were several times larger than what we made in construction. Although we continued with our construction business, I must tell you that sometimes I think that in this town the construction business is riskier than moving drugs across."

I asked Don Alfonzo if he was not concerned with the personal risks he was running. He smiled. "What do you mean?" he said. "I am just a small businessman who lends money to his employees, and what they do with that is their own business. You know, there are thousands like me. The gringos and the police here are busy chasing the big guys, and if they go after the small guys like us they will need to build a new jail the size of this whole town. The economy of this entire region would go bankrupt. No government can touch this. Why should they? The big guys give good theater and are good for politics. We don't."

Not too long after this conversation, Mexico's long-running drug wars went through another of their periodic, spectacular flare-ups. This time it turned out that the leaders of two drug organizations that had been longtime rivals, the Arellano Felix organization and the Gulf Cartel, had forged an alliance in the high-security prison in which they were being held after having been arrested in much-celebrated raids by the *federales*. From their prison lodgings the new allies were running a vicious campaign against an aggressive new player, Joaquin "El Chapo" Guzmán, an outlaw said to be sheltered by the population in his home state of Sinaloa. The warden of the prison had been bought off. As for the seriousness of the threat posed by Guzmán, it became abundantly clear when a member of President Vicente Fox's travel advance team was arrested on suspicion of ties to him.

Patterns of the past suggest that Guzman will eventually be arrested or killed, by *federales* or by other criminals. That victory too will be transient. For Don Alfonzo and the many other respectable citizens, businessmen, and officials of his ilk who help sustain the drug trade, business will keep on chugging and money will keep getting made. It's one of the seeming contradictions of the drug business that on further inspection are not contradictions at all. That one high-profile criminal rises to replace another is a fairly easy notion to absorb. But today they are the tip of the iceberg. The diffusion of the drug business into the fiber of local and global economic life is much harder to fathom, let alone combat. Its political implications are ominous. Yet, more than any cartel, kingpin, or rebel warlord, it is this pervasive global mainstreaming of the business that the fight against drugs is up against today.

DISPATCHES FROM THE FRONT

Other, perhaps more familiar paradoxes of the drug trade only confirm this realization. Consider Washington, D.C. It is the hub of the war on drugs, the most massive, expensive, and technologically advanced antidrug offensive in history. In and around the capital, thousands of federal employees report daily to jobs that exist solely to combat the drug trade and enforce drug laws. Some are Drug Enforcement Administration (DEA) agents, or staff in the White House drug policy office, home to the so-called drug czar. Others are drug specialists in dozens of other agencies and services, from

Immigration and Customs Enforcement (ICE) to the U.S. Marshals, Secret Service, FBI, Coast Guard, and more. They are cogs in a vast machinery that consumes around $20 billion per year at the federal level alone in the fight against drug use and trade. Nationally, the fight brings in 1.7 million arrests and 250,000 incarcerations each year. In Washington, 28 percent of inmates are incarcerated primarily for drug charges

Yet minutes away from these offices are Washington's sixty open-air drug markets that serve suburbanites cruising for a fix, local retailers and intermediaries who take the product to upscale neighborhoods. And the market is thriving. Supply is abundant and prices are steady, hallmarks of a volume business. The purity levels of heroin are rising. There are products for every taste and budget, from high-end sniffables for the rich kids and bankers to vials of crack cocaine and cheap heroin blends suitable only for injection and destined for the hard addicts. (The cheap stuff can always be found in the vicinity of methadone clinics.) With this market offering something for everyone, it's little surprise that nearly one Washingtonian in two above the age of twelve admits to having used an illicit drug. Meanwhile only fifty kilograms of cocaine and thirty-four kilograms of heroin were seized in the District in 2004. The numbers are trivial compared with the visible trade taking place each day on the streets. And it's consolation only to the most jaded Washingtonians that down the road in Baltimore, the situation is even worse.

In Washington, a city famously divided by income and race, the drug economy connects segments of local society more effectively than any almost anything else. Twenty percent of D.C. high school students report regular marijuana use, and 5 percent say they've used heroin. The phenomenon spreads—even thrives—in the prestigious private schools where the children of top-tier officials and political players are groomed for success. The teenagers of the power elite have at their disposal an impressive array of substances: marijuana, hashish, cocaine, heroin, mushrooms, LSD, Ecstasy, PCP, and whatever designer compounds happen to be in vogue. They are at the teenagers' fingertips—literally, no more than a cell phone call or text message away. One young woman told me that she could rustle up a bag of weed in twenty minutes. For cocaine, give her a few hours. These fifteen-year-olds told me that it is easier for them to buy a joint than a pack of cigarettes. At the command center of the war on drugs, a stronger force is winning: the market.

This is the case not just at the command center but on the front lines as well. In Afghanistan, for example, the opium poppies are back with a vengeance. In 1999, Afghanistan produced more than five thousand tons of opium, smashing its own record. The next year, the Taliban outlawed the crop, having deemed it un-Islamic. Cynics argued that the Taliban's aim was to cause a price rise and benefit by selling stockpiles at a massive profit. At any rate, production plummeted to a mere two hundred tons in 2001, all of it in the far north of the country, beyond Taliban reach. By the end of that year, the United States and its allies had driven the Islamic militia out of power, and the new government in Kabul, led by Hamid Karzai, immediately renewed the opium ban. But the poppies swept back, reclaiming prime land in all parts of the country, overrunning fields once devoted to wheat. Within a year, opium poppy acreage nearly matched its 1999 level. By 2004, Afghanistan was producing an estimated 4,200 tons of opium from 323,700 hectares. The Karzai government also launched an intensive effort to dissuade growers from planting the poppies. But no one believes that poppy growing will stop being Afghanistan's main economic activity any time soon.

The opportunity is just too rich. Even though the Afghan grower earns only a microscopic fraction of what his plants will generate down the line—after the opium has been refined into morphine, then heroin, then cut with substances like quinine or baking powder and distributed into U.S. or European streets—it is still far and away the land's most lucrative use. It is convenient, too: poppies require less water than wheat does, and the sap does not rot. Besides, Afghans are managing now to capture a bit more of the margin. In the past, opium was shipped raw; now, laboratories that refine it into higher-value narcotics are springing up all over the country. One impact of the business is to drive up the price of labor. A *Washington Post* reporter found that in one northern village, it recently cost ten dollars to buy a day of work that previously fetched only three dollars. The local police earn thirty dollars per month, assuming they're paid at all. A hundred-dollar cash bribe buys a lot of goodwill.

The news from another well-known front is not much better. In Colombia, fifteen years and billions of dollars in U.S. spending to support the Colombian military in counternarcotics efforts have netted some successes: the decapitation of the Medellin and Cali cartels and scores of arrests, extraditions, and convictions resulting in long sentences in U.S. jails. Yet the drugs still flow. The left-wing FARC guerrillas and their right-wing opponents, the AUC "self-defense" forces, both control coca-growing territory, shelter cocaine labs, and collect revenues on drug exports that make up 50 percent of FARC's and up to 70 percent of the AUC's cash flow. Trafficking interests reach high into the political and military establishment. Colombia not only produces most of the world's cocaine but has now become a serious player in heroin as well, thanks to the widespread planting of poppies from Asia in the 1990s. As for the massive crop-fumigation programs that the United States has bankrolled, the drug networks have an answer, too: research and development. Diminished acreage no longer means lower production, as the traffickers are applying the latest agronomy techniques to boost their productivity. In Colombia new strains of the coca plant that are resistant to herbicides have emerged. They also happen to be leafier, grow up to twice the height of the traditional plant, and result in much purer and stronger cocaine.

Technology has also allowed new entrants to participate in this lucrative market. The most coveted (and therefore expensive), marijuana is no longer cultivated in the tropical jungles of Colombia or Mexico. It comes from British Columbia in Canada. The variety known as "B.C. bud" is grown using advanced hydroponics and cloning techniques in special nurseries that keep the temperature and other conditions at optimal levels throughout the year. As Sarah

Kershaw of the *New York Times* reported, a rugged, hard-to-patrol border poses more problems for the police than it does for the kayakers who navigate the rapids with loads of up to one hundred pounds of B.C. bud, which sells for $3,500 a pound in California, and who coordinate deliveries by means of BlackBerry two-way devices. The B.C. bud business also involves moving cocaine and weapons back from the United States to Canada. According to Canadian law enforcement officials, this industry has grown to a gigantic $7 billion-a-year business in 2005. A decade ago it barely existed.

THE END OF ILLUSIONS

Despite the global nature of the trade, public attention is still focused on the usual fronts: the United States for demand, Colombia, Mexico, Afghanistan, and a few others for supply. It's not completely unjustified. Far and away the United States remains the single largest consumer country for illegal drugs. It is also the motor of the global response, often deploying its political or military might beyond its borders in service of its approach to drug control. At the other end of the supply chain, it is also true that Colombia and Afghanistan are the largest single sources of cocaine and heroin, respectively. These are stubborn facts that predate the 1990s.

But taken in isolation these facts imply a map of the world that is highly misleading. For during the 1990s, the number of countries reporting serious drug addiction problems steadily rose. Spikes in HIV/AIDS infections became a macabre revealer of new trade routes for injectable drugs. Amid steady growth of the world drug market, the big three—marijuana, cocaine, and opiates—lost market share to methamphetamine, rougher and more potent and addictive than heroin. The meth epidemic joins in a common crisis the small towns in the U.S. heartland and virtually every social category in Thailand, where methamphetamine is known as "yaa baa" (crazy drug) and used as a stimulant for work as well as pleasure. Other compounds—Ecstasy, ketamine, GHB, and Rohypnol—are on the rise as well.

Because these drugs are chemicals that do not depend on plant inputs, they can be manufactured virtually anywhere that some basic supplies can be obtained and a makeshift lab established. But this doesn't mean that they are restricted to a cottage industry. The meth that kills an overdosing teenager in Missouri is as likely to have come in a bulk shipment from Canada or Mexico as to have been concocted locally in someone's garage.

The global explosion of demand and supply has shattered the illusion of invulnerability that governments—or, for that matter, public opinion—harbored in many countries. Now, no country is isolated enough to delude itself or its critics into imagining that it has no part in the world drug trade. Countries that long harbored the illusion that they were only "transshipment" locations have woken up to the fact that they have become themselves major suppliers, consumers, or both. In Tajikistan, Afghanistan's neighbor to the north with hundreds of miles of porous border, only six and a half kilos of heroin were seized in 1996, so little you could fit it in a backpack with plenty of room to spare. In 2002, the Tajiks seized four tons, and an estimated eighty tons got through untouched. It is no wonder that the product has seeped out into the street. In the capital, Dushanbe, a gram of good stuff costs no more than eight dollars, and there are now 20,000 serious addicts. Clean needles being scarce, HIV and other diseases are on a rampage. The same fate has befallen China's Yunnan province, a major export route for heroin from Myanmar and, not coincidentally, the original outbreak area of AIDS in China. In Yunnan, where drug seizures have been as large as half a ton at a time, heroin addiction has rapidly spread, and teenagers sell sex for five yuan, or sixty cents. Russia, Japan, India, South Africa, Brazil, and Mexico are just a few of the countries where drug use and its side effects have become a public health emergency.

What's good for the user is good for the dealer: Traders in the drug business are a more diverse bunch than ever. They need not come from a country where drugs are produced. Twenty years ago, Nigerians were virtually unknown in the global drug business, and to this day Nigeria is a minimal producer of drugs with the exception of cannabis, which grows locally but is not a major export. Yet Nigerians today operate lucrative segments of the drug trade and distribution in far-flung corners of the world. Nigerian exporters based in Bangkok procure heroin through various local intermediaries from Myanmar—or, when Afghan product is more competitive, send couriers to buy it in Pakistan. They then ship it in bulk to Lagos by air or sea freight. When law enforcement somewhere rises from its torpor, the traffickers switch to alternate routes—perhaps overland into Nigeria from elsewhere in Africa, or avoiding Nigeria altogether in favor of South Africa, Ghana, or Ivory Coast. For the crucial entry into the United States, the Nigerians often use as mules white women—considered a low-risk category—whom they dispatch from airports in Europe. In the United States, Nigerians are in the heroin wholesale market in several cities and are dominant in Chicago, where they moved into the business in the late 1980s after the previous network—mainly Mexican—was disrupted by authorities. The Chicago wholesalers use the mail, couriers, and parcel delivery services to supply local vendors. At the retail level, the Nigerians vanish.

As this example shows, drug trafficking still employs ethnic networks for efficiency and trust, but not exclusively. In contrast to a Mafia model, in which all transactions take place among members of a crime "family," the drug trade gives rise to specialties that take advantage of location, language, local knowledge, or ability to melt into the crowd. Some drug transactions rely on the trust and mutual recognition that a common ethnic background implies; others are enforced by the threat of violence. But in a world of increasing sources of supply and product destinations, a great many drug transactions are simply that—transactions.

DEMYSTIFYING THE GAME

With this opening up of the business has come a great demystification, though the new reality is not yet fully understood. As recently as the 1980s, the drug trade was personified by legendary figures such as Pablo Escobar Gaviria, whose tales updated the popular image of the drug kingpin and earned their subject something close to a cult following. Escobar, leader of the Medellín cartel, was only one of the entrepreneurs responsible for turning Colombia, a bit player in the early eighties, into the predominant global source of cocaine by the end of the decade. But he soon stood out from the pack. His ingenuity knew no bounds: he once concealed a landing strip under mobile houses on wheels, which the inhabitants would push aside for a plane's arrival and unloading and move back into place after it took off again. His taste for violence frightened even hard-boiled fellow traffickers; he groomed a stable of killers and pioneered new techniques, such as positioning the assassin on the back of a motorcycle, a method well suited to snarled Bogotá traffic. He fancied himself a public figure, a benefactor in his home city, where he built roads and schools and made copious donations to the local Catholic good works. And he wrapped his persona in visible extravagance, from his parties to his vintage cars to his zoo, with its zebras, antelopes, and hippopotamuses.

The legend of Escobar—not to mention his longtime de facto impunity—put a face on the emerging war on drugs, focusing public opinion on a visible, describable enemy. It made disciples on the U.S. end of the business among the rising entrepreneurs of the crack game, who restyled themselves as "dons" with lavish lifestyles. Yet the days of the brash, ostentatious renegade hero were coming to an end. Too visible, too obvious, they were quick grist for the mills of the law. The American crack dons were eventually tracked down and incarcerated. And the role model Escobar, after many adventures and near misses, was killed by Colombian authorities in 1993.

A change had begun. Escobar's demise cleared the field for his longtime rivals in Cali. But they too came down in short order. Colombia remained the leading source of cocaine, both locally produced and shipped from Bolivia and Peru; enormous coca fields and processing labs sprang up in guerrilla and militia territory, soon followed by opium poppies. But the balance of power shifted. At the local level, the military movements took control. The part of the business with the highest added value, however—moving the product into the United States—shifted largely to Mexico. By the mid-1990s, the large-scale distributors that most worried law enforcement were Mexican: the Arellano Felix organization in Tijuana, the Carillo-Fuentes organization in Juarez, and Cardenas Guillen organization in Tamaulipas and Nuevo Leon.

These groups resembled the Colombian cartels in their most unsubtle aspects: the vendettas, corruption, and extreme violence. But their economics were different from their Colombian predecessors, for these groups possessed the most enviable situational advantage of all: territorial control of the approaches to the U.S. border, the single most lucrative bottleneck in the drug supply chain, the point where the most value is added. Better yet, they had years of successful experience smuggling goods of all sorts across the border, especially human beings. And the advent of NAFTA made these qualifications, already exceptional, the keys to an unprecedented bonanza.

The Mexican groups quickly adapted their business to the advantages that globalization made so valuable. This meant, first, maintaining control at all costs over their respective border-crossing corridors—Tijuana and Mexicali, Juarez, and Laredo. (By one estimate, this involved bribes to Mexican officials of up to a million dollars a week.) From this position of strength, the Mexican cartels offered partnerships to Colombian suppliers including FARC and AUC, other Mexican groups, and the new entrants brought into the picture by globalization—Russians, Ukrainians, Chinese. They also sold the rights to use "their" routes to lesser traffickers against the payment of exorbitant tolls, up to 60 percent of the value of a shipment. Despite the huge levy, the smaller players prospered thanks to the huge profit margins in the U.S. market.

In what amounted to a total recomposition of the game, product expertise was traded for functional specialty. While the Colombian cartels had been more or less vertical organizations focused on a single product, the Mexican groups focused on controlling the border and took part directly or indirectly in the movement of a wide range of goods across it. Though some still chose to specialize, others went polydrug, trading not just cocaine and marijuana but also the booming new products, heroin and methamphetamines. Through partnerships with Ukrainians, Chinese, and others, they expanded to the trade in human beings. By chaperoning other shipments against a fee, they kept a hand in just about every illicit product entering the United States. The Mexicans also excelled in the increasingly important art of large-scale money laundering. The Juarez group, for instance, was reputed for its network of twenty-six regional managers, de facto bankers located across the country.

Partnerships, diversification, the development of financial expertise—in all these respects, the Mexican cartels in the late 1990s adapted to the changing economics of the business and squeezed the maximum value from their territorial advantage. And as rivalries and physical danger grew, the business recomposition continued accordingly. By the time the elite of these groups were captured— Benjamin Arellano Felix in 2002 and Osiel Cardenas Guillen in 2003—much of their business was too decentralized, too well protected in the mainstream of the economy for the arrests to be more than a temporary setback. One Arellano Felix sister, Edenida, is a financial whiz and real estate magnate in her own right; under her leadership the group became, in the words of a Tijuana journalist, more "a corporation than a gang." Besides, since nature abhors a vacuum, new power players such as Guzman were on the rise. And throughout all this drama, small local enterprises like Don Alfonzo's side business in "transportation" have quietly prospered, no more affected by the cartel wars than by the billions of dollars the U.S. and Mexican governments have deployed to stop the trade.

What does this picture tell us? Not that the large trafficking networks are no longer the main players. They still are. But they increasingly have to share the low-end part of their trade with smaller competitors. As in any other business, competitive pressures push the large, dominant players to invest in new higher-margin products and business lines. Meanwhile the number of players has grown, their activities have decentralized, and they have become smarter and more financially savvy. The change is opportunistic, to take advantage of the possibilities that globalization affords. But it is also required to survive in the face of law enforcement challenges and competition from new entrants. In the process, the power—and greatest revenue potential—has moved to the middle of the distribution chain, to the points where the greatest opportunities exist for high-value cross-border transactions, diversification, and strategic partnerships and synergies. Not at all unlike what has happened in many legitimate global industries.

LAUNDER, BARTER, HACK

This global industry transformation would not have been possible without the innovations and tools of globalization. During the 1990s the number of reported drug seizures worldwide, which had been stagnant at around 300,000 per year, more than quadrupled to 1.4 million in 2001. This explosion should come as no surprise, for the entire legal and technological apparatus of globalization has made the illicit drug trade faster, more efficient, and easier to hide. It all starts with volume: with daily traffic of about 550 cargo containers only at the port of Hong Kong or 63 million passengers a year at London's Heathrow Airport (1,250 flights per day), the compact nature of illicit drugs makes them the equivalent of the needle in the haystack. A million-dollar retail payload of high-grade marijuana, say a thousand pounds, fits handily in a false compartment of one of the 4.5 million trucks crossing the U.S.-Mexican border every year. It takes only one kilogram of cocaine to command $12,000 to $35,000. Heroin is still more weight-efficient. A single mule who smuggles powder drugs by air or on foot, ingesting them wrapped in honey-coated condoms, can carry, fully laden, enough South American high-grade heroin to command $50,000 to $200,000.

Everywhere, the methods of the trade reflect the advance and spread of new technologies. Not only can drug wholesalers use express delivery services, but by tracking a shipment online they can know whether it has arrived or whether it has been held up, alerting them to a possible interception and narrowing the window in which authorities can intervene before the traffickers take evasive action. Drug sales are routinely arranged on cell phones that are discarded after no more than a week's use; traffickers coordinate by means of Instant Messaging, Webmail accounts, and chatrooms, often at public and anonymous computers in cybercafes. More sophisticated networks employ their own specialized hackers to protect their communications and "hack back" into law enforcement machines trying to penetrate them. The same security standards, like encryption, that make it safe to buy a book from Amazon.com or contribute to a political campaign online also help drug traffickers conceal their communications, transactions, and identities. Small-timers benefit too: the Internet brims with mail-order sales of marijuana seeds, equipment with which to grow high-potency hydroponic weed in a closet in one's home, and instructions for home-cooking methamphetamine and other substances.

It is perhaps the financial revolution of the past ten years that has most benefited the drug trade. If a packet of heroin is a needle in the haystack of world trade volumes, its monetary value is even harder to pick out in the daily swirl of financial transactions. To conceal the movement of money, pay suppliers, remunerate operatives, and recirculate the proceeds, drug traffickers make use of the complete gamut—from cash stuffed in the mail or carried in small amounts by couriers known as "smurfs" to complex laundering operations involving front companies, offshore banks, and correspondents and intermediaries in multiple countries. E-commerce, Internet banking, and wire transfer services all come into play.

In some cases, the drug-money circulation system is so entrenched and institutionalized that it develops its own "brand". In the scheme known as the Black Market Peso Exchange (BMPE), Colombian drug traffickers repatriate their proceeds by entrusting the dollars to brokers, who use the funds to make purchases in the United States on behalf of Colombian customers at a favorable exchange rate. The customers pay the brokers in pesos that the brokers pass on to the traffickers—after collecting their fee, of course. The system highlights the growing role of intermediaries and the intertwining of "dirty" and "clean" money. It also shows how law-abiding manufacturers in the United States can end up being paid, albeit indirectly, with drug money. The BMPE has worked so well that it has spawned numerous variants. It now encompasses Mexico as well, offering more opportunities for intermediaries to take shelter behind multiple frontiers. It recycles an estimated $5 billion annually.

Alongside these modern methods, more ancient ones still have their use, such as barter. Drugs make good currency in exotic settings. In-kind payments are common in many distribution networks; much of the product that seeps out along the trade routes is used as a means of payment and in the process often creates large populations of addicts in countries where only ten years ago there were none. But many large-scale exchanges in the global underworld also involve drugs as collateral or compensation. In the late 1990s, the Russian mafia supplied Mexican drug traffickers with automatic weapons, radars, and even miniature submarines in exchange for cocaine, amphetamines, and heroin. The IRA is reputed to supply the Dublin heroin market, and IRA officers surfaced in Colombia in 2001, providing technical advice and training in weapons and tactics and of course European drug market outlets to the FARC. And in remote locations where currency is scarce or impractical, heroin or cocaine make fine substitutes, easy to carry and universally valued— a modern-day salt, the prized white powder for our times.

STUCK IN SOURCE CONTROL

The drug trade has evolved; the methods to fight it, by contrast, have changed very little. The United States, which pressed for making cocaine and heroin illegal in the early twentieth century, still calls the shots—it is the heart of global illicit drug demand and the biggest spender in terms of enforcement resources. And those resources go, by an overwhelming margin, into efforts to stop the supply of drugs rather than to reduce or manage their demand. It is a strategic choice that has over the years become stubbornly entrenched: successive American administrations have reconsidered their drug policy only, in the end, to redouble their investment in police and military actions to arrest and incarcerate dealers, neutralize distribution networks, shut down border smuggling, and eliminate the raw materials wherever they are produced. The sum of these actions—the war on drugs—keeps a vast military and bureaucratic machine humming. "Source control" has an addictive quality in itself.

For more than three decades, the United States has made overseas source control an explicit and central part of its foreign policy, encouraging the spraying of coca and poppy fields with crop-killing chemicals and assaults on kingpin traffickers and their organizations. Countries that cooperate receive military, technical, and financial support. Those that do not risk the consequences: public shaming, economic sanctions, or back-channel punitive uses of American influence with international funding agencies like the World Bank and IMF. During the 1990s in an annual ritual known as "certification," the U.S. government made public its assessment of whether a foreign government had "cooperated fully" in the war on drugs, in America's interpretation. Naturally many countries viewed this process as insulting.

Eventually, the approach was discarded as it became impossible to hide that it did not work and that it was too blatantly hypocritical. A former top official of the Drug Enforcement Administration (DEA) told me that "before every trip I took to review with my counterparts in the Mexican government their efforts to combat drug trafficking, I was given a detailed briefing by our intelligence agencies about the ties between some of the high-level Mexican officials that I was going to meet and the drug traffickers. Yet after that I would go to another briefing where I was told that NAFTA was a priority for the United States and that I should be careful not to do anything that would jeopardize it. Our policy then and still now is highly schizophrenic."

Not all efforts are ineffectual and of course the dragnet does produce some victories. In 1997 the $773 million spent on "interdiction"—the interception of drug shipments headed to the United States by sea—yielded more than 100,000 pounds of cocaine and 30,000 pounds of marijuana. A week does not go by without news of a spectacular drug seizure in Florida, California, or elsewhere. In 2003, U.S. customs seized 2.2 million pounds of assorted illegal drugs, some in such containers as spare tires and teddy bears, concealed in or among wigs, boxes of corn chips and red salsa, artificial Christmas trees, and shipments of sand, and surgically implanted in a man's thigh.

The trouble is that for all these efforts and momentary successes, the flow of drugs into the United States and other major markets continues virtually unabated. According to a 2005 report released by the White House Office of National Drug Control Policy the number of marijuana users that sought treatment tripled between 1992 and 2002. According to the report this increase reflects an increase both in marijuana use and in the potency of the product available in the market.

The changes the drug trade has put itself through make it easy to see why these increases have occurred. Drugs are harder and harder to control at the source, since the sources themselves are multiplying—whether in the form of new producers of various drugs, lawless or rebel enclaves within a country, or proxy sources that have become privileged transshipment hubs for drugs of various origins. As they arrive in the high-value consumer markets, drugs are frequently combined with other licit and illicit products— not just concealed behind washing machines or inside toys in a shipping container, but embedded in complex movements of goods and money that involve numerous intermediaries and locations.

Meanwhile, "source control" and an emphasis on repression have simply added value to the drugs that make it into the market.

Borders to dodge, raids to evade, and bribes to pay out are all integrated into the cost of doing business, raising prices and profit potential without any demonstrated effect on demand. That added value is greatest where the risk is highest—for instance, crossing the United States or European Union border—but affects every segment in the supply chain. The increased cost of labor in rural Afghanistan pushes farmers to divert ever more fields from subsistence crops to poppies. Bribes become ever harder to turn down. Serving as a human courier for drugs is attractive. Cynically, traffickers know that a proportion of mules will get caught, and they accept this risk as a cost of doing business. But for single women with children—the frequent mule profile—the prospect of five thousand dollars for one drug run across the U.S. border offers a promise that no local opportunity can match.

In short, source control rests on lousy economics. But its critics, though numerous, have yet to sway any U.S. administration. In Europe, which never fully went for the approach in the first place, advocates of other strategies have enjoyed a better reception. Most European countries have simplified the problem by decriminalizing small-scale marijuana possession, either in law or de facto in police practice. Europe has been more aggressive in mandating (and funding) treatment for addicts. But at the global level the United States remains the most influential player, and as a result the certainties of the war on drugs still carry the day. If they are to be vanquished, it will not be by well-intentioned policy proposals, but rather by a stronger force: political realism. In that area too the traffickers have pulled ahead, with truly worrisome consequences.

COLLIDING WITH POLITICS

The economic force of the drug trade defies governments. It can also unseat them. Take, for example, the case of Bolivia. Strongly encouraged for years by the United States, Bolivia resolved in 1998 to eradicate cultivation of the coca leaf, the raw material for cocaine. Only a "small" legal acreage (about 12,000 hectares) would be retained, under heavy regulation, just enough to satisfy the plant's local legal use as a traditional chew. But spraying the fields and promoting alternative crops like pineapples and bananas proved nowhere near enough to change the incentives. And the plight of the *cocaleros,* the coca growers, became a rallying cause for all of Bolivia's disgruntled and unempowered: the poor, the peasantry, and the large and traditionally excluded indigenous population. An Aymara Indian socialist *cocalero,* Evo Morales, rose to become one of the country's most influential political figures. In 2002, Morales placed second by a tiny margin in the presidential election; the winner was Gonzalo Sanchez de Lozada, a liberal, free-market stalwart credited with slaying Bolivia's hyperinflation in the 1980s. The next year, *cocalero* discontent boiled over and violent protests swept La Paz. After barely a year in office, Sanchez ceded power to his vice president, Carlos Mesa, and departed for the United States. In 2005, Mesa's government too crashed under the same pressures.

Later Sanchez de Lozada told me that "narco-syndicalists, terrorist groups, and cartels" were behind his government's fall. He complained bitterly about how little economic support he received from the United States to help him improve the living conditions of poor Bolivians who had been forced to abandon their ancient coca-growing activities. "When I mostly needed financial support the Americans left me alone," he said. Two U.S.-promoted policies, the war on drugs and support for democratically elected governments in Latin America, had collided, with nefarious results. One of these is that now the *cocaleros* not only are politicized but have a natural convergence of interests with the traffickers who control Bolivia's main export industry. No longer merely tools of the trade, the *cocaleros* have become the country's main political force. Together they have achieved enormous sway over Bolivia's politics, main institutions, and international relations.

The Bolivian case is by no means isolated. Wherever the drug economy has flourished there have been political consequences. The sums of money involved are just too great. At a minimum, it is virtually guaranteed that where there are substantial drug profits, there will be corruption and official complicity—very often at the highest levels. Elite drug squads and national police units from Mexico to Russia to Cambodia have found themselves infiltrated and bought. Prosecutors and judges are no different. All the evidence suggests that we should assume corruption, not the absence of corruption. Thus, strategies based on cooperation between governments have an automatic Achilles' heel. And it is left to the honest and motivated members of a government to take on the less honest in their midst, a task that is politically costly and unlikely to get very far as long as the monetary incentives are what they are.

Other cases are more clear-cut. In Colombia the FARC and AUC territories are essentially countries within a country. With their own law, economy, and infrastructure, they are territories where the controlling authority sustains itself in large part from the drug trade. The same is true of the warlord-held zones of Afghanistan from which huge amounts of opium are exported despite the presence of tens of thousands of U.S. soldiers in that country. It is only a small step further to realize that battles between criminal organizations in northern Mexico are not just for drug-trafficking turf but for political control in areas where the official representatives of government are likely to be either for sale or too intimidated to be a threat. When a journalist spoke to the mayor of the Sinaloa town where Guzmán takes shelter, the mayor never once mentioned the criminal's name. It is fairly clear who wields the power in that relationship.

The logical next step would be for a recognized, official government to bow to economic reality and go into the drug business itself. It is a bold move, not recommended for anyone seeking cordial relations with the world's great powers. But if you feel you have nothing to lose, why not? As it happens, there is at least one country that has taken this step. According to informed accounts, North Korea began planting opium poppies many years ago. The secretive Communist nation is now, too, a producer of narcotics for the world market. It is an initiative far less known than the North Korean nuclear program. But it is set to cause plenty of potential havoc in its own right, and perhaps more, since it is not a bargaining chip but a source of much-needed revenue.

Narcotics may become yet another bone of contention in the already fraught negotiations between North Korea and the international community. But it would be a mistake to think of North Korea as an isolated case. The effect of continued huge profit margins in the global drug trade on vulnerable regions will be to produce political power that rests on drug money, and vice versa. The forms these combinations take may vary—from corruption to secession to "rogue states." The underlying dynamic, however, will be much the same.

Chapter 5

WHY IS SLAVERY BOOMING IN THE 21ST CENTURY?

Hours before dawn on June 7, 1993, an old freighter registered in Honduras and called the *Golden Venture* ran aground off Fort Tilden, near the entrance to New York Harbor. On board was an unusual cargo: more than three hundred Chinese illegal migrants from the province of Fujian. From the immobilized vessel, 120 passengers took their life in their hands and jumped into the ocean water, trying to swim ashore. Before the Coast Guard and police could scoop them all up, six were dead.

The *Golden Venture* was a wake-up call. It awoke the public to a quantum shift in the international trade in human beings. Before the *Golden Venture,* the public in rich countries was mainly aware of border passers who helped migrants enter the promised land for a fee. What the New York incident revealed instead was an organized wholesale trading business shipping bulk consignments of humans over long distances, and involving staggering amounts of money. Since the *Golden Venture* ran aground, appalling stories of human shipments around the world have proliferated. And they have largely faded from the headlines for the very worst reason: because they have become commonplace.

The *Golden Venture* also shone a light on the workings of a particular circuit—the Fujian circuit, which delivers migrants from this coastal and traditionally seafaring Chinese province to the United States, Taiwan, Japan, and Australia. The Fujian province accounted for more than one-quarter of Chinese emigration in 1995. In the early 1990s, 25,000 Fujianese were arriving each year in the United States. In 2004, 10,000 Fujianese arrived in New York alone. The Fujianese population in New York has driven Chinatown's expansion into adjacent areas and flooded restaurants and garment factories with cheap, illegal labor. The price of passage has rocketed from less than $2,000 to as much as $60,000. Typically, part is paid up front and the rest assumed in debt, by the migrant and relatives in both Fujian and the United States. The fee buys either arduous sea transport—the *Golden Venture* spent 112 days at sea—or a multisegment odyssey that involves crossing mountains into Thailand on foot, flying to another transit country and from there to Canada or Mexico, then journeying overland into the United States. Intimidation and violence are built into the process. In the early 1990s, fresh arrivals were kept awaiting further dispatch in up to three hundred New York "safe houses"—typically basements—in handcuffs or shackles, and regularly beaten, tortured, or raped. The brutal enforcement of debt payments continues long after the journey is completed. Yet once established, many of these same migrants will turn to the smugglers to help import more relatives left behind.

Tragically, much of this is typical. The Fujian circuit is just one of many. Another, for instance, involves moving South Asians to various countries in Europe. Between 1988 and 1996, a Pakistani-born Maltese citizen named Tourab Ahmed Sheikh netted $15 million in a business that quickly grew in both volume and scope. Sheikh started out sending Indians into Germany by air via Malta. Then he identified Bangladeshis as a growth segment and switched to this specialty, conveying 10,000 Bangladeshis to Italy in three years on board a flotila of chartered fishing craft. A long-distance human smuggling kingpin, Mandir Kumar Wahi, learned of Sheikh's operation and offered him a mutually beneficial partnership. Sheikh's small boats would meet Wahi's large freighters on the high seas and transfer the migrants unobtrusively to the Italian coast. Sheikh was exposed when one such deal ended, tragically, in a collision that took the lives of 283 migrants and two of his own operatives. But when one player falls, others take up the mantle. Some are long-distance operators like Wahi, others contractors like Sheikh, and still more are the "traditional" local passers who move Pakistanis or Afghans overland through Iran and Turkey for thousands of dollars at a time. All these entrepreneurs with their specialties are frequently interlocked in partnerships, subcontracting arrangements, and a maze of ever-changing deals, alliances, ad hoc collaborations.

MASS MOVEMENTS

It took the transatlantic trade four hundred years to import 12 million African slaves to the New World. Twelve million too many. But now consider that in Southeast Asia an estimated 30 million women and children have been trafficked—in the past ten years. Human trafficking is not yet the most profitable illicit trade—that honor goes to drugs—but it is very likely the fastest growing. Cross-border trafficking, which is only one part of the picture, transports an estimated 700,000 to 2 million people per year. (The purchase and sale of humans within countries pushes the total much higher.) Hard numbers are difficult to come by. They always are when it comes to illicit trade. But the governments, international organizations, and activist groups that track these flows agree on one thing: the number of people crossing borders illegally today, often in coerced conditions, has no precedent in human history.

The furious pace of growth is also without precedent. According to the United Nations, when trafficking and human smuggling are combined an overall picture emerges of a "people trade" that affects at least 4 million people every year, for a value of $7 to $10 billion. Arguably it is more, as human smuggling out of China alone has been estimated between $1 and $3 billion per year, and the FBI reckons that the Mexican people trade earns the networks $6 to $9 billion each year. While estimates on the overall value of the trade in humans vary, the consensus among leading experts is that it is larger than ever and growing at breakneck pace.

The terms *human smuggling* and *trafficking* designate, in principle, two different activities. In human smuggling, the migrant pays the smuggler for passage. In the case of trafficking, the trafficker deceives or coerces the migrant and sells her or his labor. But in reality the distinction is not that clear-cut. Many voluntarily smuggled migrants are left with exorbitant and arbitrary debts that lead them into sweatshops or other exploitative working conditions, conveniently "arranged" by their smugglers. Human smuggling and human trafficking shade into one another. Both are aspects of a vast new industry that thrives thanks to the aspirations of those who seek a better life elsewhere and the obstacles that governments place in their way.

The trade in people is surely the most morally repugnant of all the illicit trades that flourish today. But it is deeply entrenched and interwoven with the world's ever more complex migration flows. The human impulses that drive migration are age-old and hard to contain. Migrants can be driven by opportunity, hope, despair, or simply the need to survive. Human traffickers prey on these impulses and, thanks to their ability to elude government-imposed obstacles, they can turn human impulses into profits.

The opportunity is huge. Today people are moving as they have never moved before. In 2004 the world counted 175 million documented international migrants, 3 percent of humanity. Perhaps half as many again were undocumented. Still more were internal migrants, 150 million in China alone, drawn from rural hinterlands to fast-growing urban and industrial zones. Another 20 million refugees and displaced persons rounded out the picture. The United States and Western Europe remain prized destinations. The 2000 U.S. census found more than 30 million foreign-born residents, or 11.1 percent of the population. Of these, 13.3 million, or 44 percent, had arrived in the 1990s. In western Europe, close to 30 million people are foreign born. In other destinations of choice immigrants appear to make up the bulk of the labor force, as is the case in the Gulf. A full 58 percent of Kuwaiti residents are in fact not Kuwaiti. The population of the United Arab Emirates is 74 percent foreign.

However, countries today no longer neatly divide into sources and destinations of migrants. Many countries are both: part of their population leaves while at the same time illegal immigrants flock in. Morocco and the Dominican Republic are cases in point. Other countries are major transit points—or waiting areas—for those on their way beyond. Guatemalans in Mexico or Chadians in Libya are just waiting for the chance to make the move to the United States or Italy. India, Mexico, Turkey, Egypt, Spain, Portugal, and Morocco, countries that usually receive the largest sums in remittances (money sent back by nationals abroad), are themselves increasingly significant migrant destinations.

There are many reasons that the pressure to migrate is more intense and its effects more geographically widespread than ever before. Better information about opportunities elsewhere and cheaper, more frequent communications with friends and relatives abroad open many eyes and spur the motivation to try one's luck somewhere else. Cheaper communication and travel also make migration much less absolute and final, lowering a psychological barrier to departure. Another contributing factor to the rise in the movement of people was the collapse of the Soviet Bloc and its once closed borders. The new freedom to move suddenly made available millions of potential workers to the countries that needed them—and to some that did not.

There is something else. It is the hunger of employers in receiving countries. Many have a voracious appetite for labor that will accept lower salaries or the jobs that local workers spurn. In some countries economic growth creates a need for certain jobs that exceeds the local supply of labor. Elsewhere local workers are not scarce but simply seen as too expensive—especially when others are available to work at lower wages. All this results in often ambiguous and contradictory immigration policies and labor rules. Certain categories of workers are made welcome—H-1B visas for technically trained workers in the United States, or Germany's recruitment of 20,000 foreign computer experts in 2000. Others receive a retroactive welcome, for instance Spain's 2005 amnesty for illegal workers already in the country. The United States is considering a "guest workers" program for Mexicans similar to what Germany once offered Turks.

Employers frequently lobby for lighter immigration rules; public opinion is often viscerally opposed. Yet virtually no country welcomes all types of migrants with open arms. Instead today's migration flourishes *despite* barricades of quotas and prohibitions and border controls, complex arrays of visas and work permits with different rules for different nationalities and professions, special privileges for those with money to invest, and myriad other special circumstances that vary from destination to destination. The flow of migrants is not molding itself to these requirements particularly tidily. Instead it threatens to overwhelm them. That pressure makes the trade in people flourish.

It all adds up to a market—a global market for labor that is full of imperfections, with abundant legal barriers, bottlenecks, and logistical complications to overcome. And like every market, this one needs traders. But these intermediaries are not Wall Street types. Some are legal recruiters, such as agents for companies recruiting overseas, or governments themselves—for instance, the United States with its annual green card lottery. But far more players in the international labor trade are dubious or downright criminal. They deal in what Kevin Bales, one of the world's leading experts on this subject calls "modern-day slaves." The description is as terrible as it is, all too often, accurate.

THE HEIGHT OF DEGRADATION

Human trafficking is the most sordid of the ways that labor moves around in the new global economy. Its victims end up in sweatshops and plantations, factories and family farms and as household servants. One notorious dimension, though hardly the only one, is the sex trade. Numerous sex-slave itineraries thrive in the world today: Myanmar, China, and Cambodia to Thailand, Russia to the Gulf emirates, the Philippines and Colombia to Japan, and so on. A few stand out as particularly lucrative and large scale. Since the collapse of the iron curtain, tens of thousands of young women and girls have been exported from Russia, Ukraine, Moldova, and Romania into sexual exploitation in cities across western Europe and Japan. Human traffickers in London, virtually unknown in the mid-1990s, controlled half a decade later 80 percent of street prostitutes in red-light areas. In cities like Lyon, France, the resulting change in the sex business has been such that local prostitutes have launched activist movements to protest the takeover of the trade by coerced eastern European women and the consequences for their own income, health, and safety.

The trajectory of these women is particularly degrading. Recruiters who earn five hundred dollars a head round them up under usually false pretenses, typically the promise of modeling, clerical, or retail work in a rich country. Sometimes the women are simply kidnapped. Transported across borders with the complicity of corrupt officials, they are warehoused in "safe houses" in cities like Budapest or Sarajevo and conditioned there for sexual exploitation by means of drugs, beatings, and repeated rape. Finally arriving in a western European city on a forged or stolen passport or by clandestine entry, a woman is likely to spend one or more years as a sex slave, subjected to constant dehumanizing treatment until her body wears down or the trafficker decides that she has paid off her "debt"—a sum he has invented and adjusted arbitrarily. Tony capitals in western Europe conceal many such slaves. The same is true in Japan, where the girls are often from Brazil, Ecuador, and Colombia. Or Thailand, where some of the Cambodian teenagers available in the brothels have actually been sold into servitude by their desperately poor parents.

Sex trafficking operations are as efficient as they are sordid. An Interpol official estimates that the traffickers can satisfy new demand in London with fresh supplies from the Balkans within forty-eight hours. The traffickers maintain sidelines as well. One for instance is in young children, procured to turn into professional beggars or to be sold into adoption in the West. In Albania, traffickers offer poor families up to five thousand euros for a newborn baby, sometimes arranging the deal before the mother has delivered. And that's a good price. "A son for a TV," ran the title of a *New York Times* account, in 2003, of an Albanian three-year-old whose father sold him to a middleman for a television set. The child's buyer in Italy paid the broker six thousand dollars. Despite efforts to curb these practices, a 2003 report by the United Nations and the Organization of Security and Cooperation in Europe found that the trade has not suffered. "Crime bosses operate in the [Balkan] region," the report says, "and elected leaders are sometimes complicit in their crimes."

Trafficking of women for sex is common in the United States as well, although it is only recently beginning to attract mainstream attention. In 1998 Mexican sex slaves were discovered in Florida. A 1999 government report noted that immigration authorities had identified 256 brothels in 26 cities that appeared to be stocked with trafficked workers. And in a 2004 *New York Times Magazine* article entitled "The Girls Next Door," Peter Landesmann described in unflinching detail the abuse of young victims of trafficking in "normal" middle-class America. A few months later, police shut down an alleged East Asian sex slavery operation in a quiet town in Vermont. "They have done a very good job of spreading into suburban and even rural areas," Derek Ellerman of the Polaris Project, an activist group that fights human trafficking, told reporters. "Wherever there is demand for commercial sex, the traffickers will spread to those areas."

THE RESERVE ARMY OF THE UNDOCUMENTED

Knowing that a reservoir of illicit labor exists produces the temptation to use it. Employers most likely to turn to undocumented workers are those with short-term needs, notably in the restaurant, garment, and construction trades. Many are immigrants themselves. In April 2004, four Latin American women filed charges against a Korean immigrant and her two daughters, the owners of a pair of Midtown Manhattan spas called Osaka Zen. The ex-employees said they worked hundred-hour weeks for less than $250, giving massages, cleaning the premises, and even pickling kimchi, with no place to sleep but the massage tables.

Yet the recourse to illicit labor is by no means limited to immigrant businesses. Established firms, in some cases old and prestigious, stoke the demand for undocumented labor and fuel the smugglers' trade. Short-term employment agencies in New York's Chinatown known to specialize in undocumented Fujianese workers now field requests from up and down the East Coast. Their clients include Chinese and non-Chinese businesses alike. In exchange for shedding their scruples and breaking the law, employers receive from these arrangements the services of underpaid, unorganized workers with no recourse against long working hours and aberrant conditions. Employers are spared the dirty work as well: the agencies handle contracts and salaries, and employers need not even know how much their workers are paid.

Some employers have taken the next step—to actually procure illegal workers directly, eliminating the need for agencies. Both large corporations and their smaller subcontractors are regularly caught "inadvertently" employing undocumented workers. In the United States the fines and other penalties against corporations that employ illegal aliens are far from backbreaking and hardly enforced. In the United States, as one commentator argued, "A simple way to reduce illegal migration would be to enforce existing laws against employing undocumented workers. The cost of policing would then shift from taxpayers to fines on employers. . . . The current de facto policy in effect provides government subsidies in the form of tax and social security payments waivers to industries employing millions of illegals."

This lax environment for the employers of illegal workers is global. In some countries it gives certain industries their competitive edge. Around the world, garment industry sweatshops have become prime magnets for undocumented workers. These factories, where the typically female labor force is paid by the piece, ensuring long work hours and docile behavior, and often subjected to intimidation and violence, have been the focus of activist campaigns for their links to major apparel manufacturers. The U.S. territory of the Northern Mariana Islands has become a prime destination for illegal migrants from Asia. They are lured there by the traffickers' claim that they will be able to freely continue to the mainland United States. In reality the migrants are handed to garment factories, sometimes owned by Asian organized crime syndicates, to work off their debt. No surprise that Saipan, the territory's capital, has become a sex trade destination. It's a logical progression.

In rich countries that are the poles of attraction for migrants, the flood of undocumenteds is wreaking havoc on labor markets that have already suffered recessions and structural shifts like outsourcing. And if labor protections are under attack and union membership declining, undocumenteds become nothing less than a "reserve army" in the sense Marx used—a pool of cheap, docile workers whose availability drives down the price of labor and the quality of work conditions. The alarm of trade unions in the United States, for instance, is therefore no surprise. Neither are the common accusations that corporations have a vested interest in conditions remaining as they are. But in a repetition of historical experience the influx has also caused wrenching conflicts within immigrant communities, between earlier arrivals who have unionized, often at the cost of great struggle, and the new migrants and traffickers who are seen to be pushing wages back down.

Yet seen from another perspective—that of the neighbors and kin the workers leave behind—smuggled and trafficked migrants can be sources of remittances, just as legal migrants are. Many will eventually pay off their travel debts and move into more stable arrangements. This makes them potential investors back home, as well as sponsors of future arrivals. An estimated $100 billion flows each year in remittances by emigrants to their home countries, typically in small increments of $250 or so, which even low earners can spare. Remittances to Latin America are growing by 7 to 10 percent per year and have already exceeded the equivalent of 10 percent of

GDP in Haiti, Nicaragua, El Salvador, Jamaica, the Dominican Republic, and Ecuador. In Colombia remittances are equal to one-half of coffee exports; in Mexico, they are equal to tourist revenue. In recent years funds sent home by Latin American workers in the United States have exceeded the total investment flows of multinational corporations into the region. These trends only make the prospect of migration more attractive—by any means necessary.

In the tiny Chinese hamlet of Langle, it is easy to recognize the homes of families with female children. Journalist Howard French reports that families with girls have houses with tiles and air-conditioning. Those who don't are very poor, and their males still hunt in the wooded hills with bow and arrows. The main reason that homes with daughters are more prosperous is that the daughters are no longer there. They work as prostitutes in Thailand and Malaysia, and the money they send home is what makes the socioeconomic difference. "All the girls would like to go [to foreign lands to work in the sex industry] but some have to take care of their parents," twenty-year-old Ye Xiang, who herself went to Thailand, told French. He also notes that exporting daughters has become a major or even the only route for a better life for most families in the region, and that the practice does not seem to bring shame to their women or their families.

In another small town at the other end of the world similar realities and attitudes have set in. Reporter Somini Sengupta tells the story of "Becky," a thirty-four-year-old woman who returned home to Benin City, Nigeria, after ten years as a prostitute in Italy. "As far as her friends and neighbors were concerned there was no shame in her work; the shame was coming back without a nest egg," reports Sengupta. For just as in Langle, proceeds from the prostitution of the women of Benin City are transforming its physical and social landscape. The so-called Italos, Sengupta writes, "returned home and built proper houses. They sank private boreholes to supply running water day and night. They introduced four-wheel drives to the unpaved roads of Benin City." Many of these women had left for Italy with not their family's consent but their enthusiastic encouragement.

DRAGONS, COYOTES, SNAKEHEADS

"It's like a dragon—although it's a lengthy creature, various organic parts are tightly linked." This statement, which a Chinese smuggler used to describe to a researcher the structure of his business, aptly portrays much of human smuggling and trafficking today. The creature is indeed lengthy. The routes smuggled migrants follow can be tortuous and bizarre, with any number of detours and transit points. The route from China to the United States might go through Southeast Asia, Africa, and Latin America. By one estimate, on any given day up to 30,000 Chinese migrants are stashed in safe houses around the world; at one time there were 4,000 Chinese in transit in Bolivia. There are as many as 300,000 illegals in Moscow at any time from Asia, Africa, and the Middle East, awaiting onward shipment. A network dismantled in early 1998 that brought Iraqis and Palestinians into El Paso, Texas, employed "smuggling stations" in Jordan, Syria, the West Bank, and Greece, along with "staging stations" in Greece, Thailand, Cuba, Ecuador, and Mexico. If anything, examples like these have grown commonplace.

Who runs the trade? The operations vary in complexity and scale, from smallish mom-and-pop enterprises—often literally family businesses—to syndicates involved in multiple illicit businesses. But no single enterprise does it alone, so numerous and dispersed are the tasks. In an earlier era, when the typical smuggling operation involved just crossing one border, the iconic smuggler was a lone local entrepreneur. On the U.S.-Mexico border this passer was known as a coyote. A borderland archetype of the 1980s, the coyote has since become a second-tier player. He and his peers elsewhere are just one of the dragon's "organic parts." In Mexico itself, the old-fashioned coyote may soon be obsolete, as the rise in traffic along with heightened border controls has pushed up the price of passage (from three hundred dollars in the mid-1990s to two thousand in 2001) and given the advantage to more organized groups with counterparts across the border and access to technology.

The Chinese call these players snakeheads. Snakehead-class traffickers now look to coyotes as contractors and hire them for local services as needed. In 2005 authorities estimated that more than three hundred identifiable groups had the capability to operate illegally across the U.S.-Mexico border. One for instance was the Salim Boughader organization, named after its boss, a Mexican of Lebanese descent. This network specialized in the transportation of illegal immigrants from the Middle East, most of them Iraqi Christians escaping religious persecution in Saddam Hussein's Iraq. Another smuggling ring, the "M" organization, traded mostly in Egyptians who would travel to Brazil as tourists and from there to Guatemala and then Mexico en route to the United States.

Around the coyote and snakehead types, a wide range of associated roles are all vital to a successful human smuggling or trafficking operation. They include recruiters (or "small snakeheads"), procurers of documents, transportation providers and agents, corrupt officials, enforcers, debt collectors, so-called employment agents, pimps, ships' crews, local guides, and miscellaneous others. One Afghan refugee told a reporter of landing in Sumatra only to be greeted by a stranger bearing a cell phone; on the other end of the line was the Afghan's Pakistani smuggler, providing instructions for the next stage of the journey. Individuals like the stranger with the cell phone play a role in the supply chain that is as effective as it is elusive. The relationships can be ad hoc or established, governed by contracts or by trust-based partnerships within an ethnic community.

What drives people into the human smuggling business can sometimes seem surprising, the result of unintended consequences. The top U.S. immigration official for much of the 1990s, Doris Meissner told me how Taiwanese fishermen switched from tuna to humans. "When Pacific fishing nations agreed in the early 1990s to limit seine fishing in the tuna industry to reduce dolphin deaths,"

Meissner said, "Taiwanese fishermen had excess boat capacity that could no longer be used for fishing. Because Taiwan is close to Fujian, Chinese migrants became the new commodity."

People smuggling and other forms of illicit trade and crime have some evident connections. As Miguel Angel Carranza, a veteran law enforcement agent whom I met in San Antonio, told me, "It was only natural for the Mexican groups with long experience smuggling illegal immigrants to the U.S. to 'double their take' by occasionally forcing their clients to carry 'small packages' with them across the border. . . . Several small packages every day quickly become a very large package. If this large package is cocaine, it will have a street value infinitely bigger than the fee paid by the poor laborers that carry the small package, often under a death threat."

Carranza continued: "Once the large drug trafficking groups discovered the flexibility, effectiveness, and relatively low risk of using this 'small package' approach to smuggle large shipments of drugs, they developed very close partnerships with the organizations that controlled the coyotes."

One of the most surprising and organizationally complex collaborations between different illicit trades is the one that has emerged between counterfeiters and people smugglers. How do Chinese manufacturers of counterfeit watches, for example, manage to coordinate so effectively their worldwide retail distribution channels? The same high-end copied watches can be found on the corners of Paris or across the street from New York's Grand Central Station. Who are the merchants? Typically they are street vendors from sub-Saharan African countries who have been smuggled into Paris and New York by a global network that has some sort of arrangement with the Chinese counterfeiting networks.

Even a sophisticated mass-consumer, multinational corporation would have a hard time successfully pulling off such a dizzying array of coordinated activities in the fields of manufacturing, international trade, transportation logistics, inventory control, human resource management, distribution, product fulfillment, and financial control—not to mention security and secrecy. The existence of organizations with such fantastic managerial capabilities points to a business model capable of not only attracting talented managers but also generating huge profits. Sadly, it also points to the limited impact of government controls. These governmental failures are common everywhere; although many factors go into this, paramount among them is that in many countries those in charge of curbing these illicit businesses are in fact personally profiting from them. The complex operations of the trade are impossible to pull off so successfully and for such a long period of time without the help of complicit officials.

GET YOUR PAPERS HERE

In late 2001, at the height of the conflict between the United States and the Taliban, *Newsweek* reporter Melinda Liu set out to procure in Peshawar, Pakistan, all the documentation she would need if she were an Afghan seeking asylum in the West. She found it remarkably easy, and not particularly expensive. A local photographer produced snapshots that made her look vaguely Afghan. She bought a genuine Afghan passport, backed up with an identification card, driver's license, and birth certificate. All these items cost less than three hundred dollars. Her suppliers added crucial documents needed to support an asylum claim: an Afghan Communist Party card and a police summons from the Taliban. They even offered to have an article printed in the Peshawar press claiming that her Afghan alter ego had been attacked by unknown assailants.

Liu ended the experiment at this point, but not before establishing that visas for transit countries were available as well, for up to four thousand dollars. All these items were available on the local market. And equivalent kits could be constituted in a number of countries around the world. Often at lower cost: for instance, the journalist Peter Laufer reports that illegal Mexican immigrants could cheaply obtain crucial documents in Bowling Green, Kentucky. "A set of U.S. identification papers, from a driver's license to a Social Security card, takes about three hours to procure on the

Bowling Green black market," Laufer writes. "The going rate rarely exceeds $20 a card."

Access to plausible documents is a crucial resource for human smugglers and traffickers. Ronald Noble, the secretary general of Interpol, admitted in 2005 that one of his most vexing problems was how to deal with the stock of more than 20 million lost or stolen passports of which only 5.8 million were registered in databases.

Again, the role of corrupt and complicit officials is crucial. Chinese snakeheads collude with employees of state-owned labor export agencies, and the Chinese coast guard conveniently disappear when boats loaded with illegals take to sea. Many snakeheads are themselves former or even current government employees. Easily corrupted officials make a country attractive as a transit point. At many airports, a hundred-dollar bill can go a long way when slipped into a false passport at the immigration counter. And on the smuggling routes of eastern and southeastern Europe, traffickers often meet border officers to have a sheaf of passports stamped over drinks and cigarettes—perhaps serving up some women to cement the arrangement. Italian officials sent to Greece to keep smuggled migrants off ferryboats to Italy need to be rotated frequently, according to an Italian diplomat I interviewed in Athens, because after a few weeks they often join their Greek colleagues in sharing bribes from the traffickers. And the trade's success only reinforces the pattern, making bribes easier to dole out and harder to turn down.

Human smugglers orchestrate their transactions in other ways as well. With official complicity, they mingle migrants into delegations with official passports; alternatively, they disguise migrants as tourists and place them on tour buses. A more sophisticated ploy prized by Russian traffickers is to set up a bogus company with offices in several countries, then apply to transfer "employees" from one to another. Passers have forged family relationships or even, in some cases, legally married the migrant to a person with the appropriate citizenship or residency—not exactly a high-volume approach, but useful as a last resort.

For transportation, smugglers employ virtually every method known to man—aircraft, boats, buses, private cars, animal-drawn carts, and long marches on foot over mountains or through deserts. Women destined for the sex trade in the United States have been forced to trek across the Sonora Desert or clamber in the California foothills in work clothes—high heels, short skirts. Transportation altered for human transport ranges from blunt—sealed secret compartments in trucks, for instance—to highly imaginative. One Mexican operation transformed the interior of a fuel tanker truck, lining it with benches.

Safe houses—another key component—can be just as well disguised. In some cities there is no need for such measures, as the police are inept or complicit. Elsewhere a dank basement or warehouse is considered enough. In February 2004, however, 136 illegal migrants were found packed "wall-to-wall people" in a home in the posh suburb of Scottsdale, Arizona, just by a golf course's edge. Neighbors had noticed a bit too much traffic at the house, much of it vans and pickups, and complained to the police. It turned out that the migrants, all from Latin America, had paid six thousand dollars apiece to enter the United States and were now being held until relatives coughed up still more money. (On the very same day, another 64 migrants were found in a safe house in the town of Perris, southeast of Los Angeles.)

As with their colleagues in other illicit trades, the spread of consumer technology has given the traffickers a boost and helped them keep the edge over their pursuers. Human smugglers make extensive use of encrypted radios, prepaid and disposable cell phones, Web-based e-mail, and Internet cafés. Increased patrolling on the U.S.-Mexico and other borders has made access to technology a near-prerequisite for a successful crossing, to monitor the border patrol and exchange instructions with accomplices on the other side. The fullest use of new technology, however, is in the sex trade. The boom in trafficking women and children for sex has utilized the Internet to display the wares in the cyberspace equivalent of slave auctions. Suppliers of "mail-order brides"—an antiquated term for a transaction that today takes place online with all the technical conveniences of searching, sorting, and pricing—may be front operations for traffickers. And women are listed "for sale" on the Web at several points on the supply chain, at central European transit points for brothel operators to purchase and down the line for individual customers to order. The degree to which sex trafficking owes its success to advanced consumer technologies makes for a powerful contrast with its fundamental reliance on brute violence.

THE LAW TRIES TO CATCH UP

The people trade has become the object of a sudden flurry of activity in international law. Strictly speaking, not all of it is new: one United Nations instrument, a convention on migrants' rights, was first drafted in 1978, signed in 1990, and entered into force only in 2003, when Guatemala became the twenty-first ratifying country. By early 2005, only twenty-seven countries had ratified the treaty and therefore agreed to be bound by its provisions, which set out a range of rights for migrants, from legal due process and fair employment standards to the right to remit money back home. Unfortunately the ratifying countries are almost all net exporters of migrant labor; to date, no major destination country has joined. Moreover, experts argue, this treaty is not worth ratifying, as it sets too low a standard while creating a false sense of progress when in fact little is being achieved.

Measures more directly focused on the people trade have enjoyed greater success. The UN General Assembly in 2000 passed a convention against transnational organized crime, with a protocol against "Smuggling of Migrants By Land, Sea, and Air" and another to "Prevent, Suppress, and Punish Trafficking in Persons, Especially Women and Children." The trafficking protocol reached its threshold level of forty signatures in late 2003, and the smuggling protocol in early 2004. (The United States has signed both but so far ratified neither.) Other multilateral efforts include the development of common standards against smuggling and trafficking within the

European Union, and the International Criminal Court's expansion, in 2002, of the definition of "crimes against humanity" to include the forms of enslavement that occur in human trafficking.

All of these initiatives reflect an effort to define, standardize, and codify the offenses involved in the people trade. The UN protocols set out definitions of smuggling and trafficking that are broad and detailed, with attention to the role of intermediaries and facilitators, not just the principal operators and their victims. Countries that ratify the protocols commit to make a range of activities illegal, enforce these laws, cooperate to protect and repatriate victims, exchange information, and work together to secure borders. In addition, both try to differentiate victim from criminal. They emphasize that illegal migration in itself is not a crime under international law, and they demand compassionate treatment of the victims—such as guaranteeing the right of victims to be returned to their home country rather than detained where they are busted.

These efforts are far from merely academic. On the contrary, they address a fundamental problem of law enforcement, namely the absence in most countries until recently of laws to enforce. In the United States, the immigration service devised its antismuggling policy only in 1997, and an antitrafficking act was passed in October 2000. And the United States is a pioneer in the matter. In Turkey, for instance, a major transit country, smuggler arrests grew from 98 in 1998 to 850 in 2001—but only on minor charges, for there was no law against human smuggling. Many destination and transit countries have only begun to frame the question. And even where smugglers and traffickers risk prison terms, the penalties are low compared to those for other illicit trades. In the United States a smuggler caught with a load of marijuana faces more jail time than one caught smuggling people.

The United Nations and other international agreements to combat smuggling and trafficking have helped speed the passage of laws. Albania and Romania, for instance, both made human trafficking illegal for the first time in 2001. In a related effort, the United States now ranks countries every year in three tiers, according to their role in human trafficking and their prevention and enforcement efforts. It threatens to punish the poorest performers by withholding cooperation and aid. But perhaps the most valuable result is the moral suasion that "naming and shaming" those who are not cooperating with international efforts makes possible.

The not-so-hidden dynamo behind these global efforts is an armada of activist groups that have put the spotlight on modern-day slavery and on the victimization of women and children by traffickers. The success of these groups rests in part on the sheer moral repugnance of many of the practices involved. In addition, the people trade lies at the crossroads of a great many types of advocacy: on violence against women, child exploitation, labor standards, refugee rights, and human rights in general. The shocking nature of the material has helped make sex trafficking the focus of front-page feature stories and even personal crusades by concerned journalists and opinion writers. In 2004, Landesmann's "Girls Next Door" exposé and the columns of his *New York Times* colleague Nicholas Kristof, who "bought" two young women in their Cambodian brothel and returned them to their families only to see one return to the brothel the next year, helped to raise public indignation about the people trade in the United States. Similar stories published in Japan and Europe have also mobilized public opinion and stirred politicians into action.

If there is a downside to this attention, or at least a necessary caution, it is that the focus on sex trafficking should not obscure other forms of human trafficking, debt bondage, and the like involving nonsex work in factories or workshops. As David Feingold, a noted expert on the trade, points out, the fact remains that the world market for cheap labor exceeds even the market for cheap sex. Besides, labor coercion frequently entails sexual violence and vice versa.

TRADING ON DESPAIR

Yet, consider the people trade on entirely moral grounds, and there is a risk that something essential to understanding it will get lost.

And that is the economics. It isn't only that the traffickers and smugglers are running a business that must be confronted in its financial and commercial dimensions, not just for its moral abhorrence. All of that is true. But when parents in Albania trade children for television sets, small towns in Nigeria live on remittances from their migrants even when they know the terrible cost, and young women bought back from Cambodian brothels find their way there again for lack of anything better, economic calculus shows the trade in all its ambiguity far more accurately than a moral reading can do on its own.

When the human trade is considered as any other illicit trade, its workings become more legible. The smugglers and traffickers are networks of efficient intermediaries who take advantage of restrictive laws and international borders to connect supply and demand at a high price. Seen this way, ending human trafficking will require more than even the most aggressive law enforcement can do. Governments need not only laws they can enforce but specific policies that drive the value—the money—out of the business. They need to drive up the risk and down the reward that traffickers get from the human trade.

It's a tricky undertaking, because traffickers are adept at turning small differences in national laws into revenue-making opportunities. Around the world, governments are constantly tweaking and tampering with their migration laws for reasons that range from the high-minded to the xenophobic. This activity results in an ever-shifting global picture, with some country-to-country flows of people being legalized, others criminalized, and still others left in a gray area all at the same time. The picture keeps shifting, precisely at a time when the traffickers are more flexible and adaptive to these changes in the business environment than they have ever been and that government bureaucracies can be.

All this—plus sheer outrage at many of the practices of the people trade—means that governments are treading lightly when it comes to attacking the trade by driving out the value. The approaches include enforcing labor standards to do away with sweatshops or adopting a public health–driven rather than repressive approach to prostitution. There are extremely complex lines here that have to do with sexual exploitation, child labor, improper labor conditions, usury, and other scourges. Trading in children and the vulnerable or enslaving any human being deserves the harshest punishment. The problem is that governments are showing themselves to be increasingly unable to catch the culprits and dole out the punishments.

Moreover, so long as all countries have not one labor market but in practice two—one legal or tolerated, another underground and unregulated—certain kinds of labor such as garment manufacturing, domestic work, and sex will keep producing huge profits for human smugglers and traffickers.

Faced with these dilemmas, destination countries—and particularly the United States—have sought instead to stop the trade at the source, the countries of origin, by pushing for laws and enforcement and ranking source countries by the quality and effectiveness of their efforts. But this approach, with its echoes of the "source control" emphasis of the war on drugs, collides with the fact that source countries typically lack the judicial infrastructure and enforcement capability to deter or prohibit the trade. It also flies in the face of every political and cultural trend since the end of the cold war, in an era marked by increasingly open borders, inexpensive travel, and record numbers of border crossings. Globalization seen from this perspective acquires a very different connotation.

But beyond globalization there is a still deeper force driving the human trade. Tragically enough, it is a very basic aspiration—the human desire to find for oneself and one's children a better life. Economists and sociologists have concluded that what drives migration is not absolute deprivation, or poverty, but relative deprivation—the sense that one would be better off in some other place. It is this sense that pushes a Fujianese onto a cargo boat in the South China Sea, or an Albanian family to sell their infant child to traffickers who will take him to Italy. And the perceived rewards to those who persist—who make it through despite the ordeal of the journey, and eventually start sending money back home—only underscore that sense of relative deprivation and make the temptation more intense.

Morocco is hardly the world's poorest country. Indeed, many countries would gladly accept Morocco's standard of living. Yet Morocco is also a major source of illegal and smuggled migrants. Why? Because the closeness to Spain and Europe makes the difference hard to tolerate. So Moroccans by the dozens attempt each day the crossing, many washing up dead or alive after their makeshift vessels capsize. Parents pay smugglers to take their children to cities across the water, where local Moroccans will take them in. One father who had sent his fifteen-year-old son to Italy on false papers for five thousand dollars told *El País* that going deep into debt to raise another four thousand to send his second son away was an easy decision to make. "To live in Morocco is like being dead," he said. "If the raft sinks, it will not be the smuggler's fault, but the hand of Fate."

Chapter 6

THE GLOBAL TRADE IN STOLEN IDEAS

It happened to Bill Gates and to the rock star Bono. To General Motors and to General Mikhail Kalashnikov, the Russian inventor of the assault rifle that bears his name. To J. K. Rowling, who created Harry Potter, and to Pfizer, which created Viagra. All of them had their ideas stolen.

"It's never nice to have a thief in charge of your release campaign," reflected Bono, the lead singer of the group U2, upon learning that their 2004 album *How to Dismantle an Atomic Bomb* had been pirated and was available on the Internet ahead of its official release date. In 2003 Microsoft found advance copies of its new Longhorn operating system—months from release anywhere in the world—selling for two dollars in Malaysia and Singapore. General Motors has accused a Chinese carmaker of copying one of its models. In 2004 General Kalashnikov sued the United States for purchasing pirated AK-47s to equip the Iraqi police. About 100 million units of the weapon are in circulation today around the world, and many of them are perfect clones. "What can we do?" complained General Kalashnikov. "These are our times now."

Whether you call them knockoffs, replicas, bootlegs, copies, or simply fakes, counterfeits are everywhere. Think of any product in any industry, and in all likelihood it has suffered the onslaught of copycats. Weapons and perfumes; cars, motorcycles, and running shoes; medicines and industrial machinery; watches, tennis rackets, golf clubs, video games, software, music, and movies—none is immune.

Ordinary shoppers who buy knockoffs typically face little risk, or none at all. Yet counterfeits are stolen goods—stolen because they result from the theft of someone's trademark, design, and ideas. Nevertheless, they are exceedingly easy to find. Most cities, in fact, have a specific market or neighborhood that is notorious for cheap illicit copies of just about any consumer item—Canal Street in New York City's Chinatown, for instance. These markets offer thickets of knockoff handbags and mounds of watches and sunglasses of dubious origins, presented to the buyer in one cramped storefront after another. The storefronts are the tip of the iceberg. Within the shops are glossy catalogs of particularly valuable fakes—ones hard to produce or particularly desirable at the moment—which runners fetch from hideaways once a deal is struck. Warehouses stockpile the goods, often floor upon floor of contraband delivered by truck from the ports where it had arrived in forty-foot shipping containers, eluding inspection by fortune or deceit. Such markets are a truly global phenomenon: in rich and poor countries alike, they often feature the very same merchandise, in similar-looking storefronts and stalls. Often the merchants themselves are from the same ethnic group, regardless of the city or even the continent.

Where does the cargo originate? Typically in Asia: China, Taiwan, and Vietnam are likely sources, though far from the only ones. There the goods or their components often come off the same production lines that produce the brand-name items they copy. Other production facilities are more or less underground and hidden from authorities. That is, when they are not sheltered by them. In China, provincial governments and the People's Liberation Army (PLA), China's military, have been found to have stakes in production of various fakes, and the prison system is widely assumed to provide forced labor to this end. But in other countries the facilities that produce illegal copies of trademark goods might well be state-of-the-art factories that offer the best employment around.

By the time they hit the street, most counterfeits have been traded and transported enough times that the conditions under which they were produced are difficult to trace. Not that most consumers care. Stronger impulses and desires are at play here. The flood of counterfeits on the market responds to powerful forces: the intense consumer appetite for brand-name products, and the irresistible temptation of a bargain. Companies that own the brands hope they can get consumers to pay the full price. Counterfeiters are happy to offer an alternative approach. The battle between the two—not for hearts and minds but for the contents of your wallet—is one of the great economic conflicts of our time.

REVENGE OF THE BRANDS

"We have met our enemy, and it is us": the famous saying might well be echoed, in a moment of clarity, by the principals of Adidas, Guess, Calvin Klein, Sony, Black & Decker, and every other company that has sought to make itself or its products an international household name. Ironic but true: the desirability and image of attainment they have successfully infused in their products, driving up prices and revenues, are precisely what make them ideal targets for rip-offs and forgeries. As a rule of thumb, the more successful a brand, the more it will be counterfeited. Vulnerability to copycats is the Achilles' heel of brand identity.

Just like the brands they mimic, counterfeits have come a long way. Once they were easily spotted and laughably primitive in quality and style. Because the items were almost impossible to confuse with the genuine products, their manufacture and sale seemed like the epitome of a "victimless crime." No longer. Counterfeits today carry huge costs, first and foremost to the companies whose revenue they displace and whose reputation they erode. U.S. companies, for instance, estimate between $200 and $250 billion the annual revenues they lose because of counterfeiting. The European Union estimates that about 100,000 jobs are lost each year to the counterfeit trade. But illegal copies also cost governments, both in enforcement and in tax revenues foregone. In 2003, trade in counterfeit goods in the state of New York reached an estimated $34 billion, depriving the state of $1.6 billion of tax revenue, according to state officials.

Not least, counterfeiting harms unaware consumers with, in the case of pirated medicine or substandard vehicle parts, potentially deadly consequences. Nevertheless, counterfeits are ubiquitous, increasingly sophisticated in their quality of manufacture or subtlety of deceit, and flooding the global marketplace in vertiginous proportions. Since the early 1990s, according to Interpol, trade in counterfeits has grown at *eight times* the speed of legitimate trade. Twenty years ago, commercial losses around the world due to counterfeiting were estimated in the $5 billion range; today, they are around $500 billion. That puts the cost of counterfeiting between 5 and 10 percent of the total value of world trade, on a par with, say, the GDP of Australia. And still it grows, at least measured by the number of customs seizures of counterfeit goods. In the European Union, these seizures grew 900 percent between 1998 and 2001, only to double again the following year. Seizures by U.S. customs increased 12 percent between 2002 and 2003, and Japan reported substantial increases as well.

One reason for the boom is the constant expansion of the range of fake brand-name goods on the market. Once, counterfeits traded across borders were highly concentrated in the fashion industry and focused on luxury goods: Pierre Cardin shirts, Gucci handbags, Louis Vuitton luggage, and the like. These remain popular rip-off targets, of course, but so too now are industrial bolts, cigarettes, DVDs, detergent, garbage bags, video games, shock absorbers, asthma inhalers, marine gauges, cigars, and champagne. Deficient valves bearing the logo of reputed Italian makers, pressed into the steel in exactly the right place, have been appearing in the Middle East. Good-quality videos of new feature films appear across Asia well before their release date. Twenty percent of Japanese schoolteachers admit to having knowingly bought fake-label clothes or accessories. And factories in Mexico purchase raw materials from India with which they formulate and package fake medicine, its active ingredient watered down or simply absent, which they sell to Americans in Tijuana or on the Internet.

Counterfeits have nearly saturated some markets, and few more than China, ground zero of the trade. At least $16 billion in counterfeit goods are sold each year within the country. Forty percent of "Procter & Gamble" and 60 percent of "Honda" products are not the original item—neither is 95 percent of business software. Fake medicine abounds, of both the Western and the traditional Chinese variety. But China is probably the world's biggest exporter of counterfeits as well. Other leading sources include Taiwan, Vietnam, the Philippines, Malaysia, Russia, and the former Soviet republics, but also countries in Latin America and Africa as well. Some have developed specialties: Ukraine for optical discs, for instance, or Russia for software and Paraguay for cigarettes. Distribution is global, by means of the same tools that legitimate trade employs. The Internet only makes it more so: by one estimate, on the order of $25 billion in counterfeit goods is traded each year online. Internet shops are easy to set up and connect buyers and sellers discreetly and fast; e-mail and file-sharing have turned electronic copies of movies and songs into goods that can be purchased and sold.

Another reason for the boom in counterfeits is that the facilities and equipment their manufacture requires have spread around the world—not least thanks to the original manufacturers themselves, who have shared technology and know-how with overseas subsidiaries, suppliers, and licensees in order to penetrate new markets. In fact, the reproduction of commercial products is one of capitalism's most powerful tools. Franchises and licenses are essential to establishing a company's distinct identity—its "global brand" around the world. Many items we think of as luxuries—high-end cosmetics, for instance, or fancy designer apparel—are made to the brand owner's specifications by mass-production factories that work for multiple clients. A fancy perfume sold in glitzy malls and high-end boutiques may come from the same factory as a cheap chain store. A branded and more expensive TV or washer and dryer set may be the same as a nameless "clone" available for a fraction of the price. Brand names suggest quality, unity, and consistency, but they conceal the global diffusion of the facilities, labor, and skills that go into making each product.

Innovation and technology cut both ways. New technologies mean new products—miniaturized cameras, erectile dysfunction remedies, gel-enhanced sneakers—and therefore more items to fake. New manufacturing processes benefit illicit producers as well as rightful brand owners, and often with little or no time lag. Laser printers and scanners have revolutionized the art of forging packages, labels, and instruction booklets. Widely available optical disc manufacturing technology means that two-dollar Ukrainian pirated DVDs have little to envy, by way of quality, their thirty-dollar Hollywood originals. The tools of the trade may themselves be forgeries—from the unlicensed AutoCAD software used in designs to industrial production lines that are entirely counterfeit.

Particularly in developing countries, people often seem unfazed by the prevalence of counterfeit goods, even ones that function poorly or, like pirated drugs, can sicken or kill. Partly it's because they have little choice. The pharmaceutical industry estimates that one-quarter to half of the African market is counterfeit; a survey of pharmacies in Lagos, Nigeria, found 80 percent counterfeit. Under such conditions, you learn to adapt, to find lines of knockoffs and vendors you trust. In nearby Togo, *all* legal music distribution companies have either withdrawn or shut down, so the only access to recordings is through pirated CDs, which are sold in abundance on the local market and shipped across West Africa. The risk or inconvenience of a defective product is an understood facet of daily life. And counterfeiting can be seen as a lesser evil that, at least, generates local jobs and revenue, as police attempting to raid a toy factory in central Thailand found when a thousand people came out to block them.

So long as they are of sufficient quality, unauthorized replications of commercial products are sometimes welcomed, not shunned. One driver of the rise of generic medicines—which health insurers often require pharmacies to dispense when available—was the unauthorized manufacture of copies of popular drugs by companies in India and Brazil, which reverse-engineered the originals to discover their formulation method, much as one might disassemble a car to put it together again. Today, activists and health experts argue that unauthorized generics can help in the greater cause of fighting global scourges like malaria, tuberculosis, and AIDS. Unauthorized reproductions of musical recordings are credited with spurring artistic innovation—remixes, sampling, electronica. An entire movement of computer programmers and software engineers makes all its work available for free reproduction under the banner of "open source," arguing that to do otherwise would be to stifle innovation and prevent useful tools from seeing the light of day.

Of course, a technically proficient Linux application has nothing to do with a fake Prada leather purse marked "Prado" that will fall apart in three weeks, let alone with vials of tap water passed off as meningitis vaccine. Yet just where we draw the line as consumers is not always clear-cut. Counterfeits are often purchased not by necessity but by choice, by customers who have other options. Some urbanites have adopted the ten-dollar watch that lasts a few months as a lifestyle solution. Many women in Korea and Japan keep their expensive purses for special occasions and take the knockoffs with them on errands or in the rain—much as one might wear cubic zirconias or costume jewelry and save the real diamonds for worthy, and secure, occasions. "I have several fake handbags and I don't know any one of my friends who doesn't own one," admits a wealthy New York socialite who surely can afford to own only originals.

Yes, brands are a very powerful magnet. So are discounted prices. And to billions of consumers, the combination of the two is simply irresistible.

INTELLECTUAL PROPERTY IS HOT PROPERTY

To define what is and what is not a counterfeit, we look to the concept of intellectual property. The term can be slightly misleading, because not all of what it covers is "intellectual" as in scholarly. Rather, intellectual property law governs the right to use or benefit from anything that is an original idea: drug compounds, auto designs, feature films, short stories, board games, sneaker models, synthetic fabrics, as well as the distinctive names and symbols used to identify them. Nike's "swoosh" shape and McDonald's golden arches are symbols that help lure customers and generate revenues; therefore they are valuable assets. In short, intellectual property is "the idea that ideas can be owned."

Three major instruments are used to mark intellectual property. Trademarks cover words, pictures, and symbols used to identify or distinguish a product or firm; patents cover inventions; and copyright governs works of literature, art, music, and software. Although virtually every country makes use of these three devices, the laws and practices surrounding each one vary from place to place, not to mention the way they are enforced.

If ideas can be owned, it follows that they can be traded. Intellectual property may be licensed for others to use, under a contract and in return for a fee. The greater the share of a product's market value that resides in its brand—what makes a Mickey Mouse stuffed toy different from any other stuffed toy—and not in its material components, the more companies will pay to protect it. Counterfeiting is a parasitic attack on this value; counterfeiters pay for their own inputs and labor, but they "borrow"—or, more accurately, steal—the brand value and pocket as much of it as they can get away with.

The battle over intellectual property has become an important international economic conflict. The countries where most intellectual property owners reside—and where brand value generates the most revenue—argue that guaranteeing these ownership rights is an indispensable requirement for the continuous progress of humankind. Without guaranteeing ownership rights—and income—to the creators of new, valuable ideas, the incentives for inventors will disappear and innovation will dwindle. It's a logical argument, and even countries that are short of inventors, patent holders, and corporations that own major brands understand the principle. In fact, many agree with it, and their governments have promised that they too will do everything they can to stop the illicit use of intellectual property. Yet progress has been less than encouraging. As industry after industry has discovered to its chagrin, the incentives to counterfeit are simply too strong.

THE INVENTORY:
FROM TOMMY HILFIGER TO SEWER PUMPS

Counterfeits are a diverse lot. They vary by quality and by the level of deception involved. Some counterfeiters take pains to replicate each and every identifying mark, while others simply suggest a well-known brand, with less attention to detail. Some fakes are described forthrightly as copies, while others insist they are genuine. Sometimes copycats expect their buyers to know the products are fakes; in other cases they rely on deceit. Some counterfeits are perfectly adequate, functioning products; others are duds and potentially dangerous. A quick tour through several of the most affected industries—apparel, industrial goods, software, music and video, and medicine—reveals the counterfeiters' range, well-honed opportunism, and boundless creativity. It also shows that counterfeiters are serving a market as willing to buy their illicit wares as they are to sell them.

APPAREL AND ACCESSORIES. In June 2004, a raid on New York's Canal Street uncovered $24 million in bogus famous-label handbags. In Europe, counterfeits have displaced $8 billion in designer apparel and shoes and $3 billion in cosmetics. In Italy, Europe's most fashionable country and the victim of some of the more sophisticated fakes on the market, up to 20 percent of purchased clothes are designer rip-offs, and domestic fake leather-good sales are estimated at $1.4 billion. In cosmopolitan Hong Kong and Singapore, the numbers are higher.

The hot new items in fakes are the "supercopies"—meticulous imitations of luxury goods that have confounded even Chanel employees on the Champs-Elysées in Paris. The supercopy capital of the world is South Korea, with output of perhaps one million items a year that can retail for one-tenth of the real thing. One Korean counterfeiter admitted to selling his supercopy of the famous Hermès Kelly bag for $3,900—still cheaper than the real thing, which can retail at $25,000 because of Hermès's extraordinary brand premium. What permits him to pull off this deceit are the sophisticated production methods behind supercopies, which rely on state-of-the-art technology and even expert artisans from the European luxury industry who sell their skills on the sly—"rogue craftsmen" not unlike the rogue scientists of the illegal weapons trade. Supercopiers know what they want: burglars who broke into the headquarters of an Italian fashion house in the summer of 2001 stole samples of the 2002 spring/summer collection and nothing else.

The rising quality of fakes is cause for alarm among brand holders. Two hundred thousand fake Rolexes seized in Italy between 2000 and 2004 were so well made, all the way down to hypersecret internal markings, that they could fool even the company itself. Even well-heeled, demanding customers are finding that the quality of fakes is now so high that paying several times more for an original is losing its appeal. Some manufacturers are hoping that by opening high-design, trendy retail outlets in top malls, they can combat this trend by turning the whole buying experience—not only the product, but the trip to the mall to get it—into something wealthy shoppers would wish to flaunt.

Not all brand owners confess to being alarmed, however. Some high-luxury houses worry less about counterfeits because they are sure that these displace very little of their highly self-selected clientele—and even do some good, as a sort of early-warning system to advise the upwardly mobile of the brands they should seek out once they've arrived. Sometimes the facts seem to back this up: for instance, sales of $12,000 Omega watches have been up for several years, despite the profusion of $80 knockoffs on the street.

Privately, however, brand owners know they don't hold all the cards. The CEO of one of the world's best-known Swiss watchmakers told me: "We now compete with a product manufactured by Chinese prisoners. The business is run by the Chinese military, their families, and friends, using roughly the same machines we have, which they purchased at the same German industrial fairs we go to."

He continued: "The way we have rationalized this problem is by assuming that their customers and ours are different. The person that buys a pirated copy of one of our five-thousand-dollar watches for less than one hundred dollars is not a client we are losing. Perhaps it is a future client that someday will want to own the real thing instead of a fake. We may be wrong, and we do spend some money to fight the piracy of our products. But given that our efforts do not seem to protect us much, we close our eyes and hope for the better."

Closing one's eyes and hoping for the best is a luxury only a few companies can afford. For those that sell cheaper products like garments, music, or videos, counterfeiting is a scourge that has the potential to take down whole companies.

INDUSTRIAL PRODUCTS. If you are a carmaker with a stake in China, you are probably embroiled in some kind of dispute with a Chinese manufacturer over a product that happens to look, feel, and drive just like your own. The googly-eye headlights of the Chery QQ, for instance, mirror those of a General Motors product called the Chevrolet Spark, and so do many of its other features. But in the Ya Yun Cun car market on the north side of Beijing, the QQ sells for little more than five thousand dollars—a full 20 percent less than the Spark. Yet it is difficult for GM to outright accuse Chery of stealing its design. Chery's part-owner, SAIC, is none other than GM's Chinese joint venture partner; and both Chery's and SAIC's principal owners are the governments of Chinese provinces. Neither is there a favorable precedent: Toyota's claim that another Chinese manufacturer, Geery, copied its logo, was dismissed by a Chinese court. Little chance either that Nissan will successfully argue that the Great Wall Sing SUV mimics its Paladin model. It seems apparent that the Chinese government tacitly encourages this sort of emulation—a sort of technology transfer accelerator. Automakers have little choice than to accept this as a cost of doing business in the ever-expanding Chinese market.

Cloned whole cars have yet to turn up in the export market, but surely not for long. Fake Honda motorcycles are sold by the millions in China for about three hundred dollars each, roughly half the price of the original, and many are being exported. Cloned car parts are estimated to have conquered a $12 billion market worldwide, mostly originating in India, China, Taiwan, and South Korea. France estimates that one-tenth of car parts sold in Europe are counterfeits, and DaimlerChrysler estimates counterfeiters have grabbed about 30 percent of its market for car parts in China, Taiwan, and Korea. American manufacturers have found rip-off versions of brand-name filters, brakes, shock absorbers, pumps, batteries, and windshields. The fakes are not always benign: bogus brake pads have been found made of compressed sawdust, and low-grade crude oil has masqueraded as transmission fluid. More worrisome still is the spread of fake aircraft parts. In one instance, a vigilant United Airlines mechanic came upon fake parts, complete with boxes and paperwork, with a lifespan of 600 hours compared to the 20,000 hours of the original.

No product seems immune. The Jordanian agent of a reputable Italian valve manufacturer called headquarters to ask why they were selling valves directly in his market at a 40 percent discount. The offending items were high-quality forgeries, down to the logo stamped in the metal of each piece. An Ohio maker of sewer pumps blamed the loss of $5 million in revenue and twenty-five jobs on companies it found in Brazil and China copying its products, including advertising and manuals. And the list goes on. Although there are many different countries of origin, one common point is China, where the manufacturing base, the skill at reverse-engineering, and the omnipresence of foreign companies doing business through agents and licensees almost guarantee opportunities to counterfeit. In response, many companies have given up on shutting down the supply of fake goods, preferring instead to tighten control of their distribution channels.

MUSIC AND VIDEO. Music isn't usually measured by weight. But in Spain, for instance, producing and distributing one kilogram of counterfeit music and films is five times more profitable than selling one kilogram of hashish. In the first half of 2002, U.S. customs seized 2.1 million pirated discs, up 66 percent from the previous year. Between 2000 and 2003, the number of CD plants in Russia doubled; Russia now exports pirated CDs to at least twenty-six countries. Ukraine is considered another major source, as is Taiwan, where the disc-pressing capacity vastly outweighs the volume of legitimate sales. Nine out of ten recordings sold in China are pirated; in some African and Latin American markets, there is nothing but counterfeits, because the legitimate music industry has simply pulled out. The quality may be spotty, but it's better than nothing.

Prerecorded compact discs are only part of the problem, of course. Global music industry sales have declined for several years, and the rise of Internet downloading is also to blame. In total the music industry estimates $4.5 billion in yearly losses on illegal copying, and in the United States at least it has taken stern action to identify and shut down the principal culprits. Facing the music, so to speak, the major labels have launched their own pay-to-download services or joined up with software manufacturers, with varying degrees of enthusiasm. Yet despite the commercial success of legal online music stores such as Apple's iTunes, piracy remains, according to an industry survey, "rampant."

There's no question that online and pirate distribution is changing the music industry, forcing major chains to consolidate and old-fashioned record stores to shut down. Less clear is whether the industry's rearguard efforts can do much to stop the trend. In early 2004, for instance, an Atlanta DJ called Danger Mouse put online the "Grey Album"—an electronically crafted combination of the Beatles' *White Album* and the *Black Album* by the rapper Jay-Z. This blatant violation of two separate copyrights earned critical raves from the *New York Times* on down as an augury of musical innovations to come. After the recording industry threatened to sue, 170 Web sites posted the tracks on the same day.

Similar trends affect the film industry. Video files can take hours to download, yet an estimated 1 million movies are illegally available online, with up to a 500,000 downloads each day. But the big money is still in pirated DVDs produced in Asian "video factories" and sold around the world, costing the legitimate trade $3 billion in lost revenue. The challenge of releasing DVDs as fast as possible has pushed the counterfeiter's art to new heights. The actor Dennis Hopper once bought in Shanghai an "excellent" copy of a movie he was working on, complete with voice tracks he'd recorded in a Hollywood studio just two days earlier. Chinese Harry Potter fans could buy their hero's movie months before local release for $1.20. DVD piracy is a crisis for the film industry, which makes up to 80 percent of its revenue in the aftermarket—video sales, cable, pay per view. At the epicenter of supply and demand for pirated DVDs, the Hong Kong industry has withered, producing fewer movies each year.

SOFTWARE. Two weeks before Microsoft released its Windows 95 operating system, an international ring called DrinkorDie with members in the United States, Australia, Norway, Finland, and Britain was distributing the product online. Since then the software mastodon has time and again butted heads with "freelance" distributors around the world. Microsoft is the largest victim, but it is not the only one. Adobe, which makes the software that produces .pdf files, estimates that 50 percent of software sold under its name is pirated. And lest the 90-plus percent piracy rates in China, Vietnam, and Ukraine and 80-plus in Russia, Indonesia, and Zimbabwe leave the impression that the problem is confined to "over there," it's worth noting that about one-quarter of business software in the United States is unlicensed, and the same is true for up to 50 percent of Spain's. After all, who hasn't run into a not-quite-legal version of Microsoft Word?

Counterfeit software is very big business, costing the industry an estimated $13 billion per year worldwide and thousands of jobs per year in the United States alone. The volumes and sophistication can be impressive. In November 2001, for instance, authorities in Los Angeles seized 31,000 copies of counterfeit software from Taiwan, worth $100 million. They also found counterfeit security devices, manuals, bar codes, registration cards, end-user agreements—along with 85,000 cartons of counterfeit cigarettes. Microsoft, whose antipiracy team has expanded from 2 employees in 1988 to more than 250 today, is also the driving force behind the Business Software Alliance, an industry group that lobbies for software copyright enforcement worldwide. It claims some progress in curbing the "one-disc country" phenomenon, in which just one legitimate copy could beget enough counterfeits to flood the local market. At the same time, however, schools, universities, businesses, and NGOs in developing countries often feel they have no alternative, given the costs, than to employ unlicensed, copied software.

MEDICINE. Horror stories involving counterfeit medicine are legion. In 1995, a spurious meningitis vaccine killed thousands of people in Niger. The next year, eighty-nine children in Haiti died after ingesting cough syrup adulterated with antifreeze. More than one-third of a particular antimalaria pill in Southeast Asia were found to be fake in 1999. In China, some veterinary drugs are repackaged for human use. The government-owned Shenzhen Evening News estimated that 192,000 people died in China in 2001 because of fake drugs, between the toxins contained in some counterfeits and the absence of curative effect from fakes devoid of their active ingredient.

The World Health Organization estimates that 8 percent of world drug supply is counterfeit, for a value in the $32 billion range. (This is likely an underestimate: fake drugs are often not reported, because the evidence disappears into the patient.) According to one study, nearly half the fakes on the market contain either no active ingredient or the wrong one, including the 10 percent laced with contaminants. The rest may not be legitimate but are nonetheless drugs—perhaps expired and relabeled, perhaps correctly compounded but distributed with false or misleading packaging or labels. Millions of people have little choice than to turn to counterfeit drugs—knowingly or not—to treat their ailments.

The risk of running into a fake increases with the popularity of the drug in question and the premium the brand owner commands. Antibiotics, inhalers, treatments for common diseases, AIDS drugs: all are lucrative targets. So is Viagra, the stunning popularity of which makes it a prime candidate for counterfeiting. The mail-order Viagra offers that are the scourge of e-mail users usually to lead to impostors. In a 2002 case, fake Viagra was shipped from factories in China via intermediary firms in China, India, and the United States to Internet vendors based in Colorado and Nevada. The drugs arrived in the States concealed in stereo speakers and stuffed toys, then made their way to the customer by mail. One distributor boasted that he could deliver millions of pills per month.

The counterfeit drug trade is well organized, with a supply chain that is truly global, comparable to those of the largest and most sophisticated multinational enterprises. India and China, the two largest suppliers of active ingredients to the legitimate industry, are the primary source for counterfeiters as well. Other countries such as Mexico specialize in formulating and packaging the drugs. Dispersal among multiple countries makes fake drugs hard to trace, let alone eradicate. In the Haiti case, the trail of the so-called cough syrup implicated Haitian, Chinese, German, and Dutch companies, yet in the end investigators never learned where the product was made. Even within countries production sites are dispersed or camouflaged. A batch of 1,800 cartons of drugs made in China but labeled as manufactured in India and Pakistan under license from multinational companies turned out to involve ten copycat manufacturers in five provinces, using five different suppliers for packaging. Manufacturing sites range from small household workshops to legitimate factories: a firm that produces a drug under license need only run an extra shift with substandard inputs. Workers on the production line might never know they were doing anything wrong.

In short, any popular product of any type is vulnerable to the copycats. But the copycat industry isn't a perfect mirror image of the legitimate manufacturers. Quite the contrary: free of the costs of developing their own ideas, counterfeiters move easily from product to product, combining them with one another and mixing legal and illegal goods in the same shipments—or the same production facilities.

BRANCHING OUT ON ALL SIDES

Counterfeiting networks are multicountry, multiproduct, and decentralized. A 2003 bust in Los Angeles uncovered $9.7 million in counterfeits of brands that included Black & Decker, Sony, Rolex, Makita, and DeWalt, along with pirated DVDs. The goods came from China but none of the five people arrested was Chinese. In a New York bust the same year, six Brooklyn men were charged with importing 35 million counterfeit cigarettes from China, hidden in shipping containers behind cooking pots. They sold the goods through a business on a Native American reservation in upstate New York, as well as on the Internet. Two were charged as well with importing fake batteries from China, transiting in Lithuania. All were under investigation in Europe as well.

These and other cases reveal a disaggregated supply chain, with raw materials, components, assembly, packaging, and distribution dispersed among multiple locales. Made possible by communication technology and global shipping networks, this strategy minimizes and disperses the risk. And breaking down supply into its components makes it easier, at each stage, to piggyback unobtrusively on legitimate operations. The Internet compounds these advantages: the boundless profusion of publicly accessible sites, chat rooms, and message boards where obviously fake goods are listed for trade illustrates best of all just how comfortable the traders feel in cyberspace. For consumers, finding a knockoff or bootleg is as easy as logging on to a global sales site like eBay.

Powerful interests often protect the counterfeit trade. The sums of money to be made are too great to withstand the threat of corruption. In some cases powerful political interests have turned themselves into direct investors or operators in the counterfeit trade, perhaps none more so than the Chinese military. In theory, the PLA has been shedding its business assets, by government order, since 2001. But the policy suffers numerous exceptions, and many PLA officers who ran business operations have officially retired and retained both corporate control and their influential connections; others are in the hands of relatives and cronies. Unraveling the role of PLA companies, or for that matter ones owned by the national or provincial governments, might be close to impossible, even with the most diligent political will.

Similarly, product piracy involving labor in Chinese prisons has long been assumed but often been hard to prove. In December 2004, however, information emerged that Sony had documented counterfeit manufacturing of PlayStation2 consoles using prison labor. According to the *Financial Times,* Sony found ten pirating networks producing up to 50,000 consoles each day; at least one used labor from inmates at a prison in Shenzhen near Hong Kong to assemble the units. Needless to say, cracking down on prison labor raises the same thorny political issues as targeting PLA companies. And China isn't the only country where counterfeiting enjoys semi-official investment, connivance, or assistance through corruption. In some cases, the counterfeiters leave public servants no choice: disc pirates, for instance, warned Malaysian officials to let them operate—or be killed.

Counterfeiting overlaps with other illicit trades, organized crime, and terrorist networks. A natural connection, given the similarities in product and format, is between the fake medicine and illegal drugs trade, which have come to follow many of the same routes. There are indications as well that organized crime has entered particular branches of the counterfeit trade—Russian and Asian gangs, for instance, in the CD/DVD trade.

Ties with the trade in humans appear at the distribution level. In Spain, for example, music and video counterfeiting networks flood the streets with 150,000 copied CDs *each month.* These networks are organized by ethnicity, with Indians, Pakistanis, and Bangladeshis in charge of production and sub-Saharan Africans responsible for retailing. New Moroccan and Chinese competitors are vertically integrated and control both production and retail. Many "employees" are illegal immigrants who must work sixteen hours a day, seven days a week, to meet their production or sales quotas—all to repay the debts they owe the traffickers who smuggled them into the country.

But of all the nefarious links of the counterfeit trade, it is those with terrorist networks that have caused the most alarm. As noted in previous chapters, there is ample evidence that decentralized terrorist cells on the al-Qaeda model have used the trade in counterfeits to support their operations. The perpetrators of the first World Trade Center bombing in 1993 sustained themselves in part from the sale of counterfeit T-shirts from a Broadway storefront. In 1996, a haul of 100,000 fake Nike brand and Olympic logo T-shirts, intended for sale in the run-up to the Atlanta Olympics, led to followers of Sheik Omar Abdel Rahman, the imprisoned cleric. The September 11, 2001, hijackers may have supported themselves by the tried-and-true cigarette scam, which involves purchasing bulk cigarettes in a low-tax part of the United States, such as North Carolina, and selling them at a discount where taxes are higher. And the militants suspected of the March 2004 train station bombings in Madrid operated a home-based business in counterfeit CDs.

Numerous militant groups appear to have turned to this line of business. The intended beneficiaries of a shipment of counterfeit German brake pads and shock absorbers caught in Lebanon were supporters of Hezbollah. Both the IRA and the Basque ETA are widely assumed to trade in all sorts of counterfeit goods, from handbags and clothes to perfumes and DVDs, including, in one instance reported in Northern Ireland, pirate copies of *The Lion King*. Yet as much as the "war on terror" has focused attention on these scams, it has done so because of the terrorist link and in the context of a shift in law enforcement resources toward terrorism and away from other priorities. Little chance, therefore, that the current interest in terrorist hustles will have much of a long-term impact on the half-trillion-dollar global counterfeit trade.

A BATTLE OF TITANS

The battle over counterfeits pits against each other two formidable antagonists. Multinational corporations that own valuable brands obviously seek to cultivate consumer appetite. But that same consumer appetite for brands is how counterfeiters identify an opportunity. The scale of counterfeiting worldwide shows that shoppers tend to succumb to the dual temptation of seeking out both legitimate brand-name products *and* the cheap counterfeits this interest generates. The trend has all the looks of a never-ending cycle.

In this clash of titanic forces, governments and their laws are often relegated to the sideline for sheer lack of relevance, since the market evolves much faster than governments can catch up. Yet governments play a crucial role in shaping the copycat trade, for they set the rules of the game with the intellectual property laws that they pass and enforce—and that vary widely. A first offense of counterfeiting in the United States can draw a fine of $2 million and a long prison term; in China, it can carry a fine as low as $1,000. In Malaysia, where even a small narcotic drugs offense can trigger the death penalty, counterfeiting CDs or software draws a fine of 100,000 ringgit, roughly $26,000. Meanwhile, the maximum fine for counterfeiting medicine was only 25,000 ringgit, or $6,500.

In any case, local laws are of limited use against a trade that hopscotches borders with ease. International treaties, on the other hand, have at least the benefit of providing a common and mandatory frame of reference—a first step toward carrying charges and prosecuting cases across national boundaries. Protection of intellectual property rights has benefited from the strong self interest of large multinational firms, which have helped push it up on the agenda of international talks. Perhaps the most useful result of such talks thus far has been to make international disagreements on copyright, patent, and trademark rights subject to the arbitration of the World Trade Organization (WTO)—a facility limited to disputes between governments, and thus not fully adapted to combating counterfeits, but a significant step nonetheless.

Still, governments can't match the economic motives of both brand owners and copycats in what is above all a business battle. Faced with the incapacity or in some cases lack of interest of governments in taking up the fight, businesses have turned themselves into the protectors and enforcers of their own brands, so much so that brand protection has become a commercial specialty. At a 2004 international congress on counterfeiting held in Brussels, all the companies listed as sponsors and supporters were specialists in new technologies that aim to authenticate products and make them harder to copy. Security consultants like Kroll and Pinkerton, along with local subcontractors in targeted countries, do a brisk business in intellectual property protection. At the very least, the fight against counterfeits has spawned its own thriving industry.

It is a historical pattern that as economies develop, local business assigns a greater importance to the protection of intellectual property, for the simple reason that it is generating more inventions and ideas of its own. India's generic medicine manufacturers—authorized at the time under Indian law to reverse-engineer drugs patented elsewhere—violated intellectual property rights but helped develop local scientific skills. Now that these skills are paying off in the form of Indian technological innovations, Indian firms are warming to patent protection. Chinese firms are now finding themselves vulnerable to counterfeiting, and intellectual property law is receiving increased local scrutiny. (One expert on the topic, Professor Zheng Chensi, suffered the ignominy of having his own books on intellectual property protection in China pirated and posted on the Web.)

Yet the far stronger pattern is the sheer increase in the volume, quality, and global penetration of counterfeit goods of all sorts. All the incentives point that way. It is simply too easy to produce, ship, and retail counterfeits—and too easy for customers to lay their hands on them. The more brand owners invest in creating the desire to purchase their products, the stronger the temptation to purchase them from counterfeiters at a deep discount. And while the demand exists, the supply will too.

Owners of intellectual property may be very motivated to protect their rights and the ability of their intangible assets to generate revenues. But they will never be more motivated than the networks that stand to make billions from supplying hungry customers with what they want. Governments forced to stand in the middle of this battle will only see the frustration and corruption in their ranks soar. Companies would likely see better results from constant innovation— research and development to make products that are hard to copy, as well as affordable—than from relying on the deployment of armies of lawyers and lobbyists in the battle to protect their brands.

Chapter 7

THE MONEY WASHERS

Just how cheap is a human life?

In the depressing aftermath of carnage, it can seem very cheap indeed. It cost the terrorists who carried out the September 11, 2001 attacks on New York and Washington less than a half million dollars to take about three thousand lives, including their own. Which works out, in a morbid sort of logic, to less than two hundred dollars per person.

The immediate investigation established this much. The trail of evidence was barely concealed; after all, the hijackers had no intention of surviving the operation. It involved some utterly ordinary transactions: a rental car in Portland, Maine; meals at Florida chain restaurants; airplane tickets; groceries. Much of these expenses was run up on Visa cards issued by the South Florida bank where Mohammed Atta, the group's leader, set up his account in June of the previous year. Three months later he would receive a wire transfer in the amount of $69,985 from a Gulf emirate bank. The amount and origin were notable enough to trigger a suspicious transaction report to the Financial Crimes Enforcement Network, the government's crack intelligence unit devoted to such matters. But FinCEN, as it is called, receives many such reports every month; not every one leads to action, and this one did not.

Within minutes of the World Trade Center attack, counterterrorism officials knew they were dealing with Osama bin Laden's al-

Qaeda organization. But in the days after September 11, the wire transfers, cash advances, and credit card receipts were almost the only clues they had to understand how America's new enemy prepared its attack. Just finding witnesses—the waitress at the diner, the rental counter agent—involved tracing the hijackers' expenditures. But following the money trail back further held out the promise of a far bigger prize: uncovering the sources and conduits by which these and other terrorists funded their operations, in order to neutralize them by shutting off their access to money and to capture them by staking out their transactions.

"Money sets Osama bin Laden apart from other Middle Eastern fanatics and murderers," one columnist wrote a few weeks later. "It was jet fuel that caused the Trade Center's towers to burn and implode on September 11. And it was oil money that enabled bin Laden" to set up shop in Sudan and Afghanistan and launch his organization. But that high-level logic was of little use to counterterrorism experts. They knew that bin Laden had likely already drawn down his personal fortune. Their questions were far more practical: How did each al-Qaeda cell subsist on its own? What were the network's sources of revenue, and how did it move its money about? Which of the parties involved at each level—banks, businesses, individuals—were knowingly complicit, and which were being deceived? With each of these queries, investigators stepped further into a complex and expanding world: the world of money laundering and the international trade in dirty money.

A fair amount was already known. Ramzi Yousef, a perpetrator of the original World Trade Center bombing in 1993, had used donations from a company that imported holy water from Mecca to Pakistan. Some funds used in the bombing of American embassies in Kenya and Tanzania in 1998 had been delivered under cover of Mercy International Relief Agency, a Saudi-based charity. In fact a string of charities in the Arab world but also in the Philippines, Croatia and the United States had known or suspected links to al-Qaeda. So did businesses in several countries, in the fisheries, livestock, transportation, construction, honey, and leather trades. Some terrorist cells ran scams in the countries they infiltrated—black market cigarette sales, for instance, or counterfeit CDs. Thanks to this and other information, a map of terrorist financing was starting to emerge. But as events sadly proved, it was not yet enough.

There were two ways to look at all this information. From one point of view, terrorist financing was complex and diverse; there were myriad players, many out of reach in obscure or lawless locations, involved in any number of other criminal practices, and all of them hard to pin down. But seen another way, terrorist finance was strikingly simple: as exotic as deals in the background may have been, it took only a few wire transfers and credit cards to commit the actual crime. Just as a terrorist cell's communications might melt into the noise of millions of cell phone calls and anonymous Web mail messages, so too could its money merge into the torrent of currency moving at all times around the globe. To successfully "follow the money" would lead you to a place where the exotic and the ordinary were tightly interwoven.

That paradox isn't limited to terrorist finance. Instead, it's common to all financial crime today, whether it's laundering the proceeds of illicit trade, assembling the resources to commit a terrorist act, or hiding income beyond the tax man's reach. Many techniques are old classics: anonymous bank accounts in permissive jurisdictions, for instance, or front companies in cash-intensive businesses like restaurants and Laundromats. Others are brand new, made possible by global financial integration. But all of them have made "dirty money" more agile, mobile, and elusive than ever before. Most of all, the barriers that once kept small-town savings deposits and international ill-gotten gains at opposite ends of the financial world have largely fallen. It is increasingly difficult for any bank, mutual fund, wire transfer provider, check casher, or other financial agent to be absolutely, positively sure that 100 percent of the funds it moves are "clean."

The multiplication and "mainstreaming" of dirty-money opportunities has drawn a determined and often creative response from regulators and law enforcement in many countries. Yet by the summer of 2001, those efforts seemed at risk: leading nations squabbled as to which activities to criminalize and how to avoid overly weighing down the financial markets. Competition between countries to attract deposits by offering the most attractive conditions, often meaning secrecy and confidentiality, also interfered with international collaboration.

The September 11 attacks restored a sense of purpose, and urgency: as al-Qaeda's inner workings came to light, they exposed new vulnerabilities, focusing the public eye on such previously obscure entities as *hawalas*—trust-based remittance agents used by immigrants—and Islamic banks and charities. (In the same period, corporate scandals such as the collapse of Enron, which had barely paid any taxes since 1996, were spotlighting the spread of offshore shell companies. Few drew the connections, however.)

But the alarm over terrorist finance also challenged authorities to focus their efforts. After all, swift movement of money is one of globalization's benefits. Money laundering, terrorist financing, tax evasion, and fraud take place amid foreign direct investment, portfolio investment, immigrant remittances, credit card transactions, e-commerce, and more. The trouble is that the interweaving of licit and illicit activity offers money washers camouflage within the global financial system on which we all depend.

MORE MONEY, MORE WAYS TO HIDE

To understand the profusion of money laundering opportunities today, it helps to stand back and consider the big picture. The global financial system today is fundamentally different from what it was a mere fifteen years ago. For one, the system ballooned. The assets of the world's leading national monetary authorities grew from $6.8 trillion in 1990 to $19.9 trillion in 2004. But it grew not only in volume but also in complexity. Countries opened their economies, deregulated their financial sector, and allowed their local domestic financial systems—commercial banks, financial companies, stock markets, brokerage houses—to hook up with partners in other countries, and even invest in one another. This created operating and control structures that became far more difficult to monitor and regulate than when finance was a more local affair. And new financial products were launched: from ATM cards to fiendishly complex derivative contracts capable of moving massive quantities of money in ways that only specialists could understand. Behind this growth in size and complexity were not just new policies but also new technologies that lowered transaction costs and made geography far less relevant. The direct cost to a bank of a typical transaction drops by 40 percent when the client conducts it over the phone instead of showing up at a branch in person. And it plummets 98 percent if it is done online, regardless of where the customer is located.

The decline of the importance of distance and national borders as obstacles to the international movement of money was boosted by several policy changes that became fashionable among governments during the 1990s. Four of these financial reforms were of particular consequence to money launderers.

First, most countries abandoned exchange controls. It was no longer necessary to obtain government authorization to convert local money into foreign currency, or vice versa. That trend had begun prior to the 1990s, but it was during the early part of that decade that most countries joined the movement toward the relaxation or outright elimination of foreign exchange controls. As a result, the global *daily* volume of currency exchanged has skyrocketed, from $590 billion a day in 1989 to $1.88 *trillion* in 2004, while some countries have merged their currencies—the euro, obviously—and others have adopted the dollar or euro as a quasi-official second currency. Naturally, this is good news for money launderers, tax evaders, and the like, because it expands the playing field, adds flexibility, and multiplies the opportunities.

Second, freely convertible currencies led in most places to more open local capital markets. Closed financial systems are now the exception, not the norm. The foreign ownership of local banks, a practice formerly banned in many countries, is now commonplace. Governments and local firms routinely compete for capital on the global market by issuing bonds and shares, and today far more local stock exchanges allow foreigners to purchase securities. Rating agencies and fund managers judge them not just on their own merits but by how they compare to the field. Governments that used to screen and restrict the entry of foreign multinationals began to actively lure them into investing in the country. This turnabout set vast amounts of money in motion: since 1990, international portfolio investment has gone from less than $5 billion a year to nearly $50 billion in 2000; annual foreign direct investment in projects and ventures on the ground grew from $209 billion in 1990 to $560 billion in 2003. This too is good for money launderers. More transactions mean more potential piggyback opportunities for illicit money to unobtrusively reenter the mainstream.

Third, the hallmark of global finance is competition for capital—among countries and companies that issue securities but also among banks, brokers, wire transfer services, asset managers, and all the other intermediaries who vie for the opportunity to deliver capital to its destination. This suits money launderers because they have cash on hand: they can reasonably expect that sooner or later a banker or broker will accept their funds without asking inconvenient questions—particularly if they sweeten the deal by paying a bribe or an above-market fee.

Finally, the transformation of global finance owes everything to the information revolution. Banks were among the earliest and fastest adopters of new technology. The electronic backbone of the financial system has delivered instantaneous transactions that can be executed from almost anywhere in the world. Obviously not a bad thing if you are an internationally mobile money launderer keen on staying ahead of law enforcement agents who are far less agile when operating internationally.

Thus, the increased convenience of illicit transactions draws its impetus from the same advances that legitimate users have come to expect and require to manage their money. Just because many of these changes are now familiar does not mean that the consequences of this much-altered international financial system are well understood. The new wave of money laundering is one such effect. Unconstrained by the niceties of corporate decision making and bureaucracy, money launderers were probably among the quickest to adapt to financial liberalization and integration in the 1990s. They were perfectly positioned to discover before anyone else that the range of vehicles and methods that became available in the 1990s to hold, move, and employ illegal funds had no historical precedent.

DISCRETION IN DEMAND

How easy it has become to launder funds would not matter much if the demand for illicit financial services was drying up. But, unfortunately, business is booming. There is more money than ever on the market in search of discreet financial services that elude the law. The rule of thumb to estimate the scope of money laundering today is between 2 and 5 percent of world GDP, or $800 billion to $2 trillion. Some estimates run as high as 10 percent of global GDP. Add to this tax evasion, which is inherently hard to quantify; and various kinds of fraud, and there is more than enough liquidity and demand to sustain a profitable industry.

Evaluating who accounts for what share of the total is impossible. But it is clear that every time any illicit trade activity experiences a surge it pushes more money into the laundering cycle. And every time these trades reorganize or alter their global routes, new needs for illicit financial services in new locations immediately spring up. Money laundering is not just a trade in itself but an irreplaceable mechanism of every other illicit trade. In a sense, money laundering is a mirror of the global underground economy.

In recent years, the spotlight has shone especially on the finances behind international terrorist operations. But connections also occur on a more flexible, opportunistic, and decentralized basis. For a time, Mexican drug interests are believed to have partnered with Hezbollah associates in the importation of pseudoephedrine, a component of methamphetamine, from Canada to the United States. Local terrorist cells have been shown to rely on illicit trade as well. In the 1990s, U.S.-based associates of Hezbollah and of Sheik Omar Abdel Rahman, the patron of the first World Trade Center bombing in 1993, used illegal interstate cigarette distribution, store coupon scams, and counterfeit T-shirt sales to fund their operations. And the suspects behind the March 11, 2004, railway station bombings in Madrid also ran a business in counterfeit compact discs.

These ground-level, practical ties illustrate a convergence in the organization of terrorism and illicit trade that is born of both necessity and opportunity. Both employ adaptive, flexible networks as the best means to confound law enforcement while exploiting the conveniences of globalization. Though their ultimate ends are different, their operational interests are very similar. And they can cooperate on the ground, because both are so decentralized and so well camouflaged that a properly handled local collaboration need not blow either side's cover. This means that any investigation of "terrorist finance" is almost certain to merge into the bigger picture of money laundering and global illicit trade. But by the same token, terrorist finance represents only a small part of the underground financial system—a sobering caution worth bearing in mind.

Traffickers and terrorists are two sets of users of illicit financial services. A third set is corrupt individuals, who are often both accessories to other people's transactions and at the same time principals in their own. These range from tax evaders to regulators, customs officials, and others in key governmental positions, involving the grand corruption of politicians and heads of state. Of course, generations of autocrats have stashed away the proceeds of their country's wealth into numbered Swiss accounts. New methods and opportunities are available, however, which can only amplify the siren call of illicit gain. Needless to say, democratically elected leaders are not immune.

All of these practices can be called criminal without much second thought. Tax evasion, however, is a bit more ambiguous. Only a few tax evaders operate by evacuating suitcases of money in the dead of night. More often, tax evasion is a quasi-legal practice that makes use of offshore financial services to reduce tax liabilities—infringing the spirit of the law but not its letter. Moreover, each country's tax code has its own particularities, so that any person or company in more than one jurisdiction has, to some degree, a legitimate opportunity to move assets, revenues, expenditures, and liabilities across borders to minimize the tax bill. All this makes it exceedingly difficult to determine where tax evasion crosses the line.

In one instance detected by U.S. authorities, the border between tax avoidance and tax evasion was crossed to the tune of $200 million. In 2005 the IRS accused Walter C. Anderson, a tycoon who had become wealthy in the 1990s in the telecommunications industry, of hiding $450 million offshore to evade taxes estimated at $200 million. Anderson argued that he was not guilty and that the money went to his Panamanian foundation, which was devoted to advancing human rights, arms control, family planning, and the development of space. While claiming that his companies in tax-haven countries did not break any laws, Anderson recognized that "[f]or every [legitimate] company that is located in a tax haven there are 50 that are committing fraud. They're there to hide assets from your partner, they're there to hide assets from the IRS."

A whole class of professionals has sprung up to help direct money to best advantage, depending on its holder's appetite for risk, need for discretion, and degree of willingness to break the law. These include professional money launderers, who take charge of the whole operation against a fee—and sometimes go further, acting as asset managers for the laundered proceeds. An armada of lawyers and brokers is available to help conceal transactions from scrutiny and buttress them against prosecution. It could be argued that professional tax advisors who scour the globe for locations in which to set up real or shell interests play a part of their own in sustaining the financial underworld. It is still relatively easy to find a lawyer willing to serve as the director or even owner of an offshore company that holds assets that in effect belong to another anonymous person.

The more stringent rules imposed after 9/11 undoubtedly increased the risks for money launderers. But not significantly or, much less, to the level at which they create a major deterrent to illicit global financial flows. For the most part the new controls have merely increased the transaction costs and the fees that front men charge for their services. The most comprehensive and rigorous evaluation of the anti–money laundering regime in place in the United States concluded in 2004 that "the risk of conviction faced by money launderers is about 5 percent annually. Data from other industrialized nations indicate even lower levels of enforcement."

THE NEW OFFSHORE

Like some kind of migratory bird, money has long had special places to go when it wishes to reproduce in peace. The financial world beyond the reach of the law and the appetite of tax authorities has long been called "offshore." And at one time, offshore was a quite tangible notion, a set of places you could locate on a map. But pinpointing the safe havens of illicit capital is no longer so easy to do.

Defined by the book, *offshore* is a term of art that designates financial facilities that a country or territory (a "jurisdiction") makes available to noncitizens. Offshore financial facilities, therefore, have the express aim of attracting capital from other countries, which they reward with more lenient rules than it would encounter at home. The host nation benefits by charging fees for the issuance of various licenses and documents, such as articles of incorporation or licenses for banking services and mutual and hedge funds.

What caused the term to stick was that so many of the territories that offered these arrangements were, in fact, islands. And the most famous were convenient to the major financial centers: Bermuda or the Cayman Islands, a short flight from New York or Miami, or the Isle of Man and Channel Islands, a quick hop from London or Paris. It took only a jaunt to file paperwork, renew licenses, or escort a suitcase of cash. There were some other landbound players, such as Monaco, Panama, Liechtenstein, or Switzerland with its famous bank secrecy. These "islands" had in common with the others that they were small—sometimes very small—countries with few natural resources, making a play for revenue and relevance by offering these amenities.

This part has not fundamentally changed. In fact, the number of territories that specialize in offshore services has grown; and yes, many new entrants are actual islands. The Pacific state of Nauru, population 12,000, is home to 40,000 registered corporations including an estimated 400 shell banks that in practice just consist of a small office and a brass plate on the door. Other havens in the offshore game include the Bahamas, Bahrain, Cyprus, Malta, the Netherlands Antilles, Grenada, Antigua, Seychelles—as well as autonomous regions like Madeira, or even deliberately carved-out real or virtual zones such as Malaysia's Labaun Island or the Bangkok International Banking Facility.

Obviously not all of these zones aim specifically to attract illicit funds. Yet as this list suggests, countries and territories enter the offshore services market with different degrees of credibility, and they tend to attract clients to match. The more established venues have been at pains to distinguish themselves from the shadier lot. At one end of the spectrum, the Cayman Islands (population 43,000) has become a major financial center in its own right, with close to six hundred banks, including all but three of the world's top fifty, along with several thousand mutual funds and tens of thousands of offshore businesses. Concerned with their standing and competitive edge, the Caymans innovate with new financial products, for instance pioneering insurance "captives"—single-purpose vehicles set up by noninsurance companies to cover a specific risk. At the other end of the spectrum one might find Tuvalu, another microstate in the Pacific, which leased its Internet suffix—the tantalizing .tv—to a broker and earns a small fee every time an address is registered. Tuvalu also leased its international telephone prefix, 688, to a phone sex operator.

The idea of leasing out a country's sovereign assets—such as its identity in an international registry or its official seal to back up financial documents—is not a recent invention. So-called flags of convenience have existed in the shipping business for decades; 60 percent of the world's commercial vessels today are registered to Liberia, Panama, or Greece. In fact, Liberia's shipping registry is run by a company in suburban Washington, D.C., sparing registrants the need to visit Monrovia. (Aircraft owners, as well, know which countries offer registration free of onerous requirements such as safety inspections.) In offshore finance too, new entrants have successful predecessors like the Caymans to emulate. But in reality, many are driven to offshore finance for lack of any obvious resource to sell or labor to export. The most lucrative asset of a Seychelles, Niue, or Tuvalu is its international recognition as a legitimate territory or state: its sovereignty.

As the association of *offshore* with exotic islands, prestigious or shady, has persisted, so too has a certain stereotype of the offshore life, replete with playboys and ne'er-do-wells, secretive bankers and gentleman thieves. Even if this lifestyle persists, the image it conveys is deceptive. There are many more places to launder money than in merely a collection of raffish island venues. More rough-and-tumble, but no less useful to the trade, are strategic locations at the edge of the law—or perhaps just beyond it.

One such venue is Ciudad del Este, a Paraguayan city of 300,000 at the "Triple Frontier" with Brazil and Argentina, and thanks to this helpful position a major rendezvous for smugglers of all types. Ciudad del Este is a crossroads for virtually every illicit trade, including counterfeit software and electronics, smuggled imported goods, and reportedly weapons. Locally represented ethnic communities including Taiwanese, Indians, Lebanese, and Syrians have been associated with these activities. Members of the Middle Eastern communities in Ciudad del Este have been suspected of fund-raising and commerce on behalf of Hezbollah, Hamas, and perhaps even al-Qaeda. But what truly makes the place hum is drug money: cocaine revenues from the Andean countries, which the other trades—assisted by the city's fifty-five banks—all serve to recycle. In 1997 Ciudad del Este laundered this way an estimated $45 billion in drug proceeds.

What makes towns like Ciudad del Este attractive for the business is that regulations are weak, governments are passive, and law enforcement is irrelevant or on the take. These laundering havens must also possess some modicum of a financial and telecommunications infrastructure. Where there are no banks, no ties to the global market, money laundering prospects dwindle severely. The ties that link these often remote locations to the rest of the world need not be varied or complex. In fact many of these places are quite primitive and isolated and have only weak linkages with the outside world—except that banks and companies from around the globe claim them as their legal domicile. In this sense Ciudad del Este for example is not that different from Transdniester near the Black Sea or Afghanistan's Badaskhan province. They provide either a service (illicit financial services), a product (weapons), or a commodity (poppies) that the rest of the world wants in spades.

BIG BANK, LITTLE BANK, BOGUS BANK

Money laundering has worked its way into the sinews. No segment of the global banking system is completely immune to it. The great financial centers like New York and London had their own rich histories of money laundering scandals to begin with. They are now more exposed than ever.

In part, this results from sheer volume. Banks around the world exchange over two trillion transfers and other instructions annually. To police each one with respect to origin, purpose, and destination certainly strains most banks' capabilities. And the number of players in the game has exploded. More and more institutions are allowed to move money across borders, both banks and nonbanks. Thanks to technology, any small-town financial institution can be a convenient, near-instantaneous source or destination of funds to anywhere.

Consumer convenience is paramount. The ATM card pioneered

banking portability and individual control; now, a few technological advances later, the spread of e-banking is inexorable. Virtual banks have opened, Internet-only entities that never meet a customer face-to-face. Virtual money is gaining use as well, in the form of smart cards that preload value on an embedded chip—a manifold improvement over traveler's checks, and with great potential for anonymity. And adding to both customer convenience and market splintering, Western Union and competitors make transfers available from counters in supermarkets, bus terminals, and bodegas. A constant pulse of interbank transactions and electronic settlements keeps the system humming at all times.

A new sense of post-9/11 political urgency, new legislation, new forms of international collaboration, and new technologies are all working to make these tools less convenient and more risky for money launderers to use. But the reality is that in this arena, too, governments are playing catch-up to a group of illicit traders that are running faster and farther than those in charge of stopping them. That is because the financial system has built into it so many amenities, institutions, rules, and even incentives that money launderers can put to profitable use. Accounts with legitimate banks are a common tool for laundering the proceeds of illicit trade. One money launderer who moved $36 million in U.S. cocaine profits back to Colombia by way of Europe did so using a hundred accounts spread across sixty-eight banks in nine countries. Electronic transfers and other banking conveniences have made it viable for launderers to break down their holdings into inconspicuous chunks, a key first step in a laundering scheme. Separating out each transaction now adds so little cost that disaggregating and reaggregating funds is no hassle for launderers. Remote banking—by electronic card, telephone, Internet—allows extra discretion and dissimulation. Despite powerful new technologies available to law enforcement agencies and regulators monitoring these transactions, catching the ones that need to be caught is a near impossible challenge.

Banks have forged new relationships, too, that can open the

door to illicit transactions. One such relationship is correspondent banking. To anticipate the needs of their clients or just to keep pace with the expansion of financial markets, brand-name banks have hurried to establish themselves in every marketplace, either directly, by opening their own branches or acquiring local banks, or indirectly, by setting up networks of preferred banking partners around the world. These correspondent banks play a vital role in global finance, conveying money to and from far-flung locations, to the benefit of overseas investors and emigrant diasporas alike. But they also open a conduit to the international bank's global network that it cannot directly monitor and police, and through which funds can pass at the stroke of a computer key.

Correspondent banking surged in the 1990s on the strength of the emerging markets boom. By the end of the decade some of its pitfalls were starting to become clear. In 1999, a scandal broke out at the venerable Bank of New York, in which 160 correspondent relationships in Russia, along with wire transfer services, banks chartered in Nauru, and the criminal intent of a former executive and her husband helped channel into the United States $7 billion of dubious Russian money over a period of three years. These transactions had earned the Bank of New York millions of dollars in fees. The scandal raised the issue of correspondent banking and led to congressional scrutiny. Yet the problem is not easily solved, because not only is the practice widespread, but it fulfills an actual need if integrated global markets are to function to their full potential.

Terrorists as well have used correspondent banking. During his time based in Sudan, from 1991 to 1996, Osama bin Laden employed accounts at Khartoum's al-Shamal Islamic Bank to access the world banking system. Although established only in 1984, not to mention located in a country considered at the time to be a dusty backwater, al-Shamal was a local correspondent for Crédit Lyonnais, Commerzbank, Barclays, and a Saudi affiliate of ABN AMRO. It was this way, for instance, that in 1993, bin Laden's Sudanese construction interests wired $179,955 to a Dallas branch of Bank of

America to fund the purchase of an aircraft that al-Qaeda would later use to transport Stinger missiles from Pakistan to Sudan. In the aftermath of September 11, 2001, al-Qaeda interests were found to enjoy banking facilities in Sudan, Yemen, Cyprus, Germany, Hong Kong, South Africa, and the United Kingdom.

From such examples, it might seem that some risk of exposure to dirty money is hot-wired into the global banking system. There may be not just technical conduits that render this possible, but also commercial incentives that make it likely. Competition for markets, customers, and fees naturally encourages bankers to err on the generous side when evaluating a new relationship. The same competitive pressure drives countries to offer offshore services and shady brokers to look the other way.

Recent governmental initiatives have made "looking the other way" more costly and risky. But the incentives to launder money continue to be enormous and the need is there: Where would otherwise go all the billions generated by the booming illicit trades? Moreover, the profits involved can more than compensate for the added costs, while the mechanisms, institutions, and technologies that now exist to mitigate the risks make them if not negligible, at least bearable.

An extreme solution for money launderers is to go whole hog and buy their own bank. This is not particularly hard. Many offshore specialty jurisdictions make it easy to establish a shell bank. In Nauru, for instance, it takes only $25,000. But countries that are highly corrupt yet relatively significant in the global economy—for instance, Russia and Nigeria—are perfect places to buy a bank as a way of infiltrating global finance. There are fears that illicit traders are increasingly turning to this method, particularly in Africa and Latin America.

LAYERS AND FRONTS

Having succeeded in injecting dirty money into the global system undetected, launderers can start thinking about "layering" it—the rinse and spin cycles of money laundering, in which funds are recirculated until their origins are untraceable. The classic method is the front company—some sort of cash-intensive business into which laundered funds can be quietly injected. But the front company has grown in sophistication, no longer the pizza parlor of yore or the instantly suspect all-purpose "import-export" firm.

One approach is the "brass plate" business, incorporated in a specialty jurisdiction but with no tangible physical presence. Some places—Nevis in the Caribbean, the Cook Islands and Niue in the Pacific—even allow corporate trusts that conceal the identity of the actual owners. But the front can also be a full-fledged, functioning business in virtually any industry. And it could just as well be based in Delaware: according to Nigel Morris-Cottrill, who edits the *World Money Laundering Report*. "Money launderers seeking a legal framework that provides them with shelter could do worse than to choose the United States," where some states offer relaxed reporting requirements.

Some experts have found weaknesses in European business laws that they fear could benefit front companies. Seemingly esoteric legal differences from country to country have become as many potential opportunities for concealment and arbitrage. "London's Dirty Secret: Crooks Can Launder Money Through Trusts and Companies," editorialized the *Financial Times* in late 2004. It argued that the United Kingdom accounted for an estimated 10 percent of all funds laundered globally because "British authorities are less willing to crack down on money-launderers than other financial centers." Ironically, the British authorities had forced offshore financial centers to strengthen their rules while neglecting to apply the same regulations "onshore"—that is, in England. During the 1990s, twenty-three London-based banks laundered more than $1.3 billion stolen by General Sani Abacha, the former Nigerian dictator. Not a single institution or individual was named let alone prosecuted by British authorities for participating in or perhaps even engineering this operation.

Prosecuting money laundering cases is not easy. A front company can recycle laundered funds by any number of techniques. Overbilling, underbilling, and reporting inflated shipping costs are all standard methods. So is investing in still more front companies to permit bogus deals among them, as well as to bury the money trail in a mountain of miscellaneous *and mostly legal* purchase orders, invoices, shipping bills, and other paperwork. *Matrioshka,* the name of the Russian grandmother dolls made of wood that fit tightly inside one another, now also refers to eastern European front companies that are affiliated with one another in an endless chain. In Italy they are called Chinese boxes.

The Internet only broadens the horizon, adding a whole new range of businesses that can function as money laundering fronts. From pornography sites to online casinos and sports gambling, these are businesses in which regulation is at best tentative, anonymity is easily maintained, and there is no clear jurisdiction to assess complaints. Despite the gaming industry's protestations to the contrary, money launderers appear to have moved full bore into this sector.

Offshore havens, lawless frontier towns, prestigious financial capitals, and the virtual realm all harbor potential for money launderers (as well as tax evaders and fraudsters of all kinds) to "work the system" and disguise or conceal illicit financial flows. And the substantial intertwining of these practices with institutions and systems familiar to innumerable legitimate users—major global banks, local "community" banks, ATM cards and electronic banking, e-commerce, immigrant remmittances, emerging-market investments—has helped to bring about a blurring of the lines. The boundary between licit and illicit movements and uses of funds is by no means clear. And no institution in the integrated global financial system can credibly profess that *all* the money it churns is untouched by criminal hands. Surveying this landscape, one critic, Ronan Palan, describes an emerging "offshore world" made of "sovereign markets, virtual places and nomad millionaires." So long as one is connected in some way to the modern financial system, it's safe to say that there's a little bit of offshore in every one of us.

CASH AND CARRY

All the sophisticated means available to money launderers to penetrate the banking and business mainstream might suggest that the briefcase stuffed with banknotes is obsolete. It is not. Large amounts of cash travel the world unreported every day. Some ride with mules, individuals paid to carry bills just as they would carry drugs. Money entering and leaving the United States is often divided among couriers into $10,000 increments, the legal limit above which sums must be reported. Bulk wads of cash travel by DHL and FedEx. At border posts, specially trained dogs sniff for money concealed in various goods. American authorities have intercepted cash destined for Colombia secreted into cars, dolls, television sets, and shipments of refrigerated bull semen.

Wire transfers have their informal, outside-the-system equivalent too. These are schemes that transfer value by means of offsetting transactions in each place. Such trust-based remittance systems, which avoid both the expense of legal currency exchange and the risk and hassle of illegal transfers, are an age-old enterprise. The *hawalas* employed by Muslim communities around the world are one such kind of operation that garnered attention during the crackdown on potential al-Qaeda conduits in the aftermath of 9/11. But *hawalas* and their equivalents such as the Chinese *fie chen* ("flying money") are as much vital services for emigrant diasporas as they may be cover for illicit deals. A Pakistani construction worker in Dubai who needs to send money to his family gives it to his trusted *hawaladar,* who instructs his counterpart in Karachi to release the same sum to the designated recipient, minus the commission. Outstanding balances that accumulate between the *hawaladars* are settled weekly or monthly, mostly with in-kind payments that range from carpets to diamonds and gold. In one famous case weapons and drugs were delivered to Pakistan and onward to Afghanistan inside containers filled with much-coveted Sudanese honey.

These arrangements solve problems associated with cash, such as that it is cumbersome and that large quantities are liable to draw attention. Another way around these obstacles is to convert cash into easily carried high-value commodities. Dubai, for instance, boasts a winning combination for money launderers: a transportation hub, offshore banking, and one of the world's major gold markets. Diamonds too have proven an attractive means to store value—as al-Qaeda is reported to have used in one remarkable case. According to the *Washington Post*'s Doug Farah, after the 1999 U.S. freeze on assets tied to al-Qaeda, the network sheltered several million dollars by purchasing illicit diamonds from rebels in Sierra Leone through connections in Liberia. Lebanese and Pakistani intermediaries appeared in the region between 1999 and 2001, and for a time purchased all the diamonds on the market at a premium to the local price.

Illicit trade in minerals represents a form of money laundering, and because it takes place in conflict areas or where governments are corrupt, it tends to reinforce trends of violence and political decay. The mineral coltan, for instance, used in chips that go into cell phones, comes from a region of the Congo that has been wracked by civil war for a decade. This conflict doesn't prevent coltan from coming out—under the auspices of rebel groups, mercenaries, and foreign armies. Timber for high-value flooring plays a similar role in Indonesia, West Africa, and Brazil. In one reported case, Brazilian criminals set up timber companies through which they used drug revenues to purchase illegally logged timber, tying together a variety of illicit businesses and adverse impacts in the sort of neat circle that is all too common.

Drugs can themselves become a substitute for money in the laundering process, not just the source of money to be laundered. Portable and compact, a packet of heroin or cocaine takes up much less space than would its equivalent value in banknotes. Often drugs and other commodities help conceal money, not the reverse. In the global illicit economy, far stranger things have happened.

PEER PRESSURE

It was thanks to drugs, in fact—that is, thanks to the boom of organized drug trafficking in the 1980s—that money laundering vaulted onto the agenda of international crime fighters with a real sense of urgency. By general admission, the problem until then was little understood, and treated mainly as a ramification of domestic organized crime. The spectacular growth of the cocaine and heroin trades in the 1980s awoke governments to the flood of drug money crossing borders: the drug trade, they estimated, generated each year around $85 billion available to be laundered. And by the same token, there was potential to attack the drug cartels by disabling their financial operations.

The methods, however, were missing. Some countries had domestic laws against financial crime; but at the international level there was little cooperation or shared awareness, in fact no agreed definitions or rules. The late 1980s saw a flurry of efforts to change this. In December 1988, the United Nations passed its Vienna Convention on drug trafficking, which required participating countries to criminalize money laundering and cooperate in investigations and extraditions. The same month, the Basel Committee on Banking Supervision, part of the organization that groups the world's central banks, listed basic principles banks should follow to prevent money laundering. None was revolutionary—identifying customers, keeping good records, refusing to execute suspect transactions—but it was the first time this banking common sense had been formally set out as a public statement of principles.

But the most significant advance came in 1989 when the G-7 group of industrialized countries decided to set up a task force to pool their money laundering expertise. The new Financial Action Task Force (FATF) would have no bureaucracy, only a small secretariat. It would be a voluntary and practical grouping, with only the G-7 countries and several other European countries invited to participate at first. And it would function by means of strenuous mutual evaluations—peer reviews—to spread "clean" financial practices. By 1995, the FATF had completed its first round of member evaluations. New members joined and similar groups were begun in other regions.

This pragmatism immediately distinguished anti–money laundering programs from older, more ponderous methods of international cooperation. Still, the problem was growing worse. Outside the FATF countries, volumes of laundered money were booming, with new cases and new tools discovered at a much faster speed than the authorities could counter or even just monitor. New jurisdictions offering offshore facilities and only paying lip service to the FATF were popping up at a quick rate; even within the FATF, not everyone was implementing the group's recommendations at the same pace. As for the national agencies, they tended to have different priorities and enforcement approaches, shaped by each country's politics. All of these differences represented opportunities for dirty money to flow. As if to taunt the regulators, egregious and very public cases kept springing up, from the $70 billion moved from Russia to Nauru during the 1998 ruble crisis to dictators like Slobodan Milošević moving funds around unimpeded. Estimates of global money laundering were reaching the trillion-dollar range—crisis proportions by anyone's definition.

Spurred in particular by the Clinton administration, the governments of powerful countries changed tack in about 1996, directing their focus to countries and territories that specialized in offshore services and using the various new mechanisms to that end. The G-7 began to divide offshore jurisdictions into three groups: high, medium, and low quality. In 2000, the FATF laid down the law: it declared twenty-nine offshore jurisdictions to be deficient, and labeled the fifteen worst "non-cooperative countries and territories." A similar OECD initiative prepared a listing of tax havens. The G-7 then signaled that it was prepared to use these blacklists as the basis for sanctions against the worst offenders—such as forbidding relationships with member country banks.

It was a serious threat, and some of the targets responded with alacrity. Within a few months, the Bahamas, Cayman Islands, Cook Islands, Israel, Liechtenstein, the Marshall Islands, and Panama had all taken major steps—new laws, stepped-up oversight and enforcement—toward complying with the emerging standards. Likewise, a few of the countries the OECD targeted were able to remove themselves from its list of tax havens. But none of this happened without misgivings and resistance. A few countries refused to act altogether, such as Nauru, or introduced legislation that got mired in process, such as Russia. Several complained that they were being forced to take measures that the OECD and FATF countries themselves had not uniformly applied. They had a point: the FATF's own reports acknowledged that several of its members were not up to speed. In fact the wealthy countries had yet to agree on just what flows of money should be illegal in the first place. This was the case for tax evasion, which some considered tantamount to money laundering and others barely criminalized.

The powerful countries were by no means speaking in one voice. Quarrelling and mutual mistrust became common. And instead of a multicountry joint venture to pursue and curb the international trafficking of illicit money, FATF meetings often turned into negotiations not unlike those that are common at the World Trade Organization over trade rules, with each country protecting its own interest. If not in complete reversal mode, the ten-year anti–money laundering crusade appeared to be running out of steam.

RUDE AWAKENING

The attacks of September 11, 2001, made for a rude awakening. Within days, newspapers were running exposés of the al-Qaeda network and discussions of terrorist financing. Facing emergency requests to freeze the assets of terrorist-linked individuals and groups named in U.S. executive orders, banks reported a host of difficulties. A small British "thrift," or savings institution, found 1,800 customers that might—and then again might not—have a connection with names on the list of terrorist suspects. Banks struggled to convince authorities that combing through their records would take weeks and not hours.

These realizations resulted in an rapid turnabout in U.S. policy. Declaring "war on terror," the United States demanded tightened global rules on sharing financial records, lifting bank secrecy and executing asset seizures against suspect individuals. "The attitude of the international community must . . . change, quickly and permanently," hectored a report signed by the then treasury secretary, Paul O'Neill, and the attorney general, John Ashcroft. "Like it or not," a justice official told a gathering of U.S. bankers, "you are going to be on the front lines of the coming war on terrorism." Within weeks the United States was endorsing customer identification rules it had only recently rejected. Many were included in the USA-Patriot Act. The global response was sympathetic. At the United Nations, the Security Council required member countries to criminalize the collection of funds for terrorist purposes, and to freeze the assets of suspected terrorists. And virtually every anti–money laundering organization catapulted terrorist finance to the top of its agenda.

The challenge of unraveling and suppressing terrorist finance breathed new life into international efforts to combat money laundering. Yet it raises questions of its own. One fear is that the anti-terrorist focus will cause harried officials to lose sight of the trillion-dollar big picture of money laundering. Another legitimate fear concerns coordination and information between agencies. The secrecy imperative can make it difficult for financial regulators to understand what they are being asked, let alone carry it out. The top finance regulator of the Netherlands, himself a former head of the country's secret service, complained in 2004 that the "lack of feedback puts regulators in a worse position than the man hunting for the proverbial needle in a haystack." He continued: "We are not even told whether we should be looking for a needle or a pin."

Yet while confusion, inefficiency, and turf battles still plague efforts to combat money laundering, there is no doubt that September 11 gave it a priority that it never had before. This means that the best technology available will be deployed by some governments to track, detect, and seize the illicit money that travels the world. Some of these tools are already available, while others are being rapidly developed. Law enforcement agencies have also been actively recruiting the best and the brightest accountants, systems engineers, and financial experts to enforce anti–money laundering laws and develop new systems and controls that will make it harder for launderers to move and use money undetected or with impunity. International collaboration has acquired a new urgency. These are worldwide trends.

But there are others. They have to do with stubborn realities that will inevitably hinder the efforts of the governments keen on controlling money laundering. The most obvious problem is that not all governments attach the same priority to the activity. Even among those that do see it as a top priority, many lack the financial, technological, and organizational capabilities to fight it effectively. As Rudolf Hommes, a former finance minister of Colombia, told me: "It was obvious that for us money laundering was a major problem. I clearly remember how agonizing it was for me to decide to spend what, for Colombia, was a lot of money to fund our financial crimes unit, while knowing perfectly well that it was still a fraction of what was really necessary. I was aware that the amount we were spending was tiny compared to the resources of the narcos. And I also knew that while we were going to spend money on this, there were other important social needs that would remain underfunded."

Hommes is known for integrity and competence. But not all finance ministers are. In fact, a safe assumption is that not all of his peers in Latin America or other regions are committed to fight money launderers. It is also safe to assume that for some countries the deployment of an effective, global anti–money laundering regime may not be in their national interest. It may be too expensive; it may hinder their international financial competitiveness; it may spur capital flight; it may be a threat to powerful political constituencies—and in some countries it may even run against the *personal* interest of leading politicians, government officials, and top military officers. And herein lies another stubborn reality. For the fight against dirty money to have any hope of success it has to be a multilateral effort, with many countries sharing similar goals, priorities, and commitment.

The relative effectiveness and impunity that money launderers enjoy rest in their ability to move funds across borders and jurisdictions, often at great speed. This means that unilateral combats between single—or even a few—governments against the launderers are tilted in favor of the latter, regardless of the technology and resources available to the governments involved. Of course, if a powerful nation like the United States decides to make it a priority to apprehend a specific money launderer or a network in a certain foreign jurisdiction it may be able to do so, thanks to its resources and its ability to coerce or persuade the host nation to help. But this "lone ranger" approach cannot substitute for an international anti–money laundering regime that is stable and reliable and in which the voluntary and active collaboration among all the parties involved—or most of them—is an indispensable requirement. Germany's deputy finance minister, Caio Koch-Wieser, put it to me this way: "Unless more top-level government attention, better thinking, and much-enhanced international cooperation is applied to curbing the money laundering abuses that are common in the international financial system, societies will be fighting a losing battle."

Unfortunately, when societies fight losing battles some groups and individuals do very well. I met in Zurich a private banker who specializes in "wealth management" for "high-net worth" clients. "If someone wants your services to 'manage,' say, fifty million dollars," I asked him, "how much harder is it today for you to help this person to keep the money hidden away from authorities, compared to what it was ten years ago?" He smiled and replied: "The main difference is that now I charge more."

Chapter 8

WHAT DO ORANGUTANS, HUMAN KIDNEYS, GARBAGE, AND VAN GOGH HAVE IN COMMON?

The German man was only thirty years old, and four years of dialysis for kidney disease were robbing him of his vitality and his youth. He needed a transplant, but the waiting list stretched far beyond the available supply of kidneys, meaning the prospect of a many years' wait. Finally friends decided to speed things up: they gathered a large sum of money to help obtain a kidney by other means. An Israeli broker appeared and offered the man several options. For a quarter of a million dollars, he could receive a quick transplant under top-flight hospital conditions with full medical documentation and follow-up in a choice of locations: Germany, South Africa, or the United States. But Turkey was available, too, at a deep discount: $160,000. The man went for the bargain. Weeks later he emerged from an Istanbul hospital blessed with a new lease on life, his body now hosting the kidney of a stranger whose name, gender, or nationality he would never even learn.

Just another day for the illicit trade networks; just another satisfied customer, just another tidy profit on what many of us would consider a precious part of our bodies but to the traders is just another product. For if nature abhors a vacuum and greed is part of human nature, then greed too abhors a vacuum. That is why profit opportunities never go untapped for too long, not even when it is illegal to seize them. It should come as no surprise that the networks with the capabilities to move illicit goods across borders have diversified into new geographies and added new product lines to their existing ones. As is often the case in business, newcomers are the first to detect new opportunities and set to exploit them before or instead of the established players. It is new entrants who often take advantage of untapped market niches that appear thanks to a new source of supply, a new set of customers, or new technologies.

The international trade in human kidneys is a market that did not exist for most of human history and is now booming, thanks to new technologies. The widespread looting of Baghdad in 2003, including its main archaeological museum, renewed the worldwide supply of stolen antiquities, as did the collapse of the Soviet Union. Our new environmental awareness begets new government regulations that make handling garbage and industrial waste more expensive and thus creates an opportunity for those who know how to make it disappear quickly and cheaply. In this case, quickly and cheaply often means illegally and in another country. Beyond the five huge trades described in the previous chapters are many more illicit global markets that have grown immensely in the last decade or so and that are driven by the same forces. The networks that move other more obscure or "niche" products—human organs, endangered species, hazardous waste, stolen art—operate by the same methods as the better-known trades. Indeed, they are often the same.

These trades—and still others behind them, such as stolen cars, illegal logging, or smuggled cigarettes—are "secondary" only in the sense that they have not earned as much official scrutiny or media coverage or sparked the same degree of public alarm as the more notorious forms of trafficking discussed in previous chapters. They are also still catching up in value with some of the larger trades—though this is difficult to ascertain, precisely because national and international laws are still vague about their definitions and the available data is insufficient. What is beyond doubt, however, is that all are growing. And that is no surprise, because each is in its own way a by-product of the same technical, political, economic, and social changes that have accelerated since the 1990s. The organ trade results from the major scientific innovations and the widespread dissemination of new transplantation equipment, drugs, and surgical methods meant to extend human lives. Trafficking in endangered species is closely tied to the spread of human settlements, our need for natural resources, and our tastes in food and leisure. The waste trade results, simply put, from consumption. And trade in stolen art—although it dates as far back as art itself—has expanded as political turmoil spurs supply and market reforms and strong economic growth boosts demand by swelling the ranks of the wealthy. Call it the darkness within the light—the advances we cherish and seek also produce nefarious opportunities for trade and profit.

ORGANS WITHOUT BORDERS

Kidneys are big business. So are other body parts: corneas, livers, pancreases for transplantation; hearts and lungs and genitals for traditional medicines and preparations. Some bodily substances are already for sale: in many countries blood and sperm "donations" are renumerated, and plasma and marrow are traded among medical establishments. Internal organs are a different matter, however. There is no international law that defines and regulates their trade. National laws vary, from countries that have prohibited all organ sales to ones that allow organ brokers to freely ply their trade; many have never considered the possibility of organ sales, leaving the matter in a legal gray area. Meanwhile supply and demand are growing rapidly. The spread of medical technology and extension of human lives in rich countries produces hordes of transplant candidates. Bleak life prospects and immiseration make live organ donation a perfectly acceptable, even attractive option for the poor in many countries, and lack of legal protection means that deceased donors—dead of illness, accident, or execution—have little choice in the matter.

All in all, perfect conditions for a global market. And to connect the willing buyers with the (more or less) willing sellers, a highly developed global system has sprung up that includes doctors and surgeons, brokers, transporters, safe house operators, donor recruiters, and public officials who knowingly participate in the organ trade in exchange for bribes or fees. Hub countries for illicit live-donor transplants are ones that combine high-quality hospital facilities with lax or corruptible oversight. Some, like India, China, and Brazil, are themselves major suppliers of organs. Others, such as Turkey and South Africa, tend to host transplants for "donors" brought in from elsewhere: Brazil, Mozambique, Romania. Many known brokers have operated from Israel, where laws in the matter have long been permissive; others float in cyberspace, offering services and linking buyers and sellers via the Internet, alongside doctors who advertise directly in a bid to eliminate the middleman. As a result, transactions span borders and oceans. One operation shut down in 2003 rippled from Recife to Tel Aviv, with surgeries performed at a top South African hospital.

Dead-donor organs are booming too, with the advantage that they can sometimes be ordered and shipped in bulk. Given the right packaging and relatively brief transport time, you could bring an organ on an airplane in your carry-on belongings or, depending on means, in your privately chartered jet. Transplant technology, once highly unusual and specialized, is now widespread; cyclosporin, a drug that reduces the risk that a host body will reject an implanted organ, is commonly available. As a result, transplant surgeons need no longer be rare gurus of extreme skill and attainment; any competent surgeon with access to the right equipment could, in theory, set up a clinic for transplants. And many do.

Kidneys are the motor of the traffic. There are nowhere near enough kidneys available to supply the demand for transplants in rich countries, and the gap is only growing worse. In the United States, for instance, donations from deceased organ donors grew only marginally in the 1990s, while the waiting list for transplants more than tripled. As a result, only 8,000 kidneys become available each year, while the backlog of patients is close to 80,000. Similar shortfalls prevail in other rich countries. Renal disease is universal, of course, but in wealthy countries longer life spans and better overall health means patients are less likely to succumb and more likely to seek a transplant. In developing countries, recipients of trafficked organs overwhelmingly come from the economic elite.

And there is no shortage of sellers. In Brazil, India, the Philippines, Romania, and elsewhere, selling a kidney has become a commonplace way to earn money, typically for young men and women, who sometimes openly advertise themselves, sparing scouts the need to recruit actively. The going rate rarely exceeds $10,000. The more common $2,000–$5,000 range is usually enough to attract sellers from regions where it exceeds a year's average wage. As for the prices charged to recipients, reported figures vary by locale but are universally high. A forty-year-old Israeli paid $100,000—a bargain-basement price—for a transplant in South Africa. By contrast, one broker solicits wealthy Arab patients for transplants in "reputed overseas hospitals" for up to half a million dollars. With margins like these, quality service is a must. Some brokers complement the operation with first-class air travel and local sightseeing tours. The kidney sellers enjoy no such luxuries. They are held in safe houses and whisked in and out of the transplant country and hospital as quickly as possible. There is no follow-up, no protection from complications. Tragically, the international traffic in human organs is closely intertwined with the international trafficking in people. The pool of poor, illegal immigrants, scared, hungry, and with no legal protection, is an attractive hunting ground for the international networks that need to supply an almost infinite demand for organs.

At least these cases involve willing sellers. Horror stories of forcible "donations" abound. India and Brazil are rife with stories of patients coaxed into surgery for minor conditions who wake up minus a kidney—not urban legend, but big business. (One woman was informed after surgery that her ovarian cyst had grown so large that it encircled her kidney.) In some cases donors are lured by the prospect of overseas employment and, once taken overseas, have no means of escape when they learn the broker's real intention. When the subject is dying or dead, any number of organs can be harvested, which opens the door to a variety of gruesome scenarios. Orphans or "street children" with absent parents—a growing demographic in many countries, thanks to economic distress, war, drugs, and HIV/AIDS—are especially vulnerable. In Azerbaijan children have disappeared in transit from orphanages to hospitals, and the government suspects that they are killed for organs. In Afghanistan, recruitment of children to export through Pakistan for domestic or sex work or organ harvesting is one and the same process, the only difference being the child's ultimate fate.

Prisoners have been used for organ supply under dictatorships at various times in Argentina, Brazil, and Taiwan. Today the Chinese prison system is a major supplier of organs for both the domestic and international market. On Hainan Island an intermediary offered a bulk deal to the activist Harry Wu, who was working undercover: fifty prisoners' organs over a year, at prices ranging from $5,000 for a pair of corneas to $25,000 for a liver. In another case, a doctor reported witnessing both kidneys being extracted from a still-living prisoner due to be executed the next morning. The proceeds of prison organ harvesting go to the authorities. Some researchers suspect that the lucrative organs market is one additional reason that China has broadened the range of capital offenses: more executions mean more profit.

Not all organs serve the transplant market. Some go into pharmaceutical research, and medical schools require whole cadavers. In several African countries accounts are common of body parts—brains, hearts, lungs, livers, male and female genitals—used as ingredients in traditional medicine, either locally or for export. Areas with ongoing civil wars are particularly propitious sources. In the war-torn northeast of the Democratic Republic of Congo, for instance, there is strong speculation that militias sell body parts to overseas buyers—just one commodity alongside the coltan, copper, diamonds, weapons, child soldiers, and sex slaves trafficked under cover of conflict in the zone. In 2004 a Brazilian nun in Mozambique was murdered after she began investigating the discovery of adult and child corpses with their vital organs removed.

It may seem shocking that in so many places the human body has become more valuable as a source of spare parts than for its intelligence or labor. Yet international economic disparities, illness, and conflict on one side, and ease of advertising, recruitment, and travel on the other, have created conditions for a lucrative traffic. Even where the trade is explicitly banned, traffickers have found ways to bypass the laws. Investigators in Brazil have witnessed kidney "gifts"—ostensibly unpaid, therefore legal—between patients of obviously differing circumstances and no prior acquaintance, but they have been helpless to intervene without concrete proof of a transaction. The recourse is not clear, and fraught with difficult legal and ethical challenges. While some campaigners argue for tighter laws and enforcement, others, including in Israel and the United States, have begun to advocate establishing some form of legal, regulated organ transplant trade. For now, the sheer force of supply and demand and the immense profits to be made render dim the prospects of ending the trade by any means.

OF CAVIAR AND ORANGUTANS, BIG TREES AND CACTI

Trade in endangered species means a great deal more than ivory and animal hides. More than 30,000 species of animals and plants are considered protected, and trade in 1,000 of them is entirely banned. To monitor and update the list is a task of CITES, the Convention on International Trade in Endangered Species of Wild Fauna and Flora—one of the more long-standing international agreements, initially signed in 1963 and now adopted by 166 countries. An international network of government and private conservation groups known as TRAFFIC monitors the illicit trade and acts as a sort of research clearinghouse for CITES, analyzing the global trade and evaluating legal and economic methods to increase compliance. In addition, most countries boast their own endangered species protection laws and national parks or sanctuaries, and conservation—of animals in particular—is a popular cause in Western public opinion. Compared with some other victims of illicit trade, endangered and protected species do have their advocates.

Yet the market still finds plenty of uses for them. Animal heads and hides are still valued for decoration, as are animal body parts in traditional Chinese and African medicine. European collectors seek out unusual plants such as rare breeds of Mexican cactus. Protected woods appear in the furniture catalogs of household-name chains. The demand for nontraditional pets is higher than ever, not least in the United States, which is the main market for such exotics as pythons, boas, macaques, capybaras, peacocks, and the like—many of which have found their way out of captivity and are happily breeding in the tropical climate of South Florida. Poachers still kill elephants for ivory, which finds its way to Guangzhou, China, where merchants display it openly despite the total world ban on the trade. According to TRAFFIC, the six countries most involved in the ivory trade are China, Thailand, Cameroon, Democratic Republic of Congo, Ethiopia, and Nigeria. But they are far from alone. Singapore, for instance, is known as a major transit hub, yet reports no seizures. And of course there is a persistent demand for culinary delicacies of all sorts that come from species at risk. It includes whale meat in Japan (one of the few countries that still permit whaling), contraband caviar from endangered Caspian sturgeons, and the Patagonian toothfish, a restaurant favorite when sold under its commercial moniker of Chilean sea bass.

Not all of these uses are illegal in all places, but the distinction matters less and less to a global trade in which animal cargos can mix species, purposes, and destinations. In many cases it is difficult to determine whether a given shipment complies with the rules. Monitoring relies largely on paperwork. In the crocodilian business (crocodile, alligator, and caiman), for instance, a system of certificates of origin is supposed to ensure that a hide being tanned or a wallet or pair of shoes on offer in a luxury boutique conform to global standards and quotas. In practice, these certificates, like end-user certificates in the arms trade, are easily forged or purchased. For these and other species, licit and illicit supplies in practice merge smoothly into a single, global wholesale market.

Some wildlife trafficking routes are well worn; others spring up as the market evolves. For reasons that are not entirely clear, Germany and the Czech Republic have become top destinations of the cactus trade, with shipments intercepted at their and other European airports. The seizure in Tibet in 2003 of a shipment including the skins of 31 tigers, 581 leopards, and 778 otters helped to unearth a major trafficking circuit between India, Nepal, and China, with the tiger hides—trade in which CITES bans altogether—becoming decorations in fancy homes. A shawl made with the wool of Tibetan antelope fetches $15,000 in the boutiques of Milan or Paris. In 2004, a truckload of 600 pangolins—a sort of anteater—intercepted by Thai forest police confirmed the widespread trade in protected species from Indonesia and Malaysia through Thailand and Laos and onward to China to be eaten. Thailand is something of a hub: in a three-month period in 2003, authorities there recovered from traffickers 33,000 animals, from tigers and bears to 1,000 protected bird species. And the Amazon basin has become a major supply area with multiple exit routes through Brazil, Peru, Venezuela, and Colombia. (Serving two unpleasant purposes at once, a shipment of boa constrictors intercepted at the Miami airport were found to have multiple condoms full of cocaine in their digestive system. Few of the snakes survived.)

The networks that trade in wildlife are difficult to unravel, with arrests typically landing the bit players—poachers, truck drivers, retailers—who are not essential to the business. Regular seizures of animal parts and skins in South Africa, Mozambique, and elsewhere rarely result in arrests further down the chain. Often suppliers and brokers carry on dubious activities in full view, protected by ambiguous or incomplete laws, corruption, or political favor. A Belgian animal dealer specializes in purchasing "surplus" rare animals bred in British zoos and reselling them to any buyer without asking the destination or the purpose.

The "Taiping Four" offer an iconic example of this trade. These were four young and rare gorillas that were poached in 2001 in Cameroon, then smuggled to Nigeria and from there sold for $1 million to a zoo in Taiping, Malaysia. When activists denounced this illegal deal, the zoo decided in 2004 to ship the Taiping Four to another zoo in South Africa, which expects the four gorillas to help lure 6 million visitors in the next decade. Technology is also having an impact on trade in endangered species. A TRAFFIC report concluded that the United States was both one of the most aggressive countries in seizing illegal ivory and a major market for this contraband. Why the paradox? One factor is eBay, which in 2004 averaged one thousand ivory auctions *per week*. "We can't say no to the sale of ivory, because it wouldn't be fair to those who sell legal ivory," an eBay spokeman told the *Washington Post*. But TRAFFIC contended that Chinese dealers were using these auctions, offering their products as "bones."

In Indonesia, a company owned by a member of parliament, Abdul Rasyid, illegally logged a protected hardwood called ramin in the heart of a national park; when investigators from an advocacy group appeared, company staff held them hostage and beat them. Sold by Malaysian brokers, the wood has appeared in major retailers' products, according to the Environmental Investigation Agency advocacy group.

The plunder of Indonesian forests illustrates the vicious cycle effects of illicit trade. Close to three-quarters of Indonesian logging takes place under illegal conditions; a similar percentage of Indonesia's original forests has been lost. By limiting their habitat, this only increases the threat to endangered animals such as orangutans, already poached for meat or captured for private collectors. In numerous countries illicit logging has exposed human settlements to mud slides and floods by depleting the soil. Still more sinister implications are on the horizon. Researchers link the spread of an unchecked, unregulated world animal trade to the rising incidence of zoonosis—the transfer of animal diseases to human carriers, in the manner of SARS from civet cats and Ebola from monkeys.

WHEN WASTE MEANS WEALTH

In the spring of 1987, the concept of the "wandering barge" sprang into the public consciousness. For several months two hulking barges, one from New York and one from Philadelphia, ambled about the oceans in search of a place to dump their cargo, tons of toxic incinerator ash. The *Mobro* returned to New York after three months of rejections from one Caribbean country after another. The *Khian Sea,* operated by a Bahamian company and registered in Liberia, was off on a much longer adventure. Turned away from the Bahamas, Bermuda, the Dominican Republic, the Netherlands Antilles, and Guinea-Bissau in West Africa, it eventually appeared in Gonaives, Haiti, where it dumped 4,000 tons of ash on the beach. The port paperwork specified that the cargo was fertilizer. Still heavily laden, the barge decamped back to Philadelphia only to turn up in Yugoslavia renamed the *Felicia,* and eventually in Singapore, now free of ash. The captain had simply dumped the remaining 10,000 tons into the ocean.

Yet those early days of international trash dumping were in retrospect a simpler time. Today, the illicit trade in hazardous waste is part of a broader phenomenon of "environmental crime," complete with specialized networks and all the new standard trappings–front companies in multiple countries, a sophisticated financial structure, deep links with politicians, generals, and law enforcement agents in key countries, and a global scope of operations. The traffic includes not only chemical residues and ashes, but also components of computers and televisions, mobile phones, refrigerators, ships, and more. At the same time, old-fashioned dumping continues apace. According to Italian campaigners, Somalia, without an effective national government since 1991, now hosts three enormous dumps of radioactive materials that workers handle with no protective equipment. Sudan, Eritrea, Algeria, and Mozambique are four other suspected destinations of Italy's radioactive trash, which is dumped either on land or by sinking containers—or entire ships—in their territorial waters.

The global trash business reflects both political realities and a sort of grim economic efficiency. Generators of huge volumes of detritus, rich countries have taken the "not in my backyard" logic to the extreme of seeking to export trash whenever possible. Poor countries—or ruling elites within them—can be tempted to accept the proposal. Moreover, toxic and "clean" trash can be difficult to distinguish in the context of a vast and legal trade in recycled goods—from ancient city buses to secondhand cars to the piles of multiply used clothes that have become the standard garb of a whole generation of African youth. The recycling business creates jobs and incomes: ship-breaking is a main line of business for Indian and other shipyards and in a more dispersed and haphazard way, scavenging detritus is a major source of materials in a variety of street trades in developing countries.

Those professional scavengers and recyclers are most at risk. When Formosa Plastics of Taiwan deposited mercury-laced ash (resulting from the manufacture of PVCs) near a Cambodian village in 1997, locals unaware of the contents used their bare hands and even their teeth to scavenge the plastic sheeting that covered the ash blocks. And in China, Pakistan, India, and African countries, workers who dismantle used electronics and household goods are exposed to acid, lead, and toxins from burning the remnants. At least two areas in China, Guiyu and Taizhou, have become centers for this activity and suffered extreme pollution; according to campaigners, all the wells in Guiyu are contaminated and water must be brought in by truck.

Laws on the trade of hazardous waste are not fully developed. The Basel Convention on this commerce, signed in 1989 and in force since 1992, has 160 ratified members; alone among developed countries, the United States has not ratified the treaty. Yet even in the European Union, where hazardous waste exports are theoretically banned, an official study of six major ports determined that close to a quarter of waste exports were illegal. Standard methods involved falsifying paperwork or moving the substances around from port to port within the EU to complicate the trace, repacking and relabeling it along the way. Often, the hazardous materials found their way out simply because port authorities had trouble distinguishing approved from illicit cargo.

As usual, trafficking networks are exploiting these ambiguities. In Italy, where such trafficking is common on the domestic as well as international level (toxic trash from the north is dumped in the south), the term *ecomafia* has passed into the vocabulary, designating both the perpetrators and the practices themselves. And indeed, a considerable number of domestic incidents have been connected to the *Camorra, 'Ndranghetta,* and *Cosa Nostra* organizations—reminiscent of the cliché of Mafia involvement in the waste business in the United States. But as Italian campaigners point out, the term *ecomafia* is misleading. In fact, in Italy and elsewhere, trash trafficking involves networks that may or may not involve organized crime, and in which legal and illegal enterprises coexist, partner up, or provide services to one another as opportunities dictate.

TRADING THE ATMOSPHERE

Commonly used in refrigeration, chlorofluorocarbons (CFCs) have long been recognized as a prime agent of ozone depletion. And the international agreement to end their use, known as the Montreal Protocol, is by some measures one of the world's most successful. Its membership has grown from the 27 initial signatories in 1988 to 188 countries in 2004. The protocol has earned high praise for its pragmatic approach: It permits trade of used CFCs that are reclaimed from industrial equipment. It gives developing countries extra time to discontinue use of the chemicals, allowing them to keep consuming a "basic domestic minimum" while substitute chemicals and new technologies are phased in. In principle, CFCs should be entirely out of circulation by 2010.

But the market has a different idea. As rules to control CFCs have come into force, trade in violation of these rules has sprouted up and flourished, to the tune of 30,000 tons and $300–$450 million annually. As a result, developing country industries are not converting to substitute chemicals at the planned pace; the price of CFC on the market remains low while that of the substitutes, which one would expect to fall as use became more widespread, has instead failed to come down. The European Union, where a total use ban is now in force, remains a major producer of CFCs for the legal international market. But CFCs from this production also turn up as contraband, the cylinders deceptively labeled or smuggled among permitted chemicals, or the CFCs poured into smaller cans that are concealed within crates of other goods, or labeled as lubricant or paint. And illicit shipments of CFCs turn up in the United States as well, labeled for other destinations or certified as recycled chemicals, which the United States permits, when in fact they may be freshly produced.

Manufacturers and consumers of CFCs are rarely in contact. Instead, the business works through brokers and intermediaries, who mix their illicit commerce with allowed transactions and trade in other goods. Campaigners from the Environment Investigation Agency sent operatives to Singapore—a hub of the trade, along with Dubai—posing as a trading company seeking to ship CFCs to South Africa, which bans such imports. They had no difficulty securing offers for immediate delivery; brokers openly discussed "creative" methods to circumvent the ban, including deceptive paperwork, falsely labeled cylinders, and transit through neighboring countries with lax controls. The brokers made clear that they employed layers of intermediaries, allowing them to remove their own names from the transaction as fast as possible and leaving the risky business to locals more familiar with the lay of the land, and with the requisite connections. "The forwarder will have the contact with their own customs," a broker told the undercover team, "and they can do what they want."

The permitted trade in recovered gas has generated its own opportunities. Another EIA team uncovered a scam in which fresh CFCs were smuggled into South Africa and used to replace barely depleted gas from chillers in gold mines, which in turn was sold to the United States as recycled. Old-fashioned land smuggling by truck is also rife, following evershifting routes as demand and enforcement dictate. Few CFCs enter India from Nepal these days; smuggling along the far more passable Bangladesh border is flourishing, using such simple methods as handing cylinders over the border fence. In Pakistan, evidence has accumulated that the CFC and heroin trade go hand in hand; not only narcotics but also CFCs have flooded into Pakistan over the Afghan border since the Taliban regime was brought down in 2001.

THE SUBLIME MEETS THE CRIMINAL

Art theft was once the province of the well-educated "gentleman thief" whose elegant tastes offset his craven motives—or so the portrayal went. Nothing gentlemanly about today's art robberies, which occur with remarkable frequency and increasing violence in the world's museums and private homes. Improved security means that nimbleness and cunning are out and full-fledged stickups are in. The brazen theft of Edvard Munch's *The Scream* and *Madonna* from the Munch Museum in Oslo in August 2004 took place in broad daylight and at gunpoint. In Caracas' well-stocked Museum of Contemporary Art, a multimillion-dollar Matisse, *Odalisque in Red Pants*, has gone missing.

Where do these masterworks go? International registries keep lists of stolen and lost art, some of which stay that way for decades. According to a *New York Times* tally, the world is missing 551 Picassos, 43 van Goghs, 174 Rembrandts, and 209 Renoirs. Only infrequently do such works turn up on the legitimate market, for obvious reasons. Many art thieves are left with few options given the uniqueness and recognizability of their quarry. Some in the art world speculate that the average art thief is in fact a small-time crook with no clear plan.

But this activity too changed in the 1990s. There are indications, for example, that the many works of stolen art in circulation may form a sort of reserve currency and an option for concealing illicit gains. In 2001, two New York art dealers offered an undercover agent in Boston two paintings, Modigliani's *Jeune femme aux yeux bleus* and Degas's *La Coiffure* for $4.1 million, along with a referral to a broker for money laundering services: how to organize resale, move the money, and exchange cash, gems and arts as needed. In another case, a Saudi prince and his lover, along with a Swiss-based Spanish banker and a Colombian, were implicated in a 1999 deal that moved $20 million in cocaine from Caracas to Paris by private jet and somehow resulted in the apparition in Miami of a painting by Goya and anothter by Tsuguharu Foujita, a noted Japanese artist.

With large sums of money seeking discreet uses, the market for stolen masterpieces may not be shrinking after all, but shifting to new opportunities. Supply is not the problem, with infusions such as the troves of the old Soviet museums (many of them originally confiscated by the Nazis). An international registry for stolen art established in 1991 with 20,000 entries now lists more than 145,000.

The truly booming market in stolen art, however, is in antiquities. From China to Cambodia to Peru, ancient artifacts are continually unearthed and frequently plundered before authorities can secure them. In January 2001, people in a town called Jiroft in southwestern Iran happened upon a major undiscovered archaeological site containing artifacts that dated back to the fourth millennium BC. By the time news traveled to Teheran and the Ministry of Culture sent a team to view the site, what they found was a massive organized excavation by the locals—each family prospecting a designated plot—which went on for a year before the police finally came to shut it down. Since then Jiroft artifacts have turned up on the international art market, including in some of the most prestigious auction houses. A London art journalist reported eighty pieces for sale for close to a million dollars, and personally saw another collection in "a prominent London gallery." Moreover, the dealer told him, forgeries were arriving on the market as well, potentially manufactured at Jiroft itself—after all, both the materials and models were there.

Accumulation of wealth on the world art markets have driven the prices of Asian and other antiquities to great heights, and traffickers have taken note. Antiquities offer several advantages. First, locals deputize themselves to do the dirty work—finding sites and excavating them. They also bear the greatest risk, as they are exposed to police crackdowns—China has been known to execute petty looters while the traffickers remain elusive—and they need not be paid much. The bulk of the profit from antiquities traffic goes to the layers of individual middlemen and organized networks of intermediaries that include art galleries, auction houses, transportation companies, complicit museum curators, government officials, and bankers. Second, antiquities undergo nothing like the level of scrutiny that the old master paintings and sculpture receive. Dealers have proven less fastidious about origins when it comes to Asian, African, and other antiquities, especially when some are only recently unearthed and barely documented.

Art traffickers need not be specialists. In Italy, a major hub of the dirty-art business, Mafia groups have simply added art to their range of commercial activities. Moreover, the tools of trade are the same: exploiting loopholes and differences in the law between countries, falsifying documents, and of course corruption and official complicity. The attempted sale for $1.6 million in the United States of an ancient Peruvian artifact, for instance, involved a former police colonel as well as a Peruvian diplomat, who imported the piece to New York in the diplomatic pouch.

Still, there are some distinguishing facts to the illicit art trade. First, there is no clear international agreement on laws and penalties; traffickers can move sculptures, icons, or ancient coins at far less risk than, say, weapons or drugs, and potentially for much greater profit. Second, enforcement relies a great deal on self-regulation by museums and auctioneers, along with whistle-blowing: an eccentric Dutch solo investigator, Michel van Rijn, himself a reformed art thief, is responsible for setting in motion some of the most visible recent investigations. A far larger tide of trafficked works and artifacts, particularly from developing countries with ancient civilizations, has garnered far less attention and so far proven impossible to stem.

ORGANS AND SCRAPS

What do these trades have in common? For one, they operate in ways that have more in common than their different product offerings would suggest. Second, they have been relatively low-profile until now, for reasons mainly attached to the products, none of which has stirred opinion or driven new laws to the extent, for instance, that drugs have. Yet the products are increasingly available together, in combinations and mixed with legitimate goods and services, so the more obscure trades will not remain so for much longer.

Perhaps there is more. Perhaps a reason that this set of trades has garnered less critical attention is because they so clearly link to the insatiable consumer demand of wealthy countries. Rich-country demand for transplants drives the international organ trade. Luxury furnishings, clothes, accessories, are the motor of the endangered species business. The ultimate buyers of stolen art and looted antiquities are, at root, the world's wealthy. And there is no more telling illustration of the interweaving of global illicit trade with economic inequalities than the movement of hazardous waste.

Organs in one direction; scraps in the other. As it always has done, illicit trade simply flows with the tide. Only now, the tide has become a swell stronger than the world has ever before seen.

Chapter 9

WHAT ARE GOVERNMENTS DOING?

Customs, meet border patrol. Immigration, meet Coast Guard. In the winter of 2002–3, a ten-person team of officials from the United States' various border control agencies traveled to a sampler of the country's main ports and border towns—New York, Baltimore, Detroit, El Paso, and others—visiting one another's facilities, exchanging information about their mission and comparing their organizational procedures, resources, and technology. They wondered why they hadn't done this before and often. For all their proximity on the front, they hardly knew each other. Some, like the Agricultural and Plant Health Inspection Service (APHIS), whose officials control animal and vegetal products entering the country, labored in near-total obscurity despite working side by side with customs and immigration. Some offices had overlapping missions. It didn't help that each had a different boss: customs belonged to the Treasury Department, immigration to Justice, APHIS to the Department of Agriculture, and so on.

All that was about to change, and fast. On the first day of March 2003, all these disparate agencies were to come under one roof in the new Department of Homeland Security, the U.S. government's landmark administrative response to the new security climate resulting from the attacks of September 11, 2001. And the planners in Washington felt it might be useful for the organizations to get to know each other a little better in advance of their shotgun marriage, which was the reason for the border tour. The mutual unfamiliarity on display during that journey exemplified the problems that the new department was meant to fix.

Bringing together twenty-two federal agencies representing 186,000 employees and, at $36 billion, a budget larger than the entire economy of many nations, posed an unprecedented challenge. And any mistake could cost thousands of lives and imperil the national security of the United States. So it was only natural that anxiety, stress, doubts, and bitter political fights accompanied the birth of this mammoth. Its proponents argued—or hoped—that having all these functions and agencies under one single institutional roof with one boss, one budget, and clear lines of responsibility would greatly enhance the overall effectiveness of the U.S. government in the crucial task of securing the nation's borders and neutralizing terrorists. One immediate consequence of the move would be to change the way the United States managed its frontiers. Customs and border patrol would be combined in one bureau. And the policelike functions of the customs and immigration services were merged into a single force, the Bureau of Immigration and Customs Enforcement—soon to be known by the flashy acronym ICE.

Led by a sharp young prosecutor from Brooklyn, Michael Garcia, ICE was to become an important player in shaping much of the U.S. response to the onslaught of global smugglers. With a background in terrorist investigations—he had worked on the first World Trade Center attack in 1993 and the thwarted 1995 al-Qaeda plot to down twelve U.S. airliners over the Pacific at once—Garcia knew well that terrorists often used trafficking to finance their cells. But he may have been less prepared for the challenges within his new department. Merging some (but not all) of the customs service with some (but not all) of the immigration service meant welding together separate cultures, skill sets, computer networks, standard operating procedures, and lots of employees upset over or unsure of their new duties. Customs veterans resented the use of immigration's computer system, which they found inefficient and dated, and some returned to pen and paper. Customs officers needed crash courses in immigration law, and vice versa. A quarrel broke out over guns: Should the new agency adopt the custom service's nine-millimeter pistol or the immigration agents' forty-caliber handgun? Meanwhile, detention centers lacked sufficient beds. Office space was scarce. No one knew who was in charge of what. Many agents didn't know their own new job description.

Neither was it clear how ICE would do its work even after figuring itself out. With more than 20,000 employees, it billed itself as the "second-largest investigative agency" in the government, second to the FBI, and the brass lobbied to rename the unit Investigation and Criminal Enforcement. After the FBI announced that no other agency could use the word *investigation,* a year of high-level negotiations over names ensued. In the meantime, ICE officers went without badges—for what would the badges say? The FBI ended up winning that battle. Meanwhile, the Drug Enforcement Administration (DEA) was also taking stock of its upstart new partner. The powerful DEA had stayed put within the Justice Department. But its gambit to annex the customs' antinarcotics team during the merger upheaval was rebuffed. The team went to ICE instead, leaving the two agencies with overlapping missions and a simmering mutual suspicion over budget, turf, and prestige.

Frustration and anxiety festered. One senior customs veteran told me: "I used to lose sleep wondering what new trick the smugglers and crooks and—since September 11—the terrorists would pull on us, but now I found myself awake worrying sick because I knew that our own internal strife was making life far easier for all of them at a time when we needed to be at our most effective. I knew how quick, creative, and dangerous the bad guys are. And here we were spending all the time in meetings and watching PowerPoint presentations by lawyers and politicians." It didn't help that ICE soon found itself charged with additional duties that seemed removed from its original mission, including running the Federal Protective Service (FPS), responsible for the safety of government buildings, and the Federal Air Marshals program, which put undercover cops on airplanes to thwart hijackings. It was also given the task of protecting the Washington, D.C., airspace. Still other surprises shaped the early stages of the new agency. Mysteriously, Garcia chose to devote ICE's first high-profile crackdown not to narco-terrorists, human traffickers, or contraband arms dealers but to pedophiles and online child pornography: a noble venture, but not exactly at the heart of the mandate. "ICE seems like a revamped INS [the old immigration agency] with a sex crimes unit," one puzzled agent told a reporter. In truth ICE was still looking for its niche, a specialty to call its own, insulated from the turf battles. By all indications, that quest continues.

"IT CAN'T BE DONE"

Coordination problems among agencies battling global smugglers are not a U.S. exclusive. Almost everywhere these agencies tend to be fragmented and unwieldy. All too often their activities fall prey to powerful, distorting forces: vested interests, corruption, bureaucratic inertia, politicization, or sheer ineptitude. Russia, for example, established in 2003 a new drug-fighting organization, the Federal Drug Control Agency, which with its army of 40,000 is four times larger than its U.S. counterpart, the DEA. But then, as Susan Glasser of the *Washington Post* reported, "Resources that could have been devoted to fighting big-time drug traffickers or cracking down on Chechen guerrillas have gone instead to campaigns against veterinarians, physicians, and dentists, vendors of popular T-shirts bearing images of marijuana leaves and bookstores that sell tomes on the medical uses of illegal narcotics."

The U.S. Homeland Security Department and Russia's drug squad are just two among the many initiatives governments are taking to respond to the advances of global traffickers among other scourges. Having explored the nature of trafficking in our times and the behavior of today's illicit traders, here we turn to the other side of the battle lines and to those who lead the counterattack: our governments. How have they dealt with the challenge? With what tools? Who are the soldiers fighting these wars on our behalf?

The answers, of course, vary from country to country and even between agencies in the same country. The background and training of agents fighting money laundering are different from those of the ones who fight the traffic in human beings or drugs. Nonetheless, there are some common patterns. The most illustrative examples come from the efforts of the United States. They have been so intense, massive, and (to America's credit) thrashed out in public that dissecting them produces illuminating insights about this enormously important kind of government work, and the challenges it is up against.

It begins of course with the September 11, 2001, attacks. After 9/11, major changes in the ways governments fight transnational criminals and terrorists took place in almost every country from Asia to Europe to Latin America. But nowhere were these reforms as sweeping as in the United States. And nowhere have they been so illustrative of how difficult governments have found it to make anti-terrorism and antitrafficking efforts go together. A 2004 report by the inspector-general of the U.S. Justice Department, Glenn A. Fine, noted that the FBI, having shifted its focus to antiterrorism efforts, was paying far less attention to its fight against organized crime. Between 2000 and 2003 the FBI units fighting organized crime and drug trafficking lost 758 agents to antiterrorism, with the cuts concentrated in units fighting Mexican cartels. Two years later Porter Goss, the new head of the CIA, told the U.S. Congress that he worried that al-Qaeda was trying to smuggle its operatives through the Mexican border.

Alarming as that may be, it is only the start of the problem. As we saw, these people- or drug-smuggling networks may no longer be just Mexican, and they can be quickly retooled to smuggle any merchandise. And to that challenge governments have yet to provide good answers. Instead, they are focusing on beefing up border controls—at a time when borders are inherently harder and harder to police. Here again, the United States offers a compelling example. Each year, 60 million people enter the country on more than 675,000 commercial and private flights, and 370 million enter by land. In addition, 116 million vehicles cross the land borders. More than 90,000 merchant and passenger ships dock at U.S. ports. They carry 9 million containers with 400 million tons of cargo. Another 157,000 smaller vessels call at U.S. harbors. The notion that a government agency, even with 186,000 employees, can seal such a porous border in this era is challenging, to say the least. Robert Hutchings, who headed the CIA's National Intelligence Council between 2003 and 2005, put it to me bluntly: "It can't be done."

AGENTS, ANALYSTS, ENFORCERS

Shocking? Maybe—at least when compared with public concern over security and political claims that the Department of Homeland Security was already making America safer. But not shocking for anyone used to working for a bureaucracy or dealing with one. Since the pioneering studies of Max Weber, sociologists have shown how the first purpose of an administrative agency is to perpetuate itself; and political scientists explain that government institutions are "sticky"—once you set them up, they are very hard to dismantle. As loud as the clarion call of September 11 might have been, it was no match for the inner clamor of bureaucratic preservation and rivalry.

No one should have expected otherwise. Big process-driven bureaucracies are a fact of life in government. And it is to governments that we look, first and foremost, to respond to the traffickers. To do so, they have employed their standard tools: budgets, laws, organizations, courts, police, civil servants, international treaties. Today most countries have their own armada of agencies devoted in one way or another to curbing illicit trade, each one home to multiple units, specialties, and personnel. For several centuries illicit trade was mainly perceived as a border control problem—endemic, but localized and usually the work of small-time players, such as local bands that roamed across borders of neighboring countries. That made it a problem mainly for customs and border patrol. But in the twentieth century, traditional notions of "neighboring countries" were shattered by the advent of mass travel and trade. Today, in terms of the drug trade Colombia and Spain can be considered "neighbors," as can Nigeria and Italy for human smuggling rings. The rise of the term *trafficking*—with its implicit associations with organized crime—transformed our understanding of illicit trade. It also thrust forward the role to be played by the police in fighting it.

Policing itself was quite recent, at least in what is now its familiar form. But by the early twentieth century, policing as a public function had become the norm in "advanced" societies, and as a craft it had grown sophisticated and developed discrete specialties. No two countries organize and operate their police the same way. Although the roots of policing are local, many countries today have a national police service divided into branches under a single unified command. The United States is an extreme outlier, with more than 18,000 separate forces, of which 60 operate nationwide. In many countries the police took over border control from the military. But the more important innovation with respect to organized crime was the establishment of powerful and prestigious investigative units, such as the American FBI (founded 1908) or France's *Police judiciaire*, established in 1907.

Yet customs and police are just part of the picture. As the art and science of government were perfected in the twentieth century and government service grew as a profession, so did specialization. As a result, the fight against trafficking involves government employees of many kinds: not only cops, soldiers, and customs agents but also lawyers, prosecutors, accountants, diplomats, communications and technology experts, researchers, analysts, and spies. Just which professions lead the effort depends on which trade they are fighting. Money laundering, for instance, involves accountants, computer specialists, and lawyers deployed in specialized financial intelligence units. The repression of drug trafficking is a traditional police activity; most countries have some form of national drug squad, though its structure and the supervision vary. Responding to the illicit arms trade usually falls to the military or state security services, while fighting counterfeiting is normally the responsibility of commerce or trade ministries.

All this specialization is a mixed blessing. It has bred considerable expertise, but also created a need for immense coordination efforts and often nurtured a debilitating organizational myopia. Officials in charge of fighting drug trafficking tend to know or worry far less about human traffickers, and vice versa. Yet as we have seen, traffickers have reached the point at which they can shift easily from product to product and market to market. Many of the global networks have the capacity to arrange the procurement, transport, and payment of whatever "merchandise" needs moving at any given time.

Beyond the shortsightedness that specialization can breed, governments are also impaired in their effectiveness by two other built-in obstacles. One is that bureaucracies tend to be organized in rigid hierarchical fashion, making them less nimble in sharing information or coordinating efforts with others outside their vertical lines of command. The second is their dependence on standard operating procedures. From purchases to resource deployments, staff promotions and pay, administration relies on predetermined rules and routines. These standards create stability, predictability, transparency, and homogeneity in government operations. But they are also the source of much rigidity and slow down the response time to unanticipated circumstances. Enormous efforts have been invested in understanding how to "reinvent government" and make agencies more agile. But the fact remains that the public sector is bound by many written and unwritten rules that seem to create the same organizational behavior almost everywhere.

It's virtually an axiom that teamwork across divisions of a ministry or a police force is complicated by rivalries, turf battles, and competing personal and institutional interests. The same is true—often more so—across organizations. And the barriers are nearly insurmountable when the coordination needs to occur across national borders. According to the first U.S. Homeland Security secretary,

Tom Ridge, "Homeland security is about the integration of nations. We must . . . share information and best practices and develop next-generation technologies that will protect us long into the future." It's a tall order. If the CIA and the FBI had trouble sharing even the most basic information that perhaps could have prevented the 9/11 attacks, just imagine the difficulty of making sure that the FBI and its Russian or Thai or Bulgarian counterpart coordinate their action and share resources as quickly and effectively as the international networks they fight.

Beneath the commonly decried "insider politics" and jostling for resources and influences lurk more fundamental concerns about commitment and trust. Because the civil service relies on rigid pay scales that are usually lower than private sector wages, rewards to individual antitrafficking professionals don't vary greatly relative to performance. Of course, many in the public sector are motivated by a deep sense of duty, patriotism, and the defense of values in which they are deeply invested personally. But alongside them often serve less competent and even venal coworkers.

Ineffective enforcement often reflects low levels of commitment by public servants who don't earn enough in government to pay their bills, leading them to shirk on their work and moonlight, as is common in all but a few countries. Demotivation exposes government agents to corruption, of course—all the more so because traffickers have the cash to offer. Cooperation between government agencies requires a level of trust in one another's commitment, dedication, ethics, and plain competence that is extremely rare in practice. It is most difficult of all to induce among agencies of different countries. "Do you really think I am going to share the names of my informants inside the Solnetsevo Brotherhood with the police here?" asked with a grin on his face a U.S. agent I interviewed in Moscow, referring to one of the Russian criminal networks known to have "friends" in high places.

Improving interagency collaboration—even among agencies of the same government—takes far more than reorganizing their reporting lines, as the ICE agents discovered to their chagrin. And the hindrances built into law enforcement—some of them bureaucratic, but others necessary to maintain accountability and public trust—contrast mightily with the organizational innovations of traffickers, financiers, and intermediaries in illicit trade. Consider how many agencies are involved in the basic unit of antitrafficking success, the "bust." A typical large-scale catch usually requires the participation of dozens of national or local agencies. Neither the methods nor the results have changed markedly in the past few years, despite the post-September 11 mentality. But traffickers have adapted their operations in ways that exploit precisely the obstacles that weigh governments down.

ILLICIT, ILLEGAL, ILL DEFINED

It may seem banal to point out that illicit trade is a type of crime. After all, illicit trade by definition takes place outside the rules. But herein lies a complicating problem: *whose rules?* They are hardly uniform from nation to nation. And that too is a strategic difference that the traffickers have learned to exploit.

Of course, some forms of trafficking are both morally abhorrent and criminal everywhere. But not all cases are that straightforward. Since late 2004, for instance, it is no longer a criminal offense in the United States to own a military-grade assault weapon. As Andres Pastrana, the former president of Colombia, told me, "While our police officers and soldiers are being constantly gunned down by narco-guerrillas, the U.S. facilitates the possession and commerce of the world's most dangerous machine guns. If we had done that, the U.S. State Department would probably include us in some blacklist." To take another example, while the U.S. federal government is cracking down on illegal aliens, many states are giving them driver's licenses. And anyone caught smuggling a shipment of cocaine into the country faces far stiffer punishments than do the "coyotes" who smuggle people across the border. And that is the United States, where antitrafficking laws are advanced. Many countries have yet to write laws or establish punishments for some of the most prevalent kinds of illicit trade.

So in practice what may be "illicit" in one country may not be in another. Often, the laws have to catch up with the evolution of illicit trade, creating new concepts and definitions such as "cyber crime" or "digital piracy" in order to draw lines between innovative practices that are considered positive for society and ones that are viewed as harmful. Sometimes the laws redefine an old problem: the notion of "human trafficking," for instance, helps focus attention and establish rules and penalties for a series of practices that might otherwise be underestimated or ignored. But even when two countries agree to view a particular practice as criminal, they may give it a different political or even moral weight, resulting in differences in the penalties they impose. And of course what is permissible in practice in a given country often goes beyond what is legal, sometimes because law enforcement is swamped or understaffed or corrupt, and sometimes because lawmakers haven't yet caught up with the latest criminal innovations. For traffickers, all these differences—multiplied across the world's two-hundred-plus countries—produce a rather special kind of world map. To them it is a map of incentives to trade, where the grayer the area, often the greater the opportunity for profit.

The rules are always a work in progress, challenged not only by traffickers but by political quarrels, manipulation by experts in gaming the system, and often the rush of innovation and new circumstances. The distinction between tax evasion and tax avoidance is often the matter of an accountant's skill rather than clear and enforceable rules. Exactly what financial practices constitute money laundering is a matter in constant flux, not just because of political differences but because the range of available financial transactions keeps growing more plentiful and more complex. This ambiguity in no way reduces the moral abhorrence of much of illicit trade. But traffickers tend to operate beyond moral considerations anyway. For them, constantly changing rules can spell opportunity. Take any two countries, and chances are that a sufficiently skilled trafficker will find a way to take advantage of all their differences—in laws, tax codes, banking regulations, environmental regulations, labor standards, and more.

WORKING TOGETHER: HARD BUT NECESSARY

Binding and functioning international laws might clarify the picture. But it should come as no surprise that devising common international rules to combat illicit trade has been an elusive and tedious task. The discipline of international law was reshaped in the wake of World War II, but it remained focused on relations between states, not on crimes committed by individuals. Criminal infractions were left to each country to handle on its own. Only recently has a flurry of international law–making activity set out anything approaching global standards on trafficking. Yet the effectiveness of these standards has been limited by the tool most commonly used to enshrine them—the international treaty.

In the past century the scope of treaties has broadened not only to cover the results of military conflict but also to codify the agreement of countries to tackle particular problems, and sometimes the methods to do so. The formal names of these agreements have multiplied—conventions, protocols, and the like; so have the number of participants. The establishment of the United Nations created a logical forum and host for this sort of discussion, along with all of the drawbacks evoked by the sneering term "international talking shop." The results have been the establishment of specialized UN agencies responsible for researching and sharing knowledge on illicit trade, notably the UN Office on Drugs and Crime, based in Vienna, at the very same time that many UN members openly flout the office's recommendations.

The record of treaties against illicit trade is similarly ambiguous. Prior to 2000, only one major international agreement had trafficking as its central concern: the International Opium Convention, first enacted in 1912. Other forms of illicit trade did not earn the same attention as narcotics. It was the limited effectiveness of these agreements that set off the new wave of international antitrafficking treaties when the dramatic expansion of the narcotics trade in the 1980s drew political attention and spurred a legal breakthrough. For the first time, legal scholars and judicial authorities began to think of international law as governing more than the activities of states. A term of art emerged, *transnational crime,* defined as "an activity that is considered a criminal offense by at least two countries." The United Nations Convention Against Illicit Traffic in Narcotic Drugs and Psychotropic Substances—the latest incarnation of the old opium accord, enacted in 1988 and in force two years later—put this concept into practice. For the first time, it committed participant states to make a list of drug-related activities criminal offenses and grounds for extradition.

Throughout the 1990s, specialists labored away to define different forms of trafficking crime and propose global standards for confronting it. In 2000 and 2001 several UN conferences delivered their results to the world stage. The signature of the UN Convention Against Transnational Organized Crime, in Palermo, Sicily (a venue not selected by accident), in December for the first time established global norms on a wide range of illicit trade offenses. The convention provided for criminalization, extradition, and related procedures, including mutual assistance and training programs to help carry out the commitments. It came garnished with important addenda: two separate protocols, one on the smuggling of migrants and the other on trafficking in persons, which states could opt into.

Yet the United Nations, without which these agreements would probably not have seen the light, can do little to ensure that they are implemented. For member countries, voting the convention into existence was the easy part. Actually signing on to the convention, then ratifying it, and finally enforcing it represent as many "big ifs" over which no international organization has control and that are subject to all manner of political and practical obstacles. In 2004, for instance, the tally of countries that had actually ratified the Palermo Convention stood at ninety-four; the protocols on migrant smuggling and human trafficking sixty-four and seventy-six respectively. Another protocol, this one on the illicit arms trade, is under negotiation but has yet to be agreed.

The greatest value of these instruments is that they establish norms and definitions—and thus the basis for moral authority, diplomatic pressure, advocacy, and public awareness. But no matter how widely these treaties are eventually adopted and ratified, they cannot create trust from thin air. In international affairs, suspicion always carries the day.

COPS AGAINST BORDERS

"Crime is international. So is the law." This solemn voice-over opened every episode of *Man from Interpol*, a British television series that launched in 1959. The Man in question was Anthony Smith, a British detective assigned to the international police organization; in the role was Richard Wyler, an actor who had returned to England after failing to make it in Hollywood. In the show, the debonair Smith pursued miscreants across borders for thirty minutes' worth of madcap adventures before the requisite happy ending. The Man faced murderers, kidnappers, con men, extortionists, and of course smugglers, including traffickers in diamonds, counterfeit cigarettes, and what was still called "white slavery." Without taking itself too seriously, the series nonetheless evoked the awesome power of police forces working together, liberally splashed with glamour and intrigue—a sort of poor man's James Bond.

But the image was misleading, because the premise was false. The law was pointedly *not* international—not on paper or in practice, let alone in enforcement. Police cooperation was still in the throes of a prolonged infancy—limited, experimental, cagey. Its concrete manifestation, Interpol, lacked staff, funds, and authority. It did little more than channel communications between national police forces by Morse code. The rest of the TV show's voice-over introduction conceded as much: "In constant touch with the police forces around the world is . . . the Man from Interpol." Not exactly swashbuckling.

Technological breakthroughs at the turn of the 20th century had opened the door to police cooperation. The telegraph, telephone, and automobile made teamwork possible—as well as necessary, for the same advances were expanding the criminal opportunities and the perpetrators' range of action. But advances such as reliable fingerprinting methods gave police strong reasons to share knowledge. A series of international police conferences held in Europe from 1888 onward resulted in the formation of the International Criminal Police Commission in 1923. Championed by the police chief of Vienna, the new group made its headquarters in that city. But the ICPC was not a standard international organization with the authority of state backing; instead it was a voluntary association of police forces. When the Nazis took over Austria in 1938, there was little to prevent them from commandeering the ICPC. Partners dropped out, and it eventually ceased to function.

After World War II, European police forces revived the institution, with France now taking the lead. Before long, it became known by its telegraphic address, Interpol. Its members were now more established, more centralized, and more powerful. Most European countries had formed national police forces. The United States had the FBI, led by the indomitable J. Edgar Hoover. New nations emerging from the decolonization process were setting up their own national agencies. Interpol seemed to have potential for criminal investigation and pursuit, and although it remained obscure to Americans, it developed in Europe a certain mystique. The report on the morning news that "Interpol has been alerted" lent the crime in question extra gravity, made its perpetrators seem more sinister and sly. Yet all it really meant was that the suspects had crossed the border and vanished; having lost the trace, authorities issued the equivalent of a global all points bulletin. For all the efforts of a few visionaries, international police cooperation still did not amount to much.

INTERPOL OR MINIPOL?

Sixty years later, the difficulties persist. Once again, new technologies have made the technical side of police work more advanced and effective than ever before: the generalization of DNA analysis and other forensic advances, instantaneous encrypted transmission of data almost anywhere in the world, biometric technologies that conclusively identify individuals through individually unique information such as iris scans. But police work is also inherently secretive and territorial, and each country's attempts to collaborate with police departments across borders butts up against both legitimate sovereignty concerns and those fundamental issues of trust that have barely faded over time.

The contradiction leaves Interpol in an ambiguous position. Until the mid-1990s it had remained a rather stolid institution. A terrorist attack in 1986 by a European anarchist group had resulted only in a change of headquarters, from a nondescript building in the Paris suburbs to a highly fortified modern compound in Lyon, France's second-largest city. Inside, however, things proceeded at a mellow pace. For one thing, Interpol ran like a bureaucracy, not a police force—on a nine-to-five, Monday–Friday schedule. (Lyon's famously rich cuisine must have resulted in long lunches, as well.) It carried out its mission—linking police forces and hosting a central data warehouse on criminals and their activities—in rapidly obsolescing ways. Communications employed Morse code and Interpol's own coded language; the archives were rows and rows of paper files among which analysts would slide on rail-mounted chairs. Only in 1994 did Interpol start implementing a modern communications system. And as late as 2000, it was still dipping its toes into the online world, tentatively beginning to switch its internal network to an IP system.

That year, Interpol got its first non-French secretary general— the top job—in decades. Ronald Noble had been a Treasury official in the Clinton administration, responsible for the customs service and the Secret Service, among others. He'd also represented the United States on Interpol's executive board and was both intrigued by the organization's potential and alarmed by its fading relevance. Fluent in several languages and the son of an African-American father and a German mother, he was an internationalist by instinct. He campaigned heavily for the job and took office in November 2000.

As a manager, Noble began change from the top. He worked late into the night and moved Interpol to a 24/7, year-round operating schedule within his first year. He quickly reduced the time Interpol took to distribute a "notice"—its term for advisories of various kinds to its members—from up to three months down to three days. Even this, of course, wasn't enough. Noble launched a technology agenda with the aim of producing a Web-based system that every police force in the world could use to search a global database and communicate notices in real time. He moved more personnel into direct communication roles with the member police forces around the world. The September 11, 2001, attacks only galvanized him further, convincing him of the urgency of his task.

In theory, Noble's agenda makes sense. More than almost any law enforcement specialist, he sees the explosive growth and continual mutation of the global underground economy—the trafficking networks, the terrorist cells, the parallel markets—and realizes all too well how governments aren't keeping up. Both this visible need and the advanced technologies available to upgrade police work ought to point to a huge opportunity for Interpol. Yet Interpol has no authority over its members and has had to live with noncooperation in even the areas most fundamental to its work.

A first constraint is money. Interpol's budget has increased since 2000, but it remains tiny: about $50 million in 2004, just 2.5 percent of ICE's budget for the same year, or one-fifth of the funds estimated to have been available to Osama bin Laden in 2001. That forces Noble to play less the part of a top cop than that of a lobbyist and fund-raiser, traveling the world to "sell" the new Interpol to member countries and exhort them to contribute funding, much as a university president spends time not teaching but courting major donors. It would be easier to fund Interpol, of course, if all its member countries were fully committed to its mission. But the actual extent each country is willing to "play" varies a great deal, often impeding Interpol's work in some of its most fundamental activities. To this day, for instance, its "red notices"—international arrest warrants—aren't honored in the United States.

It's all too easy, unfortunately, to understand why Interpol's members are so cagey. Inherently, they face the challenges of cooperation among bureaucracies with proprietary information, set operating procedures, proud yet parochial cultures—all exacerbated by the considerations of national sovereignty. Yet even if an idealistic police reformer might succeed in pushing these barriers aside, the visible extent of corruption among many of the organization's own member countries could only give him or her pause, and quickly vanquish the lofty ambitions. Russia's new drug squad, for instance, quickly fell prey to corruption. In Mexico, the elite *federales,* or federal police force, established in large part to parry endemic corruption in local police forces, have been sapped themselves by corruption, internal conflict, and defection to crime groups. The disincentives to full and frank collaboration in such partnerships, let alone open information sharing, are obvious.

There is an inherent limit, then, to what Interpol can achieve. No surprise then that it has sprouted rivals: regional agencies like the European Union's Europol or Aseanapol in Southeast Asia, explicitly built on Interpol's own model but made more effective by the growing political ties among member countries—not to mention their greater willingness to pour in resources. Interpol's backers respond that there is still a need for a research and notification system with true global reach. For now, though, the trends point to police cooperation that is regional at best, and always constrained by a healthy degree of suspicion.

SUCCESS . . . AND ITS LIMITS

On an early-March day in 2004, a DEA team approached a roadside restaurant outside Buffalo, New York, trailing a vehicle they'd been watching since it crossed over from Canada. While the driver went to eat, an agent with a master key entered the car and drove away while others simulated a theft by spreading glass shards in the parking spot. When they stopped to inspect the car, the agents found 30,000 tablets of Ecstasy, with ten pounds of high-grade pot for good measure—just as the tipster had told them.

The swoop was just one incident in the final stages of a three-year investigation, dubbed Operation Candy Box, involving sixty-four law enforcement agencies in the United States and Canada. According to authorities, the network it targeted supplied at one point up to 15 percent of U.S. Ecstasy, drawing on Canadian labs capable of manufacturing a million pills every month. At the heart of the network was a series of front companies linked to two women. Authorities arrested Ze Wai Wong, a Chinese immigrant who was charged with directing the distribution network, while Mai Phuong Le allegedly coordinated the money laundering through Vietnamese businesses in over a dozen cities, including otherwise legitimate money transfer services. A great deal of cash moved about, some of it with couriers or hidden in cars, much more by electronic transfer. U.S. banks had accepted sizable sums for deposit and wired the money to accounts all over the world, without suspicion. Less than three weeks after the Buffalo caper, the investigation wrapped up with a bang: 150 coordinated arrests in nineteen cities, from Toronto to Jacksonville and Boston to San Jose.

As this story shows, the law enforcement fight against trafficking isn't all bureaucratic depression and gloom. Agents are working hard, teaming up, and busts are going down. Every week, an announcement from a leading police force boasts of a major takedown or seizure. Within a few weeks of Candy Box, Operation Streamline shut down a channel that moved hundreds of pounds of extremely pure heroin from Colombia to the United States via Nicaragua and Argentina and laundered the proceeds by means of wire transfers or cash swallowed in condoms by couriers. Operation Decollo (Italian for "takeoff") culminated in seventy-five predawn arrests by Italian *carabinieri,* with simultaneous swoops in Spain and Colombia; for four years, agents from eight countries had tracked massive cocaine shipments from Colombia and Venezuela to destinations in Australia and Europe, on a trail that led them to the Calabrian Mafia. Operation United Eagles (these cops have a way with names) produced the arrest by Mexican *federales* of two notorious members of the Arellano Felix organization, with support from more than a dozen U.S. and Mexican agencies. And a French navy vessel intercepted on the high seas a Togolese tugboat moving two tons of cocaine from Venezuela to transshipment points in West Africa.

Successes like these are the good news. Some—like the interception of the cargo BBC *China,* which helped unroll Dr. A. Q. Khan's business in nuclear centrifuges—have major implications for global security. Others, however, seem to repeat year after year without denting the supply of illicit goods for more than a brief period, and that, of course, is the bad news. One reason for this problem is that the trade networks don't reduce to ringleaders anymore: the capture of a Vietnamese money launderer in Canada, a Calabrian Mafia boss, or a Mexican cartel lieutenant takes a number of people out of circulation, but their network of direct and indirect, regular and occasional, knowing or unaware business partners suffers, by its very nature, only a temporary injury.

Multiyear, multiagency international investigations are impressive and have the advantage of being voluntary and targeted. They involve a limited number of personnel who have both time and cause to get acquainted and develop trust. They do not involve whole organizations and, importantly, they don't require anyone to divulge all they know. In law enforcement information is power, and people hold their cards tight. And the fundamental law enforcement model hasn't changed. A senior official in the George W. Bush administration, John Bolton, described the U.S. antitrafficking strategy as favoring these sorts of operations over more structured types of cooperation. "Rather than rely on cumbersome treaty-based bureaucracies," he wrote, "this administration has launched initiatives that involve co-operative action with other sovereign states." He presented this policy as an innovation, of course, but it harkened as well to the pre-treaty era.

Somewhere between the two poles—treaties and opportunistic partnerships—a glimmer of a third model has appeared, specifically in the fight against money laundering. The Financial Action Task Force, described in Chapter 7, has succeeded in coordinating banking rules in the G-8 countries (minus Russia) and a growing number of their peers by combining traditional strategies in new ways. The FATF committed member countries one by one, on a voluntary basis, until all the main "on-shore" financial centers were on board; it then turned to countries known as money laundering harbors and threatened to cut them off from the world's capital markets and banks. The FATF relies on peer review: each member country has its financial sector inspected by an expert team of fellow members, who identify needed reforms and supervise their implementation. As radical a willing suspension of sovereignty as the antitrafficking milieu has seen, this type of review is hard to imagine applied to police forces. But in the financial sector at least, it has functioned better than in other areas of global crime fighting.

Yet the FATF is less the success of a new approach to combating illicit trade than a reasonably effective adaptation to some of the limits that fight has encountered. That the most effective antitrafficking approach has been the one that relies the most on accountants and analysts behind computers in head offices speaks to governments' lack of success in penetrating illicit trading networks with undercover agents and reliable field operations. In addition, the FATF has had to alter its agenda to maintain the support of the powerful governments that back it. It suffered a near-death experience in the summer of 2001, when the newly installed Bush administration considered relaxing U.S. antilaundering rules; target countries, emboldened, prepared to oppose the task force's demands. It took September 11 to reverse the administration's stand. The trade-off has been the political requirement that the FATF—

and other organizations—focus resources and labor on terrorist finance. An important task to be sure, but just one small part of the problem.

LABOR OF LOVE

Governments are gravely impaired by all kinds of obstacles in fighting the global trafficking networks. Still, there sometimes surfaces from the murk of bureaucracy and interagency squabbling a surprising secret weapon: a hero. Antitrafficking still attracts some remarkable, dedicated public servants who are willing to incur the most enormous personal costs to stop the criminals. More than dogged determination, it is a labor of love, perhaps even obsession.

These professionals ply their trade in some of the most hazardous environments—countries like Colombia, for instance, where the infiltration of public life by traffickers has reached the level of a cliché. Already a risky place to be a journalist, Colombia is even more dangerous for judges and prosecutors. Few people would call Maria Cristina Chirolla's job desirable, for instance.

When Chirolla became chief of the money and asset laundering division in the Colombian state prosecutor's office, she took charge of some of the most dangerous law enforcement activities in the world. It became her duty to shut down Colombia's jungle drug labs, seize the traffickers' villas and aircraft and luxury goods, and infiltrate the financial networks that repatriate cocaine and heroin earnings from the United States. Chirolla, an intense and dedicated lawyer in her forties, would call the shots. She also confronted the enemies within—corruption and graft. All the officials whose help she'd need to get her job done were potentially vulnerable to payoffs: the investigators, the regional governors, the police and military brass, the judges. During raids, unsupervised soldiers might grab cash and drug stashes for themselves. Chirolla's colleagues were not immune, either. Within a short time, allegations of ethics violations had claimed the careers of her peers responsible for antidrug and anticrime operations. Chirolla took over their portfolios, instantly becoming the nation's most important and visible crime fighter—and therefore, assassination target.

It's hard to imagine that the zest for prosecution alone would motivate Chirolla to take on this role, or that ambition might have blinded her to the lethal risks. The backstory to her ascension was a great deal more personal and complex. Chirolla had joined the public service in the early 1990s as an aide to the mayor of Bogotá, responsible for outreach for and rehabilitation of prostitutes. It was her time with the street workers that exposed her to the realities of the drug world—not the flash and danger of international trafficking, but the sordid descent of the prostitutes into a never-ending spiral: drugs to ease the pain, sex to pay for drugs. Chirolla helped the women form an organization to raise funds and sponsor treatment and job programs to break the cycle of sex work and addiction. Eventually, she'd leave city government and serve as their advocate, until one of the ex-prostitutes was ready to take her place.

The story might have stopped there, but Chirolla would soon see Colombia's drug crisis from the other end of the telescope—no longer the street-level perspective of addiction wrecking already desperate lives, but the no less catastrophic truth of Colombia's role in the global drug trade. Joining the Ministry of Justice, Chirolla was appointed to oversee the country's compliance with international treaties and conventions. In practice, this meant drugs: interpreting global treaties, devising new laws, assisting other government branches in fighting drug production and trafficking to bring Colombia into compliance with its official commitments. Her expertise became such that she was next appointed to head the Controlled-Substance Division of the Health Ministry. There her vision broadened again, in a way she did not expect. She grew aware of a paradox—while Colombia was fighting drug trafficking and sales, patients in Colombian hospitals and clinics were suffering in unnecessary pain because of a lack of standard narcotics like morphine. The volumes involved were low, but the human cost high. Moreover, launching a public program to actually *distribute* narcotics would require cooperation and close control by health officials all the way down to the hospital level. Yet not only did Chirolla succeed, but the system she devised became a model for other countries, endorsed by the Organization of American States.

As a top prosecutor, Chirolla returned to enforcement and repression "aware that there is not just one side in the drug world." Her personal journey, in which she witnessed the cocaine and heroin trade not only as a crime but also in its complicated social, medical, and economic aspects, gave her an enviable depth of perspective and ability to target her efforts. But that journey, that commitment, may also be what drove her to accept ever-greater levels of personal risk as her career advanced. Featured in a British television documentary in 2004, she spoke of learning that she was the target of a specific assassination plot with involvement of Colombia's right-wing paramilitaries—and of facing the prospect of execution or exile, and finally tallying up the personal costs, yet still feeling the call to go on. "It's strange," Chirolla once told me, "but you do learn to live with the thought that there are very nasty people trying to kill you."

She is not alone. Every country has its committed crusaders who carry on the fight no matter how frightening or demoralizing the conditions. And in the end, the massive application of state power and resources to fighting illicit trade—burdened by bureaucracy, eroded by corruption, complicated by protocol and practical obstacles—boils down to characters like these. Individuals compelled to their craft by personal motivations usually far deeper and psychologically complex than the mere desire for a civil service job and state pension, they are a loose fraternity facing the onslaught of globalization's tide—each a lone ranger on one of the fight's myriad fronts, and usually pronounced heroes only after they fall.

Chapter 10

CITIZENS VS. CRIMINALS

The investigators scored a big break. Posing as buyers seeking to ship to China a load of merbau, a high-quality tropical wood that Indonesia forbids exporting, they found a broker in Jakarta who was more than ready to tell them, quite candidly, the many ways in which he and his colleagues broke the law. "In Indonesia," Yaman Yeo told them, ". . . everything is possible." He explained that his timber concession in the remote Papua province was guarded by army soldiers in his pay, told how he used fake documents from Malaysia to dissimulate the wood's real origin, and assured the investigators that he knew people with official connections to guarantee that they could ship the wood out—of course, for a fee. His boldness matched his candor, as his firm described itself on its Web site as an "environmentally conscious operation." In reality, as the investigators knew, Yeo and his peers took advantage of legal gray areas, intimidation of local indigenous populations, and outright graft and official complicity to advance deforestation of Papua, the world's third-largest tropical forest area and home to thousands of unique plant and animal species, by an area the size of Switzerland each year.

The undercover agents were putting the pieces together. In Papua itself, they found community members willing to explain how the timber traders lured villagers into signing a cooperation agreement that granted them access to tribal lands in exchange for small payments—a motorcycle, a church for the town—dwarfed by the immense profits of the trade. When the villagers attempted to protest, they were met with threats from soldiers allied with the trafficking. Following the trade through brokers in Singapore and Hong Kong, the agents ended up in Zhangjiagang, a port town near Shanghai that has become in just five years "probably the largest trading center for tropical logs in the world," where vast amounts of timber arrive to supply China's construction and housing boom as well as its flooring and furniture exports. Around 600,000 cubic meters of illegal Indonesian merbau arrive there each year, a Hong Kong trader told the agents, accompanied by fake documents. "They make a whole set [of documents]," he told them. "I am expert on this."

Juicy evidence, thanks to great undercover police work. Except, these agents were not cops. They were activists from the Environmental Investigation Agency (EIA), which is not a police department but a nonprofit nongovernmental organization (NGO) based in London, and from their Indonesian partner group Telapak, based in the town of Bogor. Their methods, however, showed how far NGOs have progressed from the stereotype of "charities," as they are sometimes still called. Surveillance, forensics, and undercover buys are part of the new stock in trade for activist groups combating illicit trade.

So are sting operations. In March 2003, at about the same time that the EIA team was beating the bush around remote villages on the tip of Papua, another NGO undercover team was rousting up police in Cambodia for a joint raid on traffickers of another type: those who rent children for sex. In this case, the agents worked for an American organization called International Justice Mission, based in suburban Virginia. Their targets were the brothels of Svay Pak, a ramshackle village outside Phnom Penh famous in the sordid demimonde of pedophile sex tourists. Here all day long touts dispatched teenage girls to proposition the expatriates and tourists who refreshed themselves at the dusty outdoor tables of makeshift taverns. In the brothels the children were far younger. Many were trafficked within Cambodia or from Vietnam and China, often to be resold in Malaysia or Thailand. None of this stopped Svay Pak from functioning in plain daylight. One British reporter watched a local cop stroll up to a brothel gate and casually collect an envelope—a common transaction.

Svay Pak was clearly ripe for shutting down. The problem was, it had been shut down before, in police swoops from the capital that the touts always seemed to know about in advance. Pimps and madams had time to close shop. Those the police picked up generally found their way back quickly, simply bribing their way out of custody. All this was familiar, almost ritualistic. One such bust occurred just two months before IJM arrived. Then, the local police chief had told a reporter that "the closures were permanent this time." But Svay Pak was soon back to its old, ghastly ways. So the IJM team took a new approach. Not only did they hire former police officers, local investigators, and at least one global security firm to document the activities in the brothels; they also brought with them on the day of the raid a crew from the popular American television program *Dateline NBC*. A few days earlier, the TV reporters had joined investigators on an undercover visit to the brothels with hidden cameras. Now they were back to capture the raid for their viewers.

As it turned out, the raid was not a complete success. Some touts smelled a rat and stayed away from the "safe house" where the agents tried to lure them. Still, a number came and were promptly arrested, and thirty-seven victims were taken to a shelter that a local NGO operated. Several later scaled the walls, probably to return to the brothels. But for IJM, an evangelical Christian organization, every single rescue had meaning.

DAY OF THE ADVOCATES

As these stories vividly show, the fight against illicit trade is by no means limited to governments and international organizations. Quite the contrary: NGOs have become an essential part of the picture, both because they have grown extremely active in the past decade and because they bring tools and capabilities that governments usually lack. So do corporations and business organizations, which have taken the lead in fighting the segments of illicit trade that stand to harm their reputation and profits. The hackneyed term that social scientists use, "civil society"—or, even worse, "nonstate actors"—does little to convey the incredible diversity and vitality of private parties that have become involved in the fight—and that have a crucial role to play in the solution.

This boom is a hallmark of the 1990s, which saw not only a flourishing of new nongovernmental organizations, particularly in developing countries, but also the international expansion of existing ones. Some were born global: Transparency International, for instance, a nonprofit group whose aim is to fight corruption, was created in 1993 with an explicitly global scope of operations and with local chapters in many countries. Others include grassroots campaigns, traditional relief organizations, and activists of all sorts working in groups or increasingly as free agents. Foundations, think tanks, and research institutes play an active part as well.

Businesses too have become increasingly involved in international advocacy through trade organizations, philanthropic programs, public relations campaigns, and attempts to be good "corporate citizens." The role of the media has been transformed as well: although editorial pages have always functioned as bully pulpits, the explosion of a free press in country after country after the end of the cold war has made the marketplace of news, reporting, and opinion more vibrant and aggressive than ever before. And new communication tools and technologies from satellite video links to minicameras to blogging have only intensified the trend.

With its fast pace and geographic scope, the rise of international advocacy resembles that of international crime. After all, the same new politics and technologies that help criminal networks work abroad also help civic-minded networks to do the same. The intimate collaboration of the EIA and its Indonesian colleagues at Telapak could not have functioned twenty years ago. Neither the political conditions nor the practical tools existed. But NGOs can now work with like-minded counterparts across the globe with ease, just as different spokes of criminal networks can coordinate their activities with nearly no geographic limitations—giving both an immense advantage that governments can only struggle to follow but never match.

Armed with this advantage, the NGOs distinguish themselves in the fight against trafficking by doing what governments cannot or will not do. First, they are able to work across borders without the need for tedious diplomatic negotiations. A top echelon of global NGOs—with familiar names such as Human Rights Watch, Greenpeace, Oxfam, CARE—maintain offices in dozens of countries, staffed by expert local personnel. But grassroots local NGOs have also been empowered by access to international partnerships and the resources, technical assistance, and skills that established organizations in rich countries can bring. These include global NGOs as well as international funders like the Ford Foundation or the Open Society Institute.

Second, the NGOs are able to raise funds—internationally, if needed—and dedicate these resources to a very specific goal of interest to their supporters, unlike governments, which must allocate money to antitrafficking activities in competition with hundreds of other budget priorities. It is impossible for a taxpayer to determine if she is getting value from her investment in fighting illicit trade. It is much easier for her to gauge whether the NGO to which she contributed last year has carried out its promises and is deserving of her funds this time around. The competition for funding can sharpen the focus of advocacy groups, and a small start-up group can grow influential in a short time if its work is seen as crucial and well handled. An NGO called the Polaris Project, for instance, grew out of a two-person campaign by students at Brown University to draw attention to the plight of Korean sex slaves in the city of Providence, Rhode Island. It took Polaris less than five years to grow into a reputed Washington advocacy group with staff who testify at congressional hearings.

Another advantage advocacy groups possess over governments is their ability to expose corruption. They can also galvanize the media by pitching stories to journalists and through the use of sophisticated public relations campaigns. Advocacy has become a full-fledged global profession, with its innovators, best practices, and iconic figures—along with lawyers, PR firms, fund-raisers, nonprofit consultants, and other service providers eager to sell their skills. For all the noble goals of many advocates, more mundane considerations—method, competence, financial integrity, communication skills, recruitment, and so on—have the most to do with the results they achieve. All of which contrasts yet again with the professional culture that is characteristic of government agencies and security services.

Most of all, the advantage that NGOs bring to the table is their capacity—in some cases, predilection—to push the envelope, to find aggressive new ways to document the issues of concern and push for awareness and enforcement. To a considerable extent this is because many advocates are idealists—but so are many who choose to enter the profession of government. Governments are not only constrained by their own frontiers but are also limited by procedure: for accountability's sake we expect government agents to follow methods and rules that are set out in laws, and we become concerned when they do not. But private actors are free to do anything that is not specifically forbidden—that is, they experiment with new approaches, change the focus of their work, subject only to the interests of their supporters and the ability of their staff.

What they do with this latitude varies, of course. The NGOs that address illicit trade typically have moral motivations: to end human exploitation and slavery, to protect endangered species, to prevent environmental depredation, to help drug addicts break the habit, to stop the flow of funds to rebels and dictators. But their ideas about how to do so, whether deriving from political ideology, religion, or simple compassion, can be wildly divergent or clashing, which inevitably leads to differences in methods as well. In Southeast Asia, for instance, the IJM activists working to shut down the child brothels have had difficulties collaborating with local NGOs such as the Cambodian Women's Crisis Center or Afesip, a group that a French-Cambodian couple founded. Not because they disagreed on the evil of child trafficking, but because of their methods, with the local groups complaining that the IJM emphasis on spectacular but short-lived "rescue" raids was counterproductive to the long-term task of rehabilitating the victims and helping them learn skills rather than return to the brothels.

Sometimes differences in approach stem from the way NGOs see the issue from the point of view of their main concern. Human trafficking can be seen as an issue of women and children's rights, poverty, or labor conditions. The Solidarity Center, for instance, an NGO that is an arm of the AFL-CIO, the main U.S. trade union federation, links human trafficking to sweatshops and unfair trade practices—less lurid an angle than slavery and coerced sex but important nonetheless. Working with still less fanfare are networks of organizations that aim to protect smuggled migrants, with a focus on their human rights.

Yet these differences may also mask less altruistic motives. One debate that can affect work against human trafficking is the one that opposes those who see all prostitution as exploitation against those who see a place for legal sex work. In Russia a dispute along these lines took shape between the Angel Coalition, which favors outlawing and repressing prostitution as a tool for ending sex trafficking, and other civil society groups that argued for liberalization—but that the Angel Coalition suspected were in fact a front for corrupt politicians involved in the sex trade. And of course some NGOs are wary of antitrafficking measures because they fear these will harm their own constituents; the National Rifle Association in the United States, which has opposed international small-arms regulation efforts, is a noteworthy example.

SELLING THE ISSUE

Do the advocates deliver? If the measure is information and awareness, then the answer is yes. Many of the leading, most reputed, and complete sources of information on illicit trade are not international organizations but rather NGOs, foundations and institutes that have specialized in each field. The annual Small Arms Survey, for instance, has become a key source of global information on the weapons trade. It may not grace many private bookshelves, but it is influential in policy circles. It is the product of the Graduate Institute of International Studies, a research institute based in Geneva. Human Rights Watch, Global Witness, Amnesty International, Greenpeace, and Oxfam are among the organizations that have become references in their field. And small-scale NGOs in developing countries are pioneering efforts where governments have failed. Viva Rio, an antiviolence NGO in Brazil, launched the country's first civilian-run gun collection center. In a savvy prevention policy, its workers disable the guns *before* handing them over to the police.

Their command of the data has allowed NGOs to speak with growing authority to governments, with the successes measured in the passage of new legislation or the allocation of funds toward the antitrafficking goals that the NGOs advocate. Here again some of the most visible efforts have addressed human trafficking. The Victims of Trafficking Protection Act that the United States passed in 2000, for instance, owes much to the combined push of evangelical Christian organizations and liberal advocacy groups. Similarly, in Russia leaders of the Angel Coalition helped draft the country's first antitrafficking law in 2003.

Along with pressure and support to pass laws, advocates play a major role as incubators and distributors of new ideas. One such contribution is the concept of "harm reduction," which advocates usually apply to the drug trade. This notion entails taking the total effect of drugs and their trade and gauging every new measure by whether it reduces harm rather than increasing it. In practice this means moving resources into prevention and treatment, and considering the decriminalization or legalization of some drugs. It can be politically sensitive material, and accordingly its proponents tend to couch it in technical terms, making the argument on grounds of economics rather than politics. Ethan Nadelmann, an influential advocate of harm reduction in the United States, is no radical activist but rather a respected social scientist and author with Harvard degrees in law and political science. He stumbled into drug policy almost by accident while searching for topics in graduate school. Since 1994 he has led a U.S. group, now known as the Drug Policy Alliance, that is a leading proponent of harm reduction and has received funds from the philanthropist George Soros.

Information is good; ideas are better still. But what about concrete results? There are many cases of small-scale success—raids on traffickers and their stashes, exposure of corrupt politicians, passage of new laws—that owe much to the efforts of the private advocates. Yet the continued expansion of illicit trade since 1990—during the very same period that the boom in international civil society activity has taken place—shows that the advocates can't turn the tide on their own. One reason is that for all their operational advantages over governments, advocates are just as constrained as are bureaucracies by two factors: resources and tunnel vision. If governments have a hard time matching the resources that the traffickers can muster, then nongovernmental organizations face an even harder struggle. But like governments they are also impaired by their specialized and therefore partial vision: the intense focus on one aspect of the issue, one part of the elephant, at the risk of ignoring the connections on which the traffickers thrive. Advocacy groups in fact are almost forced to some degree of tunnel vision since they must compete for funds from the public and for its short attention span.

And it is no secret that some issues "sell" better than others. In general, the more intense and vivid the focus—on, say, ending the sex trafficking of minors in eastern Europe; promoting conservation of endangered species; or training coca farmers in the cultivation of alternative crops—the easier to sell the cause, raise funds, and become a relevant voice at the policy table. How activists choose their issues represents the result of a kind of competition among social issues, or at least among the words and images that advocates use when they convey the issues to the public. Their competitive skill in this landscape can make an enormous material difference in the resources that become available to them. Advocates might draw support and funding from philanthropists, corporate boards, worshippers in churches and mosques, or small donors who leave their pocket change in donation envelopes on airplanes, sponsor a marathon runner, or buy a calendar. And many worthy groups work perennially on meager means and far outside the spotlight.

Thus, the strength of the NGOs is also their crucial weakness when it comes to fighting illicit trade. Their ability to raise money and awareness by skillfully framing a problem can make them vastly influential. But it forces them also to specialize, and honing in on just one form of illicit trade matches up poorly against the increasingly nonspecialized approach of illicit traders, who as we know move in and out of different "product lines" with flexibility and speed.

Also, there is not much guarantee that NGO initiatives that are "sold" to the public (and to financial contributors) in wealthy countries will be helpful to local activists in developing countries, which often confront illicit trade in entirely different terms—in the context of grinding poverty, accelerated economic and social changes, or civil wars. Many of the most successful NGOs focus their efforts and apply money raised from the Western public to the "source countries" of slaves, animals, drugs, and the like. Although many such programs are laudable in themselves, they are unlikely to make a lasting dent in illicit trade until they can mobilize the same Western public to curb its own demand for the products the traffickers help to supply.

BUSINESS BRIGADES

Meet the software police. No, this is not an official police force either. But as with the NGO investigative groups, efforts by major corporations to take matters into their own hands when it comes to fighting illicit trade are beginning to look like traditional police functions. The software police, as it is known, is the Business Software Alliance, the consortium of twenty-six global big names from Adobe to Veritas by way of Avid, Intel, Microsoft, and Symantec. Since the mid-1990s the BSA has made a mission of cracking down on unlicensed and fraudulent software wherever it is in use. And as we saw in Chapter 6, that means everywhere. In response, the BSA has established offices on three continents with activities in dozens of countries, including hotlines to report fraud.

The group does a lot more than just collect tips. It enforces. With its own professional investigators, others that it hires, and when possible the help of local police, the BSA has made a practice of swooping on the sites of illegal software manufacturing and use—the white collar crime par excellence of the cyber era. The fifteen-hour raid it conducted on a Singapore manufacturer of CD-ROM software in 1997, for instance, had little to envy of professional police raids in the home countries of the American, Australian, and Hong Kong investigators involved. Singapore police were present but left the main role to the private investigators, who followed the scent from an earlier undercover purchase of 10,000 illegal CD-ROMs from another Singapore firm.

It is not cheap to deploy a global police force when that is not your regular line of business. But manufacturers will tell you they have no choice. The scale of counterfeiting is such, and the disadvantages of governments against counterfeiters so glaring, that industry has had to assume much of the burden. In China pharmaceutical manufacturers hire private security firms to assist in rooting out counterfeits of their brand-name products. It is frustrating work: the *Washington Post* reported in 2002 the case of a security contractor in Guangzhou called Smiling Wolf Consultative that had carried out ten raids on fake drug manufacturing locations but never found anyone on the premises to take in. The head of the company, Liu Dianlin, admitted to the *Post* that the task was Sisyphean. "You close one, they move to another," he said. "It's really basically impossible to eradicate this problem. We're managing it more than solving it." Which might be good for Liu's business, but not at all good for his corporate clients.

Yet there is no alternative. These raids came *after* the Chinese government set its own wheels in motion to crack down on counterfeits. Even with laws and orders from the top, local police have little incentive or resources to crack down on nimble counterfeits—if they are not connected to them in the first place. In China and elsewhere corporate investigators must often take it on themselves to prod and cajole authorities into a sting, often by supplying the evidence and providing the vehicles for the operation—not to mention wining and dining police chiefs in order to build the necessary goodwill.

Corporate police loves informers, and knows how to cultivate them. In Britain, a whistle-blower who reveals a software infraction of sufficient magnitude—for instance, an entire midsize company running unlicensed programs—stands to earn a reward of up to 10,000 pounds. Turning from police to prosecutor, the BSA or its local counterpart then informs the company that its wrongdoing has been detected and offers to negotiate a settlement. The offer serves multiple purposes. First, it allows companies genuinely unaware of their infraction a chance to make good, on the (relatively) cheap. Second, it spares the BSA the cost of proceeding to the next step, the lawsuit. But there is a third motivation, and this is where the police analogy no longer holds. The software industry would rather not sue when it might benefit instead from turning the user of unlicensed products into a legitimate, and therefore profitable, customer.

Clearly trade associations are not what they used to be. Lobbying public officials for various laws and regulations is a time-honored practice and still endures. The BSA, for instance, lobbied China to make software piracy a civil offense, which then permits the association to sue violators, and in 2002, the Chinese supreme court issued a ruling to that effect. But the urgency of the threat from illicit trade has forced industry groups to expand their role or face irrelevance. Fewer golf tournaments and luncheons for politicians; more minicam surveillance, undercover buys, and monitoring of Internet activity. At stake is something business understands very well: profits. A measure of the concern with the avalanche of copycat products, stolen designs, and pirated software that make up the global market for counterfeits is that it has vanquished barriers of competitive suspicion and secrecy, turning rivals into partners for common survival. And trade associations, the best placed for hosting such initiatives, have now become centers of research, data collection, advanced publicity campaigns, investigation and enforcement bureaus—the whole portfolio of modern advocacy and then some.

Most aggressive have been the industries that have gained the most from the advent of new information and communication technologies and therefore have the most to lose. Along with the BSA, the Motion Picture Association (MPA) and the International Federation of Phonographic Industries (IFPI) are most active, combating bootleg CDs and DVDs and unlicensed downloads off the Internet. The roots of these organizations reflect the composition of each industry. Based in Washington, the BSA reflects the dominantly American composition of its membership. The MPA is a direct emanation of the Motion Picture Association of America, long symbolized by its famous and politically influential head Jack Valenti, who retired in 2004. As for IFPI, in keeping with the somewhat broader origins of the main record companies, it is based in London and is also, logically enough, the oldest of these associations. But everyone is affected, and counterfeiting is as much on the agenda of motor or valve manufacturers as it is for makers of Rolexes and video games. Reflecting this realization, the Paris-based International Chamber of Commerce launched in 2005 an ambitious multiindustry initiative that it called Business Action to Stop Counterfeiting and Piracy (BASCAP).

For business to fight counterfeiting is understandable enough. But industry has also had to take a role in combating other forms of illicit trade—the ones where its products are likely to be misused, for instance. The American Chemical Council, for example, routinely works with the U.S. Drug Enforcement Administration to spot suspicious purchases and deliveries of chemicals that might be precursors for cocaine labs. Banking associations have established specialized units focusing on anti–money laundering standards and best practices and often try to develop their own rules ahead of those imposed by regulators. The trade associations and the professional standards board of the accounting profession are also developing tools to counter money laundering and fraud. Business has other less direct but still significant effects on the landscape for illicit trade: lobbying for work visas for highly trained workers in Europe and the United States has effects on the world market for illegal immigration "assistance." At a certain point these activities merge into the general effect that big-company decisions have on the political and economic environment around them. Yet the lesson of the software police and its equivalents is that industry's natural instinct to help itself can—potentially—be a positive force in the fight against trafficking.

REPORTERS IN THE CROSSFIRE

The nongovernmental enemies of the traffickers take risks. Some have died in the process. Investigators with NGOs and business groups have found themselves undercover in dicey situations. But among the traffickers' enemies, it is journalists who are most often in the line of fire. Quite literally. A significant number of the journalists who are killed and attacked each year—a tally maintained by the New York–based Committee to Protect Journalists, another NGO—are the victims of traffickers whose operations they were working to unravel. Which says a great deal, it its macabre way, about just who it is that the traffickers consider their most dangerous threat. Yet although the general public is quite aware of the high-profile cases of journalists abducted and killed by terrorists, the stories of investigative journalists attacked for their reporting on traffickers are far less known. Few have heard, for instance, of the Pakistani investigative reporter Sufi Mohammed Khan, shot dead in Karachi in 2000 after reporting on prostitution and drug smuggling. Although the assassin was quickly nabbed, those behind him remained in the shadows. They allegedly include a family involved in smuggling women into forced prostitution in India.

Sometimes the victims are among the top of the profession in their country. That was the case of Georgy Gongadze, a Ukrainian journalist who was decapitated in 2000 and whose case remained untouched by the government until after the "orange revolution" that brought opposition leader Viktor Yushchenko to power four years later. A Brazilian television reporter, Tim Lopes, won his country's equivalent of the Pulitzer Prize for a report on the drug trade in Rio de Janeiro in 2001. The next year enforcers loyal to one of Rio's drug entrepreneurs kidnapped Lopes, beat him, and condemned him to death in a mock trial, enforcing the "sentence" with a sword.

Not surprisingly, ground zero for much of the world's illicit trade is also the most dangerous place to be an investigative reporter: on the Mexican border with the United States—which means in practice a wide swath of northern Mexico, coast to coast. In Matamoros on the Gulf Coast, newspaper editor Antonio Martínez Guttiérez was tortured and then killed with four shots to the head in March 2001. Theories about the perpetrators included drug traffickers and migrant smugglers, both of which his paper had investigated. A crusading syndicated columnist, Francisco Arratia, suffered a similar fate in August 2004. Over in Tijuana, the most famous local reporter covering trafficking, Jesus Blancornelas, the founder and editor of an independent magazine called *Zeta,* was badly wounded in a gun attack in 1997 but survived. But in June 2004 his coeditor, Francisco Ortiz, was not so lucky. After many years of living under the watchful eye of bodyguards, Blancornelas ended up growing weary. He told Reuters in 2005, "I regret founding *Zeta.*"

Clearly the risk to the media is in proportion to the importance they hold in the eyes of the traffickers. Reporters enjoy a pulpit that few NGOs can match, even the largest and most influential ones. One intrepid journalist can file a story that results in a particular trafficking cell or enterprise being taken down. Investigative journalists also often muster the persistence, even obsession, necessary to track down illicit trade. One U.S. watchdog organization, the Center for Public Integrity, acknowledged as much when it formed an investigative unit made up of journalists to apply their skills to its projects. The initiative, dubbed International Consortium of Investigative Journalists (ICIJ), has gone on to produce detailed research on the international arms trade, among other topics.

Yet all the evidence makes clear that journalists can't unravel the networks alone, let alone do more than briefly disrupt one or another supply chain or distribution operation. Paradoxically, it may be popular fiction in books and film that stands the highest chance of conveying to the public the complex realities of illicit trade. Yet for each work like the Stephen Soderbergh film *Traffic* (2000), which many officials praised for its documentary-like accuracy, there are several that offer portrayals of trafficking networks that are at worst absurd and at best outdated.

SMALL BATTLES, LARGE WAR

In 1997 Jessica Mathews, currently president of the Carnegie Endowment of International Peace, wrote a much-cited article titled "Power Shift." In it she argued this:

> The end of the Cold War has brought no mere adjustment among
> states but a novel redistribution of power among states, markets,
> and civil society. National governments are not simply losing
> autonomy in a globalizing economy. They are sharing powers—
> including political, social, and security roles at the core of
> sovereignty—with businesses, with international organizations, and
> with a multitude of citizens groups, known as nongovernmental
> organizations (NGOs). The steady concentration of power in the

hands of states that began in 1648 with the Peace of Westphalia is over, at least for a while.

Mathews was right. And illicit trade is no exception to the dynamic she identified. As governments have struggled to combat trafficking, more and more private organizations have sprouted up and mobilized to fill the vacuum. They are part of the more benevolent segments of the new groups of civil society suddenly empowered by globalization. The trouble is that they are up against an enemy that is empowered by the very same factors. As a result they have won some battles, but they are embroiled in a deep and long war.

In that combat they have some inherent weaknesses. One is that they are fragmented. Unlike illicit traders, who are motivated by the universal value of profit, the advocates are often motivated by ideals, which differ enormously from activist to activist, group to group. So far that fragmentation has been the downside of the focus that NGOs and business groups have managed to shine on specific issues and places—sex tourism in Cambodia, tropical wood in Indonesia, "conflict diamonds" from Sierra Leone, pirated CDs in New York City. With the victories on these specific fronts comes the frustration of knowing that the trafficking networks adapt and regroup even when a company stops buying suspect supplies or dealers are taken off the streets.

The advocates have ulterior motives as well. They may be altruistic and yet conflicting, because they stem from different worldviews and moral systems. Religious motivations are particularly fraught. Nuns have been killed in Brazil and Mozambique, for instance, for threatening to blow the whistle on illicit traders of timber and human organs respectively. But on the other hand some religious activists have faced criticism for proselytizing among the populations—of victims of trafficking, for instance—they have come to assist. The alliance of feminist and evangelical groups to push for antislavery legislation in the United States must be counted as a significant success, but it is also inherently fragile and unlikely to carry over into many other initiatives.

Similarly, economic and moral motivations at some point are bound to collide, breeding potentially drastic differences between business and activist approaches to an issue of mutual concern. While activists can agree with pharmaceutical industry organizations, for instance, on the need to curb the spread of potentially dangerous or defective counterfeits, opinions tend to diverge when it comes to deciding how to accelerate the distribution of cheap drugs in developing countries.

Those disagreements don't necessarily stand in the way of working together. More ominous is the danger that the traffickers will penetrate the advocacy groups. And the new focus on civil society in international aid funding has led, inevitably, to a mushrooming of self-declared NGOs in many countries with backers that are not necessarily easy to determine. Another component of civil society—the media—can help to spotlight what works and unmask the impostors. But media attention of course tends to be spotty and brief.

Still, don't blame the advocates for ineffectiveness. They have been effective in their areas of focus—enough at least to bring down some criminals, relieve some victims, and disrupt illicit trade by shuffling the risks and rewards. But to erode the growth of trafficking as a whole is a much vaster project, one that plainly goes beyond the scope of what is reasonable to ask of an issue-based civic or business group. Without widespread public awareness of illicit trade as an integrated whole, an interwoven aspect of the "legitimate" global marketplace—and government policies that respond to this reality—there is little that private and civic groups can do other than fight small-scale battles that can't win the war.

Chapter 11

WHY WE ARE LOSING

What do all the illicit trades have in common? The most immediate answer is that they are large and growing. The corollary of this conclusion is that in all cases and despite massive efforts, governments are failing to stem the tide of illicit trade. A third conclusion from our tour around the main illicit markets is that these businesses could not achieve their large scale without the active complicity of governments, or without a solid business infrastructure that includes corporations that are often legal, large, and visible. Illicit trade is deeply embedded in the private sector, in politics, and in governments.

Since the 1990s ushered in the current wave of intense globalization, illicit trade has transformed itself in three ways. It has grown immensely in value; it has extended its scope of products and activities; and the different illicit trade specialties of old have come together, with brokers and intermediaries taking the ascendancy over suppliers. The combined operation of these three trends amounts to nothing less than a massive reorganization of illicit trade, not unlike the upheavals that major industries go through from time to time to become more competitive, productive, and efficient.

As business school case studies teach, major industrial upheavals occur when new revolutionary products are introduced, when new technologies drastically change the way a product is manufactured or delivered to clients, when consumers' preferences change, or when there is a surge in new customers, often as a result of the opening of new geographical markets. The equilibrium is also lost when new competitors challenge traditional ones, when governments change the rules of the game, or when long-standing, often tacit arrangements and pacts among dominant firms are broken. As we saw in the previous chapters, *all* of these forces transformed the illicit markets—some of which had been rather stagnant for centuries and others that did not even exist. Moreover, all of them have been spurred by sustained and rapidly growing demand, new sources of supply, and ineffective government regulation.

This new landscape has rewarded the traffickers with superb results. But perhaps the most important transformation of all is that the main participants in illicit trade have achieved political influence in direct proportion to their enormous profits. This political influence has gone beyond the traditional "purchase" of politicians or bureaucrats. It also includes the prolonged "capture" of certain state and local governments, almost sovereign control over territories that may or may not coincide with political boundaries, and in extreme cases control of crucial decision-making centers within national governments. It follows that in some cases a country's national interest is completely aligned with the furtherance and protection of international illicit activities.

The business and politics of illicit trade have changed dramatically. What has changed far less is the way we look at illicit trade, and the way we and our governments mobilize and organize to confront it. That gap in perception—and ultimately in action—is not shrinking despite the growing daily evidence of its importance and our ineffective ways. Sometimes we hone in on a particular line of business when current events and media attention point that way. The discovery of A. Q. Khan's nuclear components network, for example, attracted this sort of global public attention. The persistence of widespread people trafficking has sparked popular outrage. Yet we rarely put the pieces together—and neither, surprisingly, do most governments and law enforcement agencies. In contrast, merely by following the money and adjusting their operations to market opportunities, the traffickers are blazing a trail on which all of us—

governments, businesses, civic organizations and citizens—are fast losing the trace.

Only by confronting the new reality of global illicit trade and understanding why we have been so powerless to stop it can we start to find a better way forward. This chapter is about taking stock and facing our predicament.

It begins, once again, with globalization. Since 1990 the phenomenal spread of political reforms aimed to lower barriers to trade and investment, and the accelerated pace of technological change, have infused global commerce with unprecedented energy. Illicit trade received the same boost for the same simple reasons. And so in the first decade of the twenty-first century, illicit trade has reached a point it had never reached before—in terms of geography, profits, and the share of the world's population that it touches. The stories in the preceding chapters abound in examples.

But scratch beneath the surface and consider exactly *how* all these changes have affected illicit traders in particular, and the conditions for their economic success. As the costs of doing business have gone down, so has the cost of all the transactions along the complicated chain that links suppliers to final consumers of the product, be it heroin or ammunition or counterfeit DVDs or illegal domestic labor. And that has permitted the supply chain to extend well past the point that was once its viable limit. Today, labyrinthine routings of contraband across multiple continents are commonplace and easy to execute. Front companies are easy to set up, so it is not a big hassle to set up a dozen fake fronts or more in order to blur one's trace. As a result, intermediaries in the international commerce of illicit products, services, and humans have increased their profile and their profits. It is brokers, for example, who control today's illicit arms market, and brokers who set up the deals and make the big money from illicit kidney transplants. That preeminence extends across all the illicit trades.

Still infused with images of cartels and syndicates—rigid, top-down organizations—we are not accustomed to thinking of flexible, even unchartable networks of intermediaries that operate across many borders and provide different services. Some are permanently linked and others vary in their composition, activities, and geographical scope depending on markets and circumstances. Thus, brokers and agents with access to multiple suppliers, conveyors, and buyers are more significant in the drug trade than are old-fashioned "kingpins." For all of these brokers, expanding into new product lines, legal or illegal, is just a logical business step.

The result takes the form of illicit trade value chains that mock conventional wisdom. Yes, at first sight Chinese producers of fake luxury watches have little in common with the sub-Saharan African gangs that transport desperate emigrants from villages deep inside Niger or Mali into Italy or Spain. But a closer look reveals a global value chain that employs illegal African immigrants in European capitals as street vendors of counterfeit watches. When Nepalese drug smugglers operate in Thailand on behalf of Nigerian criminal groups that refine the product in Lagos before exporting it to the United States in the luggage of European women through Brussels or Frankfurt, it is fairly certain that some of the parties in the sequence are dealing in other goods, too—perhaps exotic animal skins from Southeast Asia, or bootleg CDs or child labor. And no one should be surprised if they are carrying on perfectly legal and above-board import-export transactions as well. Business is business.

This makes it hard to pin down where the front lines of the "war on drugs" or any other offensive against illicit trade lie. Is the war on drugs to be fought in Colombia or Miami? Myanmar or Milan? Where are the battles against money launderers being fought? In Nauru or in London? Is China the main theater in the war against the infringement of intellectual property, or are the trenches of that war on the Internet? These questions are harder and harder to answer because they make less and less sense to ask.

GOVERNMENTS ARE FAILING

In the fight against global illicit trade, *governments are failing*. So are businesses and civic groups. Despite all our efforts, we are losing this battle.

This failure emerges from the panorama of the previous chapters, not as a subtle hint but as an indisputable conclusion. There is no evidence that a sustained, irreversible governmental victory over any of these illicit trades has taken place. It does not even seem reasonable to expect that in the foreseeable future a major event or new technology will turn the tide against global trafficking. There is simply nothing in the cards that points to an imminent reversal of fortune for the myriad networks active in illicit trade. It is even difficult to find evidence of substantial progress in reversing or even just containing the growth of these illegal markets.

Of course, the fight has its high moments. Every single day we learn that a government somewhere was able to detect a shipment, freeze a trafficker's bank account, dismember a global criminal network, or board a vessel laden with prohibited cargo. Unfortunately, too often these dispatches relate isolated events and do not reflect a trend. In fact, even the specific successes can quickly fade away until the point where they could just as well not have happened. Consider the following report from Thailand in *Jane's Intelligence Review*:

> At a heavy cost in human life and government expenditure Thailand's
> highly publicized 2003 "war on drugs" severely disrupted trafficking
> and distribution networks in the Kingdom. . . . One year later however
> it is apparent that new networks are developing and that the flow of
> both amphetamine-type stimulants and heroine into the Kingdom is
> again on the rise. . . . Thailand has no decisive victory to celebrate.

After an offensive, a reversal. Variations on this theme recur around the world and across the illegal markets. The death of Pablo Escobar in Colombia did nothing to stem the production and export of drugs. In Mexico the spectacular arrests of leaders of the Arellano Felix organization and of the Gulf Cartel in 2002–3 have not led to a reduction in trafficking, but simply to a readjustment: new players have sprouted up, new alliances have formed, and the arrested leaders, once bitter rivals, were revealed in early 2005 to have forged an alliance in prison. "The good news is that the government of Mexico has arrested more kingpins and dismantled more cartels," a Mexican crime expert told the *New York Times*. "The bad news is that it means nothing."

Money laundering provides another example on a broad scale. It is the facet of illicit trade where joint efforts by governments have been the most intense, and the results have garnered the most praise. Yet even here the results are far from promising. The international economist Ted Truman and the expert on the economics of crime Peter Reuter undertook an exhaustive, three-year study on the effectiveness of anti–money laundering efforts in the wake of September 11, 2001. They found little to cheer:

> Critics argue that the [global anti–money laundering] regime has done little more than force money launderers to change their methods. Felons' lives are a bit more difficult and a few are caught, but there is little change in the extent or character of either laundering or crime. Critics may well be right.

Common sense and daily observation already suggest that the fight against illicit trade is not going well. We know that the price of drugs is going down while addiction is on the rise, from prescription drugs in U.S. high schools to methamphetamine in American small towns and throughout Europe, to heroin along the trade routes of China and Central Asia. We also know that procuring weapons does not seem to be too difficult for those determined to have them. Enough civil wars and regional conflicts are under way at any given time to make this clear. It turns out that the research supports this commonsense observation. No country can claim that it has significantly decreased the flow of illegal immigrants. Despite all the rhetoric and colossal resources devoted to stemming the tide, governments are universally losing the battle against traffickers.

THE LATEST, GREATEST EPISODE

The war against traffickers pits the force of governments against the force of the market. History and common sense say that, in the long run, market forces tend to prevail over those of governments. In this sense, modern trafficking has much in common with the age-old smuggling that appeared as soon as governments first imposed barriers to trade. The valued commodities and methods of the trade may have changed. But the economic incentives are ancient. Salt, for instance, was for centuries an important and universal repository of value. In the third century B.C., the Chinese imposed on it the world's first-ever commodity trade monopoly. The Romans allowed it to be privately traded, but at mandatory prices set by the imperial government. Ancient texts tell stories of the harsh punishment meted on those who broke these laws. They show that the economic incentives to breaking the laws were compelling, and that not even harsh punishments were enough to stop many from trying—as is the case today.

The story continues: In the sixteenth century, French smugglers profited from differences in salt taxes, which were high in some parts of the country but in others barely existed. Women crossed the Loire River carrying bags of salt hidden in their underwear and in false buttock compartments. In the nineteenth century, contraband salt was rife in British India and imperial China. Only about a hundred years ago did salt smuggling lose its appeal, as the relative value of the commodity faded compared with newer, more profitable goods. From this historical perspective not much has changed—except the size of the markets, the diversity of the products in global demand, and the almost unfathomable scale of the profits involved.

Today, conditions for trafficking are the best they have ever been. Now able to gauge demand and assess opportunities on a global scale, traffickers can make the most of exploiting price differences between countries or the cost advantages produced by theft. A Chinese cook working at a Manhattan restaurant makes in a month or two what he would make in more than a year of similar work in China. A gram of cocaine in Kansas City is thirty times more expensive than in Bogotá, and flooring wood is two hundred times more expensive in London than in Papua. Fake Italian valves are 40 percent cheaper because counterfeiters don't have to cover the costs of developing the product. Copies of miracle drugs launched in the United States or Europe can be purchased a few weeks later in China at a tenth of their price. A well-funded guerrilla group will pay anything to get the weapons it needs—especially if it is well funded by the proceeds of other banned trades.

In every instance, the incentives to trounce government-imposed limits to trade are simply enormous. As a result of their new global scope and the political influence their money buys, the smugglers have accumulated immense power. They are no longer dependent on one or few suppliers but can procure what they need on a global basis, shopping for price, availability, logistics, and other risk and profit factors. Likewise, their clients are no longer a few "regulars" in traditional markets; they can now venture as far as their supply chain and initiative take them. A typical result is that they no longer must sell their goods at home or in nearby countries but can now supply clients in other continents. Just a few years ago it would have been outlandish to expect to find Nigerian traffickers operating in Thailand or Colombian women shipped to Japan for prostitution.

THE NETWORK TRANSFORMATION

None of these advantages would be enough to propel traffickers as far ahead of governments as they are today were it not for the organizational adaptation that distinguishes today's traffickers—and that governments are inherently blocked from adopting themselves. Today's illicit trade is carried out by networks. Preceding chapters have frequently alluded to these networks and shown examples of their functioning and successes. But to understand just how essential an asset the network structure has been for illicit trade, it helps to examine briefly the nature of networks and how traffickers have put them to use.

So just what is a network, anyway? The consensus definition is minimal: a network is a system of nodes connected by ties. Those nodes could be anything: people, companies, objects. And their relationship could be acquaintance, transactions, radio signals, or anything else. Some networks are inanimate; others highly deliberate, as the use of the word as a verb—*to network*—indicates.

Consider now human networks. Some are bound by ties that are not particularly deliberate: a neighborhood could be considered a network, but a block association gathering many of the same people suggests a much stronger tie. Members of the block association are bound by shared interests and by common goals that advance or protect these interests. A group of "friends of friends" is a network, but an online service that permits them to meet and communicate displays a potentially much more robust type of tie. There is no universal qualification that draws a clear line between networks and non-networks. And if you seek out networks in social organizations, chances are you will find them everywhere.

What is possible, however, is to compare networks by the structure they take, the functions they serve, and the way their members construct their ties. Networks come in three canonical types. One is the single-strand network: a simple chain, in which each node has one connection in either direction, like a string of Christmas lights or the players in a game of telephone. The second is a hub with spokes, familiar from airline route maps. Third is the multistranded network in which all the participants are linked to one another. Think of people with an ethnic or national tie—for example, all the Colombians in Queens, or the Senegalese in Paris—who enjoy a connection to one another, exclusive to the group and universal within it.

A second distinction among networks is the function they serve, and the extent to which they are put to use. That shared origin among immigrants might support community banking, newspapers, or matrimonial agencies, but political conflict back home could just as easily tear those ties apart. The directors of a company form an official network that meets regularly according to a schedule, but the company's softball team or happy-hour regulars might form a looser but more resilient (some might say more useful) network. Networks may have layers of purposes or no specific purpose at all.

And the tie that binds members might be as instinctive as mutual recognition, or as self-conscious and selective as a shared political goal or a shared religion.

Which suggests a third distinction among networks: do their members construct them through their actions, or are they assigned to them by birth or upbringing? Some networks are embedded: they gather individuals who have in common an identity characteristic such as ethnicity, religion, nationality, or caste. Other networks are entirely constructed: McDonald's franchisees, Greenpeace activists, soccer referees. The lines aren't always clear. The network of Yale graduates, for instance, is in part constructed (attending Yale was a choice) but in part embedded as well, since a graduate is a member whether he or she wishes to be or not.

Every network has its own mix of attributes. Nevertheless, identifying where it fits into the known ranges—of simple and complex structures, latent or active functions, embedded or constructed identities—is key to understanding what makes the network tick; how its members join or drop; what makes it sustainable over time; and what weaknesses might cause it to malfunction.

What does all this tell us about illicit trade? Illicit trade networks are quite deliberate, because they have a clear goal—profit by breaking laws—and when deliberate networks take form and function, it is because they help solve a problem. To be successful, illicit trade networks must be a) lucrative, and b) secure. But those prerequisites do not by themselves dictate the structure of a successful trafficking network. Ethnic groups, for instance, have always been conduits of trade. But an ethnic connection is neither necessary nor sufficient to produce a successful trading operation.

Since the 1990s, however, illicit trade networks have taken on a distinctive form. This winning structure marks a huge departure from the model of organized crime cartels or from even earlier models. Today trafficking networks are highly decentralized, even atomized. Their cells—or participants—tend to be autonomous and self-sustaining. Participants transact across borders in chains that can be long and complex yet highly adaptive and effective. Interactions are as likely to be transient as they are to be permanent. A deal is as likely to be one-off as it is to be part of a pattern.

As the previous chapters showed, every major illicit trading organization has experienced a network transformation of this sort since the 1990s, transforming its own business and linking it with others. Networking has permitted, for instance

- **THE RISE OF GLOBAL PRODUCT SOURCING, FORMULATION, OR ASSEMBLY.** Today, Mexican plants that compound and assemble counterfeit medicine with chemicals from India and packaging from China play a crucial role in illicit trade. So do heroin labs in Nigeria that process opium from Afghanistan or Myanmar that has transited through Pakistan, Uzbekistan, Thailand, or China; or the plant in Malaysia that assembled centrifuges for Libya with Pakistani blueprints under Sri Lankan supervision and funding from banks in Dubai.

- **A SHIFT IN THE ROLE OF WAY STATIONS ALONG TRAFFICKING ROUTES.** Once merely "safe houses" where smugglers could bivouac, they can now be virtual warehouses in which to stock goods until conditions are right. Houses in Bolivia, Mexico, Spain, and Hungary have become holding pens for dozens of smuggled migrants from China or Afghanistan, or sex slaves from Moldova and Ukraine. Warehouses make possible as well a wholesale business where buyers and sellers meet on neutral, inconspicuous ground—or, thanks to the Internet, never meet at all.

- **THE EMERGENCE OF A WELL-FUNCTIONING, ILLICIT INTERNATIONAL FINANCIAL MARKET.** Long gone are the days when narco-traffickers struggled to transport and use their mountains of cash. The piles of cash are still collected and big profits abound, but now their owners have many more tools and arrangements to transport and use their ill-gotten gains. From hawalas to sophisticated financial networks that tie offshore banks with money-center ones, illicit entrepreneurs now have many more options. Also, the financing of large, risky transactions no longer need come from a small group of associates. Large deals can be broken down into different parts with different networks financing each part, sometimes without even knowing who else is involved. Techniques such as project financing and loan syndication are no longer the exclusive preserve of reputable corporations.

- **THE END OF COMMAND-AND-CONTROL.** If trafficking operations relied on instructions relayed from a headquarters, they might be easier to trace. But they don't. The cartel model no longer applies. Instead, trafficking networks are decentralized and appear to possess multiple leaders or no leader at all, so that "no precise heart or head can be targeted." Networks are about multiplying options; and the operating autonomy that each cell possesses makes it easy for it to blend into its local environment.

A MARKET IS BORN

For illicit traders today the decentralization that networks allow improves on all prior arrangements for at least four reasons.

First, it reflects advances in technology. Illicit traders tend to be early adopters and have made good use of the dispersal of operations that today's information and communication tools permit.

Second, decentralization lowers the cost of illicit trade operations because it lowers the risks, especially the risk of discovery. By dispersing their operations across borders, traffickers slow down the opposition and reduce the chance that one arrest in the chain will shut down the trade. Multistranded networks can cope with an arrest or a raid, because alternative channels are always available.

Third, since decentralization and dispersal are no longer costly, traders can use them to wrest market control, and the biggest profits, from the supply and demand ends. Low contract and inventory commitments and the ready ability of financing—be it a letter of credit from a cooperative banker or a wire transfer through myriad agents—make it possible to structure a "soup to nuts" deal in record time. The more flexible the network structure and the more options available to a trader at any given time, the faster it is to forge a transaction. As in any business, the successful traders are the ones who have options.

Finally, the more options a trader has, the less bound he is to a particular product. Thus the proliferation of multiproduct transactions such as drugs for weapons, or drugs plus counterfeits for cash. It follows as well that each transaction is potentially a one-off deal that the parties need not repeat to sustain their revenue. Just because a suspect is involved in a DVD scam does not make him a DVD specialist: his next transaction might involve entirely different goods.

Today's illicit trade hasn't gotten rid of all product specialists. But players in the network who are most closely bound to a particular product are almost all concentrated in supply or distribution. The flexibility and the real power now lie in between. Look carefully, and all of the stock characters and notorious individuals associated with a particular trade have long since widened their scope beyond it. They range from Victor Bout, who has augmented his arms brokerage with "conflict diamonds," frozen fish, cut flowers, and even transportation services for the U.S. authorities in Iraq, to groups in Tirana, Casablanca, or Tijuana who will smuggle anything and anyone across the border to Italy, Spain, or the United States if the price is right.

Illicit trade is no longer a collection of arcane and dangerous specialities. Instead, it's something much closer to a full-fledged exchange in which legal, illegal, and gray-area goods can be endlessly substituted and combined, and agents (traders, service providers, financiers) are at once more autonomous and better connected—a marketplace that keeps growing more efficient. It is not a pure market, of course. Because illicit trade by definition cannot take place in the open, perfect information—one of the features of an economist's ideal market—is out of the question. And so, because cocaine, weapons, bootleg videos, and sex slaves aren't traded on commodity exchanges, with price tickers beamed to computer terminals worldwide, the market for these items is patchy and affected by local conditions, not just global supply and demand.

But a flexible network structure does a good job smoothing over this patchiness. Using the full gamut of twenty-first-century technology, a dispersed network can match participants with opportunities quite effectively. At the same time, it limits risk by insulating parties from one another: no one need know the identity of network members more than a link or two away. It offers alternative routings for each transaction and reduces the risk that a deal gone sour will pollute other ones under way.

Organizational structure doesn't account for everything, of course. The transformation of illicit trade reflects the creativity of "business leaders" as well, innovators responding to the limitations of the earlier model. But for all the innovators' acumen, the shift owes as much to freelancers, mom-and-pop types, and quasi-accidental new entrants like Don Alfonzo, the Mexican businessman we met in Chapter 4—all of whom have taken advantage of lower barriers to entry. It owes as well to the brokers and intermediaries—from bankers to transporters to complicit officials—who've mastered the art of blending illicit and licit transactions in inconspicuous ways. Together these pioneers have created a business environment in which fewer of the decisive signals come from themselves and many more come from the market. And that may prove to be the distinctive strength of illicit trade in the twenty-first century: the more it takes on the characteristics of a global market, the greater the likelihood that it will keep on ticking on its own.

AN UNFAIR FIGHT?

Now compare these traits with those of governments. The key reason that governments are losing the battle against global criminal networks is not some perverse characteristic of globalization. Rather, it is because they are governments and the networks are, well, networks. Far from wordplay, this is a fundamental reality that defines the asymmetry between the two clashing organizations. Regardless of their money and technology, the heroic idealism and commitment of their agents, or the creativity and boldness of their tactics, the fact remains that the government agencies in charge of fighting international criminal networks are bureaucracies. And public bureaucracies everywhere tend to exhibit certain predictable patterns.

STRUCTURE. Bureaucracies have a propensity to organize according to hierarchies in which authority and information flow vertically from the top and back, rather than across units. Thus coordination and collaboration among units that are not part of the same vertical line of command are always a struggle and seldom emerge naturally. The *9/11 Report,* containing the findings of the commission that investigated how terrorists could strike so effectively against the United States, abounds in examples of the lack of "interagency coordination" creating opportunities for al-Qaeda. The same is true for illicit trade. In all the interviews I conducted for this book, the difficulty of synchronizing the activities of hundreds of different agencies involved in the fight against illicit trade was unanimously singled out as a fundamental obstacle to progress. In fact many of the experts and practitioners I interviewed called the task virtually impossible.

BUDGET. Government bureaucracies also tend to be budget-oriented. This means that for public sector agencies, maximizing the budget received from the national coffers takes precedence in the minds and for the time of their leaders over any other priorities. Of course, for the leaders of the government agencies fighting the criminals, responding rapidly to the threats, opportunities, and other signals they receive from their external environment may be a priority. Many officials are highly driven by their mission. But paying attention to the external environment may be futile if they first do not secure an adequate chunk of the public budget. Fighting the networks is an expensive undertaking, and without adequate public budgets, it is a pointless one.

POLITICAL AND LEGAL LIMITS. Governments are political entities. And not even the most politically insulated government bureaucracies are immune to the distortions of politicization and patronage in their decisions about staffing or the procurement and allocation of scarce resources. Government agencies are also limited by law in what they can do. They are allowed to operate only within the confines of their charter—which usually tends to be updated more slowly than the changes in their environment.

BORDERS. Finally, all government bureaucracies have a hard time working effectively outside their country, assuming they have the opportunity to do so thanks to a partnership or diplomatic agreement. Their natural habitat is at home, not abroad. A government agency needs as much training and specialized equipment to operate in another national jurisdiction as a diver needs to operate underwater. Public bureaucracies of one country usually do not do well operating outside the legal and political environment of their own country.

This description of government agencies is admittedly a stylized one, but it is essentially valid. Compared with the equally stylized description of global illicit trade networks, the differences are striking. The networks draw their resources from their customers, not from the public budget. Concrete outputs and successful results are the only drivers of revenues: no deliveries means no revenues. Missing or misreading a market signal or a clue from the operating environment may be catastrophic. Profits and personal survival drive the staff's motivation. They are as comfortable at home as they are "abroad"—a concept that has less and less meaning to them. Whereas government agencies can only do what the law explicitly permits, those outside government can do all they want, except what is explicitly prohibited by law. Criminal networks do both: that which is not explicitly banned, and activities that are explicitly prohibited as well.

Thus, whereas governments are rather rigid, vertically organized bureaucracies with limited range of motion, the networks behave like mercury. Once one tries to grab it, it slips through one's fingers, forming many smaller droplets. The difference is that successful networks do not stay small for long; and their newfound global mobility has endowed them with a propensity to grow very fast.

THE TROUBLE WITH SUPPLY-SIDE

The quantum leap in the economic power and mobility of the networks has confounded governments. Their efforts to curb illicit trade are hampered by bureaucratic entanglements, national boundaries, legal jurisdictions, conflicting diplomatic goals, and sensitive political concerns. Not that governments are idle. Governments do try to curb or constrain end-user demand for illicitly traded products. They lock up drug users and distributors, "name and shame" prostitutes' clients, harass college students who download unlicensed copies of movies and songs, fine banks that fail to "know their customer," and penalize employers of illegal immigrants.

Governments also work hard at reducing the supply of the illicit goods. For this they rely on border interdictions of illegal aliens, weapons, counterfeits, and drugs, on spraying coca and poppy fields with herbicides, shutting down rogue laboratories for pharmaceutical compounds and the precursor chemicals used for transforming leaves into narcotics, tightly controlling arms manufacturers, and forcing other governments to close down factories that make pirated products.

Well and good, in theory—except that the networks have shown enormous speed and flexibility in factoring these changes into their comparisons of each market's supply and demand, and adapt their operations, staffing, procurement, pricing, and distribution strategies to changes in their threat environment, as any prudent business would. They certainly do not lack the resources or motives to pursue their trades regardless. Often government interference is nothing more than another cost of doing business, and as often it just serves as a price-boosting intervention.

Yet one crucial pattern that emerges from the global illicit trades is that in all cases—and despite their rhetoric to the contrary—the preferred strategy used by governments everywhere is to attack the supply. Governments deploy most of their antitrafficking money, personnel, and technology in pursuing producers, transporters, and suppliers. The norm is that efforts at curbing the supply always exceed by a wide margin the efforts governments make to curb the demand. The U.S. government devotes far more resources on interdiction—for example, chasing the traffickers' speedboats and small airplanes in the Caribbean or spraying poppy fields—than on curbing the lucrative market that makes it worthwhile for traffickers to risk their lives to bring the drugs into the United States. The Brazilian teenager caught at Kennedy Airport with cocaine-filled condoms in her bowels faces a far more harrowing future in the hands of the U.S. legal system than the college student of the same age caught snorting coke at a frat party. Employers in Europe who create the huge demand for illegal African immigrants face a far less aggressive threat from their authorities than the aliens who risk their lives crossing the Mediterranean in rickety boats. The street peddler of the fake Cartier watch faces disproportionately larger risks and penalties than his strolling customers, who in fact run no risk at all. In most countries the police chase the women selling sex, not their clients.

Why this persistent preference for attacking the supply side? The reasons are manifold. For governments, protecting national borders from foreign intruders is a more automatic response than developing complex efforts to dissuade citizens from consuming the products or hiring the services. Blaming foreign criminals is politically profitable, but putting the onus on one's drug-consuming compatriots or the businesses and families that employ illegal aliens could amount to political suicide. Curbing demand requires complex and often untested changes in values, education, domestic institutions, and other "soft" social policies—for politicians, a risky terrain. Attacking supply means relying instead on the tried and true: the use of force, coercion, and law enforcement. Even the tools used to curb the supply are more telegenic: helicopters, gunboats, heavily armed agents, judges, and generals. The same world that we sometimes like to call a world without borders is one where we are still addicted to border control.

Most of all, the supply-side bias reflects a vision of the threat of illicit trade that still draws a clear line between good guys and bad guys, when the reality is far more ambiguous. It suggests that traffickers can be encircled and apprehended, when in fact not only do they blend into the landscape but their networks extend into mainstream life: banks that help move the money wittingly or not, legitimate businesses with trafficking sidelines that not everyone in the firm is aware of, the many government agents—and not just in poor countries—who choose the trafficker's bribe, and many more. Attacking supply tends to underestimate the prevalence, the persistence, and the influence of these trends. It also suggests that illicit trade can be confined geographically, when all the evidence shows that it is more mobile than it has ever been.

Our common assumptions simply do not match up with the way illicit trade networks have come to operate, and prosper. The question is whether, by taking the time to rethink the nature of the threat, we can find the ways to do better.

Chapter 12

WHAT TO DO?

It isn't hopeless.

The same convergence of new technologies and changing politics that empowered criminals and weakened governments in the 1990s reappeared in a new form after 2001—this time with the potential to change the trend in favor of governments.

It began when an unexpected event at the dawn of the new century set in motion a new refashioning of the global landscape in which transnational criminals operate. On September 11, 2001, complacency and general lack of awareness of the new capabilities of stateless criminal networks collapsed into the rubble of the World Trade Center's twin towers. Acquired in pain, the realization that these networks had hitherto unimagined destructive capabilities fueled a seemingly boundless appetite for new laws, institutions, and technologies—ones that could contain and ideally stamp out the new threat. Everywhere a new hunger grew for more effective methods to ensure public safety and protect borders from the entry of unwanted people and goods. The public demanded these measures, and the politicians obliged.

Suddenly borders were important again, even paramount, as bulwarks against infiltration. Public employees—firemen, police officers, custom officers, and soldiers—became the new heroes while international financiers and global traders lost some of the allure they enjoyed in the 1990s. Homeland security was the new priority, not international business. Fears of terrorist attacks employing smuggled materials, and of their use of the financial system to fund their misdeeds, gave new urgency to the fight against illicit trade. The exuberant claims common in the 1990s that the new interdependence would fuel global prosperity now gave way to an apprehensive mood about "the dangerous outside world." Cross-border movements of goods and people became inherently suspect. Governments weighed new laws, police methods, and procedures, innovative forensic techniques, and new forms of international collaboration. The public's resistance against government encroachments on privacy and civil liberties abated.

Within weeks after 9/11, heightened demand for security was generating its own supply, in many forms. By year's end, new anti-terrorism laws had been enacted in Britain, Canada, France, India, Japan, and the United States. Most governments created blue-ribbon commissions and task forces to study the new terrorist threat and recommend solutions. Many countries began to reorganize their security and intelligence agencies, and national budgets were expanded to make room for new spending. Consulting firms started new practices geared to the market for security. Universities established new institutes to study terrorism and homeland security. Training centers began offering courses in emergency preparedness, disaster relief, civil defense, border control, surveillance, encryption, how to do business in dangerous places, and how not to get kidnapped. Firms that sold screening machines, new-generation holograms, or electronic devices to authenticate people, goods, and documents saw their share prices soar. The outgoing mayor and police chief of New York retired and began selling their advice to cities around the world, raising the profile and reputation of a consulting trade long associated with recycled spooks and hardened Israelis.

The dragnet compelled a new attention to the different aspects of what had been called, more or less indistinctly, international or transnational crime. Terrorism took pride of place, of course. But the evidence pouring in—9/11, the October 2002 bombing of a Bali nightclub, the March 2004 strike on the Atocha train station in Madrid—made clear that terrorism was tied to illicit trade. The two phenomena functioned in much the same way, by means of highly effective, decentralized mobile networks. They enabled and fed on each other. Terrorist cells used illicit trade to support themselves, equip themselves, and move funds around. Unraveling terrorist finance often led directly into illicit trade.

In this changed atmosphere, the fight has intensified. Of course, dedicated investigators and advocates have been combating traffickers all along. But as we have seen time and time again, all their efforts in the 1990s were not enough to keep up with the explosive growth of illicit trade. Today, government officials, activists, technology developers, university researchers, and others have redoubled their efforts.

The question is how to make sure that all this new effort pays off.

There can be no doubt that succeeding in the fight against illicit trade requires substantially changing the way we carry it out. The approaches of the past have plainly failed. Yet it seems that we have been repeating them over and over, reinvesting in strategies that have borne little fruit while failing to acknowledge the persistent blind spots that have narrowed our thinking. Thus the first task is to decide to break this cycle and get rid of the collective learning disability that has blocked progress in the fight against global crime.

The second is to step back from the temptation of resorting to moral indignation as the basis for public policy. Of course most of what takes place under the umbrella of illicit trade violates not just laws but also widely held beliefs as to what is right and wrong. Yet over time we have allowed moral exhortations to substitute for honest analysis of the problem, and that is a dangerous tendency. It breeds complacency toward solutions that don't work and increases the risks and obstacles for politicians and citizens who seek to innovate.

But there is a way forward. If we learn from the mistakes of the past and step back from the temptation of moral pieties, we are in an excellent position to understand what we are up against and how to engage it. We can then make the most of new technologies and ideas and change our domestic and international strategies against illicit trade in ways that give us a fighting chance.

THE FOUNDATION: APPLY WHAT WE KNOW

Illicit trade need not be a mystery. We have all the information we need to update our understanding of how it works and why it has become so pervasive and powerful. Therefore, before thinking about new public policies, laws, institutions, or strategies, it is important to draw on the knowledge we have amassed. There are a few simple, yet often ignored, baseline realizations to keep in mind.

ILLICIT TRADE IS DRIVEN BY HIGH PROFITS, NOT LOW MORALS. It should be obvious. And yet the fundamental motivation of illicit trade seems all too often to be a blind spot in our thinking. We are quick to resort to moral language to condemn illicit trade. It is true that many of the characters involved in illicit trade are abominable criminals. But what drives them are profits and a set of values that is often impervious to moral denunciations. Illicit trafficking is an economic phenomenon, not a moral one. And the tools of economics do better at making sense of it than do the insights offered by the study of ethics and morals. Supply and demand, risk and return, are trafficking's primary motivators. Economic incentives explain how traffickers and their networks have continually adapted and refined their activities, even at the cost of temporary setbacks that would give most people pause, such as long jail sentences or the constant threat of death. Unless and until traffickers face diminished incentives to trade—less demand, lower margins, higher risks—it is more or less futile to talk about other remedies.

ILLICIT TRADE IS A POLITICAL PHENOMENON. Illicit traders cannot prosper without help from governments or accomplices in key public offices. Indeed, some governments have become traffickers themselves. We now have a mountain of evidence to show that trafficking is political. It infiltrates governments, and it can go so far as to control the government of an entire province or even take over a weak or failed state. Again, the enormous incentives associated with the profits involved in these trades drive this criminalization of politics and public service. Trafficking is political in another sense as well: public opinion and politicians define many of the expectations and constraints that shape antitrafficking efforts. These include the definition of what is criminal, the severity of penalties for different crimes, and the budgets allocated to fighting these crimes. Illicit trafficking may never be fully understood or effectively acted upon if we do not place the economics and politics that drive it at the center of the analysis and the recommendations.

ILLICIT TRADE IS MORE ABOUT TRANSACTIONS THAN PRODUCTS. We are accustomed to parsing the illicit trades into separate product lines. So much so that we usually task different government agencies or international organizations with fighting each distinct trade. But the trades are no longer distinct. Illicit traders move in and out of product lines as economic incentives dictate and practical considerations permit. Only at the highly localized, extreme ends of the chain is it common to find product specialists: the Bolivian coca farmer or the bootleg CD peddler in an Asian night market. But these are marginal characters. We need to shed once and for all the illusion that the different illicit trades can be kept separate and start thinking of illicit traders as economic agents who have developed functional specialties, not product niches. Instead of distinguishing between traffickers, smugglers, pirates, coyotes, snakeheads, mules, and smurfs, we would do better to think of illicit traders in the roles they truly perform: investors, bankers, entrepreneurs, brokers, transporters, warehousers, wholesalers, logistics managers, distributors, and more. When we consider illicit traders as profit-minded, opportunistic economic agents, it becomes clear that they should have no reason to stick to just one product.

ILLICIT TRADE CANNOT EXIST WITHOUT LICIT TRADE. All illicit businesses are deeply intertwined with licit ones. Indeed, traffickers have strong incentives to combine their illicit operations with legitimate business ventures. The extraordinary profits they accumulate, for example, exert a natural pressure to diversify. Often this means investing in activities that are legal and completely unrelated to the criminal side of the trafficking businesses. And whether complicit or innocent, the professions that get caught up in proving the tools for illicit trade to function so well are numerous and varied: banks, airlines, shipping companies, freight forwarders, truckers, courier companies, jewelers, art galleries, doctors, lawyers, pharmaceutical and chemical manufacturers, international money transmitting companies, and myriad others that provide the infrastructure that enables illicit trading to operate swiftly, efficiently, and stealthily.

ILLICIT TRADE INVOLVES EVERYONE. To think of a clean line between good guys and bad guys is to fail to capture the reality of trafficking today. The fact is that illicit trade permeates our daily lives in subtle ways. Some are intentional: the customs official, plant manager, or private banker who assists in some illicit trade activities yet draws the line at others, or financial advisors who stash funds beyond the reach of the Treasury at the cost of infringing a "minor" law or two. But others are widespread and casual: citizens who always pay their taxes and never run red lights, yet smoke an occasional—or not so occasional—joint, listen to music illegally downloaded from the Internet, purchase knockoff Louis Vuitton bags—all are among the faces of illicit trade today.

The point is not to compare ordinary shoppers to international criminals. Of course the ringleader of a band that traffics in women for sexual exploitation deserves the harshest possible punishment. But what about the men who purchase these services? Or the families that rely on illegal aliens for the domestic help that allows both parents to pursue a professional career? Are the crimes equivalent? Of course not. But we will never make progress if all our attention is placed on the suppliers of illicit goods and not the upright citizens whose appetite for them creates the incentives that make it all possible. In too many instances fighting the illicit trades is not a battle of "us"—honest citizens—against "them"—criminals, often foreign. In reality the differences between "us" and "them" are frequently blurred. Any solution needs to include the customers: "normal" members of their communities who have habits, needs, and behaviors that feed the demand that makes illicit traders immensely rich.

GOVERNMENTS CAN'T DO IT ALONE. Antitrafficking strategies based on government action alone are doomed to founder on government's inherent limitations—national frontiers and bureaucratic processes—that traffickers have so adeptly turned to their advantage. And if governments can't curb illicit trade within their own borders alone, it follows that they can't do it beyond their borders, either. Illicit trade is a bigger problem than any one country, police force, or military or spy agency can tackle alone. This holds true for powerful governments that have the capability to intervene outside their own borders as much as it does for less powerful and more resource-constrained nations. Unilateral action can produce occasional and spectacular short-term results, but it has yet to score a long-term victory in the fight against illicit trade.

But governments do have to be part of the answer. The biggest part, in fact. Battling illicit trade calls on lawmaking and law enforcement, pure prerogatives of government. It requires legal, police, and intelligence cooperation across borders. Without the legal authority and coercive power of governments, the fight is lost. That makes it all the more worrisome that illicit trade has managed to penetrate governments—and not just in poor and unstable societies—to the extent it has. And it makes it crucial that we find ways to equip government for the fight. This is not just a matter of reorganizing agencies or boosting budgets. More crucially, it is a matter of setting realistic goals and clear, reasonable public expectations.

With these basic points in mind, we can trace a path for success against global illicit trade. It involves six steps. They follow from one another, and they depend on one another for success. None is pie-in-the-sky. They involve extending and capitalizing on the most promising developments already under way. The hardest part is not devising the strategy but mobilizing the political will to make it happen. But if we stay true to what we have learned, we can do this too.

ENHANCE, DEVELOP, AND DEPLOY TECHNOLOGY

The extraordinary pace of technological development is beginning to yield tools with unprecedented potential to help fight illicit trade. In fact, we are using the tools of the new century to tame the effects of the tools of the 1990s.

Since the watershed date of 9/11, the direction of research and development has substantially changed. It is now a priority to break the link between trade expansion and increased vulnerability. Scientists and engineers have honed in on tools that counteract the anonymity-enhancing developments and border porosity of the recent past. Identification, surveillance, tracing and detection are the new watchwords of research and development. They are producing a tide of commercial innovations that will throw obstacles in the path of illicit traders. Many of these are already in circulation, spreading into our daily lives more or less unobtrusively. Here are some examples.

RFIDs. Perhaps the fastest-spreading new tools with anti-trafficking applications are radio frequency identification devices (RFIDs). This technique is poised to overtake the now familiar bar code as the best way to identify an item and confirm its authenticity, register its origin and date of manufacture, and record its price. An RFID conveys radio signals that a specialized reader can collect and confirm. Some RFIDs have their own power source; others respond to the signal that the reader sends to them. Applications already range from inventory management in supermarkets to authentication devices on packages and bottles of medication. Likewise RFIDs are a potential tool for passports and visas: the United States has begun to issue RFID tags to foreign visitors at several border crossings with a view to possibly generalizing the practice.

PACKAGE AND PRODUCT TAGS. A cornucopia of other innovative tags are becoming available to mark both packages and products. They include specialty inks and dyes, watermarks, holographs, wraps, and foils. Chemical and biological tags are minuscule enough to be applied to individual products no matter how small. Some can be engineered to synthesize or occur in the process of manufacture. These technologies will make it possible to identify and track products as well as their users.

BIOMETRICS. Also very quickly coming into practice is biometrics: the use of unique physical characteristics to identify a person. Voice recognition technology has come a long way beyond the crude and fallible methods used on dictation devices. But devices that recognize the iris of the eye or the shape of the hand or face are more reliable and secure, and will soon be familiar to anyone who travels internationally. The European Union is on a timetable to comprehensive adoption of biometric indicators on its passports, and the United States is making biometric recognition mandatory for foreigners entering the country. Biometrics has the potential to deeply disrupt the market for the millions of passports that are lost around the world each year.

DETECTION AND SECURITY DEVICES. Another set of tools travelers will soon know well are new detection devices that can identify suspect items or pick up traces of drugs and explosives far more reliably than the standard X-ray machines and metal detectors. They include backscatter portals—scanners that mercilessly contour the body to reveal any foreign items—and "puffers," which blow air on passengers and analyze the particles set loose—ideal for picking up traces of drugs or explosives. At container port and railway terminals, large-scale scanners are being deployed that use three different technologies: X-rays, gamma rays, and neutron activation.

SURVEILLANCE AND EAVESDROPPING. These days and especially in wealthier countries, traffic intersections, bank transactions, building lobbies, stores, parking garages, and even some streets are constantly monitored, videoed, and photographed. The combination of the Internet with digital cameras has made monitoring a very common and inexpensive activity—even at great distances or from high up in the sky. Satellites or submarines that can listen to conversations transmitted via phone cables on the ocean floor are more versatile and reliable than ever. New scanning devices can home in on conversations and decipher certain people, specific locations, or patterns of words. A highly classified project called Echelon consists of a worldwide eavesdropping capability that in theory enables its users to listen to any conversation—anywhere.

SOFTWARE. Powerful computer models and data-mining tools are taking detection to an extraordinary new level. Banks, for example, are spending considerable sums to implement AML, or anti–money laundering, software in order to conform to the requirement that they "know their customer." Behavior detection applications can monitor the hundreds of millions of transactions that a large global bank processes and immediately spot events that fall into suspicious patterns. Government crime fighters are turning to similar software for "social mapping"—logging huge numbers of transactions and interactions to establish the structure and behavior of networks.

TRACKING HUMANS. A set of tools with rich commercial prospects are those that track human beings, in particular using global positioning satellite (GPS) location-tracking technology. Cell phones loaded with GPS software are becoming popular among parents of teenagers in various countries, to help them make sure that the kids are going where they say they are—or simply that they are safe. As the kidnapping business expands in numerous countries, such tools take on a very powerful value. In one instance that feels extreme for now but may seem less so in years to come, some wealthy businessmen in Sao Paulo, Brazil, have begun wearing microchips implanted under their skin to help locate them in the event of abduction.

BIOTECHNOLOGY. The revolution in biotechnology will do more than just help with DNA-matching identification methods. A U.K. biotechnology company called Xenova, for example, has tested an anticocaine vaccine that helped 58 percent of the users tested to shed their habit. Biotechnology combined with microelectronic and nanotechnologies is expected to spawn a powerful arsenal for governments intent on curtailing illicit trades.

But the list of privacy-invading technologies is also offensive and threatening to anyone who considers governmental intrusion in our individual life unacceptable and even dangerous. Governments armed with detailed information about the private lives of their citizens—their jobs, possessions, income, family, and even personal habits—have been prone to misuse it. Justified fears of incompetence and abuse make the public balk at the idea of granting those in power access to their personal information. And history is full of tragic instances when governments have harmed innocents based on incorrect data or used their privileged access to intimidate or repress political opponents. Times when lists of citizens have been employed for the political persecution of entire social groups, even genocide, of course loom large in any debate about how much governments may snoop into people's lives. That is why many constitutions enshrine the individual right to privacy. In the United States, famously, the Fourth Amendment to the Constitution sets out that "The right of the people to be secure in their persons, houses, papers, and effects, against unreasonable searches and seizures, shall not be violated."

But just what is "reasonable"? As we saw after 9/11, the public is capable of major shifts in attitude toward privacy. Different countries will reach different results when attempting to balance public safety and personal privacy, homeland security, and civil liberties. And some societies, particularly the United States, exhibit a perplexing tolerance for private companies to "mine" personal data. Citizens often willingly share confidential information with the anonymous employees of private corporations, yet furiously resist government access to even a fraction of the same information.

The inevitable reality is that the technologies that enable those in power to be more intrusive in our lives are here. How widely they are adopted will depend on how good governments are at using them and how effectively they help fight criminals and terrorists. After all, successful technology development does not guarantee successful, widespread international implementation. Research doesn't come cheap. Rich countries have a natural edge, and they will be leery of sharing the resulting tools with governments they do not trust. At the same time, nothing guarantees that wealthy countries will always invest wisely. As we know from so many other areas of human activity, technology may be a necessary condition for progress, but it is never sufficient. Indeed, believing that technology alone can save the day in the fight against illicit trade can be a fatal mistake.

DEFRAGMENT GOVERNMENT

It is easy to expect too much from technology and fall into a technocratic fantasy in which problems that have deep socioeconomic and political roots are solved by throwing new technologies at them. Technology alone never works if the people and organizations that have them don't use them well. If governments don't change their ways, the new technologies amount to waste that creates the illusion of progress when in fact it opens up huge new vulnerabilities.

Take for example the project that the FBI code-named Trilogy and that critics came to call "Tragedy." In March 2005 the bureau found itself forced to write off $170 million that it had invested in a case management database system that didn't work. It was an appalling waste not only of resources, but also of precious time. More than three years after 9/11, FBI agents were still without a tool crucial to their daily work. "I am frustrated," the FBI director Robert Mueller said when he announced the failure of the project. "I am frustrated that we do not have on every agent's desk the capability of a modern case management system." The reasons for the failure were very illustrative. The project was plagued by "escalating costs, imprecise planning, mismanagement, implementation problems, and delays," said one U.S. senator familiar with the situation. The contract for the "virtual case file" system had been changed thirty-six times.

Similar stories are common at the Department of Homeland

Security, which the *Washington Post* described in 2005 as remaining "hampered by personality conflicts, bureaucratic bottlenecks and an atmosphere of demoralization, undermining its ability to protect the nation against terrorist attack, according to current and former administration officials and independent experts." Its Immigration and Customs Enforcement (ICE) branch suffered so severe a financial crisis for more than a year, the article said, that the use of agency vehicles and even photocopying were at times banned—this at the government agency charged with confronting some of the wealthiest criminals of all time. Ironically, ICE was at the same time part of the domestic security agency with the world's largest budget. Similar stories of waste inefficiency and misguided efforts also hampered the agencies in charge of increasing the security of ports and airports in the United States.

These problems are not exclusive to the United States, of course. They plague all governments; in fact, it can be argued that the U.S. public sector is more competent and better endowed with resources, talent, and flexibility than most others. Nowhere do technologies solve interagency turf battles or even simple differences in bureaucratic outlook. Every agency has its own culture and procedures. Customs, border patrol, immigration, police, military, coast guard, financial investigators, diplomats, and spies bring different backgrounds, training, and priorities, even to fundamental shared goals. Those differences can all too easily result in tunnel vision. Even the most capable governments are hard put to make sure that one hand does not undo the other hand's work. The top crime fighters that I interviewed around the world shared a deep frustration with the seemingly congenital fragmentation of the government response to illicit trade.

So what to do? Unfortunately, the solution must involve a unified government organization—one with the scope, authority, and skills to counter the entire spectrum of illicit trade activities. This is unfortunate because smaller agencies tend to be more efficient. Yet just as illicit traders no longer distinguish between the products they move, separate government agencies for separate trades have become hindrances in the fight against trafficking. Their bureaucratic boundaries play into the traffickers' hands. So does the way these agencies typically compartmentalize disciplines. Often, police who raid warehouses and financial analysts who trace suspect bank transactions barely communicate. Complicated information-sharing procedures give traffickers a precious time advantage. In a world of decentralized, adaptable criminal networks, the time available between analysis (figuring out what is going on) and operations (stopping it) is dwindling quickly. Assigning these tasks to separate agencies is a debilitating but common practice. So is allowing them to drift apart within the same agency.

Bringing together cops, lawyers, accountants, economists, computer scientists, and even social scientists into tightly integrated, highly functional teams with operational latitude is a challenge, yes. But it is not insurmountable. Task forces drawn from different agencies—even across borders—have succeeded in dismantling trafficking operations and putting away major players in the trade. The problem is that task forces eventually dissolve, each member returning to his or her original agency, while traffickers regroup and adapt. Sustaining a "task force mentality" across multiple agencies into the indefinite future collides with everything we know about how public administrations prefer to operate. But the fight against illicit trade is too important and the opponent too potent to leave to separate agencies.

Hence an integrated view of illicit trade dictates an integrated approach to fighting it. And there is no substitute for an integrated agency with full responsibility for this task. Which raises, of course, the problem of how to make this agency work. This is what defragmenting government means: bring together scattered efforts in order to be more effective. But just as an overreliance on technology can create the illusion of a solution, integrating government efforts by just moving organizational "boxes" around and placing them under the authority of a "czar" can be an equally dangerous illusion. In the United States, the Department of Homeland Security created an illusion of unity when, in reality, rearranging the same bungling, uncoordinated agencies became a source of waste and perhaps even of heightened vulnerability. When muddled ideas are combined with huge amounts of money, petty bureaucratic politics, and an urgent, massive task, inefficiency and ineffectiveness are guaranteed.

Defragmenting government entails bringing together agencies to produce better-coordinated efforts. But this can work only if there are clear plans, multiyear budgets that extend the time horizon beyond just the most immediate emergencies, and solid, competent leadership.

But there is more. No government can be effective if its goals are unrealistic. There are no organizational solutions to the problem of bureaucracies charged with tasks that are constantly growing and increasingly unreachable. Unless the tasks of government are simplified and priorities for action are chosen more selectively, the idea that the problem can be solved by reorganization alone will continue to be an illusion.

GIVE GOVERNMENTS GOALS THEY CAN ACHIEVE

Regardless of organization or budget, no government agency anywhere can fight the law of gravity. Yet this is the mandate we give agencies in charge of curbing illicit trade. Stand between millions of customers desperate to buy and millions of merchants desperate to sell, and stop them—this is what we are asking governments to do. In most countries the results are not that different from the ones you would get trying to stop a boulder rolling down a steep mountain: the government is crushed. More concretely, it is either corrupted by the traffickers or left to believe that the daily successes it scores against them are a sign that victory is at hand. Or can be at hand—if only more resources, more technology, or more power were made available to the gravity fighters.

Unfortunately, most societies, governments, or agencies seem unwilling to acknowledge and act upon the fact that both suppliers and their clients are increasing, that the volumes of the trade are booming, and that new illicit trades are constantly appearing. Much less are they ready to accept that a different approach may be necessary. Yet any honest assessment will show that this reality is as undeniable as the law of gravity. Another approach is indeed desperately needed.

And it starts with the recognition that some of these illicit trades need to become licit. Does this mean the decriminalization of the traffic in sex slaves, nuclear material, or heroin? Of course not. But it does mean that the resources now wasted enforcing the prohibition of marijuana, all counterfeits, or temporary illegal workers should be deployed in the fight against the more dangerous illicit trades. Despite its prohibition, marijuana is readily available, as are all kinds of counterfeits. And when was the last time anyone you know had trouble finding and hiring an illegal worker? Decisions to decriminalize are difficult, controversial, imperfect, and not without risk. But so is continuing with the pretense that the current approach is taking us to a superior social situation. It is not.

Decriminalizing some of these trades is a pragmatic necessity. And it means coming to terms with a simple reality. In the era of globalization, it is simply impossible to make all borders safe against everything at all times. Even the iron curtain was permeable. With today's volumes of travel and trade, communication tools and use of cyberspace, there is no impregnable barrier. We must make choices—between the activities we focus our resources on repressing and those for which a different approach is more suitable.

Fortunately we have tools to help us make intelligent choices. A rich stream of research by economists, sociologists, public health specialists, and others helps us to understand the economic incentives to illicit trade and measure its economic and social costs as well as those of proposed alternatives. Two principles are vital to these decisions and are best applied together. The first is *value reduction*. As with any other economic activity, illicit trade grows the more value its participants derive from it. Drive out the value from an economic activity, and its prevalence will diminish accordingly.

This basic tenet of market-based reform is as valid for illicit trade as for anything else.

The second principle is *harm reduction*. Simply put, this means measuring the social harm that an illicit trade activity causes and comparing ways to fight it by the extent that they lower this harm. Researchers have honed tools to make these estimates. They underlie, for instance, the choice that many countries have made to invest in treatment over incarceration or in needle exchanges and HIV/AIDS education for addicts. Thinking of illicit trade in terms of harm is a productive alternative to the discourse of moral reprobation. And it is not as big a jump as one might think. For it turns out that the activities that most people would find highly immoral are also among the most costly in their social impact.

There is a third, more pragmatic consideration. To ignore it would be unrealistic. It is the budgetary constraint under which governments operate. To conduct a wholesale repressive strategy against every aspect of illicit trade is impossible even for the wealthiest nations. For poorer countries with such other urgent concerns as unsafe water, illiteracy, and child mortality, it is a pipe dream. Focusing the combat against illicit trade is essential if developing countries are to have a chance. And because traffickers know no borders, success in poor countries is essential to success in rich countries and vice versa.

In practice, what does this mean? Deregulation, decriminalization, and legalization have to be policy options, subject to the test that they reduce the value to traffickers *and* the harm to society. It also means that policies that have proven *not* to have this effect should be open to reevaluation. For every measure to combat illicit trade on the table, we should ask the following: Will it make trafficking less lucrative and desirable? Will it redirect traffickers from more harmful to less harmful activities? Will it lower the incentives that lead so many government officials, corporate executives, bankers, and consumers to play their part, big or small, in illicit trade? Of course, not all these questions can be answered in advance. Still, economic value and social cost should be at the heart of our response to illicit trade, rather than brushed aside at decision time, as happens all too often.

In many ways this rethinking is already quietly happening. Decriminalization of soft drugs such as marijuana is widespread in Europe and elsewhere, including Canada, whether by law or in practice, as police focus on matters of greater urgency. The result is not a proliferation of legal hash bars on the Amsterdam model. Rather, it is the end of prosecutions for possession and consumption of small quantities for personal use, which de facto legalizes the small-scale trade and allows law enforcement to focus on wholesalers who are likely involved in multiple criminal businesses. Rather than open the door to an increase in crime and antisocial behavior, decriminalization in Europe has produced a decade's or more worth of experience from which countries newer to reform might draw. Even socially conservative Chile is reforming its drug laws to distinguish trafficking from small-scale dealing and use, so that small-time users are no longer subject to heavy jail terms and the police and courts can focus their efforts elsewhere.

Drugs are not the only front where countries are sharpening their focus. In Europe and the United States the pressure to repress illegal immigration is matched by business interest in encouraging legal immigration for both skilled and unskilled labor. Periodic measures to regularize the status of certain illegal immigrants are becoming common, even if they are subject to various conditions. Such amnesties—throughout southern Europe, for example, but also in the United States—demonstrate the recognition by governments that airtight border controls are an impossibility. They also acknowledge that the laws must sometimes—often—catch up to social realities that most people have already come to take for granted.

Other, less familiar experiments are also under way. Sweden, for instance, has legalized the sale of sexual services. But that does not mean legalizing prostitution, for the purchase of such services is now forbidden. In other words, Sweden has shifted the risk from the prostitute to his or her customer, calculating that penalizing the customer is a much more effective way to deter demand—which results in lowering the value traffickers can expect to gain from bringing their chattel to the country. This example shows that paying attention to the demand side of illicit trade is by no means a euphemism for legalization. Rather, it is part of confronting illicit trade for what it is, a phenomenon driven by economics.

The same is happening with counterfeits. Companies are increasingly recognizing that technology, not lawyers, affords the best protection against copycats. Investing in new features that make counterfeiting harder or impossible is a safer strategy than relying on the patent protection prowess of the Chinese government, for example. Not all companies have this luxury, and many still actively lobby their governments to protect them against this economic law of gravity: merchandise in great demand that can be copied will be illegally copied by someone, somewhere in the world. To ask governments to fight every instance of this phenomenon is to dilute their ability to defend intellectual property where it counts the most.

Making government more effective means giving its agencies mandates that are realistic, and that in turn often means getting the government out of some activities so it can do better with other more urgent and necessary ones. "Nobody fully understands the complexity of our task," said Tom Ridge, the first secretary of the U.S. Department of Homeland Security, as he prepared to step down from his job in 2005. He was right. To have a system that makes sense we need to unburden government and simplify its tasks.

FIGHT A GLOBAL PROBLEM WITH GLOBAL SOLUTIONS

Unburdening governments is essential. But of course the benefits of even the best-thought-out government strategy run the risk of ending at that country's borders—and with them any prospects for long-term success. But illicit trade is a cross-border problem. And the only solution to a cross-border problem is a cross-border solution. Which means that international cooperation is imperative. These are unassailable facts based on simple logic. They also have fiendishly difficult implications for action.

Working with others is never easy. Working with foreigners is even less so, especially for governments. The arsenal of international treaties and conventions that govern illicit trade function better to enshrine global standards than to actually enable successful prosecution. Stories of international collaboration undermined by corruption, noncompliance, or absence of trust litter the headlines. But in the case of illicit trade, the alternative to international cooperation is to cede the field to the traffickers, who will find ways to penetrate even those countries that invest the most in patrolling their borders. In other words, the alternative is not an acceptable one. We need to find ways to make international cooperation against illicit trade work.

The ways exist. First, a smart multilateral approach to illicit trade has to be selective. Universal organizations suffer from the same pitfalls as the treaties that bring them into existence. The example of Interpol—the global police cooperation agency that is crippled by lack of trust between member forces—contrasts with the successes that many countries have enjoyed working together in pairs or small groups. Incremental, trust-based approaches deliver better, more convincing results than does starting with an ambitious global treaty from which most countries in practice defect. Bilateral treaties, technical assistance, and extradition agreements are nothing new. A more novel approach that has shown some success is peer review. Peer review is the method the Financial Action Task Force, the G-8 group of industrial countries' anti–money laundering and financial crime outfit, has employed with some real success. The FATF model is based on a few critical countries opting in by meeting a list of qualifications. Not every country is invited into the

FATF. Quite the contrary. The key to the FATF's successful operation is mutual trust, which is generated the only possible way—through a careful, deliberate process.

Despite the enormous problems faced by the European Union (EU), its attempt to tightly coordinate public policies and establish durable common institutions—the commission, the parliament, the court of justice—they strengthen its ability to deal with transnational problems. The EU makes adherence to its norms on a wide range of issues, including illicit trade, a prerequisite for new members.

The shared commitment—as well as the existence of political institutions to enforce it—means that types of collaboration at which other countries might balk are more likely to succeed among the European countries. The European police agency, Europol, is an interesting experiment. Europol was established in 1992 on the Interpol model. But Europol's secure place within the European Union earns it greater trust—and resources—from the member countries than they place in Interpol.

There are ways to pick one's partners and build trust. But what is unavoidable in all these approaches is some degree of flexibility with regard to the concept of national sovereignty. The FATF, the EU, and other groups all limit to a degree the exercise of sovereignty by their member countries with respect to a specific set of issues. This approach in fact provides the only hope to limiting the constant and far more harmful violations of national sovereignty that illicit traffickers inflict on nation states on a daily basis.

The lesson here is a difficult one for governments. It is that the most effective forms of cooperation to curb illicit trade are also the ones that invite the most mutual scrutiny—what governments are usually quick to call "meddling." It offends traditional notions of national government based on sovereign privilege, a state's prerogative to legislate as it wants and without another's opinion. Yet without allowing such "meddling," it seems unlikely that governments will ever trust one another, learn from one another, and work together fast enough to keep up with the trafficking networks. All this sounds and may even be quite naive. But it is more naive to assume that a government acting alone can make a dent in a global problem like illicit trade.

BUILD POLITICAL WILL

The tools to wage a more successful fight against illicit trade are within reach. So are new approaches that squarely confront the economic drivers of illicit trade and its social cost. Models of how to organize and equip governments for the fight are emerging. Even the vexing problem of achieving international cooperation in this most global of fights presents glimmers of possibility. It is a picture that should inspire hope.

So what is stopping us? The answer lies in politics. Consider the politicians on whom making these changes is incumbent. They weigh their interest in potential reforms and innovations by the measure of political realities in their constituency. Will their backers—voters, financial supporters, allies within their political party, vested interests in their home region or ethnic group, and so on—stand by them when they call for new policies? Is public opinion sensitive to the issue and sufficiently interested compared to other concerns? Is it worth the political risk to go out on a limb and argue for a major correction to long-established policies, a rethinking of long-entrenched interests? It is easy to blame politicians for being timorous, or following the winds of public opinion as expressed in polls and focus groups. Passing the measures required to combat today's illicit trade does involve real political risks. We can hold politicians to a standard of courage, but we can't expect them to be foolhardy.

For there are sacred cows here. The biggest is how accustomed we are to thinking of illicit trade in primarily moral terms. It is absolutely true that a full panorama of illicit trade today produces enormous shock and horror at the callousness, greed, violence, and depravity that trafficking can entail. But moral exhortations can actually stifle the kinds of political innovation we so desperately need if we are to jettison the strategies that are proven failures and have the courage to attempt new ones. Many are the politicians who have taken refuge in morally tinged denunciations as a substitute for transparency and educating the public. Unfortunately, the apparent hypocrisy of politicians often mirrors that of their voters. Few politicians have the luxury or the skills to lead their constituency beyond the moral certitudes of their times. One chagrined U.S. senator told me, speaking on condition of anonymity: "I have no doubt that what we are doing on the war on drugs is not working. But I also have no doubt that if I say it and come out in favor of legalizing some drugs, marijuana, for example, I will lose my next election." He continued: "I am ready to accept that new bold measures that break with what we have been doing are necessary. But my voters are not."

Facile moral certitudes make political innovation difficult. So do facile certitudes about national sovereignty and the outside world. Pooling some sovereignty among trusted partners is a necessary step to fight illicit trade. But it is often interpreted to the public as a sign of weakness, a surrender to a supranational authority that is unelected, unaccountable, and foreign. Giving the impression of tampering with nationhood is as much a third rail for politicians as is appearing to promote immorality. Indiscriminate nationalistic rhetoric makes it difficult to distinguish the careful, specific measures involved in peer-driven partnerships, or concepts like the EU's "subsidiarity," which determines the sovereign privileges that are pooled versus the ones member countries retain. It is paradoxical that the aversion to "meddling" so often heard in the United States finds its echo in countries that the criminal networks have penetrated, where it is invoked to ward off international scrutiny. Rabid nationalism works quite well to ensure that no foreign spotlight interferes with the business of global criminals that have long abandoned loyalty to any flag or country.

That scrutiny is more urgent than ever, for so long as the networks find safe havens in locations like Transdniester, Liberia, Ukraine, Cambodia, China, and Russia, the easier they will find it to regroup and regenerate whenever they suffer a setback. In these countries, political will to fight the traffickers must be generated and supported from outside. It is up to the less corrupt governments of other countries to bring this pressure and support by promoting openness, transparency, and democracy and by forging effective antitrafficking partnerships with other nations that widen the scope of mutual trust. But these governments must also recognize the role their own laws often play in boosting the profits of illicit trade.

GET EVERYONE INVOLVED

Governments can't do it alone; neither can politicians. Nurturing the political will to confront illicit trade is a project for us all. Politicians need public pressure to take on the issue and public support for them when they do. None of which is possible without a degree of public awareness of illicit trade that we have yet to achieve. It will take the efforts of activists, journalists, academics, clergy, educators, and even novelists and screenwriters to portray to the public the reality of illicit trade today and how it clashes with the received ideas of the past.

The key is to understand the nature of the threat. As much as the public has heard that terrorist organizations today are made of flexible, decentralized cells structured as networks, much media and political discussion of the fight against terrorism still dwells on leaders, masterminds, and rogue regimes. The point is not that masterminds or rogue regimes don't exist. Rather it is that the public has little way of visualizing what exactly these networks are, how prevalent they can be, and how far into daily life they can reach. Moreover, the discussion is still generally limited to the threat of terrorist attacks. The notion that terrorists are only a small part, with special motivations, of the global networks of illicit trade is only beginning to become clear. So is an appreciation of just how far illicit trading networks have gone to hijack the new world economy.

To understand the threat means to make the connections. The dots are there to be connected. Yet we persist in thinking of human trafficking, drug dealing, software piracy, and so on as discrete behaviors with at most incidental connections. These blinders are part reassurance. We don't like to think of ourselves as criminals, and dwelling on the interconnectedness of minor foibles like downloading a copyright-protected song and major horrors like child slavery and African civil wars is bound to make us uncomfortable. But that would be missing the point. Most of us are not criminals. Still, we gain from understanding who benefits from our activities and who pays the cost; what are the laws and incentives that make it that way; and how we can change it.

Making the connections is a task for civil society—that is, for all of us. It is what we know how to do when we are not blinkered by the hierarchical structure of governments or massive corporations. Empowered by the same tools that make the trading networks so effective—horizontal organization, irrelevance of borders, decentralized communication and leadership, viral propagation of ideas, creative freedom to exchange using new technologies—groups formed in the public interest and simply concerned citizens have an enormous contribution to make. Just as citizens band together in "neighborhood watch" groups when they realize that government can't or shouldn't monitor everything all the time, so the fight against illicit trade demands a global neighborhood watch, in which teachers and activists and the media goad, cajole, and persuade politicians into action and support and assist them when they do.

How does that happen? Through education, through mobilization, through election campaigns. It's hard work, and there are plenty of other priorities. Yet if we stand back and consider how much the world has changed and into what kind of world order we are headed, the rationale for mobilizing against global criminal networks will become clear, and also urgent.

Chapter 13

THE WORLD AHEAD

The politics of a world altered by pervasive illicit trade creates a new global opposition between two poles. It is no longer the old opposition of East and West, nor that of a rich North and a poor South. It is even less the opposition that some now see between Judeo-Christian and Islamic cultures. Rather, it is something new, the collision of geopolitical bright spots and black holes.

In astrophysics, black holes are regions in the universe where the traditional—Newtonian—laws of physics do not apply. The pages of this book are full of examples for which traditional ways of thinking about world politics and international relations do not apply either. Moreover, these pages also show that the world does not lack for regions and even countries that are not "normal" according to the standards commonly used by scholars and policymakers. In many important ways these are "geopolitical black holes."

Geopolitical black holes are the places where the trafficking networks "live" and thrive. To enter one, you need not look very far. Travel for instance to Spain's Costa del Sol, for decades the destination of middle-class package tours from Britain and Germany. Despite one of the highest unemployment rates and lowest incomes in Spain, Málaga, the main city in this well known "first world" tourist area, has experienced a 1,600 percent increase in private home construction in five years. Why? Because, as a chief police inspector told the *Financial Times,* "Criminals are businessmen these days . . .

they want good travel connections, an efficient banking sector, nice weather and anonymity. They can get all that in Málaga."

The same report notes that 550 criminal groups operate in Spain, half of them foreign. José Antonio Alonso, Spain's interior minister, said that that organized crime was "as big a threat to Spanish security as Islamic terrorism." This might come as a surprising revelation in a country reputed to be one of the prime European hubs of Islamic terrorists, and victim in 2004 of a terrorist attack that killed 191, injured 1,500, and torpedoed the government into electoral defeat. Yet the fact is that the Costa del Sol is now commonly called "Costa del Crime." In its own sunny way it has become a geopolitical black hole that all kinds of transnational traffickers whose actions contribute to global instability use as one of the multiple hubs of their networks.

Manhattan, for all its investment in fortifications and security since 9/11, remains an entrance point for the threats originating in geopolitical black holes. That is what a task force of the FBI and New York Police Department found as it investigated Russian organized crime in 2004. Posing as representatives of a terrorist organization, the team found an Armenian, Artur Solomonyan, and a South African, Christiaan Dewet Spies, ready to sell them a range of sophisticated military-grade Russian weapons including heat-seeking antiaircraft and guided antitank missiles. Delivery was available at the customer's convenience in New York, Los Angeles, or Miami. And yet more interesting products were on offer: as one agent testified in his sworn statement, "Solomonyan informed the CI [confidential informant] that he could also obtain enriched uranium for the CI which, Solomonyan suggested, could be used in the subway system."

Of course, geopolitical black holes can for a time match up with the borders of a state. "Failed states" or "rogue nations" can easily turn into geopolitical black holes. Failed states include the remote and isolated places where the rule of law is nonexistent and warlords and despotic rulers misgovern with impunity in sometimes medieval fashion. Somalia, Congo, or Haiti are iconic examples.

North Korea, Iraq under Saddam Hussein, Lukashenko's Belarus, and (until 2004) Libya have all been commonly cited as rogues.

The black holes can be "lawless"—that is to say, anarchic—regions within countries like Transdniester in Moldova, the mountain heart of Corsica, or the Mexican states that make up the border with the United States. They can be frontier regions that cross countries like the Golden Triangle of Southeast Asia or the "triple frontier" of South America. They can be systems of neighborhoods and localities, such as the Lebanese communities across the capitals of West Africa. And increasingly they are disembodied space on the Internet. Simply because they are hard or impossible to pinpoint on a map does not mean they do not exist. Quite the contrary— those qualities are what make them attractive to the networks.

The opposite of a geopolitical black hole is a bright spot. What distinguishes the two is not whether illicit networks are operating. They are, everywhere. The difference is whether in a given setting there is enough state and civic capacity to counter the networks, to get the better of them. And that is not purely the responsibility of governments or that of citizens. It is both. That is the difference between a geopolitical bright spot and black hole. It is a difference that can cleave in two a country, a city, or even a family.

BLACK HOLES VS. BRIGHT SPOTS

As sovereignty erodes and nations face growing difficulties in controlling their borders, there is every indication that the geopolitical black holes that illicit networks have come to inhabit and cultivate are only going to expand. And unless major changes take place, it is safer to assume that in the future the world will have more, not less, of these geopolitical black holes.

Governments in less-developed countries that are already weak will be further weakened as the illicit networks operating inside their territory amass large fortunes. Inevitably the networks will invest those fortunes in the pursuit of political influence and military capabilities that can rival those of the governments of the countries where they operate. At the same time, governments in rich countries will face growing difficulties in curbing the influence of black holes in their midst that are stealthily but effectively connected to others abroad. The Dutch government, for example, has been fighting an uphill battle to contain networks inside Holland that are the appendage of powerful drug trafficking networks operating from Suriname—a former Dutch colony in South America that has become a "connector" between the Andean region and Europe. Similar patterns are visible in all of Europe and in Japan, where local traffickers are operating regional networks throughout Southeast Asia and China.

Traditional thinking assumes that a nation-state has a unique, sovereign government with exclusive authority over a territorially defined jurisdiction. The German sociologist Max Weber defined government as "the organization that holds monopoly on the legitimate use of violence in its territory." Moreover, according to a commonly used definition, a nation-state has (a) a permanent population; (b) a defined territory; (c) a government; and (d) capacity to enter into relations with the other states.

None of these criteria apply to geopolitical black holes. Multiple authorities may exert control over the same territory, and inside geopolitical black holes the traffickers of illicit goods who are connected to larger global networks have a defining role in economic, political, and military affairs. Central government representatives may control the police, schools, and other aspects of civil life, but trafficking networks will have control over the production, armed protection, and international distribution of whatever that region has that fetches high prices in world markets—from opium to arms to people. Trafficking networks will also control the profits and have the coercive means to defend their activities from threats (governments) or predators (rival networks). The situation in parts of Colombia, Russia, Afghanistan, Mexico, Laos, and many places in Africa and Asia today fit this description.

A crucial factor—and one that gives black holes much of their potency—is their specialized *connectedness* with bright spots. A remote, primitive, and badly governed—or ungoverned—region is not a geopolitical black hole unless it can radiate threats to places far away. The trading networks that operate internationally serve as the channels through which these threats move from remote locations to the rest of the world.

In this future world more deeply divided between bright spots, defended and fortified, and black holes, vulnerable and overrun by international traffickers, an important paradox emerges.

It is this: The more the fortified and successful bright spots are at defending themselves, the more value there is in breaching their fortifications. The brighter the bright spot, the more attractive and lucrative it is for the networks operating from black holes to find ways to deliver their products and services inside it. Illicit trade is essentially determined by price differences: wood that is far more expensive in Los Angeles than in Indonesia, coca leaves that can be processed and sold in Miami for hundreds of times what it cost to buy them in Bolivia, Cameroonian workers who earn in London what they could never dream of making in their own country. The brighter the bright spot, the higher the prices these illicit goods can command. The darker the black hole, the more desperate its people will be to sell their goods, their minds, their work, and even their bodies to the traffickers. Together these two trends create ever-widening price differentials—and, therefore, ever more irresistible incentives to connect black holes to bright spots.

IDEAS AND CONSEQUENCES

Seen in this light, with the benefit of the evidence that is amassing each day around us, the connections between illicit trade and global security (and insecurity) are powerful, glaring, and dire. Illicit trade is pushing the world in new directions that so far have eluded our capacity to comprehend, let alone arrest. Unchecked illicit trade is making the world less safe. It empowers those who reject or care little for governance and social norms. It provides an economic shelter for rebels, crooks, and terrorists. It stimulates corruption, impairs economic development, and renders more vulnerable the rest of us, who obey the laws and rely on them for protection. All of which puts not only governments but entire societies on the defensive, with all the costs and burdens and frustrations that entails. Illicit trade is not merely a law enforcement problem that has been with us since time immemorial. It is that, but it is also a new threat that, thanks to new technologies, new economics, and new politics, has acquired the ability to change the world. This is no longer about crime rates. It is about global instability.

As we saw in the previous chapter, the situation isn't hopeless. There are things we can do. But progress in mitigating the threats of illicit trade depends on moving aggressively toward the goals outlined in that chapter, from deploying better technologies to enhancing the capacity of governments to use them effectively—an impossible task if we continue to saddle agencies with unrealistic goals or require them to act without allies abroad and political support at home. And none of this will be possible unless we change our ways of thinking about illicit trades. We need more clarity about who the main players are, what drives them, the political and social consequences, and what it means that governments have failed to contain them despite all their massive efforts and expense in doing so. Most of all we must use what we have learned to challenge the prevailing theories that leaders use to gauge world politics—theories that are failing us in the fight against illicit trade yet remain dominant to this day.

A DIFFERENT CHESSBOARD

In 2000, as the century ended, a prominent American professor at a prestigious university who at the time was advising a candidate for the U.S. presidential election wrote an article in the journal *Foreign Affairs*, describing the state of the world. Based on her interpretation of where the world stood and where it was going, Professor Condoleezza Rice of Stanford University concluded that the international priorities for the United States ought to be "building a military ready to ensure American power, coping with rogue regimes and managing Beijing and Moscow." In her vision of the world ahead, terrorism did not figure as a main concern. Rice did mention terrorism twice, but essentially as a reason to clamp down on the few "rogue" states prone to use it. She singled out Iraq ("nothing will change until Saddam is gone"), North Korea, and Iran.

The article showed that in Professor Rice's worldview what mattered most were nation-states, especially those with the strongest military capabilities. Thus, she wrote, a "crucial task for the United States is to focus on relations with other powerful states," especially China, Russia, countries in Europe and India. This last deserved attention, she explained, because even if India "is not a great power yet . . . it has the potential to emerge as one." Regarding China: "Cooperation should be pursued but we should never be afraid to confront Beijing when our interests collide."

Rice's article never mentioned Islamic terrorism in particular, or the explosive growth of transnational crime. While she surely knew about the growing threat posed by what the jargon of international relations calls "nonstate actors," she obviously thought that other priorities mattered more. In her thinking, governments were—and would continue to be—the main players on the international chessboard.

Nineteen months later Rice had to adjust her priorities. For like an earthquake, September 11, 2001, was both tragic and informative. Tragically, it was unexpected and killed thousands. The only good thing about earthquakes is that they also provide seismologists with invaluable new data about forces at work deep inside the earth's crust that could not otherwise be fathomed. And 9/11 delivered vital new information about powerful, dangerous, and hitherto almost invisible forces buried deep inside the international system.

Suddenly Afghanistan, a failed, miserable nation located at the antipodes of the United States and equipped only with a squalid army, became a new and important American enemy demanding urgent attention. An old, almost iconic adversary, Saddam Hussein, whose alleged links with the 9/11 attacks were never proved and who very likely never imagined that his destiny had been sealed in lower Manhattan on that September morning, moved back to the top of the U.S. military agenda. But the most important new information that the 9/11 earthquake revealed was that a nebulous entity called al-Qaeda—a religious group? a political movement? a network? the world's most insidious NGO? what?—had now become America's main threat.

"September 11 clarified . . . the kinds of threats that you face in the post–cold war era," Rice said in a 2002 interview, this time in her role as national security advisor to the president of the United States. But for all this newfound clarity, the American response to 9/11 demonstrated the persistence of old instincts and assumptions. Faced with the prospect of waging a new kind of war against a new kind of stateless opponent with an uncanny international mobility that allowed it to cross borders frequently and stealthily, the Bush administration chose instead to go to war against nation-states.

Set against the complexity of today's trafficking networks and geopolitical black holes, the insistence on seeking one's enemies among nation-states produces some remarkable contradictions. Take for instance a law the U.S. passed in 1999, the National Missile Defense Act, which reads: "It is the policy of the United States to deploy as soon as it is technologically possible an effective National Missile Defense system capable of defending the territory of the United States against limited ballistic missile attack." Pursuing this goal costs each year between $7 and $8 billion. Meanwhile, only about 5 percent of the 6 million cargo containers shipped annually into the United States are ever inspected. Between 2002 and 2004, the federal port security grant program had allocated only $515 million and actually spent about $100 million, far less than what the U.S. Coast Guard says is necessary.

While the need to deploy a *Star Wars*–like "shield" that protects the United States from a ballistic missile attack is a controversial proposition, the need to boost port security is not. Yet missile defense gets a huge amount of money and port security does not.

Missile defense, of course, is a program that predates the 9/11 wake-up call. But how much has the pre-9/11 mentality really changed? For instance, even as the United States and Europe were bearing down on Iran for its development of a nuclear program, the United States also agreed to wait until sometime after 2008 to secure Russian nuclear weapons and other critical material. As is well known, these materials are guarded in poor conditions, by guardians who are not that difficult to persuade to do their jobs with less than complete diligence.

But it would be grossly unfair to assume that the worldview that guided these judgments was an aberrant doctrine held by a small group of intellectual extremists in Washington. Quite the contrary: the views expressed by Rice and others echoed an eminently respectable line of thought that has dominated thinking in world politics for years, indeed centuries, and not just in the United States.

WELL-WORN LENSES

They are called "realists." Textbooks explain that those who belong to this school of thought believe that sovereign nation-states are the fundamental building blocks of the international system. Therefore, because each nation is relatively independent (sovereign) and does not have to respond to the designs of any higher authority, the system of nations is inherently anarchic. States interact with each other by wielding power in pursuit of their national self-interest. The result is "Realpolitik," the term coined by Germany's Chancellor Otto von Bismarck in the nineteenth century to describe what he saw as "the politics of reality." In other words, deal with the world as it is, not as you would like it to be.

In this view, power and other practical considerations—military capabilities, resources, geography, population—rather than ideas, values, or ethics dictate how a nation will behave toward others. If you want to predict a country's international actions, look at its needs and compare its military might with that of other countries.

That will tell you more about its likely future behavior than any statement its leaders might make.

The realist outlook has a long lineage and still enjoys wide acceptance among influential academics. In 1998, I asked Professor Stephen Walt of Harvard, one of the world's top scholars on international relations, to survey for *Foreign Policy* magazine the main schools of thought on world politics and see how each one held up in view of the changes that emerged in the 1990s. Walt concluded that "the end of the cold war did not bring an end to power politics, and realism is likely to remain the single most useful instrument in our intellectual toolbox."

In 2004, three years after 9/11, I asked Jack Snyder, another leading expert who is a professor at Columbia University, to assess what the terrorist attacks and U.S. reaction meant for the ways in which experts thought about world politics. Snyder pointed out that no institution, law, rule, or "the international community" had been able to restrain the unilateral decisions of a country, the United States, which had the military capability and the will to attack other countries in pursuit of its perceived national interest. In other words, events had unfolded very much as the realists might have predicted. Just as his colleague Walt had done six years earlier, Snyder too concluded that the realist model still offered the most reliable lenses to assess the direction of global politics.

There are alternative views, of course. One is liberalism—a term that has a very specific meaning in international relations. Rather than centering on the struggle for power, survival, and domination among nations, liberalism assigns great importance to the factors that *inhibit* nations from using force against each other. In this view, international commerce, democracy, and global political institutions create a web of constraints that reduce both the attractiveness and feasibility of going to war. The more countries are linked by trade and investment, the lower the chance they will attack each other. Moreover, liberalism argues, democracies accountable to voters are less prone to initiate wars than authoritarian regimes. And institutions like the European Union, NATO, and

NAFTA reduce the likelihood of armed conflict among their member nations.

Realists and liberals look at the future differently. Assessing the rise of China, for example, American realists would worry about China becoming wealthy enough to afford a powerful military, creating a major rival to the United States in world affairs. But from the perspective of liberalism, China's economic ascendancy is a goal worth promoting rather than fearing. Making China a member of the World Trade Organization, for instance, and ensuring that it is enmeshed in a web of trade and investment relationships with other countries does more for world peace than attempting to curb its economic ascent, simply by making it prohibitively expensive for Chinese leaders to go to war.

Another important school of thought that seeks to explain and predict world politics is idealism (or constructivism). It emphasizes the role of beliefs, ideas, culture, narratives, and social identities in shaping the behavior of nation-states and the elites that lead them. And there are still other theories, usually variations or combinations of these broad outlooks. One is the "neoconservative" approach, which became a quite popular term to describe the foreign policy and military decisions of the Bush administration after 9/11. This view and its proponents, often called the "neocons," advocate aggressive and if need be unilateral action by the United States to promote "American values"—democracy, human rights, and free markets—and to maintain America's global primacy. (In reality, few of the prominent members of the Bush team accept the "neocon" label. Neither do the leading thinkers of the neocon movement accept that its tenets correctly characterize the U.S. government's decisions during the Bush presidency.)

Policy debates among these schools of thought can rage furiously and do, in Washington and other world capitals. Yet despite their fundamental differences all these theories of international relations share the same strong propensity to think of sovereign nation-states as the central players in world affairs. They differ as to what motivates nations and what forces encroach on their autonomy, but at bottom they still make sovereign states the center of their attention and the building blocks of their arguments.

Many influential thinkers still hold dear the assumption that in the future nothing of major and lasting importance in world affairs is likely to happen without the active involvement of a nation-state. They would point out for example that across the table from A. Q. Khan's nuclear smugglers were Libya, Iran, and North Korea—sovereign governments bent on obtaining nuclear capabilities to further their national interest. This active participation of governments could be used to "prove" that sovereign nation-states are still the world's prime movers. But it is not that simple. Yes, nation-states were buying, but stateless networks were selling. And both were changing the world—together.

Still, many respected experts reject the idea that actors other than states have that much importance. In his survey of state-of-the-art thinking after 9/11, updated by the new awareness of international terrorism, Professor Snyder wrote that "States, not the United Nations or Human Rights Watch, have led the fight against terrorism. . . . Insights from political realism . . . are hardly rendered obsolete because some nonstate groups are now able to resort to violence."

And it is not just scholars. Influential policy makers too have been reluctant to accept that global networks have acquired significant capabilities and can act without the backing of a nation-state. In his memoir, Richard A. Clarke, the senior antiterrorism official at the White House from 1998 to 2003, writes that he realized "that Rice, and her deputy, Steve Hadley, were still operating with the old Cold War paradigm" born of dealing with the threats posed by the states of the Warsaw Pact and the Soviet Union before 1989. He remembers telling them, "The boundaries between domestic and foreign have blurred. Threats to the US now are not Soviet ballistic missiles carrying bombs, they're terrorists carrying bombs."

Clarke goes on to explain that when he convened a White House meeting on al-Qaeda in April 2001, some colleagues did not share his alarm over the risks facing the United States. He writes that when he stressed the need to go after al-Qaeda,

Paul Wolfowitz, Donald Rumsfeld's deputy at Defense, fidgeted and scowled. Hadley asked him if he was all right. "Well, I just don't understand why we are beginning by talking about this one man bin Laden," Wolfowitz responded. . . . I answered as clearly and forcefully as I could: "We are talking about a network of terrorist organizations called al Qaeda, that happens to be led by bin Laden, and we are talking about that network because it and it alone poses an immediate and serious threat to the United States." . . . Finally, Wolfowitz turned to me. "You give bin Laden too much credit. He could not do all these things like the 1993 attack on New York, not without a state sponsor."

As we now know al-Qaeda and bin Laden continue to be a menace even though no state openly and actively sponsors them. It was stateless networks that hit New York on 9/11 and Madrid in March 2004. And stateless networks will hit again.

ASYMMETRIC BORDERS

All borders leak, all the time. Not even the fiercest police state is able to completely seal its national borders. The *Guardian* published in 2004 this dispatch from the banks of the Yalu River, which separates China and North Korea:

> Here and there, shadowy figures can be seen on both sides of the misty river quietly carrying out an illegal—but thriving—trade in women, endangered species, food and consumer appliances that makes a mockery of North Korea's reputation as a tightly controlled and internationally isolated state.

And that is the supposedly tightly-closed North Korea. Naturally, the more politically and economically free a country is, the bigger the obstacles its government faces in exercising effective control of the borders.

Hence the theme throughout this book—that the 1990s witnessed changes in politics, technology, and economics that dissolved the sealants on which nation states had relied to safeguard their borders. These changes benefited traffickers more than governments. Of course, governments too grew more able to operate internationally in the 1990s, especially thanks to developments in travel and communication. But the changes helped traffickers more.

This makes borders lopsided, asymmetric. Although a border looks like a hard-to-overcome uphill incline when observed from the point of view of a government agency, it looks like an inviting downhill slope when seen from the perspective of traffickers. They have the tools, the resources, and the expertise to trespass borders. And of course, a pot of gold often awaits at the end of a successful crossing. Borders shield traffickers from prosecutors who cannot reach them outside the limits of their jurisdiction without the official and active engagement of the other country's legal authorities—a process that is hard to marshal, bureaucratically tedious, and subject to all manner of trust and coordination problems. And of course, it is borders that enable governments to create the differences in prices that generate the profit opportunities that make traffickers rich.

In short, borders are a trafficker's best friend and an enormous headache for those fighting him. This asymmetry is not new, but it has become more acute. And in looking toward the future, it seems safer to assume that asymmetric borders are likely to become even more so.

HOLLOWED-OUT SOVEREIGNTY

Sovereignty is one of the thorniest issues of our time. The principle of nonintervention whereby a state has no right to intervene in the internal affairs of another is increasingly overridden, often on humanitarian grounds: NATO's armed intervention in Yugoslavia to stop "ethnic cleansing" and UN peacekeeping operations in states ravaged by internal conflicts are good examples. Meanwhile, the International Monetary Fund (IMF) and World Bank constantly impose economic policy conditions on countries that depend on them for financial support, thus impinging on their sovereignty.

Traffickers, of course, violate state sovereignty all the time. And not just by smuggling. In many countries, traffickers—often backed by foreign associates—take over state or local governments by using money to influence politics and by placing accomplices in power. Through force and violence they have gained control of large swaths of territory or entire neighborhoods in large cities. In many metropolitan areas—Rio de Janeiro, Manila, Mexico City, Bangkok, Cairo—large, populous sections of the city are in practice under the control of trafficking networks and criminals, not the local government.

There are aspects of this that are not new. Sovereignty has never been absolute, and the demise of the nation-state has often been erroneously predicted. Nation-states are not about to go away and will continue to be the main building block of the international system. But thinking about sovereignty without taking into account the termites that are chipping at it—or assuming that state power can neutralize their impact by building fences or electronically sealing borders—ignores a plethora of highly apparent warning signals. Time and again, parliaments and legislatures pass laws aimed at making the nation's borders more resilient to illicit penetration. And time and again these laws are based on assumptions about capabilities that governments simply do not have and seem unable to acquire.

Almost daily, a new report issued by credible institutions documents the inability of governments to control national borders. For example, according to a study issued in 2005 by the Organization for Security and Cooperation in Europe (OSCE), human trafficking is on the increase. "The problem is not diminishing . . . but is going more underground," said the OSCE's Helga Konrad. Another report revealed that in 2005 there were three times as many illegal immigrants living in Spain as there were in 2001. And despite massive efforts and investments, the United States is failing at defending itself from the onslaught of the termites that seem to have no problem violating its borders. Despite tighter border enforcement after 9/11, the number of illegal immigrants continues to grow at the same rate as it did in the 1990s. And it is not just illegal immigrants who violate borders. The flow of all kinds of illicit goods across borders also continues unabated and in some places is accelerating.

Moreover, the governments in the examples above are among the wealthiest in the world, and their machinery is comparatively the most capable and best-endowed with talent, money, and technology. A "normal" or average nation in today's world—be it Brazil, India, Indonesia, Argentina, Thailand, or Egypt—does not have similar capabilities and is therefore even more vulnerable to the influence of trafficking networks.

In the world ahead, while the state may well be with us for a long time, its capacity to meet traditional expectations about national sovereignty is likely to continue to dwindle. That is why we need new ways to think of sovereignty. Though for many an upright citizen "national sovereignty" is a hallowed idea, for traffickers it has become a hollow one. They violate it all the time.

We need to consider the possibility that clinging to old ideas about sovereignty may be stunting the evolution of the nation-state and thus weakening the security of its citizens. It may sound difficult, even improbable, but national sovereignty, security, and public safety are more likely to be ensured by a government's close collaboration with other nations allied in the fight against illicit traffickers than through continuous attempts to plug leaking borders with sealants that do not work. "Closing the border" is certainly appealing to nationalistic sentiments and to the basic human instincts of building moats and walls for protection. But when threats travel via fiber optics, or when finding the way to move a load across the border ensures unimaginable wealth or the chance of a better life, the wisdom of relying mostly on unilateral security measures is highly questionable.

This does not mean that nations should abdicate the right to safeguard their borders or assert their culture and values. But it is an utterly naive expectation to assume that nations can successfully fend off threats just by relying on tighter border controls. Unfortunately, it is also a political promise that is as dishonest as it is appealing to voters scared by the new and bewildering threats coming from "abroad." The notion that borders have lost much of their ability to keep foreign threats at bay is not a message many voters want to hear or that politicians are eager to endorse.

CHERCHEZ L'ÉTAT

In the classic scenario of film noir, detectives applied a formula to help them solve crimes: *"Cherchez la femme."* Look for the woman. A man's atypical behavior always had the passion sparked by a woman as his main motivation. Find the woman and the puzzle would be solved. A similar instinct tends to drive thinkers and decision makers in world affairs. For them when something happens in the world, it is a case of *"cherchez l'État."* Look for the state behind it and you will be well on your way to understanding the situation.

But the global boom in illicit trading networks suggests something quite different. All the evidence from the illicit trade in arms, drugs, human beings, counterfeits, money laundering, organs, animals, toxic waste, and all the rest—to say nothing of international terrorism—points us over and over to the driving force that international networks exercise in eroding the authority of states, corrupting legitimate businesses and governments and hijacking their institutions and even their purpose.

Yes, states are involved. But not in ways that the standard theories of international relations are comfortable with. Sovereign states are supposed to be unitary. They are run by bureaucracies that rely on coordination and hierarchy (for all the dysfunctions that breeds). And they make the ultimate decisions—to deploy armies, to contract debt, to purchase arms, to levy taxes, and dispense foreign aid.

Yet the kind of links that networks are now developing inside governments, and vice versa, should force us to rethink the factors that shape the workings of the international system. Governments tend to be partially, not fully involved with the networks—through a rogue minister or state-funded scientist, a security branch that is loyal to a powerful political faction funded by traffickers, the relatively autonomous management of a state-owned company, or simply through the aggregation of hundreds of small acts of corruption carried out by minor functionaries at airports and border posts. Elite squads of the Cambodian national police raid the brothels that the local commanders of the same police protect. The top military officer in charge of Mexico's counternarcotic efforts is now serving a jail sentence after being indicted for working for traffickers. In 2004, the Lithuanian parliament impeached President Ronaldas Paksas for taking funds from a Russian businessman, Yuri Borosov, with alleged ties to Russian organized crime. The Lithuanian State Security Department recorded conversations in which Borosov told the president that he would become a "political corpse" if he did not live up to their "agreement."

Some of these may be cases of individual "bad apples." But there is mounting evidence of more structured and organized arrangements between trafficking networks and groups of individuals working at the highest levels of government. The United States has "clearly established that North Korean diplomats, military officers and other party/government officials have been involved in the smuggling of narcotics" and that "state-owned assets, particularly ships, have been used to facilitate and support international drug trafficking ventures." In Peru, Vladimiro Montesinos, the head of national intelligence and leader of the country's anti-insurgency and counterdrug efforts between 1990 and 2000, is now in jail, accused of running major international operations trafficking drugs, and weapons and in money laundering. Top Chinese military officials and their relatives are known to be involved in counterfeiting manufacturing operations. In Belarus or Transdniester, illicit trafficking is an indispensable feature of the economy. It is hard to imagine that this could become so without the active and prolonged support from top government officials. Politics and decision making in the nations of the former Soviet Union cannot be understood without considering the influence and the interests of traffickers.

The "criminalization of the national interest" is one of the greatest overlooked trends of our time. Yes, the state is a central player in world affairs, and national interests often drive its behavior. But there is ample confirmation that in certain countries these national interests have been secretly—and sometimes not so secretly—hijacked by criminals.

But this does not mean that a government found to be involved in an illicit network is necessarily fully entangled in it, or even that all its leading policy makers have complete knowledge of these activities. And it would be an even greater mistake to assume that simply because a government official or agent is involved in an illicit transaction the traders require that state's sponsorship. More often than not, government officials are cogs in the machinery, not engines. They supply the illicit traders with false documents, inflated billing statements, precious goods for sale on the world market, armed protection, and the well-timed governmental distraction that allows a trade to be successfully completed. And they may be customers as well. But they are rarely the only option. In today's world economy, illicit traders are free to swap government accomplices just as they would change their airline or their banker or their cell phone vendor. Conversely, top government officials with an appetite for extraordinary profits are also free to rotate the illicit trading network they favor.

It has become clear, for example, that while the A. Q. Khan network was deeply embedded in the Pakistani state, its sales of nuclear technology to North Korea or Iran were an expression of the financial appetite of the network's top members rather than actions calculated to further Pakistan's national interest. And A. Q. Khan is not the only private entrepreneur active as a commercial nuclear proliferator. With the arrival of the new Yushchenko government in Ukraine in 2005, it was discovered that during the previous administration weapons dealers smuggled to Iran and China eighteen Kh-55 nuclear-capable missiles that could strike targets 1,860 miles away, carrying a two hundred-kiloton bomb. According to the Associated Press, these sales were illegal and contravened the official policy of the Ukrainian government. Again these deals were motivated by profit, not politics, and Ukraine's national interest had nothing to do with the decision.

It seems likely that these deliveries of highly dangerous equipment and materials would have come to light more quickly, making possible a more timely response, if we had been actually looking for them. That is, if we had assumed from the start that the way nuclear materials were likely to spread in the globalized world economy was through stateless, decentralized networks with the opportunistic involvement of government officials—rather than through the dedicated and orchestrated efforts of "rogue" nations.

In other words, it is high time that *"cherchez l'État"* gave way to *"cherchez le réseau"*—seek the network—when attempting to explain, and eventually anticipate and prevent, troubling world developments.

THE WORLD AHEAD

For now, the trend is toward more. More trafficking, more black holes, more conflict and confusion, and borders that remain porous despite government attempts to seal them.

But is this trend irrevocable? Are we fated to descend for the foreseeable future into a world of besieged fortresses and forsaken hinterlands and ghettos?

If you believe solely and exclusively in the power of the profit motive, the answer has to be yes.

If you believe that ideas can change the world, then the answer is no.

But we have learned through history to believe both. Profit will never fully vanquish ideas, nor will ideas ever eradicate the drive to profit.

To stop the trend—to exit the downward spiral—will require putting both to use. Only an attack on what makes illicit trade profitable stands a chance of containing its rise. Only fresh ideas that take into account the profound changes that globalization has wrought on states, governments, politics, and the conduct of civic life—changes that forces like illicit trade and transnational militant and political networks keep driving forward every day—can help us understand where we are.

As we look forward to a world with less trafficking, violence, and exploitation, we can also look back to a thinker whose assessment of illicit trade—in 1776—perfectly blended an understanding of the profit motive and of the power of ideas, Adam Smith. He wrote:

> Not many people are scrupulous about smuggling when, without
> perjury, they can find any safe and easy opportunity of doing so. To
> pretend to have any scruple about buying smuggled goods . . .
> would in most countries be regarded as one of those pedantic
> pieces of hypocrisy . . .

That simple truth persists today—amplified to the scale of the whole globe and extended to every commodity imaginable. To find a way to make the world better without evading or glossing over this truth, is both our challenge and our opportunity.

REFERENCES

CHAPTER 1: THE WARS WE ARE LOSING

1   [Counterfeit Clinton biography] Oliver August, "Clinton's Mentor Was Mao, Chinese Readers Are Told," *The Times Online (London)*, July 21, 2004.

1   [Garcia Marquez counterfeit] Sergio Dahbar, "Papel Literario: Gabo deberia escribir una historia de piratas," *El Nacional*, October 23, 2004.

3   [Thai brothel operator ran for office] Weerayut Chokchaimadon, "Set a Thief to Catch a Thief," *Korea Herald*, November 17, 2003.

3   [Cambodian police—national help fight trafficking, but local take bribes from traffickers] Kathy Marks, "Cambodian Police Close Dozens of Child-Sex Brothels," *Independent (UK)*, January 25, 2003, Kathy Marks, "The Skin Trade: High-Profile Investigations into Pedophilia Are Headline News," *Independent (UK)*, January 22, 2001, pp. 4–5.

Three Illusions

5   [Number of countries having passed anti–human trafficking laws] According to the U.S. government, seventeen countries had specific, comprehensive, and enforced laws against trafficking in 2004. U.S. Department of State, Office to Monitor and Combat Trafficking in Persons, "Trafficking in Persons Report," June 14, 2004. http://www.state.gov/g/tip/rls/tiprpt/2004/33187.htm

CHAPTER 2: GLOBAL SMUGGLERS ARE CHANGING YOUR WORLD

12   [Declining cost of telephone calls in the 1990s] "International Pricing and the Death of Distance," *International Telecommunication Union, TELECOM.* http://www.itu.int/telecomwt99/press_service/information_for_the_press/press_kit/backgrounders/backgrounders/telecoms_pricing-next.html#International

14   [Volume of the people trade] David Feingold, "Think Again: Human Trafficking," *Foreign Policy*, forthcoming, 2005.

14   [Global drug seizures nearly double, 1990–2002] United Nations Office on Drugs and Crime, "2004 World Drug Report: Executive Summary," 2004, p. 17.

15   [Small arms fuel nearly fifty wars] United Nations Office for the Coordination of Humanitarian Affairs, Small Arms. http://ochaonline.un.org/webpage.asp?Page=528. Also: Small arms responsible for 4 million deaths in intrastate and regional conflicts since 1990; 14 million refugees from conflicts where small arms/light weapons are used ("The Extent and Dangers of the Illicit Small Arms and Light Weapons Trade," U.S. State Department fact sheet, July 19, 2001).

15–16   [Haiti killer counterfeit "cough medicine"] Frances Williams, "WHO Launches Drive to Stamp Out Fake Drugs," *Financial Times*, November 12, 2003, p. 14.

16   [Camdessus] Address by Michel Camdessus, managing director of the Interna-

tional Monetary Fund, at the Plenary Meeting of the Financial Action Task Force on Money Laundering, Paris, February 10, 1998.

16   [Estimates of laundered money at 10 percent of world GDP] Peter Reuter and Edwin M. Truman, *Chasing Dirty Money: The Fight against Money Laundering* (Washington, DC: Institute for International Economics, 2004), p. 13.

Globalization Happened

17   [Washington consensus and economic reforms in the 1990s] Moisés Naím, "Washington Consensus or Washington Confusion?" *Foreign Policy,* spring 2000, pp. 87–103; Moisés Naím, "Washington Consensus: A Damaged Brand," *Financial Times,* October 28, 2002, p. 15.

Reform=Opportunity

18   [Drop in average tariffs, 1980–2002] Robert Lawson and James Gwartney, "Economic Freedom Is on the Rise," *CATO Institute Daily Commentary,* July 19, 2004. http://www.cato.org/dailys/07-19-04-2.html

19   [Trade growth] Supachai Panitchpakdi, WTO director-general, "The Doha Development Agenda: What's at Stake for Business in the Developing World?" *International Trade Forum,* no. 2, 2003, pp. 4–5.

20   [Friedman, "golden straitjacket"] Thomas L. Friedman, *The Lexus and the Olive Tree: Understanding Globalization* (New York: Farrar, Straus and Giroux, 1999), pp. 83ff.

Tools of the Trades

21–22   [Gaviria] Author interview with President Cesar Gaviria. Washington, January 25, 2005

22   [Growth in daily value of foreign exchange transactions] Gabriele Galati and Michael Melvin, "Why Has FX Trading Surged? Explaining the 2004 Triennial Survey," *BIS Quarterly Review,* December 2004, p. 68; Tom Abate, "Banking's Soldiers of Fortune: Foreign Exchange Traders on Front Line of Currency War," *San Francisco Chronicle,* December 7, 2004.

23   [Growth in credit and debit cards in the United States] "A Durable Idea," *The Economist,* February 14, 2005, p. 71.

24   [Online gaming industry] Bear Stearns estimate cited in U.S. Congress. House Committee on Financial Services, *Financial Aspects of Internet Gaming: Good Gamble or Bad Bet?* Statement of Rep. Sue Kelly, 107th Cong., 1st sess., July 12, 2001.

24   [Web based drug trafficking] Marc Kaufman, "Internet Drug Ring Broken," *Washington Post,* April 21, 2005, p. A3.

New Sources, New Routes

26   [Moody] Author interview with James Moody, former senior FBI agent, January 6, 2005, Reston, Virginia.

Altered States

27   ["Failed states"] Robert Rotberg, ed., *When States Fail: Causes and Conse-quences* (Princeton, NJ: Princeton University Press, 2004); Francis Fukuyama, *State-Building: Governance and World Order in the Twenty-first Century* (Ithaca, NY; Cornell University Press, 2004).

27   [Bouterse relatives] Ivan Cairo, "Eight Nabbed in Joint Suriname-Holland Anti–Drug and Money Laundering Operation," *Caribbean Net News,* March 4, 2005.

27–28   [Tajikistan] "Tajikistan: Stemming the Heroin Tide," IRINews.org. UN Of-fice for the Coordination of Humanitarian Affairs. http://www.irinnews.org/webspecials/opium/regTaj.asp

28   [On Vladimiro Montesinos] John McMillan and Pablo Zoido, "How to Subvert Democracy: Montesinos in Peru," *Journal of Economic Perspectives* 18, no. 4 (fall 2004): pp. 69–92; author interview with Roberto Dañino, former prime minister of Peru, November 2004, Washington, DC.

28   [British intelligence] Author interview with senior agent, UK M16, London, Jan-uary 20, 2004.

28–29   [Fifty regions of little or no government control] "The Worldwide Threat 2004: Challenges in a Changing Global Context," testimony of Director of Central Intelligence George J. Tenet before the Senate Select Committee on Intelligence, February 24, 2004, Washington, DC.

29   [FARC drug trade revenues] "Las FARC ganaron $783 millones por droga en el 2003," *El Nuevo Herald (Miami),* March 8, 2003, based on an Agence France-Presse dispatch.

29   [Al-Qaeda diamond deals] Douglas Farah, *Blood from Stones: The Secret Finan-cial Network of Terror* (New York: Broadway Books, 2004), pp. 47–62.

The New Entrepreneurs

30–31   [Post-Soviet entrepreneurs and background in gaming the system] Phil Williams, ed., *Russian Organized Crime: The New Threat* (London: Frank Cass Publishers, 1997); Alena V. Ledeneva and Marina Kurkchiyan, eds., *Economic Crime in Russia* (New York: Kluwer Law International, 2000); Chrystia Free-land, *Sale of the Century: Russia's Wild Ride from Communism To Capitalism* (New York: Times Books, 2000); David Satter, *Darkness at Dawn: The Rise of the Russian Criminal State* (New Haven: Yale University Press, 2004).

Underworld No Longer

32   [Baginski] Author interview with Maureen A. Baginski, executive assistant di-rector, Office of Intelligence, Federal Bureau of Investigation, Washington, DC, November 17, 2004.

33   [Wal-Mart accused in 2003] "Wal-Mart Pays $11M to Settle Illegal Immigrant Janitors Case," *USA Today* and Associated Press, March 18, 2003.

CHAPTER 3: SMALL ARMS AND LOOSE NUKES

38–41   [A. Q. Khan network] "A Tale of Nuclear Proliferation: How a Pakistani Built His Network," *New York Times,* February 12, 2004, p. A1; Stephen Fidler and Victoria Burnett, "The Nuclear Entrepreneur: 'Khan's Network Shows Terrorists Have a Lot More Options Than We Thought,'" *Financial Times*, April 7, 2004.

38   ["Father of islamic bomb" and popularity in Pakistan] Anthony Barnett, "Revealed: How Pakistan Fuels Nuclear Arms Race," *The Observer*, January 18, 2004, p. 24; "Sold," *The Economist*, February 7, 2004.

38–39   [Gulf Technical Industries, Paul Griffin, capture of BBC *China*, KRL stickers] Owen Bowcott, Ian Traynor, John Aglionby, and Suzanne Goldenberg, "Briton Key Suspect in Nuclear Ring," *The Guardian*, February 12, 2004, p. 1.

39   [BSA Tahir, Scomi, SMB Computers] Raymond Bonner, "Salesman on Nuclear Circuit Casts Blurry Corporate Shadow," *New York Times*, February 18, 2004, p. A1.

40   [Khan's dealings with Iran, Iraq, Libya, and North Korea] Ian Traynor, "Pakistan's Nuclear Hero Throws Open Pandora's Box," *The Guardian*, January 31, 2004, p. 16; William J. Broad and David E. Sanger, "Warhead Blueprints Link Libya Project To Pakistan Figure," *New York Times*, February 4, 2004, p. A1; Stephen Fidler and Victoria Burnett, "Pakistan's 'Rogue Nuclear Scientist': What Did Khan's Government Know about His Deals?" *Financial Times*, April 6, 2004, p. 17.

40   [Chinese and "Good Looks" anecdotes] Joby Warrick and Peter Slevin, "Libyan Arms Designs Traced Back To China," *Washington Post*, February 15, 2004, p. A1.

40   [A. Q. Khan compared to Hitler and Stalin] Michael Hirsch and Sarah Shafer, "Black Market Nukes," *Newsweek*, February 23, 2004.

40–41   [Humayun Khan] David S. Cloud, "US Says Banned Technology Went to Pakistan and India," *New York Times*, April 9, 2005.

Strictly Business

43   [Khan wealth and lifestyle] Francoise Chipaux, "L'inquiétant Dr. Khan," *Le Monde*, February 20, 2004; "Business in Timbuktu," *The News International (Pakistan)*, February 1, 2004; Stephen Fidler and Victoria Burnett, "Animal Lover, Egotist, and National Hero," *Financial Times*, April 7, 2004.

45.   [9/11 commissioner] Author interview with 9/11 Commission member, Washington, DC, January 24, 2005.

45   [Haqqani] Author interview with Husain Haqqani, Washington, DC, September 16, 2004.

Up for Anything

45–50   This section draws on the International Consortium of Investigative Journalists (ICIJ), *Making a Killing: The Business of War* (Washington, DC: Center for Public Integrity, 2003).

46–47   [Minin section] Ibid., Chapter 10, pp. 134–42.

47–48   [On Monsieur] Ibid., Chapter 9, pp. 124–33.

48–50   [On Bout] Ibid., Chapter 11, pp. 143–56 (including "merchant of death" coinage); Peter Landesman, "Arms and the Man," *New York Times Magazine*, August 17, 2003; PBS Frontline World, May 2002, online at http://www.pbs.org/frontlineworld/stories/sierraleone/bout.html

48   [Khartoum "green boxes"] Brian Johnson-Thomas, "Anatomy of a Shady Deal," Chapter 1, in Lora Lumpe, ed., *Running Guns: The Global Black Market in Small Arms* (London: Zed Books, 2000), p. 21.

49   [Ruprah arrest and Bout Taliban/al-Qaeda connections] Douglas Farah, "Arrest
     Aids Pursuit of Weapons Network," *Washington Post,* February 26, 2002, p. A1;
     "On the Trail of a Man behind Taliban's Air Fleet," *Los Angeles Times,* May 19,
     2002, p. A1.
49   [Trailing Bout in Moscow] Stephen Smith, "On the Trail of the Elusive Victor
     Bout," *Guardian Weekly,* April 17, 2002, originally published as "L'insaisissable
     Victor Bout," *Le Monde,* March 26, 2002; "Russian Businessman Wanted by
     Belgians Turns Up in Moscow Radio Studio," BBC Monitoring online report of
     Ekho Moskvy radio, February 28, 2002.
50   [Bout role in U.S.-Iraq logistics subcontracting] Mark Huband, Andrew Parker,
     and Mark Turner, "UK Snubs France over Arms Trafficker: Bid to Help Dealer
     Linked To Coalition Avoid Sanctions," *Financial Times,* May 17, 2004, p. 1;
     Michael Scherer, "Dealing with the Merchant of Death," *Mother Jones,* Septem-
     ber 20, 2004; Stephen Braun, Judy Pasternak, and T. Christian Miller, "Black-
     listed Russian Tied To Iraq Deals," *Los Angeles Times,* December 14, 2004, p. A1.

A Middleman's Dream

50–51   [Production of small arms] The leading source on small arms and light
     weapons is the annual *Small Arms Survey* (Geneva: Graduate Institute of Inter-
     national Studies). See specifically *Small Arms Survey 2003: Development De-
     nied,* Chapter 1, "Workshops and Factories: Products and Producers," pp. 8–56;
     Small Arms Survey 2004: Rights at Risk, Chapter 1, "Continuity and Change:
     Products and Producers," pp. 6–41.
51   [Small arms industry recomposing] *Small Arms Survey 2003,* p. 15.
51   [Number and scope of firms involved in small arms production] *Small Arms
     Survey 2003,* Chapter 1; Pete Abel, "Manufacturing Trends: Globalising the
     Source," in Lumpe, *Running Guns,* pp. 81–104; on Heckler & Koch,
     pp. 89–96.
51   [1,249 small arms producers in 2003] *Small Arms Survey 2004,* p. 10.
52   [Darra Adam Khel] Raymond Bonner, "When It's Business, the City Sticks To
     Its Guns," *New York Times,* April 11, 2002.
52   [Ghana] *Small Arms Survey 2003,* pp. 29–32; Emmanuel Kwesi Aning and
     Nicholas Florquin, "Ghana's Secret Arms Industry," *Jane's Intelligence Review,*
     December 2004, p. 7.
52   [Central and Eastern Europe small arms industry] *Small Arms Survey 2003,* pp.
     39–49.
52   [2001 imports to the United States] *Small Arms Survey 2003,* p. 39.
52   [European gun brokers] Lumpe, *Running Guns,* pp. 131–32.
52   ["Refuges for rogue brokers"] *Small Arms Survey 2003,* p. 119.
53   [Illicit arms deliveries to Liberia] United Nations Security Council, *Report of
     the Panel of Experts Appointed Pursuant To Security Council Resolution 1395
     (2002), Paragraph 4, in Relation to Liberia,* S/2002/470, April 19, 2002,
     pp. 15–23; United Nations Security Council, *Report of the Panel of Experts Ap-
     pointed Pursuant To Security Council Resolution 1408 (2002), Paragraph 26,
     Concerning Liberia,* S/2002/1115, October 25, 2002, pp. 16–29; United Na-
     tions Security Council, *Report of the Panel of Experts Appointed Pursuant To Se-
     curity Council Resolution 1408 (2002), Paragraph 16, Concerning Liberia,*
     S/2002/498, April 24, 2003, pp. 19–33; United Nations Security Council, *Re-
     port of the Panel of Experts Appointed Pursuant To Security Council Resolution*

1478 (2003), Paragraph 25, Concerning Liberia, S/2003/937, October 28, 2003, pp. 23–29.

53–54   [Nonstate groups who are known to have MANPADs] *Small Arms Survey 2004,* chapter 3, "Big Issue, Big Problem? MANPADS," p. 89.

53   [Portable missile launchers produced, in stock, and missing, worldwide and in Iraq] *Small Arms Survey 2004,* pp. 83–89 (the SAS cites reports suggesting there are 500,000 MANPADs in existence, but argues that these are likely overestimates, and that the real number is 100,000); Dana Priest and Bradley Graham, "Missing Antiaircraft Missiles Alarm Aides," *Washington Post,* November 7, 2004, p. A24; U.S. Government Accounting Office, *Nonproliferation: Further Improvements Needed to Counter Threats from Man-Portable Air Defense Systems,* May 2004.

The Weapons Wal-Mart

54   [Togo/UNITA] United Nations Security Council, *Report of the Panel of Experts on Violations of Security Council Sanctions against UNITA,* S/2003/937, Robert R. Fowler, March 10, 2000.

55   [Montesinos/FARC] *El Espectador (Bogota),* February 10, 2002 (via "Paper Reports Flourishing Arms-for-Drugs Trade with Colombian Rebels," BBC Monitoring, BBC News online).

55   [On end-user certificates] Organisation for Security and Cooperation in Europe, Forum for Security Cooperation, *Standard Elements of End-User Certificates and Verification Procedures for SALW Exports, Decisions,* no. 5/04, November 17, 2004.

55–56   [Regional/civil conflict] Ann Hironaka, *Neverending Wars: The International Community, Weak States, and the Perpetuation of Civil War* (Cambridge: Harvard University Press, 2005); Paul Collier and Anke Hoeffler, "Murder by Numbers: Socio-Economic Determinants of Homicide and Civil War," *Centre for the Study of African Economies Series,* Ref: WPS/2004–10, Oxford University; Ian Bannon and Paul Collier, eds., *Natural Resources and Violent Conflict* (Washington, DC: World Bank, 2003).

56   [Sampson quote] Anthony Sampson, *The Arms Bazaar: From Lebanon To Lockheed* (New York: Viking, 1977), p. 340.

Own Your Own State

57–58   [Transdniester] Joby Warrick, "Dirty Bomb Warheads Disappear," *Washington Post,* December 7, 2003, p. A1; Joby Warrick, "Smugglers Enticed by Dirty Bomb Component," *Washington Post,* November 30, 2003, p. A1.

Armed Civil Society

59   [U.S. small arms stock] *Small Arms Survey 2003,* p. 61.

59   [List of "most-armed" countries] Ibid., pp. 64–65.

59   [England gun crime rates] for England and Wales; data for firearms other than air weapons. http://www.homeoffice.gov.uk/rds/pdfs2/hosb0104.pdf

59   [European arms seizures] *Small Arms Survey 2003,* p. 71.

60   [Small arms in Europe] Mark Turner, "European Citizens 'Heavily Armed,' " *Financial Times,* July 9, 2003, p. 11.

60   [Kampala, Uganda] *Small Arms Survey 2003*, p. 134.

60   [Mindanao] Ibid., p. 138.

60   ["Development denied" and direct/indirect effects] Ibid., chapter 4, pp. 125–68.

61   [Security business boom] *Small Arms Survey 2001*; referenced in *Small Arms Survey 2003*, p. 139 and fn. 30, p. 160; also see IBSSA (International Bodyguard and Security Services Association)—http://www.ibssa.org

61   [Cameroon and Nigeria examples] *Small Arms Survey 2003*, p. 140 (Cameroon) and p. 139 (Kaduna).

Ghosts and Borders

62   [On brokers] Brian Wood and Johan Peleman, "Making the Deal and Moving the Goods: The Role of Brokers and Shippers," chapter 6, in Lumpe, *Running Guns*, pp. 129–54.

62   [Rules vary country to country] Emanuela-Chiara Gillard, "What's Legal? What's Illegal?" Chapter 2, in Lumpe, *Running Guns*, pp. 41–42.

62–63   [Rwanda and Congo deals] Wood and Peleman, "Making the Deal," pp. 136–39; "Un Français est écroué pour trafic d'armes de guerre avec le Rwanda," *Le Monde,* February 2, 1995.

63   [Slovakia/Sudan story] Johnson-Thomas, "Anatomy of a Shady Deal," pp. 13–25.

63   [Antonov crash in Monrovia] United Nations Security Council, *Report of the Panel of Experts Appointed Pursuant To Security Council Resolution 1395 (2002), Paragraph 4, in Relation to Liberia,* S/2002/470, April 19, 2002.

63   [List of embargoes] Gillard, "What's Legal?" p. 33.

63   [ECOWAS moratorium] Sarah Meek, "Combating Arms Trafficking: Progress and Prospects," chapter 8, in Lumpe, *Running Guns*, pp. 194–97.

64   [UN conference] United Nations, *Report of the United Nations Conference on the Illicit Trade in Small Arms and Light Weapons in All Its Aspects,* A/CONF. 192/15, New York, July 2001.

64   [Bolton intervention] Colum Lynch, "U.S. Fights UN Accord to Control Small Arms Sales," *Washington Post,* July 10, 2001, p. A1.

64   [LaPierre comment] Jim Burns, "U.S. Fires First Shot at UN Anti-Gun Conference," CNSNews.com, July 10, 2001; "U.S. Blocks Small Arms Controls," BBC News Online, July 10, 2001.

64   [UN response] UN Department of Public Information, "Setting the Record Straight," July 2001. www.un.org/depts/dda/cab/smallarms/facts.htm

64   [Kolowa "five cows" anecdote] Karl Vick, "Small Arms' Global Reach Uproots Tribal Traditions," *Washington Post,* July 8, 2001, p. A1.

CHAPTER 4: NO BUSINESS LIKE DRUG BUSINESS

65–66   [Don Alfonzo] Author interview with "Don Alfonzo," Nuevo Laredo, Mexico, September 10, 2004.

67   [Guzmán] Chris Kraul and Cecilia Sanchez, "Mexican Border Town Tries to Clean Up Its Image," *Los Angeles Times,* February 12, 2005, p. A3; Chris Kraul, "Official Says Tijuana, Gulf Cartels Have United," *Los Angeles Times,* January 14, 2005, p. A4.

67   [Mexican organizations] "Drugs in Mexico: War without End," *The Economist,* March 4, 2004.

68   [U.S. annual antidrug expenditure] Total estimates vary due to the number of separate programs involved and are subject to political interpretation. The U.S. government estimated federal antidrug spending at $12.1 billion for 2004; unofficial estimates ranged as high as $20 billion. Moreover, adding state and local expenses may increase the total by up to 100 percent, though more likely somewhat less. See, for instance, Office of National Drug Control Policy, *National Drug Control Strategy 2004 Fact Sheet,* p. 3. http://www.whitehousedrugpolicy.gov/publications/policy/ndcs04/strategy_fs.pdf; Gary E. Johnson, "Take It from a Businessman: The War on Drugs Is Just Money Down the Drain," MotherJones.com, July 10, 2001; National Research Council, National Academy of Sciences, *Informing America's Policy on Illegal Drugs: What We Don't Know Keeps Hurting Us* (Washington, DC: National Academy Press, 2001), p. 1.

68   [drug arrests] Federal Bureau of Investigation, *Crime in America: FBI Uniform Crime Reports 2003* (Washington, DC: U.S. Government Printing Office, 2004), p. 270, table 29.

68   [DC statistics on high school students, jail, and drug seizures] "Washington, DC, Profile of Drug Indicators," Office of National Drug Control Policy, Drug Policy Information Clearinghouse, at ONDCP website.

68   [2004 DC seizures] Drug Enforcement Administration website: dea.gov, DEA State Fact Sheets, "Washington DC 2005." http://www.dea.gov/pubs/states/washingtondc.html

68–69   [on Washington teenagers' access to drugs] Author interviews with students in Washington-area private high schools, January–February 2004.

69   [Afghanistan 2004 poppy production/acreage] According to the United Nations Office of Drugs and Crime, *2004 World Drug Report* (Vienna: UNDCP, 2004), p. 206; 3,600 metric tons of opium were produced from 80,000 hectares of land in Afghanistan in 2003, according to Tom Shanker, "Pentagon Sees Antidrug Effort in Afghanistan," *New York Times,* March 25, 2005, p. A1. Production rose 64 percent in 2004.

69–70   [Afghan drug transformation; anecdotes on cost of labor and bribes] "Afghan Poppies Proliferate: As Drug Trade Widens, Labs and Corruption Flourish," *Washington Post,* July 10, 2003, p. A1; "Karzai: Don't Spray Our Poppies," CBSNews.com, November 19, 2004, at: http://www.cbsnews.com/stories/2004/11/18/world/main656576.shtml

70   [FARC and AUC drug revenue] Mark S. Steinitz, "The Terrorism and Drug Connection in Latin America's Andean Region," *CSIS Policy Papers on the Americas,* vol. 13, study 5; Angel Rabasa and Peter Chalk, *Colombian Labyrinth: The Synergy of Drugs and Insurgency and Its Implications for Regional Stability* (Santa Monica: RAND Project Air Force, 2001).

70   [Colombia: new strains of coca] Joshua Davis, "The Mystery of the Coca Plant that Wouldn't Die," *Wired,* November 2004; Andy Webb-Vidal, "It's Super-Coca! Modified Bush Boosts Narcotics Output," *Financial Times,* December 7, 2004, p. 4.

70–71   [Canadian supply of B.C. bud] Sarah Kershaw, "Violent New Front in Drug War Opens on the Canadian Border: Potent Marijuana at Center of Smuggling Chain," *New York Times,* March 5, 2005, p. A1.

The End of Illusions

71   [Global drug market statistics] *Global Illicit Drug Trends,* United Nations Office on Drugs and Crime, at http://www.unodc.org/unodc/en/global_illicit_drug_trends.html

71   [Yaa baa] Kevin Fagan, "Southeast Asia Is Reeling from Combination of Meth, AIDS," *San Francisco Chronicle,* May 29, 2003, p. A7.

72   [Tajikistan] "Drugs in Central Asia: Deadly Traffic," *The Economist,* March 29, 2003, pp. 38–39; see also Iran: Molly Moore, "Iran Fighting a Losing Drug War," and Molly Moore, "Once Hidden, Drug Addiction in Changing Iran," both *Washington Post,* July 18, 2001, pp. A1 and A26.

72   [Yunnan] "China-Burma: Heroin Is King at Border Crossing," Inter Press Service, March 26, 2004; "Condom, Needle Distribution Highlights AIDS Issue in S. W. China," *Kyodo News International,* March 9, 2004.

73   [Nigerian Southeast Asian networks] Felix Umoru, "A Tough War," *Financial Times,* December 1, 2002; Benjamin Adedeji, "Nigeria; Pains, Gains and Challenges of Certification," *All Africa,* March 29, 2001; Frank A. Aukofer and Dave Daley, "Heroin Buys Here Help Bust Ring," *Milwaukee Journal Sentinel,* October 12, 1996, p. 1.

73   [Chicago wholesale and distribution case] National Drug Intelligence Center, U.S. Department of Justice, *Heroin Distribution in Three Cities,* November 2000.

73   [Transformation of the trade] Matthew Brzezinski, "Re-engineering the Drug Business," *New York Times Magazine,* June 23, 2002.

Demystifying the Game

74   [Escobar, rise of the cartels] Colombia: Robin Kirk, *More Terrible than Death: Massacres, Drugs and America's War in Colombia* (New York: Public Affairs, 2003).

75   [Mexican drug business] Jorge Luis Sierra Guzmán, "Mexico's Military in the War on Drugs," *WOLA Drug War Monitor,* April 2003.

75–76   [Mexican collaboration with other non-Mex trafficking networks] [Russians] Susana Hayward, "Russian Mafia Helping Mexican Cartels Smuggle Drugs into U.S. Officials Say," Knight Ridder news service, August 6, 2003; [FARC] Eric Rosenberg, "Colombia Effort Raises Fears of Another Vietnam," *San Antonio Express-News,* January 15, 2001, p. 1A.

76   [Juarez group; twenty-six regional manager "bankers"] Library of Congress Federal Research Division, "Organized Crime and Terrorist Activity in Mexico, 1999–2002," Washington, DC, 2003, p. 8.

76   [Mexican organizations] "Drugs in Mexico: War without End," *The Economist,* March 4, 2004.

Launder, Barter, Hack

77   [Annual drug seizures] United Nations Office of Drugs and Crime (UNODC), *Global Illegal Drug Trends 2003.*

77   [Ease of dissimulation in volume of global trade] Kris Axtman, "Rising Border Traffic, More Drugs," *Christian Science Monitor,* May 8, 2001, p. 1; Stephen E. Flynn, "The Global Drug Trade versus the Nation-State: Why the Thugs Are

Winning," in Maryann Cusimano, ed., *Beyond Sovereignty: Issues for a Global Agenda* (New York: St. Martin's Press, 2002), pp. 44–66; Kal Raustiala, "Law, Liberalization, and International Narcotics Trafficking," *New York University Journal of International Law and Politics* 32, no. 1 (fall 1999): pp. 89–145, especially "Drugs and Liberalization," pp. 114–30.

77–78   [New technologies] United Nations, International Narcotics Control Board, *Globalization and New Technologies: Challenges To Drug Law Enforcement in the Twenty-First Century,* 2001, E/INCB/2001/1; "High Technology Boosts Dutch Marijuana Trade," *Financial Times,* August 23, 2001.

78   [early adoption of encryption techniques by Cali cartel] Author interview with César Gaviria, president of Colombia, 1990–94; New York, March 2005.

78–79   [Black market peso exchange] Oriana Zill and Lowell Bergman, "The Black Peso Money Laundering System," at PBS Frontline website, "Drug Wars." http://www.pbs.org/wgbh/pages/frontline/shows/drugs/special/blackpeso.html

79   [Description of "Russian weapons and other equipment" for drugs] Jerry Seper, "Mexicans, Russian Mob New Partners in Crime," *Washington Times,* May 28, 2001, p. A1.

79   [IRA/Dublin drug supply and FARC links] Jim Cusak, "IRA Unit in Bogotá as Part of 'Technology Exchange,' " *Irish Times,* August 15, 2001, p. 7.

Stuck in Source Control

80   [U.S. overseas drug operations] Mark Bowden, "Witness: Plan Colombia," *Prospect,* July 2001, pp. 38–44; "Latin American Poppy Fields Undermine U.S. Drug Battle," *New York Times,* June 8, 2003, p. A1; Ted Galen Carpenter, *Bad Neighbor Policy: Washington's Futile War on Drugs in Latin America* (New York: Palgrave, 2003); William M. LeoGrande and Kenneth Sharpe, "A Plan, But No Clear Objective," *Washington Post,* April 1, 2001, p. B2.

80   [Stubbornness of source control policy] Peter Reuter, "Supply-Side Drug Control," *Milken Institute Review,* first quarter 2001, pp. 15–23.

80   [U.S. certification system] Peter Reuter, "A Certifiable Drug Policy . . . " *Washington Post,* August 23, 2000, p. A25.

80–82   [Certification] Author interview with former DEA official. Miami, FL, March 5, 2004.

81   [U.S. seizures and strange hiding places] For example, see: U.S. Customs and Border Protection press release, "CBP Inspectors Find Heroin in Teddy Bear," CBP.gov, September 12, 2003; Kris Axtman, "Rising Border Traffic, More Drugs," *Christian Science Monitor,* May 8, 2001, p. 1.

81   [Increase in marijuana users seeking treatment] The White House, National Drug Control Strategy, February 2005; "More Seek Treatment for Marijuana," *New York Times,* March 4, 2005.

Colliding with Politics

82–83   [Bolivia] "Bolivian President Has Corrupt Congress, No Political Backing, but Nation's Respect," Knight Ridder/Tribune News Service, February 10, 2004; Larry Rother, "Bolivian Leader's Ouster Seen as Warning on U.S. Drug Policy," *New York Times,* October 23, 2003; "Throwing Down the Gauntlet; Turmoil in Bolivia," *The Economist,* March 12, 2005, p. 61; "A President under Siege; Bolivia," *The Economist,* March 19, 2005, p. 64.

83 [Quotes from former Bolivian president Gonzalo Sanchez de Lozada] Author interview with Gonzalo Sanchez de Lozada, Washington, DC, July 20, 2004.

84 [Mayor of Guzmán's hometown] James C. McKinley Jr., "Drug Lord, Ruthless and Elusive, Reaches High in Mexico," *New York Times,* February 9, 2005, p. A3.

84–85 [North Korea state involvement in drug trafficking] John Hill, "Korean Diplomats Face Drugs Trafficking Charge," *Jane's Intelligence Review,* January 2005, p. 6; Jonathan Mann and Mike Chinoy, "Drugs and Nuclear Weapons in North Korea," *Insight,* CNN, September 29, 2004. Also: U.S. Department of State, Bureau for International Narcotics and Law Enforcement Affairs, "2003 International Narcotics Control Strategy Report," March 1, 2004.

CHAPTER 5: WHY IS SLAVERY BOOMING IN THE 21st CENTURY?

86–87 [Golden Venture] Greg Torode, "Hong Kong Probe into Death Ship: Survivors Held as U.S. Vows to Stem Flood," *South China Morning Post,* June 8, 1993, p. 1; Sarah Jackson-Han, "Chinese Aliens Sparked Long-Term Immigration Crackdown," Agence France-Presse, June 7, 1996.

86–87 [Fujian circuit] Zai Liang and Wenzhen Ye, "From Fujian To New York: Understanding the New Chinese Immigration," chapter 7, in David Kyle and Rey Koslowski, *Global Human Smuggling: Comparative Perspectives* (Baltimore: Johns Hopkins University Press, 2001); Ko-Lin Chin, "The Social Organization of Chinese Human Smuggling," chapter 8, in Kyle and Koslowski, *Global Human Smuggling;* Michael Maiello and Susan Kitchens, "Preying on Human Cargo," Forbes.com, June 7, 2004.

87 [$60,000 price for one person smuggled from China to the United States] Author interview with Doris Meissner, U.S. commissioner of Immigration and Naturalization Service, 1993–2000; Washington, DC, February 2002, published in *Foreign Policy,* March–April 2003, p. 31.

87–88 [Tourab Ahmed Sheik/Mandir Kumar Wahi] "Le prince des trafiquants d'êtres humains enfin dans le box," *Courrier International,* November 6, 2003, p. 9; David Finkel, "Dreams Dashed on the Rocks," *Washington Post,* June 10, 2001, p. A1.

Mass Movements

88 [Size and scope of global trafficking and smuggling trade] David Kyle and Rey Koslowski, introduction, in Kyle and Koslowski, eds., *Global Human Smuggling,* pp. 3–4; International Organization for Migration, "New IOM Figures on the Global Scale of Trafficking," *Trafficking in Migrants Quarterly Bulletin,* no. 23, April 2001, and online at www.iom.int; Frank Laczko, "Human Trafficking: The Need for Better Data," Migration Information Source, Migration Policy Institute, November 1, 2002; Barbara Crossette, "UN Warns That Trafficking in Human Beings Is Growing," *New York Times,* June 25, 2000; UN Population Fund, UN Information Service, United Nations, *State of the World's Cities, 2004/2005: Globalization and Urban Culture.* UN-HABITAT (London, 2004). Also David Feingold, "Think Again: Human Trafficking," *Foreign Policy,* forthcoming, 2005.

88 [FBI estimates of Mexican people smuggling] Oscar Becerra, "Mexican People Smuggling Trade Worth Billions," *Jane's Intelligence Review,* December 2004, p. 30.

89   [Reasons for migration] "On the Move," *The Economist,* May 12, 2001; Kirstin
      Downey Grimsley, "Global Migration Trends Reflect Economic Options," *Wash-
      ington Post,* January 3, 2002; "Immigration into Germany: More Needed, Fewer
      Wanted," *The Economist,* June 23, 2001; "Knocking at the Rich Man's Door,"
      Financial Times, May 25, 2002; Alan Cowell, "Migrants Feel Chill in a Testy
      Europe," *New York Times,* April 28, 2002, p. A14.

89   [Global migration numbers, countries receiving remittances] "Humanity on the
      Move: The Myths and Realities of International Migration," *Financial Times,*
      July 30, 2003, p. 11.

90–91   [Guest worker idea in the United States] On guest-worker program: Max
      Blumenthal, "Immigration Conflagration," *American Prospect,* April 2004, p. 14.

91   [Bales, modern-day slavery] Kevin Bales, *Disposable People: New Slavery in the
      Global Economy* (Berkeley and Los Angeles: University of California Press,
      1999).

The Height of Degradation

92   [East Europe to West Europe sex trafficking, Operation Sunflower] Christopher
      Sulavik, "Facing Down Traffickers: Europe Takes on Its Fastest-Growing Crimi-
      nal Enterprise," *Newsweek,* August 25, 2003; "Preying on Children," *Newsweek,*
      November 17, 2003; "Balkan Traffic in Women and Girls 'On Rise,' " *Financial
      Times,* December 18, 2003; see also "Trafficking of People in Kosovo," Immigra-
      tion and Nationality Directorate, UK Home Office, June 25, 2004.

92   [Politicians as accomplices of people-trafficking criminals in the Balkans] Eric
      Jannson, "Report: Balkan Traffic in Women and Girls 'On the Rise,' " *Financial
      Times,* December 18, 2003.

92–93   [Sale of babies/children] "Baby Trade," *The Economist,* February 7, 2004;
      Nicholas Wood, "For Albanians, It's Come To This: A Son for a TV," *New York
      Times,* November 13, 2003.

93   [Sex slaves in Florida] "16 Indicted in Mexican Prostitution Ring," United Press
      International, April 23, 1998.

93   ["A 1999 report . . . "] Amy O'Neill Richard, "International Trafficking in
      Women To the United States: A Contemporary Manifestation of Slavery and
      Organized Crime," Center for the Study of Intelligence, November 1999.

93   [Sex trafficking in the United States] Peter Landesman, "The Girls Next Door"
      New York Times Magazine, January 25, 2004; Wilson Ring, "Experts: VT Sex
      Slavery Fits U.S. Pattern," Associated Press, July 23, 2004.

The Reserve Army of the Undocumented

93–94   [Osaka Zen spa] Nina Bernstein, "Women Complain of Hellish Life at Up-
      scale Spa," *New York Times,* April 9, 2004, p. B1.

94   [Chinese labor market in the United States] Peter Kwong, "Impact of Chinese
      Human Smuggling on the American Labor Market," chapter 9 in Kyle and
      Koslowski, eds., *Global Human Smuggling.*

94   [Corporate illegal alien scam] "Largest Corporation Immigrant Smuggling
      Ring Indicted by the INS," NPR News/National Public Radio, December 10,
      2001.

94   [Comment about implicit subsidy to U.S. companies employing illegal aliens]
      Mathias Blume, Letter to the Editor, *The Economist,* January 29, 2005, p. 14.

95 [Northern Marianas] Robert Collier, "Stalemate in Talks on Saipan Workers," *San Francisco Chronicle,* January 20, 1999, p. A1.

95–96 [Remittances] Devesh Kapur and John McHale, "Migration's New Payoff," *Foreign Policy,* November–December 2003, pp. 48–57; also, International Monetary Fund, *World Economic Outlook: Globalization and External Imbalances,* Washington, DC, April 2005, chapter 2, "Workers' Remittances and Economic Development."

96 ["Exporting" daughters in China] Howard French, "A Village Grows Rich Off Its Main Export: Its Daughters," *New York Times,* January 3, 2005, p. A4.

96 [Nigerian prostitutes return home] Somini Sengupta, "Oldest Profession Is Still One of the Oldest Lures for Young Nigerian Women," *New York Times,* November 5, 2004, p. A9.

Dragons, Coyotes, Snakeheads

97 ["It's like a dragon . . ."] Chin, "Social Organization," p. 218.

97 [30,000 Chinese in safe houses; 4,000 Chinese in Bolivia] Ibid., p. 217.

97 [300,000 clandestine in Moscow] Frank Viviano, "New Mafias Go Global: High-Tech Trade in Humans, Drugs," *San Francisco Chronicle,* January 7, 2001.

97 [El Paso network/1998] Allen Myerson, "4 Indicted on Immigrant Smuggling Scheme," *New York Times,* February 27, 1998, p. A20.

97–98 [change from coyote model to business model] Peter Andreas, "The Transformation of Migrant Smuggling across the U.S.-Mexican Border," chapter 4, in Kyle and Koslowski, eds., *Global Human Smuggling* (Baltimore: Johns Hopkins University Press, 2001).

97–98 [Price of Passage] Mary Jordan, "People Smuggling Now Big Business in Mexico," *Washington Post,* May 17, 2001, p. A1.

98 [Boughader organization and the M smuggling network in Mexico] Oscar Becerra, "Mexican People Smuggling Trade Worth Billions," *Jane's Intelligence Review,* December 2004, p. 31.

98 [Smuggler with cell phone/Sumatra] Michael Winchester, "The 'Travel Agents': On the Trail of the Syndicates Smuggling Desperate Middle Easterners through Asia To Australia," *Asiaweek,* January 19, 2001.

98–99 [Meissner] Author interview with Doris Meissner, U.S. Commissioner of Immigration and Naturalization Service, 1993–2000; Washington, DC, February 2002 (published in *Foreign Policy,* March–April 2003, p. 31).

99 [Carranza] Author interview with Miguel Angel Carranza, San Antonio, Texas, November 19, 2004.

Get Your Papers Here

100 [Afghanistan] Melinda Liu, "All Papers in Order: Getting the Documents Needed to Be Smuggled Abroad Is Shockingly Easy," *Newsweek,* November 5, 2001; Hugh Williamson, "Smugglers See Afghans as Potential Prey," *Financial Times,* November 5, 2001, p. 8.

100–01 [U.S. identification documents in Bowling Green] Peter Laufer, "My New Kentucky Home," *Washington Monthly,* January–February 2005, p. 24.

101 [Interpol's secretary-general on stolen passports] *El Pais,* January 28, 2005, p. 10.

101 [Official complicity with snakeheads] Chin, "Social Organization," pp. 225–29.

101   [Italy/Greece] Author interview with Italian diplomat, Athens, Greece, November 11, 2004.

101–02   [Examples of smuggling methods] Mary Jordan, "Smuggling People Is Now Big Business in Mexico," *Washington Post,* May 17, 2001, p. A1; Sofia Wu, "Cross-Strait Human Smuggling Ring Busted," *Central News Agency (Taiwan),* January 14, 1999; Letta Tayler, "Crossing a 'Corridor of Death,' " *Newsday,* June 17, 2002, p. A14.

102   [Phoenix and Perris, California, stories] Nick Madigan, "160 Migrants Seized at an Upscale Home," *New York Times,* February 13, 2004.

102–03   [Internet warehousing/sale of trafficked people] Landesmann, "The Girls Next Door," another source is: Graham Johnson and Dominic Hipkins, "Sex Slaves for Sale at £3,000 Each," *Sunday Mirror (UK),* December 28, 2003.

The Law Tries to Catch Up

103   [Migrants' rights convention] United Nations, "International Convention on the Protection of the Rights of All Migrant Workers and Members of Their Families," UN General Assembly Resolution 45/158, December 18, 1990.

103–04   [UN smuggling and trafficking protocols] United Nations, "Protocol to Prevent, Suppress and Punish Trafficking in Persons, Especially Women and Children, Supplementing the United Nations Convention against Transnational Organized Crime," UN General Assembly Resolution 55/25, November 15, 2000; United Nations, "Protocol against the Smuggling of Migrants by Land, Sea and Air, Supplementing the United Nations Convention against Transnational Organized Crime," UN General Assembly Resolution 55/25, November 15, 2000.

104   [U.S. policy] U.S. Department of State, *Trafficking in Persons Report,* annual; Gary Haugen, "State's Blind Eye on Sexual Slavery," *Washington Post,* January 16, 2002.

104   [Turkey arrests] "Smuggling of Humans into Europe Is Surging," *Washington Post,* May 28, 2001.

104   [Prison terms] U.S. Sentencing Commission, *Guidelines Manual* (November 2004). see: http://www.ussc.gov/2004guid/tabconoy_1.htm

105   [NGOs] See in particular Polaris Project at www.humantrafficking.com; Coalition Against Trafficking in Women at www.catwinternational.org.

105   [concerned journalists] Landesman, "The Girls Next Door"; Nicholas Kristof, "Cambodia, Where Sex Traffickers Are King," *New York Times,* January 15, 2005, p. A15; Kristof, "Leaving the Brothel Behind," *New York Times,* January 19, 2005, p. A19; Kristof, "Back to the Brothel," *New York Times,* January 22, 2005, p. A11; Kristof, "After the Brothel," *New York Times,* January 26, 2005, p. A17; Kristof, "Sex Slaves? Lock Up the Pimps," *New York Times,* 29 January 2005, p. A19.

Trading on Despair

107   [Relative deprivation] Oded Stark and J. Edward Taylor, "Migration Incentives, Migration Types: The Role of Relative Deprivation," *Economic Journal* 101, issue 408 (1991): pp. 1163–78.

108   [Morocco story] "Arriesgo la vida de mi hijo porque vivir en Marruecos es como estar muerto," *El Pais,* February 11, 2003, p. 43.

CHAPTER 6: THE GLOBAL TRADE IN STOLEN IDEAS

109 [Bono] "Names and Faces," *Washington Post,* November 27, 2004, p. C3.

109 [Microsoft Longhorn Malaysia anecdote] John Burton, "Software Pirates Circulate New Microsoft Operating System," *Financial Times,* December 12, 2003, p. 9.

109 [GM suit] Richard McGregor, "GM Probes Chery 'Piracy,'" *Financial Times,* November 12, 2003, p. 30.

109 [Gen. Michael Kalashnikov's lawsuit against U.S. government] John Ness, "Swords into Vodka," *Newsweek International,* November 22, 2004, p. 54; C. J. Chivers, "Who's a Pirate: Russia Points Back at the U.S.," *New York Times,* July 26, 2004, p. A1.

110 [Canal Street] Julia Apostle and David Gruber, "City of Phonies," at NYC24.com, issue 4, February 23, 2001; Julian E. Barnes, "Fake Goods Are Flowing under the New Radar," *New York Times,* October 14, 2001, p. C4.

Revenge of the Brands

111 [Counterfeits boom] "Imitating Property Is Theft," *The Economist,* May 15, 2003; "The Impact and Scale of Counterfeiting," Interpol, online at http://www.interpol.com/Public/News/Factsheet51pr21.asp

111–12 [New York and growth in commercial losses] "Bootleg Billions: The Impact of Counterfeit Goods Trade on New York City," New York State Office of the Comptroller, November 2004.

112 [Seizures] [Europe] "Warning as Fake Goods Flood Market," BBC News Online, August 8, 2003.

112 [United States] "Since 2000, the number of seizures of infringing goods at our nation's borders has increased by 100 percent. During the first half of 2004, CBP is setting a record pace with increases in seizures." U.S. Department of Commerce, "Results," StopFakes.gov., online at http://www.export.gov/stop_fakes_gov/results.asp

112 [Product range] "Market Pirates Lose the Taste for Luxury," *Financial Times,* July 27–28, 2002.

112 [Japanese schoolteachers] "Bags of Trouble," *Far Eastern Economic Review,* March 21, 2002, pp. 52–55.

113 [China] Ted C. Fishman, "Manufaketure," *New York Times Magazine,* January 9, 2005; "People's Republic of Cheats," *Far Eastern Economic Review,* June 21, 2001.

113 [Online counterfeit trade estimate] "Imitating Property Is Theft," *The Economist,* May 15, 2003.

114 [Africa counterfeit pharma] Tope Akinwade, "Lethal 'Cures' Plague Africa," *World Press Review* 51, no. 2 (February 2004).

114 [Togo CD industry] Matt Steinglass, "Moctar and Moctar," *Transition* 92 (2002), pp. 38–55.

114 [Thailand demonstration] "Imitating Property Is Theft," *The Economist,* May 15, 2003.

115 [Open source] Peter Wayner, "Whose Intellectual Property Is It, Anyway? The Open Source War," *New York Times,* August 24, 2000, p. G8.

115 ["I have several fake handbags"] Author interview, New York, March 14, 2004.

Intellectual Property Is Hot Property

116 [History of idea of intellectual property] "Economics Focus: Market for Ideas," *The Economist,* April 14, 2001; Suzanne Scotchmer, *Innovation and Incentives* (Cambridge: MIT Press, 2005).

The Inventory: From Tommy Hilfiger To Sewer Pumps

117 [NYC 2004 bust] "Retail Raid," *Newsday,* June 5, 2004, p. A8.

117–18 [Super copies] "Bags of Trouble," *Far Eastern Economic Review,* March 21, 2002, pp. 52–55; Jo Johnson, Fred Kapner, and Richard McGregor, "Back-Street Bonanza for the Counterfeiters," *Financial Times,* December 4, 2003, p. 16.

118 [Italy] Robert Galbraith, "Luxury Groups Battle a Wave of Counterfeit Goods," *International Herald Tribune,* September 29, 2001, p. 12; "The Impact and Scale of Counterfeiting," Interpol, May 25, 2004.

118 [Rolex seizure in Italy; also China media executive mention] Peter S. Goodman, "In China, a Growing Taste for Chic," *Washington Post,* July 12, 2004, p. A1.

118 [Genuine sales rising, example of $12,000 Omega watches] "Psst. Wanna Buy a Real Rolex?" *The Economist,* January 24, 2004.

118–19 [CEO of watch company quote] Author interview with CEO of Swiss watch company, Geneva, Switzerland, September 2003.

119–20 [Cars, other industrial products] "Heavy-Duty Forgers," *Far Eastern Economic Review,* March 23, 2000, pp. 46–47; Richard McGregor, "GM Probes Chery 'Piracy,' " *Financial Times,* November 12, 2003, p. 30; Jose Reinoso, "Coches clonados a bajo precio," *El Pais,* March 29, 2004; James Kynge, "Nissan May Sue Chinese Rival over Design," *Financial Times,* November 28, 2003, p. 21.

120 [Fake Honda motorcycles in China] Frederik Balfour, "Fakes," *Business Week* (European edition), February 7, 2005, pp. 54–64.

120 [DaimlerChrysler loss of market share in auto parts to counterfeiters] Ibid.

120 [Car and aircraft parts, United Airlines mechanic story] Murray Hiebert, "Fake-Parts Fear," *Far Eastern Economic Review,* March 4, 2004, p. 40.

120 [Valves, sewer pumps, other industrial examples] "Fakes Are Blotting the Horizon in Italy's Valley of the Valves," *Financial Times,* March 20, 2001; "Counterfeit Electrical Products Cause Damage To U.S. Markets," *Today's Facility Manager,* Online Exclusive, June 2002, at http://www.wireville.com/hots/hots0204.html#10; "Knock-offs Threaten U.S. Firms' Profitability," *Indianapolis Star,* May 24, 2004; "Chinese Counterfeiting Takes Root in U.S. Marine Industry," *International Boat Industry Magazine,* May 27, 2004.

120 [China as center of knockoff manufacture] Fishman, "Manufaketure."

121 [Music industry] International Federation of Phonographic Industries, "The Recording Industry Commercial Piracy Report 2004," July 2004.

121 [Russia CDs] Tim Burt, "Music Groups Tackle Russian Piracy," *Financial Times,* December 19, 2003, p. 12.

121 [Impact on sales] "Piracy Slashes Music Sales," *Financial Times,* April 11, 2003; Stan Bernstein, "Burned by CD Burners," *Washington Post,* September 24, 2002, p. A21.

121 [Online distribution] "Music's Brighter Future," *The Economist,* October 28,

2004; Scott Morrison, "Apparent Fall in Web Piracy Is Music To Record Company Ears," *Financial Times,* January 6, 2004, p. 10; Ien Cheng and Richard Waters, "Piracy: Overkill Gives Way to Pragmatism," *Financial Times,* April 14, 2004, p. 14; Michael Skapinker, "An Industry Fights for Its Future," *Financial Times,* October 12, 2004.

121 ["Rampant" quote] International Federation of Phonographic Industries, "A Round-Up of Anti-Piracy Actions Worldwide," January 2004.

121 [Danger Mouse] Bill Werde, "Defiant Downloads Rise from Underground," *New York Times,* February 25, 2004, p. E3.

122 [Video] "Tipping Hollywood the Black Spot," *The Economist,* August 30, 2003; "Film Industry Warns of Big Losses To Pirate Copying," *Financial Times,* February 4, 2004, p. 52; "Romancing the Disc," *The Economist,* February 7, 2004, p. 63; Amanda Ripley, "Hollywood Robbery," *Time,* January 26, 2004, p. 56; John Schwartz, "In Chasing Movie Pirates, Hollywood Treads Lightly," *New York Times,* December 25, 2003, p. C1; Chris Buckley, "Helped by Technology, Piracy of DVDs Runs Rampant in China," *New York Times,* August 18, 2003.

122 [Hopper anecdote] "Fast Track: Avenue of the Americas," *Financial Times,* January 25, 2002, p. 13.

122 [Harry Potter/China] Elizabeth Rosenthal, "Counterfeiters Turn Magic into Cash," *New York Times,* November 25, 2001, p. A1.

122 [Microsoft] "Intelligence: Slipped Discs," *Far Eastern Economic Review,* January 30, 1997; "Phonies Galore," *The Economist,* November 8, 2001; "U.S. Targets Software Pirates," *Washington Post,* December 12, 2001; "Asian Software Pirates Ahead of Microsoft," *Financial Times,* December 3, 2003; John Burton, "Microsoft Plans Cheaper Software to Combat Piracy," *Financial Times,* June 30, 2004, p. 18.

122–23 [Computers, chips, software] "Piracy Losses More Than Double," *New York Times,* July 8, 2004 (includes updated BSA numbers: "Software manufacturers lost $29 billion to piracy in 2003, more than double the previous year's losses . . . " "About 36 percent of software installations worldwide are of pirated copies. Vietnam and China had the highest rates, with pirated versions accounting for 92 percent of all computer software installed in each country. Next were Ukraine, with 91 percent; Indonesia, at 88 percent; and Zimbabwe and Russia, with 87 percent each. By region, about 53 percent of software applications on computers in the Asia/Pacific region were pirated in 2003, compared with 70 percent in Eastern Europe, 63 percent in Latin America, 55 percent in the Middle East, 36 percent in Western Europe and 23 percent in North America").

123–24 [Medicines/general] Trish Saywell and Joan McManus, "What's in That Pill?" *Far Eastern Economic Review,* February 21, 2002, pp. 34–37; "Medicine: Fighting Back," ibid., pp. 38–40.

123 [China] Peter S. Goodman, "China's Killer Headache: Fake Pharmaceuticals," *Washington Post,* August 30, 2002, p. A1.

123 [WHO estimate] Frances Williams, "WHO Launches Drive to Stamp Out Fake Drugs," *Financial Times,* November 12, 2003, p. 14.

124 [2002 case] "Five Companies, Seven People Charged with Making, Selling Fake Viagra," Associated Press, May 17, 2002.

124 [Batch of 1,800] Claire Innes, "Regulators and Drug Companies Fight Rising Tide of Counterfeit Products," *World Markets Research Center,* February 15, 2002.

Branching Out on All Sides

125   [Los Angeles bust] "Major Counterfeiting Ring Broken," Los Angeles Police Department, press release, September 12, 2003.
125   [New York bust] William Glaberson, "6 Are Charged with Selling Millions of Counterfeit Marlboros," *New York Times,* February 13, 2003, p. B3.
126   [PLA] "No More Business as Usual," *Asiaweek,* December 6, 2000.
126   [Sony/China prisons] "Sony Uncovers Piracy of PlayStation Game Consoles in Chinese Prison—Report," *Financial Times,* December 22, 2004; [China generally] Fishman, "Manufaketure."
126   [Malaysian officials threatened] U.S. Congress. House. Subcommittee on Courts, the Internet, and Intellectual Property, *International Copyright Piracy: Links To Organized Crime and Terrorism,* testimony of Jack Valenti, March 13, 2003.
126–27 [Spanish CD counterfeiting networks] Pedro Farre, "Mafias y Pirateria Cultural," *Foreign Policy (Edición Española),* December 2004–January 2005, p. 63.
127–28 [Terrorist connections] "The Links between Intellectual Property Crime and Terrorist Financing," testimony of Ronald K. Noble, secretary-general of Interpol, before the House Committee on International Relations, 108th Congress, July 16, 2003; "Al-Qa'idah Trading in Fake Branded Goods," BBC Monitoring Reports, September 11, 2002; "Militants Turn To Crime to Fund Terrorism," Associated Press, August 12, 2004; Roslyn A. Mazer, "From T-Shirts To Terrorism," *Washington Post,* September 30, 2001.

A Battle of Titans

128   [United States] "A Primer on Patents, Trademarks, and Copyrights and Trade Secrets," Olive and Olive, P.A., 2003, online at http://www.oliveand olive.com/primer.htm; "Twelve Arrested for the Manufacture and Distribution of Counterfeit Microsoft Software," *Microsoft PressPass,* February 14, 2000, online at: http://www.microsoft.com/presspass/press/2000/Feb00/LosAngRaidsPR.asp.
128   [Fines for offenses] [China] Jonathan C. Spierer, "Intellectual Property in China: Prospectus for New Market Entrants," *Harvard Asia Quarterly,* summer 1999, online at http://www.fas.harvard.edu/~asiactr/haq/199903/9903a010.htm
128   [Malaysia] American Malaysian Camber of Commerce, "Position Papers: Review of Holograms—FMCG Products," online at: http://www.amcham.com.my/action/position/position_hologramFMGCNov'04.htm
128   [Global rules] "Patent Law: Going Global," *The Economist,* June 17, 2000; Frances Williams, "Copyright Protection Reinforced," *Financial Times,* March 7, 2002, p. 12; Paul Meller, "Europe Moves to Strengthen Piracy Laws," *New York Times,* March 10, 2004, p. W3.
128–29 [TRIPS/WTO-driven reform] "China and Japan to Tackle Product Piracy," *Financial Times,* April 5, 2002; "U.S. Imposes CD Piracy Sanctions on Ukraine," *Financial Times,* December 21, 2001.
129   [Brussels conference] "Combatting Counterfeiting," First Global Congress on Counterfeiting, Brussels, May 2004. Online at http://www.anti-counterfeit congress.org/wco2004/website.asp?page=home
129   [Business enforcement] Stryker McGuire, Richard Ensberger Jr., and Tony Emerson, "Microsoft Cops," *Newsweek,* April 9, 2001, p. 20.

129   [Indian companies] "New Frontiers: Indian Companies Are Moving to Shed
       Their Copycat Image by Investing in Basic Research," *Far Eastern Economic Re-
       view,* July 20, 2000.
129   [China IP scholar] "Beijing Group Prosecuted for Book Piracy," *Financial
       Times,* January 14, 2005.

CHAPTER 7: THE MONEY WASHERS

131–32 [9/11 finance] "Bankrolling bin Laden," *Financial Times,* November 29,
       2001; "Trail of Terrorist Dollars That Spans the World," *Financial Times,* No-
       vember 29, 2001.
132   ["Money sets Osama bin Laden apart" quote] Jim Hoagland, "Dry Up the
       Money Train," *Washington Post,* September 30, 2001, p. B7.
132   [Charities and terrorist finance] "The Iceberg beneath the Charity," *The Econ-
       omist,* March 15, 2003.

MORE MONEY, MORE WAYS TO HIDE

134   [Scale of financial liberalization] BIS Reporting Banks. Summary of Interna-
       tional Positions. http://www.bis.org/publ/qcsv/anx1.csv
135   [Plummeting banking costs] Saleh M. Nsouli and Andrea Schaechter, "Chal-
       lenges of the E-Banking Revolution," *Finance & Development,* September 2002,
       p. 48.
135   [Currency transactions, $1.88 trillion in 2004] Gabriele Galati and Michael
       Melvin, "Why Has FX Trading Surged? Explaining the 2004 Triennial Survey,"
       BIS Quarterly Review, December 2004; Tom Abate, "Banking's Soldiers of For-
       tune," *San Francisco Chronicle,* December 7, 2004.
136   [International Portfolio Investment] International Finance Corporation, *Emerg-
       ing Stock Markets Factbook* (Washington, DC: IFC, several years).
136   [FDI Worldwide] United Nations Conference on Trade and Development, *World
       Investment Report, 2004* (Geneva: UNCTAD Press Unit, September 22, 2004).

Discretion in Demand

137   [Global money-laundering estimates] "Fighting the Dirt," *The Economist,* June
       23, 2001; "IRS Says Offshore Tax Evasion Is Widespread," *New York Times,*
       March 26, 2002; Nigel Morris-Cotterill, "Think Again: Money Laundering,"
       Foreign Policy, May–June 2001, pp. 16–22, Peter Reuter and Edwin M. Tru-
       man, *Chasing Dirty Money: The Fight Against Money Laundering,* (Washington,
       DC: Institute for International Economics, 2004) p. 13. For higher estimates of
       money laundering, see Friedrich Schneider and Dominik Enste, "Shadow
       Economies: Size, Causes, and Consequences," *Journal of Economic Literature*
       38, no. 1 (2000): pp. 77–114. See also Vito Tanzi, *Policies, Institutions, and the
       Dark Side of Economics* (Cheltenham, UK: Edward Elgar, 2000).
137   [Mexican drug interests/Hezbollah partnership in pseudo-ephedrin] "Drug
       Money for Hezbollah?" CBS News, September 1, 2002, online at
       http://www.cbsnews.com/stories/2002/09/01/attack/main520457.shtml
138   [Sheik Omar Abdel Rahman associates' use of cigarette, coupon scams, etc.]
       John Mintz and Douglas Farah, "Small Scams Probed for Terror Ties," *Washing-
       ton Post,* August 12, 2002, p. A1.

138   [Madrid bombing perpetrators funding through counterfeit CDs] "Militants Turn To Crime to Fund Terrorism," Associated Press, August 12, 2004.

139   [Walter C. Anderson] David S. Hilzenrath, "$200,000,000 Telecom Tycoon Used International Financial Labyrinth," *Washington Post*, April 18, 2005, p. E1.

140   [Estimate of risk faced by money-launderers] Peter Reuter and Edwin M Truman, *Chasing Dirty Money: The Fight against Money Laundering* (Washington, DC: Institute for International Economics, 2004), p. 5.

The New Offshore

140   [New offshore: marketing national sovereignty] William Wechsler, "Follow the Money," *Foreign Affairs* 80, no. 4, pp. 40–57; "OECD Attacks Tax Havens over Law Changes," *Financial Times*, June 12, 2001, p. 4; "U.S. Companies File in Bermuda to Slash Tax Bills," *New York Times*, February 18, 2002.

141   [Nauru] Jack Hitt, "The Billion-Dollar Shack," *New York Times Magazine*, December 10, 2000.

141   [Cayman Islands] Nigel Morris-Cottrill, "Think Again: Money Laundering."

141   [Tuvalu leasing of domain name and country code] Wechsler, "Follow the Money."

142   [Flags of convenience] Kerry Lynn Nankivell, "Troubled Waters," *Foreign Policy*, November–December 2004, pp. 30–31.

142–43   [Ciudad del Este] William W. Mendel, "Paraguay's Ciudad del Este and the New Centers of Gravity," *Military Review*, March–April 2002; Kevin Gray, "Paraguay Tri-Border Area Is Terror Haven," Associated Press, October 3, 2004.

Big Bank, Little Bank, Bogus Bank

143–44   [E-banking] Saleh M. Nsouli and Andrea Schaechter, "Challenges of the E-Banking Revolution," *Finance & Development*, September 2002, pp. 48–51.

144   [$36 million money-launderer] "Money Laundering," UNODC online document, May 1998, at http://www.unodc.org/adhoc/gass/ga/20special/featur/launder.htm

145   [Correspondent banking] "Through the Wringer," *The Economist*, April 14, 2001; "U.S. Banks Admit To Shortfall in Monitoring," *Financial Times*, March 2, 2001, p. 12.

145   [Bank of New York scandal] Celestine Bohlen, "Bank Inquiry's Trail Leads To Top Levels of Power in Russia," *New York Times*, February 18, 2000, p. A1; [160 correspondent banks] Thomas A. Fogarty, "Bank Chief Says Workers Used Poor Judgment," *USA Today*, September 23, 1999, p. 7A.

145–46   [Bin Laden money movements via al-Shamal Bank] John Willman, "Trail of Terrorist Dollars That Spans the World," *Financial Times*, November 29, 2001, p. 7.

146   [Buying/opening banks] Thomas Azzara, *Tax Havens of the World*, 7th ed. (Nassau, Bahamas: New Providence Press, 1999). Jack Hitt, "The Billion-Dollar Shack". U.S. Department of State, Bureau for International Narcotics and Law Enforcement Affairs, "International Narcotics Control Strategy Report, 2005," March 2005.

Layers and Fronts

147 [Front companies, layering, "could do worse"] Nigel Morris-Cottrill, "Think Again: Money Laundering"; Financial Action Task Force on Money Laundering website, online at http://www1.oecd.org/fatf/

147 [Weaknesses in European company law] Ernesto U. Savona, "Obstacles in Company Law To Anti–Money Laundering International Cooperation in European Union Member States," in Mark Pieth, ed., *Financing Terrorism* (London: Kluwer Academic Publishers, 2002).

147 [London as money laundering center] "London's Dirty Secret," *Financial Times,* October 29, 2004, p. 14.

147 [Abacha anecdote and numbers] "Britain Goes after Abacha Billions," BBC News online, October 18, 2001.

148 [Online gaming and laundering] Rod Smith, "Online Betting Growth Called Threat To Nevada," *Las Vegas Review-Journal,* January 24, 2004, p. 1D; Peter Spiegel, "U.S. to Stop Net Becoming an Offshore Tax Haven," *Financial Times,* July 11, 2000, p. 13.

148–49 ["Offshore world"] Ronen Palan, *The Offshore World: Sovereign Markets, Virtual Places, and Nomad Millionaires* (Ithaca and London: Cornell University Press, 2003). See also Vito Tanzi, *Policies, Institutions, and the Dark Side of Economics* (Cheltenham, UK. Edward Elgar, 2000), and R. T. Naylor, *Wages of Crime: Black Markets, Illegal Finance, and the Underworld Economy* (Ithaca, NY: Cornell University Press, 2002 and 2004, rev. ed.).

Cash and Carry

149 [Bull semen shipments and other concealment strategies] Patricia Hurtado, "Drugs and Money at the Crossroads," *Newsday,* June 23, 1997, p. 3.

149 [How hawalas work] Douglas Frantz, "Ancient Secret System Moves Money Globally," *New York Times,* October 3, 2001, p. B5.

149 [Chinese "fie chen"] United Nations General Assembly, Special Session on the World Drug Problem, "Money Laundering," UN Department of Public Information (DPI/1982), May 1998.

149–50 [The trade in honey used to ship drugs and weapons] Judith Miller and Jeff Gerth, "Honey Trade Said to Provide Funds and Cover To bin Laden," *New York Times,* October 11, 2001, p. A1.

150 [Farah] Douglas Farah, *Blood from Stones: The Secret Financial Network of Terror* (New York: Broadway Books, 2004).

150 [Conversion to resources] Jonathan M. Winer and Trifin J. Roule, "The Finance of Illicit Resource Extraction," photocopy manuscript dated January 13, 2002; "Gold Shampoo Washed Money," *Washington Post,* January 9, 2004, p. E3; "Infighting Slows Hunt for Hidden al-Qaeda Assets: Funds Put in Untraceable Commodities," *Washington Post,* June 18, 2002.

Peer Pressure

151 [Basel committee] Basel Committee on Banking Supervision, "International Convergence of Capital Measurement and Capital Standards," July 1998.

151–52 [FATF first phase] Andrew Parker, "Professions Join Hunt for Dirty Cash," *Financial Times,* March 1, 2004, p. 11.

152–53   [FATF sanctions/compliance] Wechsler, "Follow the Money"; "Panama helps Russia Beat Money Laundering," *Financial Times,* August 9, 2001; [Caymans] "Tax Haven Tightens Up Its Financial Regulations," *Financial Times* special section, July 16, 2001; Canute James, "Offshore Financial Centers Hit at OECD," *Financial Times,* November 21, 2001, p. 5; "Doubts over Israeli 'Dirty Money' Unit," *Financial Times,* November 16, 2001; "Tough Test in Battle to Beat Tax Evasion," *Financial Times,* February 20, 2001; "Fighting the Dirt," *The Economist* June 1, 2001; Michael Peel, "Bahamas Agrees To Tax Haven Demands," *Financial Times,* March 19, 2002, p. 6.

Rude Awakening

153–54   [Post-9/11 terrorist focus] Jonathan M. Winer and Trifin J. Roule, "Fighting Terrorist Finance," *Survival: The IISS Quarterly* 44, no. 3 (autumn 2002): pp. 87–104; Jonathan M. Winer, "Globalization, Terrorist Finance, and Global Conflict: Time for a White List?" in Pieth, ed., *Financing Terrorism,* pp. 5–40; "Terrorists Are Now Targets in Money-Laundering Fight," *Washington Post,* July 25, 2002, p. E3; "The Dirty Money That Is Hardest to Clean Up," *Financial Times,* November 20, 2001; "G7 Countries to Seek Stiffer Controls on Financial Centers," *Financial Times,* December 13, 2001; "Banking on Secrecy," *Time,* October 22, 2001; "Money Laundering Targeted in Europe," *Washington Post,* October 2, 2001, p. A12; "The Needle in the Haystack," *The Economist,* December 14, 2002; Claes Norgren and Jaime Caruana, "Wipe Out the Treasuries of Terror," *Financial Times,* April 7, 2004; "Loopholes Undermine Crackdown on Terror Financing," *Financial Times,* November 14, 2003.

154   ["The attitude . . . must change"] United States Treasury Department, *National Money Laundering Strategy,* July 2002, p. 3, online at http://www.treas.gov/offices/enforcement/publications/ml2002.pdf

154   ["Like it or not . . ."] "Task force to Discuss Financial Crackdown," *Financial Times,* October 23, 2001, p. 4.

154   [Netherlands regulator] Arthur Docters van Leeuwen, "Secrets That Block the War on Terror Financing," *Financial Times,* October 7, 2004.

155   [Hommes] Author interview with Rudolf Hommes, former minister of finance of Colombia; Bogotá, November 2004.

156   [Koch-Wieser] Author interview with Caio Koch-Wieser, state secretary of the Federal Ministry of Finance, Germany; Davos, Switzerland, January 2005.

156   [Private banker] Author interview with private banker; Zurich, Switzerland, January 2005.

CHAPTER 8: WHAT DO ORANGUTANS, HUMAN KIDNEYS, GARBAGE, AND VAN GOGH HAVE IN COMMON?

157   [German kidney transplant story] Martina Keller, "Operation Niere," *Die Zeit,* December 11, 2002.

Organs Without Borders

159   [Organ trade overall] Nancy Scheper-Hughes, "The Global Traffic in Human Organs," *Current Anthropology* 41, no. 2 (April 2000); Scheper-Hughes, "The New Cannibalism," *New Internationalist,* no. 300 (April 1998).

160   [2003 South African case] Abraham McLaughlin, Ilene R. Prusher, and Andrew Downie, "What Is a Kidney Worth?" *Christian Science Monitor,* June 9, 2004; "The Rise and Fall of the South African Organ-Trafficking Ring," ibid.; Larry Rohter, "Tracking the Sale of a Kidney on a Path of Poverty and Hope," *New York Times,* May 22, 2004; "Poor Sell Organs To Trans-Atlantic Trafficking Ring," IPS (Inter Press Service), February 23, 2004.

160–61   [Kidney supply and demand; going rates to sellers] Nancy Scheper-Hughes, "Prime Numbers: Organs without Borders," *Foreign Policy,* January–February 2005, pp. 26–27.

161   [Forty-year-old Israeli] McLaughlin, Prusher, and Downie, "What Is a Kidney Worth?"

161   [Broker solicits Arab patients] Massoud Ansari, "Life on the Line," Newsline (Pakistan) online, May 2003, online at http://www.newsline.com.pk/News May2003/newsbeat4may.htm; Scheper-Hughes, "Global Traffic in Human Organs."

161–62   [Forcible "donations" stories; also organ-snatching rumors and realities] Scheper-Hughes, "Global Traffic in Human Organs."

162   [Azerbaijan] "Azerbaijan Probes Child-Organ Traffickers," BBC News online, February 23, 2004.

162   [Afghan children] "Karzai Seeks Death for Afghan Organ Traffickers," *Financial Times,* July 4, 2004.

162   [Harry Wu] Scheper-Hughes, "The New Cannibalism"; [Hainan anecdote] "Evil Trade in Organs," *Sunday Times,* June 19, 1999.

162   [China capital sentences] Dena Kram, "Illegal Human Organ Trade from Executed Prisoners in China," *Trade and Environment Case Studies* (American University) 11, no. 2 (June 2001); Craig S. Smith, "On Death Row, China's Source of Transplants," *New York Times,* October 17, 2001, p. A1.

162   [DR Congo] Luc-Roger Mbala Bemba, "Vaste trafic d'organes humains et d'armes dans l'Est de la République démocratique du Congo," *L'Observateur* *(Kinshasa),* as reproduced online at http://www.nkolo-mboka.com/genocide _56.html

162–63   [Nun in Mozambique] "Du meurtre d'une nonne au trafic d'organes," *Info Moçambique,* March 3, 2004, as reproduced online at http://www.amigos-de-mocambique.org/info/article.php3?id_article=43

163   [Legal debate] "Q & A: 'The Kidney Is Not a Spare Part,' " and "Q & A: 'It Should Be Made Legal,' " *Christian Science Monitor,* June 9, 2004.

Of Caviar and Orangutans . . .

163   [CITES] Convention on International Trade and Endangered Species, online at http://www.cites.org

164   [Mexican cactus] Mary Jordan and Kevin Sullivan, "Riches Uprooted from Mexican Desert," *Washington Post,* February 13, 2003, p. A18.

164   [exotics at large in South Florida] Abby Goodnough, "Forget the Gators: Exotic Pets Run Wild in Florida," *New York Times,* February 29, 2004, p. A1.

164   [Ivory to Guangzhou] Marcal Joanilho, "Ivory Sellers Back in Business," *South China Morning Post,* November 11, 2002, p. 4.

164   [TRAFFIC info on six most involved countries in ivory trade] Tom Milliken, "Urgent Need for ASEA to Improve Elephant Ivory Trade Monitoring Perfor-

mance," TRAFFIC.org, March 9, 2005, online at http://www.traffic.org/news/elephant_ivory.html

164 [Contraband caviar] Carolyn Jung, "Saving Sturgeons: Value of Eggs Make Fading Fish a Target of Criminal World," *San Jose Mercury News,* February 3, 2004, p. 1.

164–65 [Crocodilians] James McGregor, "International Trade in Crocodilian Skins," TRAFFIC report, December 2002.

165 [Tibet skins seizure] "Tiger Smuggling 'Out of Control,'" BBC News online, October 6, 2004.

165 [Thai pangolin seizure] "Thailand Seizes 600 Pangolins," Xinhua News Agency, September 29, 2004.

165 [Thai 2003 recoveries] Ellen Nakashima, "Thais Fight Animal Smuggling," *Washington Post,* December 11, 2003.

165 [Miami airport boas] Jay Cheshes, "Cold Blooded Smuggling," *New Times Broward–Palm Beach,* February 4, 1999; also James Reynolds, "Organised Crime Cashes in on Wildlife," *The Scotsman,* June 17, 2002.

165 [Southern Africa arrests] "Seizures and Prosecutions," *TRAFFIC Bulletin,* 18, no. 2 (April 2000).

165–66 [Belgian wildlife dealer] Antony Barnett and Andrew Wasley, "Revealed: UK Zoos Caught in Rare Wildlife Trade with Dealer," *The Observer,* March 28, 2004.

166 [The "Taiping Four"] "Gorillas in the Midst: Trade in Endangered Species," *The Economist,* November 6, 2004, p. 82.

166 [Ivory trade on eBay] Marc Kaufman, "U.S. Is Major Market for Illegal Ivory," *Washington Post,* September 24, 2004, p. A4.

166 [Ramin logging and trade] "Australian Film on Indonesian Illegal Logging Causes Outrage," Environmental Investigation Agency (EIA), July 31, 2002; "Police Fail to Prosecute Timber Barons and Plan Auction of Stolen Timber," EIA, June 6, 2002; "Malaysia Still Laundering Illegal Timber," EIA, May 13, 2004.

166–67 [Zoonosis and animal trade] Roni Rabin, "When Animal Germs Infect Humans," *Newsday,* June 24, 2003, p. A34.

When Waste Means Wealth

167 [Wandering barge] Steven Hayward, "NIMBYism and the Garbage Barge from Hell," *Capital Ideas* 7, no. 29 (July 25, 2002); Shirley Perlman, "Barging into a Trashy Sea," *Newsday,* date unknown, online at http://www.newsday.com/community/guide/lihistory/ny-history- hs9garb,0,6996774.story?coll=ny-lihistory-navigation

167–68 [Environmental crime general sources] FBI Environmental Crime, http://www.fbi.gov/hq/cid/fc/gfu/ec/ec.htm; UK Environment Agency, http://www.environment-agency.gov.uk/; Australia Crime Prevention Division, http://www.lawlink.nsw.gov.au/cpd.nsf/pages/module_8

167 [Electronic waste] "Japan Found Dumping Toxic Electronic Waste in New Dumping Zone in China," Basel Action Network, April 21, 2004; John Vidal, "Poisonous Detritus of the Electronic Revolution," *The Guardian,* September 21, 2004.

167–68 [Somalia radioactive dumps] Jorge Piña, " 'Eco-Mafia' Dumps Radioactive Waste on Poor Countries," Inter Press Service, May 7, 2001.

168   [Ship-breaking] Prasanna Srinivasan, "Let the Trade in Waste Continue," *Wall Street Journal*, December 16, 2002.

168   [Cambodia mercury] TED Case Studies: Toxic Dumping by Formosa Plastics Group in Cambodia (CAMWASTE)—Abbi Tatton, December, 1999. http://www.american.edu/TED/camwaste.htm

168   [Guiyu, Taizhou] "High-Tech Toxic Trash from USA Found to Be Flooding Asia," Basel Action Network, February 25, 2002.

168   [Basel convention] Secretariat of the Basel Convention, United Nations Environment Programme, http://www.basel.int

168–69   [EU port study] Cited in Vidal, "Poisonous Detritus . . ."

169   [Italy "ecomafia"] Piña, "Eco-Mafia": "Online Extra: 'We Need International Cooperation,' " *Business Week* Online, January 27, 2003.

Trading the Atmosphere

169   [Montreal protocol text] http://www.unep.org/ozone/Treaties_and_Ratification/2B_montreal_protocol.asp

170   [CFC trade overall] "Lost in Transit: Global CFC Smuggling Trends and the Need for a Faster Phase-Out," Environmental Investigation Agency report, November 2003; "Curbing Illegal Trade at the Source: The Need for Cuts in the Production of CFCs," Environmental Investigation Agency briefing, November 2004; presentation of Halvart Koeppen to the United Nations Environment Programme (UNEP), DTIE Working Group on Crimes Related to Environmental Pollution, Lyon, December 11–12, 2001.

170   [Singapore sting; South Africa gold mine scam] EIA, "Lost in Transit" report.

171   [Bangladesh border] EIA, "Curbing Illegal Trade at the Source" report.

171   [Pakistan CFC/heroin overlap] "Whistle Blown on Illegal CFC Trade," BBC News Online, January 31, 2004.

The Sublime Meets the Criminal

171   [Munch thefts from Oslo, 2004] Walter Gibbs and Carol Vogel, "Munch's 'Scream' Is Stolen from a Crowded Museum in Oslo," *New York Times*, August 23, 2004, p. A6.

171   [Matisse missing in Caracas] Alexandra Olson, "Stolen Matisse Shocks Venezuela Museum," Associated Press, February 1, 2003.

171   [Stolen art registries] Anna J. Kisluk, "Stolen Art and the Art Loss Register," Art Crime: Protecting Art, Protecting Artists and Protecting Consumers Conference, Sydney, December 2–3, 1999.

171   [*New York Times* tally] Edward Dolnick, "Stealing Beauty," *New York Times*, August 24, 2004, p. A17.

171–72   [Art thieves and networks] Steve Vol, "Art of the Deal," *Philadelphia Weekly*, September 1, 2004; Marc Spiegler, "The Crimes They Are A-Changin'," *Slate*, August 26, 2004, online at http://slate.msn.com/id/2105632/; Bruce Ford, "The Good, the Bad, and the Ugly," *Australian Art Review*, February 2003.

172   [Modigliani/Degas story and Saudi prince story] Martha Lufkin, "How Drug Dealers Use Paintings to Launder Money," Art Newspaper.com, April 8, 2003. Also Larry Lebowitz, "Arrest Made in Convoluted Case of Art, Drugs, Money," *Miami Herald*, January 8, 2003, online at http://www.aberdeennews.com/mld/aberdeennews/news/nation/4899604.htm

172–73   [Jiroft] Edek Osser, "London and Paris Markets Flooded with Looted Iranian Antiquities," *Art Newspaper.com*, January 8, 2004.

173   [Antiquities trade in general] "Spirited Away," *Time Asia*, October 20, 2003 [on antiquities trade out of India, Cambodia, China]; "Big Business: Asia's Stolen-Art Trade Is Carried Out on an Almost Industrial Scale," ibid.; "Art gangs 'Looted Iraqi Museums,'" BBC News Online, April 17, 2003; "Ancient Art Traffickers Rob History for Millions," *Christian Science Monitor*, October 7, 1999.

173   [Italy art theft and "art police"] "For That Stolen Vermeer, Follow the Art Squad," *Unesco Courier*, April, 2001, p. 30; Linda Hales, "Art-Theft Cops and the Loot of All Evil," *Washington Post*, August 10, 2003, p. N1.

173   [Peruvian artifact] Catherine Elton, "Ancient Art Traffickers Rob History for Millions," *Christian Science Monitor*, October 7, 1999.

173–74   [Michel van Rijn] "The Art of Crime," *Sunday Times (South Africa)*, October 19, 2003; "Le pourfendeur de l'élite plus caustique que jamais," *Artcult*, June 2002.

CHAPTER 9: WHAT ARE GOVERNMENTS DOING?

175   [Border tour] Jason Peckenpaugh, "Under One Roof," *Government Executive*, May 1, 2003, at GovExec.com.; see http://www.govexec.com/features/0503/HSs3.htm

175–76   [DHS and ICE] Michael Crowley, "Playing Defense," *New Republic*, March 15, 2004; Jason Peckenpaugh, "Under One Roof," and Jason Peckenpaugh, "The Ties that Bind," *Government Executive*, November 15, 2003, at GovExec.com; see http://www.govexec.com/features/1103/1103s4.htm; Hector Gutierrez, "Shoring Up Borders, and a Reputation," *Rocky Mountain News*, August 26, 2004, p. 26A; Jerry Seper, "ICE Embraces Role in Homeland Security," *Washington Times*, September 13, 2004, p. A3.

176–77   [DHS integration issues] Peckenpaugh, "Ties that Bind."

177   [Disagreement over guns] Crowley, "Playing Defense."

177   [Detention centers] "Turner Says Security Gaps along Border Imperil Nation," *Lufkin Daily News*, September 9, 2004.

177   [Unsure of own job, others] Peckenpaugh, "Ties that Bind"; Crowley, "Playing Defense."

177   [Name and badges] Crowley, "Playing Defense"; Jason Peckenpaugh, "DHS Agency to Keep Its Name," GovExec.com, June 25, 2004, see http://www.govexec.com/dailyfed/0604/062504p1.htm; Michelle Malkin, "Homeland Insecurity Files," June 28, 2004, at MichelleMalkin.com. http://michellemalkin.com/archives/2004_06.htm.

177   ["I used to lose sleep . . ."] Author interview with senior customs official, Washington, DC, April 6, 2004.

178   [Child pornography operation and "revamped INS" quote] Peckenpaugh, "Ties that Bind."

"It Can't Be Done"

178   [Russia drug agency] Susan Glasser, "Russian Drug Unit Criticized over Dubious Tactics, Priorities," *Washington Post*, September 22, 2004, p. A20.

179   [Glenn A. Fine report] U.S. Department of Justice. Office of the Inspector

General. "The Internal Effects of the Federal Bureau of Investigation's Reprioritization," Audit Report 04–39, September 2004.

179 [Porter Goss concerns] James McKinley Jr., "Terror Fears Grow over U.S. Borders," *New York Times,* March 23, 2005.

179–80 [Annual border traffic] Ted Carlson, "Eye in the Sky," *Flight Journal,* June 2004.

180 [Hutchings] Author interview with Robert Hutchings, chairman, U.S. National Intelligence Council, CIA, Airlie, Virginia, October 1, 2004.

Analysts, Agents, Enforcers

180 [Studies of bureaucracy] James Q. Wilson, *Bureaucracy: What Government Agencies Do and Why They Do It* (New York: Basic Books, 1989); Ali Farazmand, ed., *Modern Systems of Government: Exploring the Role of Bureaucrats and Politicians* (New York: Sage Publications, 1997).

181 [U.S. police forces and 18,000 figure] Thomas O'Connor, "Police Structure of the United States," online at http://faculty.ncwc.edu/toconnor/polstruct.htm

182–83 [Ridge] Tom Ridge, "Global Security Depends on Joint Action," *Financial Times,* January 13, 2005.

183 [U.S. agent in Russia] Author interview, Moscow, September 16, 2003.

Illicit, Illegal, Ill-Defined

184 [Lifting assault weapons ban in U.S. 2004] "On Guard, America," *New York Times,* September 11, 2004, p. A14.

184 [Pastrana] Author interview with Andres Pastrana, president of Colombia, 1998–2002; Santo Domingo, Dominican Republic, December 2004.

184 [U.S. states and drivers licenses to illegal immigrants] "On Guard, America," *New York Times,* February 15, 2005, p. A18.

184 [Smuggling sentences] [Coyotes] U.S. General Accounting Office Report To Congressional Committees, "Alien Smuggling," May 2000; [Drug traffickers] Karen Gullo, "Federal Drug Charges Rise," Associated Press, August 19, 2001.

Working Together: Hard but Necessary

186–87 [History of "transnational crime"] David Feslen and Akis Kalaitzidis, "A Historical Overview of Transnational Crime," Chapter 1, in Philip Riedel, ed., *Handbook of Transnational Crime and Justice*.

187–88 [On use of treaties and conventions] Matti Joutsen, "International Instruments on Cooperation in Responding To Transnational Crime," Chapter 13, in Riedel, ed., *Handbook of Transnational Crime and Justice*.

Cops against Borders

188 [*Man from Interpol* TV show] "Danzingers, The Man from Interpol," online at http://www.78rpm.co.uk/tvi.htm; Austin Powell, "The Man from Interpol," JazzProfessional.com, online at http://www.jazzprofessional.com/memorial/Crombie_Interpol.htm

188–89 [Origins of Interpol] Mathieu Deflem, " 'Wild Beasts without Nationality':

The Uncertain Origins of Interpol, 1898–1910," Chapter 14, in Riedel, ed., *Handbook of Transnational Crime and Justice.*

189 [Interpol history] www.interpol.int, and "The Secret History of Interpol," *Fast Company* web exclusive, September 1, 2002, online at http://www .fastcompany.com/articles/2002/09/interpol.html

Interpol or Minipol?

190–92 [Interpol, Ron Noble] www.interpol.int; Chuck Salter, "Terrorists Strike Fast . . . Interpol Has to Move Faster . . . Ron Noble Is on the Case," *Fast Company,* no. 63, October 2002, p. 96; "The Man from Interpol," interview with Peter Nevitt, Interpol IS director, *CIO Magazine,* June 15, 2000, online at http://www.cio.com/archive/061500/interpol.html; Maggie Paine, "The World's Top Cop," *UNH Magazine* (University of New Hampshire), winter 2002; online at http://unhmagazine.unh.edu/w02/noblelw02.html
192 [Russia drug squad] Glasser "Russian Drug Unit . . ."
192 [Mexico *federales* corruption and conflict] Richard Boudreaux, "Once Superheroes, Mexico's Elite Police Fall from Grace," *Los Angeles Times,* December 17, 2004, p. A1.

Success . . . and Its Limits

192–93 [Operation Candy Box] Buffalo bust: "NAAUSA in Congress: USA Patriot Act, Section 213: Delayed Notice B Rep. Otter Amendment," National Association of Assistant United States Attorneys. Online at: http://www.naausa.org/ congress/patriot.htm; "Drug Empire Smashed," *Ottawa Sun,* April 1, 2004; DEA summary online at http://www.usdoj.gov/dea/major/candybox/
193 [Operation Streamline] "DEA Disrupts Colombian Drug Ring," DEA website, January 16, 2004, at http://www.usdoj.gov/dea/pubs/states/newsrel/ mia011604.html
193–94 [Operation Decollo] "Calabrian Mafia Dismantled in Operation 'Decollo' (Take-Off)," DEA website, January 28, 2004, at http://www.usdoj.gov/dea/pubs/pressrel/pr012804.html
194 [Operation United Eagles] "Major Cartel Lieutenants Arrested in Mexico," DEA website, June 7, 2004, at http://www.usdoj.gov/dea/major/united_eagles; Robert J. Caldwell, "Winning the Long Battle against the Tijuana Cartel," *San Diego Union-Tribune,* June 20, 2004.
194 [Togolese tugboat seizure] "Importante saisie de cocaine au large du Ghana," Agence France-Presse dispatch, July 7, 2004.
194–95 [Bolton] John Bolton, "An All-Out War on Proliferation," *Financial Times,* September 6, 2004.
195–96 [FATF near-death experience] Wechsler, "Follow the Money"; Edward Aldin and Michael Peel, "U.S. May Ease Stance over Money Laundering," *Financial Times,* June 1, 2001, p. 12; David Ignatius, "The Tax Cheats' Friends," *Washington Post,* April 29, 2001, p. B7; George Lardner, "O'Neill Targets Tax Havens," *Washington Post,* July 19, 2001, p. E13; "Banking on Secrecy," *Time,* October 22, 2001; Doug Cameron and Canute James, "Caribbean Governments Seek Global Forum on Tax Haven Issue," *Financial Times,* February 26, 2001, p. 8.

Labor of Love

196–98 [Chirolla] Author interview with Maria Cristina Chirolla, December 2004; "Wide Angle: An Honest Citizen" (documentary film), Thirteen/WNET for PBS, premiered September 16, 2004; Angus MacQueen, "The White Stuff," *The Guardian*, January 9, 2005; Maria Cristina Chirolla, "Personal Reflections: Relieving Pain and Suffering in Colombia: One Regulator's Journey," *Innovations in End-of-Life Care* 5, no. 1, January 27, 2003 (January–February 2003).

CHAPTER 10: CITIZENS VS. CRIMINALS

199–200 [Merbau Trade and EIA bust] Environmental Investigation Agency (EIA) and Telapak, "The Last Frontier: Illegal Logging in Papua and China's Massive Timber Theft," February 2005.

200–201 [Svay Pak] "Children for Sale: *Dateline* Goes Undercover with a Human Rights Group to Expose Sex Trafficking in Cambodia," MSNBC.com, January 30, 2004; "Cambodian Police Close Dozens of Child-Sex Brothels," *Independent*, January 25, 2003; "The Skin Trade: High-Profile Investigations into Pedophilia Are Headline News," *Independent*, January 22, 2003; Mark Baker, "A Sick Trade Flourishes," *The Age*, July 13, 2002; "Cambodian Brothels under Threat," BBC News Online, July 5, 2003; Christopher St. John, "Trafficking's Lasting Limbo: Former Sex Workers Face Slow Repatriation, Recovery," *Cambodia Daily*, December 13–14, 2003; "Cambodia Shuts Down Red-Light District," BBC News Online, January 23, 2003.

201 [International Justice Mission] Maggie Jones, "Thailand's Brothel Busters," *Mother Jones*, November–December 2003, p. 19; "Weblog: International Justice Mission Gets Notice and Results," *Christianity Today*, January 27, 2004; Henry Hoenig, "U.S. Group Battles Trade in SE Asia: Christian Organization Gets Federal Funds," *San Francisco Chronicle*, May 11, 2004, p. A1.

Day of the Advocates

202–4 [Rise of international civil society activism in the 1990s] See, for instance, Margaret Keck and Kathryn Sikkink, *Activists Beyond Borders: Advocacy Networks in International Politics* (Ithaca, NY: Cornell University Press, 1998); Thomas Carothers, "Think Again: Civil Society," *Foreign Policy*, winter 1999–2000, pp. 18–24; Nicanor Perlas, "Civil Society: The Third Global Power," *INFO* 3 (Germany), April 2001.

204–5 [AFESIP and IJM friction] Hoenig, "U.S. Group Battles Trade in SE Asia."

205 [Solidarity Center] "Migration and Trafficking," Solidarity Center. Online at http://www.solidaritycenter.org/our_programs/counter_trafficking/

205 [Dispute between Angel Coalition and pro-liberalization groups that it suspected of being fronts] Donna M. Hughes, "Prostitution in Russia," *National Review* online, November 21, 2002.

Selling the Issue

206 [Small arms survey] *Small Arms Survey 2004: Rights at Risk* (Geneva: Graduate Institute of International Studies, 2004).

206 [Viva Rio] "Brazilian Gun Buyback Exceeds Expectations," Associated Press, December 23, 2004.

206 [Russia, Angel Coalition helps draft antitrafficking law] "Bill Makes Human Trafficking a Crime," *Moscow Times,* February 19, 2003; Nabi Abdullaev, "Ministry Bemoans Problems of Fighting the Sex Trade," *Moscow Times,* August 28, 2002.

206–7 [Harm Reduction approach] James A. Inciardi and Lana D. Harrison, eds., *Harm Reduction: National and International Perspectives* (New York: Sage Publications, 2000), and *Harm Reduction Journal,* a journal on all aspects of minimizing the adverse effects of psychoactive drugs, at www.harmreductionjournal.com

206–7 [Ethan Nadelmann and Drug Policy Alliance] Jacob Sullum, "Mind Alteration: Drug-Policy Scholar Ethan Nadelmann on Turning People against Drug Prohibition," ReasonOnline, 1994. Online at http://reason.com/Nadelman.shtml

Business Brigades

208 [Software police] Business Software Alliance, http://www.bsa.org; on founding of BSA, see "Amnesty in May Will Let Firms Check for Software Violations," *Business Journal,* April 26, 2002, p. 7.

209 [1997 Singapore Raid] "Piracy Raid on Singapore Computer Firm, Shares Suspended," Agence France-Presse, August 13, 1997.

209–10 [Chinese pharmaceutical manufacturers hire private investigators] Peter S. Goodman, "China's Killer Headache," *Washington Post,* August 30, 2002, p. A1.

210 [seeking whistle-blowers] "Protecting Your Business from Software Piracy and the Trouble It Brings," *Broward Daily Business Review,* June 9, 2004.

210 [BSA lobbying in Asia] Bruce Einhorn, "China Learns to Say, 'Stop, Thief!'" *Business Week* Online, February 11, 2003; Phusadee Arunmas, "Software Group Concerned about Thailand's Intellectual Property Law," *Bangkok Post,* May 23, 2003.

210–11 [Other industry groups] "Music Piracy: Serious, Violent, and Organised Crime," IFPI report, January 2004; "The Pirates among Us," *CIO* magazine, April 15, 2003; [MPA and IFPI in raid] "Hong Kong Court Sentences Disc Pirate Couple To 6 1/2 Years," *Consumer Electronics Daily,* July 21, 2004; "BASCAP Operations Plan," Business Action to Stop Counterfeiting and Piracy, November 9, 2004. Online at http://www.iccwbo.org/home/BASCAP/BASCAP_Ops.pdf.; Lew Kontnik, "Counterfeits: The Cost of Combat," *Pharmaceutical Executive* 23, no. 11, November 1, 2003.

212 [American Chemical Council working with DEA] Kevin G. Hall, "Cocaine War's Neglected Front," *San Jose Mercury News,* November 22, 2000, p. 11A.

Reporters in the Crossfire

213 [Sufi Mohammed Khan] "Pakistan 2000: Country Report," Committee to Protect Journalists. Online at http://www.cpj.org/attacks00/asia00/Pakistan.html

213 [Georgy Gongadze] "Ukraine 2000: Country Report," Committee to Protect Journalists, September 20, 2002. Online at http://www.cpj.org/attacks00/europe00/Ukraine.html

213 [Tim Lopes] "Brazil: Police Arrest Suspect in Journalist's Murder," Committee to Protect Journalists. Online at http://www.cpj.org/news/2002/Brazil20sept02na.html

213 [Antonio Martínez Guttiérez] Committee to Protect Journalists statement, March 27, 2001.

213 [Francisco Arratia; Jesus Blancornelas and Francisco Ortiz] Tim Gaynor, "Journalists under Fire in Mexico Border Drug War," Reuters, February 14, 2005.

214 [ICIJ] International Consortium of Investigative Journalists (ICIJ), *Making a Killing: The Business of War* (Washington: Center for Public Integrity, 2003).

Small Battles, Large War

214–15 [Rise of the NGOs] Jessica Mathews, "Power Shift," *Foreign Affairs* 76, no. 1 (January–February 1997): pp. 50–66. See also Keck and Sikkink, *Activists Beyond Borders;* Thomas Homer-Dixon, "The Rise of Complex Terrorism," *Foreign Policy,* January–February 2002, pp. 52–62; Sebastian Mallaby, "NGOs: Fighting Poverty, Hurting the Poor," *Foreign Policy,* September–October 2004, pp. 50–58.

215 [Nuns killed] [Mozambique] "Body of Brazilian Nun to Be Flown Home," Associated Press, March 3, 2004. [Brazil] Michael Astor, "Brazilian Senate Commission Finds Wider Conspiracy in Killing of U.S. Nun," Associated Press, March 30, 2005.

215–16 [Proselytizing] Steve Hargreaves, "Cross Purposes: Federally Funded Missionaries Threaten a Southeast Asian Culture," *Village Voice,* January 29–February 4, 2003.

215 [U.S. evangelicals and feminists' coalition against sex trade] Nina Shapiro, "The New Abolitionists," *Seattle Weekly,* August 25–31, 2004; Jennifer Block, "Sex Trafficking: Why the Faith Trade Is Interested in the Sex Trade," *Conscience,* summer–autumn 2004; "Odd Coalition Unites on Human Trafficking," Associated Press, September 15, 2004.

CHAPTER 11: WHY WE ARE LOSING

Governments Are Failing

221 [Thailand] Anthony Davis, "Thai Drugs Smuggling Networks Reform," *Jane's Intelligence Review* 16, no. 12 (December 2004): p. 22.

221–22 [Mexico] Ginger Thompson and James C. McKinley Jr., "Mexico's Drug Cartels Wage Fierce Battle for Their Turf," *New York Times,* January 14, 2005.

222 [Truman/Reuter] Reuter and Truman, *Chasing Dirty Money* (Washington, DC: Institute for International Economics, 2004), p. 192; author interview with Ted Truman, Washington, February 7, 2005.

The Latest, Greatest Episode

222–23 [Salt trade] Mark Kurlansky, *Salt: A World History* (New York: Penguin, 2003).

The Network Transformation

224–26 [Networks] Phil Williams, "The Nature of Drug Trafficking Networks," *Current History,* April 1998, pp. 154–59; Peter Klerks, "The Network Paradigm Applied To Criminal Organisations: Theoretical Nitpicking or a Relevant Doctrine for Investigators? Recent Developments in the Netherlands," *Connections* 24, no. 3 (2001): pp. 53–65; Kathleen M. Carley, Ju-Sung Lee, David Krackhardt, "Destabilizing Networks," *Connections* 24, no. 3 (2001): pp. 79–92; Barry Wellman, "The Rise (and Possible Fall) of Networked Individualism," *Connections* 24, no. 3 (2001): pp. 30–32; Gerben Bruinsma and Wim Bernasco, "Criminal Groups and Transnational Illegal Markets: A More Detailed Examination on the Basis of Social Network Theory," *Crime, Law and Social Change*, no. 41, 2004, pp. 79–94; Jörg Raab and H. Brinton Milward, "Dark Networks as Problems," *Journal of Public Administration Research and Theory* 13, no. 4 (2003): pp. 413–39.

226–28   [Networks] John Arquilla and David Ronfeld, eds., *Networks and Netwars: The Future of Terror Crime and Militancy* (Santa Monica, CA: Rand, 2001), especially Phil Williams, "Transnational Criminal Networks," pp. 61ff, and also James Rauch and Alessandra Casella, eds., *Networks and Markets* (New York: Sage Publications, 2001).

An Unfair Fight?

231   National Commission on Terrorist Attacks upon the United States, *The 9/11 Commission Report* (New York: Norton, 2004). On bureaucracy, see discussion in chapter 9 above.

CHAPTER 12: WHAT TO DO?

Enhance, Develop, and Deploy Technology

243–44   [RFIDs, tags] Susan B. Schor, "RFID Tags May Not Reduce Drug Counterfeiting," CRM News, online at http://www.crmbuyer.com/story/38179.html, November 15, 2004; Eric Chabrow, "Homeland Security to Test RFID Tags at U.S. Borders," *Security Pipeline*, January 25, 2005; John Blau, "Prepare for the One-Cent RFID Tag," *Techworld*, January 14, 2005; Stephen D. Nightingale, "State-of-Art Operations: New Technologies for Food Traceability, Package, and Product Markers," *Food Safety Magazine*, August–September 2004; "Mobile Technologies Set to Revolutionise Manufacturing and Retail Sectors," Technews, May 2004, online at http://securitysa.com/news.asp?pklNewsID =14249&pklIssueID =457&pklCategoryID=13

244   [Biometrics] Shane Harris, "Biometrics Need a Measure of Security," GovExec.com, July 15, 2003; Greta Wodele, "Delays in Deploying Biometrics Aggravate Key Lawmakers," GovExec.com, May 19, 2004; David McGlinchey, "Border Chief Touts Biometrics as Security Tool," GovExec.com, September 23, 2004; "EU Biometric IDs on Track," ComputerWeekly.com, December 3, 2004; Kevin Poulsen, "EU goes on Biometric LSD Trip," *The Register (UK)*, February 3, 2005.

244   [Backscatter portal, puffers, scanners] Ryan Singel, "New Screening Technology Is Nigh," Wired News, online at www.wired.com, October 19, 2004; Matthew L. Wald, "New High-Tech Passports Raise Snooping Concerns," *New York Times*, November 26, 2004; "The Evolution of the Photofit," *The Economist Technology Quarterly*, December 4, 2004.

244–45   [Surveillance] See Robert O'Harrow Jr., *No Place to Hide: Behind the Scenes of Our Emerging Surveillance Society* (New York: Free Press, 2005);

Patrick Radden Keefe, *Chatter: Dispatches from the Secret World of Global Eavesdropping* (New York: Random House, 2005); Jason Ackleson "Border Security Technologies: Local and Regional Implications," *Review of Policy Research* 22, no. 2 (2005): p. 137ff. See also Matthew Brzezinski, *Fortress America: On the Frontlines of Homeland Security—An Inside Look at the Coming Surveillance State* (New York: Bantam Books, 2004).

245 [Anti–money laundering detection software] Jessica Pallay, "Brokers Will Spend Big on Anti–Money Laundering," Wall Street & Technology Online, www.wallstreetandtech.com, May 1, 2003; Peggy Bresnick Kendler, "Executive Roundtable: Combating Money-Laundering," *Security Pipeline,* January 30, 2005.

245 [Subcutaneous GPS chips in Brazil] David Rowan, "The Personal Microchip Is Being Touted as the Next-Generation Identity Card," *The Times (London),* February 27, 2002.

245 [Anticocaine vaccine] David Finn, "Vaccine Aids Cocaine Addicts," *Financial Times,* June 15, 2004.

246–47 [Debate on technology and rights] "Move Over, Big Brother," *The Economist Technology Quarterly,* December 4, 2004; Amitai Etzioni, *The Limits of Privacy* (New York: Basic Books, 2000).

Defragment Government

247 [FBI computer problems] Dan Eggen, "Computer Woes Hinder FBI's Work, Report Says," *Washington Post,* February 4, 2005. The U.S. senator quoted is Patrick J. Leahy (D-VT).

247–48 [Bureaucratic problems at U.S. Department of Homeland Security] John Mintz, "Infighting Cited at Homeland Security: Squabbles Blamed for Reducing Effectiveness," *Washington Post,* February 2, 2005. On the difficulties in establishing the Department of Homeland Security, see chapter 9.

248 [Waste and inefficiency in U.S. agencies in charge of port and airport security] Clark Kent Ervin, "Mission: Difficult, but Not Impossible," *New York Times,* December 27, 2004; Editorial: "Follow the Port Security Money," *New York Times,* February 28, 2005.

Give Government Goals It Can Achieve

251 [Decriminalization of soft drugs] Robert J. Macoun and Peter Reuter, *Drug War Heresies: Learning from Other Vices, Times, and Places* (New York: Cambdrige University Press, 2001); Ethan Nadelmann, "An End to Marijuana Prohibition," *National Review,* September 9, 2004, p. 7.

253 [On better policies to manage illegal immigration] Gary Becker, "The Wise Way to Stem Illegal Immigration," *Business Week,* April 26, 2004; Demetrios Papademetriou, "Responding To Clandestine Migration: Economic Migrants? Trends in Global Migration" (Toronto: Caledon Institute of Social Policy, June 2000); Demetrios Papademetriou, "The Shifting Expectations of Free Trade and Migration," *NAFTA's Promise and Reality: Lessons from Mexico for the Hemisphere* (Washington, DC: Carnegie Endowment for International Peace, 2003).

253–54 [Sweden's approach to prostitution] "Swedish Message," *The Economist,* September 4, 2004.

254 [Tom Ridge on complexity of task] Tom Ridge, "Global Security Depends on Joint Action," *Financial Times,* January 13, 2005.

Political Will

258   [U.S. senator on legalizing drugs] Author interview, Washington, DC, August 28, 2004.

CHAPTER 13: THE WORLD AHEAD

261   [Geopolitical black holes] This term was first used to describe failed states by Italian editor Lucio Carraciolo and *La Stampa* China correspondent Francesco Sisci. See Francesco Sisci, "Black Holes and Rogue States," *Asia Times* online, March 2, 2005.
261–62   [Costa del Sol] Leslie Crawford, "Hot Money Pays for Boom on Spain's Costa del Crime," *Financial Times*, March 23, 2005. For a fictionalized account of criminal activities in the Costa del Sol and its global connections, see Arturo Perez Reverte, *Queen of the South* (New York: Putnam, 2002).
262   [FBI busts Russian arms dealers in New York City] *United States v. Artur Solomonyan, Christian Dewet Spies, et al.* United States Magistrate Judge, Southern District of New York, March 2005, p. 20; Julia Preston, "Arms Network Is Broken Up, Officials Say," *New York Times*, March 16, 2005.

Black Holes vs. Bright Spots

264   [Dutch government fighting trafficking network from Suriname] U.S. Department of State, "International Narcotics Control Strategy Report, 2003," Bureau for International Narcotics and Law Enforcement Affairs, March 2004; Suriname Drug Information Network, "Annual National Report, 2002," December 30, 2002.
264   [Weber] Max Weber, "Politik als Beruf (Politics as a Vocation)," speech given at Munich University, Munich, Germany, 1918; translated in Max Weber, *From Max Weber: Essays in Sociology* (New York: Oxford University Press, 1946), p. 78. ("A state is a human community that claims the *monopoly of the legitimate use of physical force* within a given territory.")
264   [Commonly used definition of nation-state] Article 1 of the Montevideo Convention on the Rights and Duties of States, a treaty signed at the Seventh International Conference of American States on December 26, 1933, in Montevideo, Uruguay.
264   [Multiple authorities exert control over the same territory] James Anderson, "The Shifting Stage of Politics: New Medieval and Postmodern Territorialities," *Environment and Planning: Society and Space* 14 (1996): pp. 133–53; Stephen J. Kobrin, "Back To the Future: Neomedievalism and the Postmodern Digital World Economy," *Journal of International Affairs*, spring 1998; and Bruno Tesche, "Geopolitical Relations in the Middle Ages: History and Theory," *International Organization* 52, no. 20 (spring 1998): pp. 325–58.

A Different Chessboard

266–67   [Condoleezza Rice's pre-9/11 opinions about the main challenges facing the United States] Condoleezza Rice, "Promoting the National Interest," *Foreign Affairs,* January–February 2000, pp. 45–62.

268 [Condoleezza Rice's post-9/11 comments] James Harding and Richard Wolffe, " 'We Worry a Good Deal More . . . September 11 Clarified the Threats You Face in a Post-Cold-War Era': Interview with Condoleezza Rice," *Financial Times,* September 23, 2002, p. 21.

268 [National missile defense goals and budget] U.S. Congress. *National Missile Defense Act of 1999.* 106th Cong., 1st Sess., H.R. 4 (January 6, 1999); U.S. Department of Defense, Missile Defense Agency, "Historical Funding for MDA, FY85–05," 2005.

268 [Low investment in U.S. port security] Department of Homeland Security, Office of the Inspector General, "Review of the Port Security Grant Program," OIG-05-10, January 2005.

269 [2008 deadline to secure Russian nuclear material] Peter Baker and Walter Pincus, "U.S.-Russia Pact Aimed at Nuclear Terrorism," *Washington Post,* February 24, 2005, p. A1.

Well-Worn Lenses

269 [Realist theories and thinkers] John Mearsheimer, *The Tragedy of Great Power Politics* (New York: Norton, 2001); Robert G. Gilpin Jr., "Realism," *Encyclopedia of U.S. Foreign Relations* (New York: Oxford University Press, 1997), pp. 462–64; Fareed Zakaria, *From Wealth To Power: The Unusual Origins of America's World Role* (Princeton, NJ: Princeton University Press, 1998); Michael C. Williams, *The Realist Tradition and the Limits of International Relations* (Cambridge and New York: Cambridge University Press, Cambridge Studies in International Relations, 2005).

269 [Otto von Bismarck and Realpolitik] Henry Kissinger, *Diplomacy* (New York: Simon & Schuster, 1994), p. 121; Otto Pflanze, *Bismarck and the Development of Germany* (Princeton, NJ: Princeton University Press, 1990).

270 [Recent reviews of international relations theories] Stephen M. Walt, "International Relations: One World, Many Theories," *Foreign Policy,* spring 1998, pp. 29–45; Jack Snyder, "One World, Rival Theories," *Foreign Policy,* November–December 2004, pp. 52–62. Also Louis Klarevas, "Political Realism: A Culprit for the 9/11 Attacks," *Harvard International Review,* fall 2004, pp. 18–23.

270–71 [Liberal tradition in international relations] Bruce Russett and John R. Oneal, *Triangulating Peace: Democracy, Interdependence, and International Organizations* (New York: Norton, 2001), and G. John Ikenberry, *After Victory: Institutions, Strategic Restraint, and the Rebuilding of Order after Major Wars* (Princeton, NJ: Princeton University Press, 2001). See also Andrew Moravcsik, "Taking Preferences Seriously: A Liberal Theory of International Politics," *International Organization,* autumn 1997.

271 [Constructivism in international relations] Alexander Wendt, *Social Theory of International Politics* (New York: Cambridge University Press, 1999); Margaret E. Keck and Kathryn Sikkink, *Activists Beyond Borders: Advocacy Networks in International Politics* (Ithaca, NY: Cornell University Press, 1998); Alexander Wendt, "Why a World State Is Inevitable: Teleology and the Logic of Anarchy," *European Journal of International Relations* 9, no. 4, pp. 491–542.

271 [Neocons and their role in the Bush administration] Max Boot, "Think Again: Neocons," *Foreign Policy,* January–February 2004, pp. 20–28. See also Robert

Kagan and Irving Kristol, "A Distinctly American Internationalism," *Weekly Standard,* November 29, 1999.

272 [Snyder] Snyder, "One World, Rival Theories."

272–73 [Pre-9/11 meeting at the White House] Richard Clarke, *Against All Enemies* (New York: Free Press, 2004), pp. 231–32.

Asymmetric Borders

273 [Smuggling in North Korea] Jonathan Watts, "Frozen Frontier Where Illicit Trade with China Offers Lifeline for Isolated North Koreans," *The Guardian,* January 9, 2004.

Hollowed-Out Sovereignty

274–75 [Sovereignty] John Ruggie, *Constructing the World Polity: Essays on International Institutionalization* (London: Routledge, 1998); Stephen D. Krasner, *Sovereignty: Organized Hypocrisy* (Princeton, NJ: Princeton University Press, 1999); and also Krasner's two articles: "Think Again: Sovereignty," *Foreign Policy,* January–February 2001, pp. 20–29, and "Sharing Sovereignty: New Institutions for Collapsed and Failed States," *International Security* 29 (fall 2004): pp. 85–120.

275 [OSCE report; Helga Konrad] Special representative on Combating Trafficking in Human Beings, *Stop Human Trafficking,* Organization for Security and Cooperation in Europe, March 11, 2005; "Report Says People-Smuggling on Increase in Europe," *Reuters,* March 31, 2005.

275 [Illegal immigrants tripled in Spain between 2001 and 2005] David Unger, "An Immigration Experiment Worth Watching in Spain," *New York Times,* March 20, 2005.

275–76 [Illegal immigrant flows to the United States same as during the 1990s] Sylvia Moreno, "Flow of Illegal Immigrants to U.S. Unabated," *Washington Post,* March 22, 2005.

Cherchez l'État

278 [Mexican commander jailed] Julia Preston and Craig Pyes, "Mexican Tale: Drugs, Crime, Corruption, and the U.S.," *New York Times,* August 18, 1997; Procuraduria General De La Republica, Mexico, Press Release No. 510/00, September 28, 2000. Online at http://www.pgr.gob.mx/cmsocial/press00/sep/pr510.html

278 [Lithuanian president Paksas impeached] Mark Galeotti, "The Paksas Affair," *Jane's Intelligence Review,* January 2005, p. 25.

278 [U.S. government accusations of North Korean officials' involvement in drug trafficking] U.S. Department of State, Bureau for International Narcotics and Law Enforcement Affairs, "2003 International Narcotics Control Strategy Report," March 1, 2004.

278 [Montesinos in jail] "New Jail Term for Peru Spy Chief," BBC News Online, June 29, 2004.

278 [Chinese military officials involved in counterfeiting] "No More Business as Ususal," *Asiaweek,* December 6, 2000; Ted C. Fishman, "Manufaketure;" "People's Republic of Cheats," *Far Eastern Economic Review,* June 21, 2001.

279   [Pakistani government's relationship with A. Q. Khan's nuclear smuggling]
"State Department Spokesman Adam Ereli Has Unequivocally Absolved the
Pakistani Leadership of Any Role in Dr. A. Q. Khan Proliferation Network's Op-
eration," *The Nation,* March 21, 2005; U.S. State Department daily briefing,
March 17, 2005; author interview with Pakistani expert Husein Haqqani,
Washington, DC, September 16, 2004.

279   [Sale of nuclear-capable missiles by Ukrainian arms dealers] Aleksandar Vaso-
vic, "Ukrainians Sold Missiles To Iran, China, Prosecutors Say," *Washington
Post,* March 19, 2005.

The World Ahead

281   [Smith] Adam Smith, *An Inquiry into the Nature and Causes of the Wealth of
Nations* (New York: Modern Library, 1994), book 5, chapter 2, article 4.

Andreas, Peter, and Timothy Snyder, eds. *The Wall around the West: State Borders and Immigration Controls in North America and Europe.* New York and Oxford: Rowman & Littlefield, 2000.

Arquilla, John, and David Ronfeld, eds. *In Athena's Camp: Preparing for Conflict in the Information Age.* Santa Monica, CA: Rand, 1998.

———. *Networks and Netwars: The Future of Terror, Crime, and Militancy.* Santa Monica, CA: Rand, 2001.

Azzara, Thomas. *Tax Havens of the World,* 7th ed. Nassau, Bahamas: New Providence Press, 1999.

Bales, Kevin. *Disposable People: New Slavery in the Global Economy.* Berkeley and Los Angeles: University of California Press, 1999.

Bannon, Ian, and Paul Collier, eds. *Natural Resources and Violent Conflict.* Washington: World Bank, 2003.

Barabasi, Albert-Laszlo. *Linked: The New Science of Networks.* Cambridge MA: Perseus Publishing, 2002.

Barnett, Michael, and Raymond Duvall, eds. *Power in Global Governance.* Cambridge, UK: Cambridge University Press, 2005.

Barnett, Thomas P. M. *The Pentagon's New Map: War and Peace in the Twenty-First Century.* New York: G. P. Putnam's Sons, 2004.

Becker, Jasper. *Rogue Regime: Kim Jong Il and the Looming Threat of North Korea.* Oxford, UK: Oxford University Press, 2005.

Bhagwati, Jagdish. *In Defense of Globalization.* Oxford, UK: Oxford University Press, 2004.

Bobbitt, Philip. *The Shield of Achilles: War, Peace, and the Course of History.* New York: Anchor Books, 2003.

Brown, Michael E., Owen R. Cote, Sean M. Lynn-Jones, and Steven Miller, eds. *New Global Dangers: Changing Dimensions of International Security.* Cambridge, MA: MIT Press, 2004.

Brzezinski, Matthew. *Fortress America: On the Frontlines of Homeland Security; An Inside Look at the Coming Surveillance State.* New York: Bantam Books, 2004.

Carpenter, Ted Galen. *Bad Neighbor Policy: Washington's Futile War on Drugs in Latin America.* New York: Palgrave, 2003.

Casella, Alessandra, and James Rauch, eds. *Networks and Markets.* New York: Sage Publications, 2001.

Chalk, Peter, and Angel Rabasa. *Colombian Labyrinth: The Synergy of Drugs and Insurgency and Its Implications for Regional Stability.* Santa Monica, CA: RAND Project Air Force, 2001.

Clarke, Richard. *Against All Enemies.* New York: Free Press, 2004.

Cusimano, Maryann, ed. *Beyond Sovereignty: Issues for a Global Agenda.* New York: St. Martin's Press, 2002.

Dahlby, Tracy. *Allah's Torch: A Report from Behind the Scenes in Asia's War on Terror.* New York: William Morrow, 2005.

Dixit, Avinash. *Lawlessness and Economics: Alternative Modes of Governance*. Princeton, NJ: Princeton University Press, 2004.

Encyclopedia of U.S. Foreign Relations. New York: Oxford University Press, 1997.

Environmental Investigation Agency. *Lost in Transit: Global CFC Smuggling Trends and the Need for a Faster Phase-Out*. London: EIA, November 2003.

Etzioni, Amitai. *The Limits of Privacy*. New York: Basic Books, 2000.

Farah, Douglas. *Blood from Stones: The Secret Financial Network of Terror*. New York: Broadway Books, 2004.

Farazmand, Ali, ed. *Modern Systems of Government: Exploring the Role of Bureaucrats and Politicians*. New York: Sage Publications, 1997.

Federal Bureau of Investigation. *Crime in America: FBI Uniform Crime Reports, 2003*. Washington, DC: U.S. Government Printing Office, 2004.

Finger, Michael J., and Philip Schuler, eds. *Poor People's Knowledge: Promoting Intellectual Property in Developing Countries*. Washington, DC: World Bank, 2004.

Freeland, Chrystia. *Sale of the Century: Russia's Wild Ride from Communism To Capitalism*. New York: Times Books, 2000.

Friedman, Thomas L. *The Lexus and the Olive Tree: Understanding Globalization*. New York: Farrar, Straus and Giroux, 1999.

———. *The World Is Flat: A Brief History of the Twenty-first Century*. New York: Farrar, Straus and Giroux, 2005.

Friman, Richard R., and Peter Andreas, eds. *The Illicit Global Economy and State Power*. New York: Rowman & Littlefield, 1999.

———. *NarcoDiplomacy: Exporting the U.S. War on Drugs*. Ithaca, NY: Cornell University Press, 1996.

Fukuyama, Francis. *State Building: Governance and World Order in the Twenty first Century*. Ithaca, NY: Cornell University Press, 2004.

Hironaka, Ann. *Neverending Wars: The International Community, Weak States, and the Perpetuation of Civil War*. Cambridge, MA: Harvard University Press, 2005.

Ikenberry, G. John. *After Victory: Institutions, Strategic Restraint, and the Rebuilding of Order after Major Wars*. Princeton, NJ: Princeton University Press, 2001.

Inciardi, James A., and Lana D. Harrison, eds. *Harm Reduction: National and International Perspectives*. New York: Sage Publications, 2000.

International Consortium of Investigative Journalists (ICIJ). *Making a Killing: The Business of War*. Washington, DC: Center for Public Integrity, 2003.

International Federation of Phonographic Industries. *The Recording Industry Commercial Piracy Report, 2004*. London: IFPI, July 2004.

International Monetary Fund. *World Economic Outlook: Globalization and External Imbalances*. Washington, DC: IMF, April 2005.

Kahin, Brian, and Hal R. Varian, eds. *Internet Publishing and Beyond: The Economics of Digital Information and Intellectual Property*. Cambridge, MA: MIT Press, 2000.

Kaplan, Robert D. *The Coming Anarchy: Shattering the Dreams of the Post Cold War*. New York: Random House, 2000.

Keck, Margaret, and Kathryn Sikkink. *Activists Beyond Borders: Advocacy Networks in International Politics*. Ithaca, NY: Cornell University Press, 1998.

Keefe, Patrick Radden. *Chatter: Dispatches from the Secret World of Global Eavesdropping*. New York: Random House, 2005.

Kirk, Robin. *More Terrible than Death: Massacres, Drugs, and America's War in Colombia*. New York: Public Affairs, 2003.

Kissinger, Henry. *Diplomacy*. New York: Simon & Schuster, 1994.

Krasner, Stephen D. *Sovereignty: Organized Hypocrisy.* Princeton, NJ: Princeton University Press, 1999.

Kurkchiyan, Marina, and Alena V. Ledeneva, eds. *Economic Crime in Russia.* New York: Kluwer Law International, 2000.

Kurlansky, Mark. *Salt: A World History.* New York: Penguin, 2003.

Kyle, David, and Rey Koslowsky, eds. *Global Human Smuggling: Comparative Perspectives.* Baltimore: Johns Hopkins University Press, 2001.

Lal, Deepak. *In Praise of Empires: Globalization and Order.* New York: Palgrave Macmillan, 2004.

Laufer, Peter. *Wetback Nation: The Case for Opening the Mexican-American Border.* Chicago: Ivan R. Dee, 2004.

Lennon, Alexander T. J., ed. *The Battle for Hearts and Minds: Using Soft Power to Undermine Terrorist Networks.* Cambridge, MA: MIT Press, 2003.

Library of Congress, Federal Research Division. *Organized Crime and Terrorist Activity in Mexico, 1999–2002.* Washington, DC: Library of Congress, 2003.

Lumpe, Lora, ed. *Running Guns: The Global Black Market in Small Arms.* London: Zed Books, 2000.

Macoun, Robert J., and Peter Reuter. *Drug War Heresies: Learning from Other Vices, Times, and Places.* New York: Cambridge University Press, 2001.

Marez, Curtis. *Drug Wars: The Political Economy of Narcotics.* Minneapolis: University of Minnesota Press, 2004.

Mearsheimer, John. *The Tragedy of Great Power Politics.* New York: Norton, 2001.

Miron, Jeffrey A. *Drug War Crimes: The Consequences of Prohibition.* Oakland, CA: Independent Institute, 2004.

Nadelman, Ethan A. *Cops across Borders: The Internationalization of U.S. Criminal Law.* University Park, PA: Pennsylvania State University Press, 1993.

Napoleoni, Loretta. *Modern Jihad: Tracing the Dollars behind the Terror Networks.* London: Pluto Press, 2003.

National Commission on Terrorist Attacks upon the United States. *The 9/11 Commission Report.* New York: Norton, 2004.

National Research Council, National Academy of Sciences. *Informing America's Policy on Illegal Drugs: What We Don't Know Keeps Hurting Us.* Washington, DC: National Academy Press, 2001.

Naylor, R. T. *Wages of Crime: Black Markets, Illegal Finance, and the Underworld Economy.* Ithaca, NY: Cornell University Press, 2002, and 2004 rev. ed.

Nordstrom, Caroline. *Shadows of War: Violence, Power, and International Profiteering in the Twenty-first Century.* Berkeley and Los Angeles: University of California Press, 2004.

O'Harrow, Robert Jr. *No Place to Hide: Behind the Scenes of Our Emerging Surveillance Society.* New York: Free Press, 2005.

Oneal, John R., and Bruce Russett. *Triangulating Peace: Democracy, Interdependence, and International Organizations.* New York: Norton, 2001.

Organisation for Security and Cooperation in Europe, Special Representative on Combating Trafficking in Human Beings. *Stop Human Trafficking.* Vienna: OSCE, March 11, 2005.

Palan, Ronen. *The Offshore World: Sovereign Markets, Virtual Places, and Nomad Millionaires.* Ithaca and London: Cornell University Press, 2003.

Papademetriou, Demetrios. *Responding To Clandestine Migration: Economic Migrants? Trends in Global Migration.* Toronto: Caledon Institute of Social Policy, June 2000.

————et al. *NAFTA's Promise and Reality: Lessons from Mexico for the Hemisphere.* Washington, DC: Carnegie Endowment for International Peace, 2003.

Perez Reverte, Arturo. *Queen of the South.* New York: Putnam, 2002.

Pflanze, Otto. *Bismarck and the Development of Germany.* Princeton, NJ: Princeton University Press, 1990.

Pieth, Mark, ed. *Financing Terrorism.* Boston: Kluwer Academic Publishers, 2002.

Rabkin, Jeremy A. *Law without Nations: Why Constitutional Government Requires Sovereign States.* Princeton, NJ: Princeton University Press, 2005.

Reuter, Peter, and Edwin M. Truman. *Chasing Dirty Money: The Fight against Money Laundering.* Washington, DC: Institute for International Economics, 2004.

Rheingold, Howard. *Smart Mobs: The Next Social Revolution.* New York: Perseus Books, 2002.

Riedel, Philip, ed. *Handbook of Transnational Crime and Justice.* Thousand Oaks, CA: Sage Publications, 2005.

Robinson, Jeffrey. *The Merger: The Conglomeration of International Organized Crime.* Woodstock, NY: Overlook Press, 2000.

Rotberg, Robert, ed. *When States Fail: Causes and Consequences.* Princeton, NJ: Princeton University Press, 2004.

Ruggie, John. *Constructing the World Polity: Essays on International Institutionalization.* London: Routledge, 1998.

Sampson, Anthony. *The Arms Bazaar: From Lebanon To Lockheed.* New York: Viking, 1977.

Satter, David. *Darkness at Dawn: The Rise of the Russian Criminal State.* New Haven: Yale University Press, 2004.

Schwartz, Peter. *Inevitable Surprises: Thinking Ahead in a Time of Turbulence.* New York: Gotham, 2004.

Scotchmer, Suzanne. *Innovation and Incentives.* Cambridge, MA: MIT Press, 2005.

Slaughter, Anne Marie. *A New World Order.* Princeton, NJ: Princeton University Press, 2004.

Small Arms Survey 2003: Development Denied. Geneva: Graduate Institute of International Studies, 2003.

Small Arms Survey 2004: Rights at Risk. Geneva: Graduate Institute of International Studies, 2004.

Smith, Adam. *An Inquiry into the Nature and Causes of the Wealth of Nations.* New York: Modern Library, 1994 edition.

Stares, Paul B. *Global Habit: The Drug Problem in a Borderless World.* Washington, DC: Brookings, 1996.

Tanzi, Vito. *Policies, Institutions, and the Dark Side of Economics.* Cheltenham, UK: Edward Elgar, 2000.

United Nations Conference on Trade and Development. *World Investment Report, 2004.* Geneva: UNCTAD Press Unit, September 22, 2004.

United Nations Office on Drugs and Crime. *2004 World Drug Report: Executive Summary.* Geneva: UNODC, 2004.

————. *Global Illicit Drug Trends.* Vienna: UNODC, 2003.

United Nations Population Fund and UN Information Service. *State of the World's Cities, 2004/2005: Globalization and Urban Culture.* London: UN-HABITAT, 2004.

United States Department of Justice, National Drug Intelligence Center. *Heroin Distribution in Three Cities.* Washington, DC: November 2000.

United States Department of Justice, Office of the Inspector General. *The Internal*

Effects of the Federal Bureau of Investigation's Reprioritization. Washington, DC: September 2004.

United States Department of State, Bureau for International Narcotics and Law Enforcement Affairs. *International Narcotics Control Strategy Report, 2003.* Washington, DC: March 2004.

———. *International Narcotics Control Strategy Report, 2005.* Washington, DC: March 2005.

United States Department of State, Office to Monitor and Combat Trafficking in Persons. *Trafficking in Persons Report.* Washington, DC: June 14, 2004.

United States, Government Accounting Office. *Nonproliferation: Further Improvements Needed to Counter Threats from Man-Portable Air Defense Systems.* Washington, DC: May 2004.

United States Treasury Department. *National Money Laundering Strategy.* Washington, DC: July 2002.

Weber, Max. *From Max Weber: Essays in Sociology.* New York: Oxford University Press, 1946.

Wendt, Alexander. *Social Theory of International Politics.* New York: Cambridge University Press, 1999.

Williams, Michael C. *The Realist Tradition and the Limits of International Relations.* Cambridge: Cambridge University Press, 2005.

Williams, Phil, ed. *Russian Organized Crime: The New Threat.* London: Frank Cass Publishers, 1997.

Wilson, James Q. *Bureaucracy: What Government Agencies Do and Why They Do It.* New York: Basic Books, 1989.

Wolf, Martin. *Why Globalization Works.* New Haven: Yale University Press, 2004.

Yergin, Daniel, and Stanislaw Joseph. *The Commanding Heights: The Battle between Government and the Marketplace That Is Remaking the Modern World.* New York: Simon & Schuster, 1998.

Zakaria, Fareed. *From Wealth To Power: The Unusual Origins of America's World Role.* Princeton, NJ: Princeton University Press, 1998.

ACKNOWLEDGMENTS

I wrote this book while simultaneously working full-time as editor of *Foreign Policy* magazine. Therefore, my first words of gratitude are for my boss, Jessica Mathews, president of the Carnegie Endowment for International Peace, publisher of *Foreign Policy*. The ample autonomy that she, along with the Board of Trustees of the endowment, have afforded me in running the magazine is a privilege for which I will be forever grateful. Readers familiar with Jessica's own pathbreaking writings will recognize her intellectual influence on this book. She also offered valuable comments on an earlier draft.

I am especially grateful to my colleagues at *Foreign Policy*, who kept the magazine firmly on its successful path during my absences: Lynn Newhouse, Will Dobson, Travis Daub, Mark Strauss, Carlos Lozada, and James Gibney. James also helpfully commented on a few chapters. My thanks to them as well as to my current and past *FP* colleagues: David Bosco, Laura Peterson, Mike Boyer, James Forsyth, Kate Palmer, Amy Russell, Jai Singh, Jeff Marn, Sarah Schumacher, Kelly Peterson, Jen Kelley, Elizabeth Daigneau, Melinda Brouwer, and Leslie Palti. Eben Kaplan tracked down references and prepared the index with intelligence and dedication.

I owe very special thanks to Siddhartha Mitter. His contributions to this book as editor and intellectual interlocutor were essential. Siddhartha deployed his considerable talents in quickly mastering the ideas and the data on which this book is based, and in so doing became an indispensable colleague.

Early versions of the book were greatly improved by the comments and suggestions of a knowledgeable and thoughtful group of individuals who generously made time in their busy schedules to read preliminary drafts. My thanks to David Beal, John Deutch, Bill Emmott, Thomas L. Friedman, Francis Fukuyama, Jamie Gorelick, Ethan Nadelmann, Demetrios Papademetriou, George Perkovich, Strobe Talbott, Stephen Walt, Phil Williams, Jonathan Winer, and Fareed Zakaria. Thanks also to former presidents Ernesto Zedillo from Mexico and César Gaviria from Colombia, who also read the manuscript and offered useful comments.

I have benefited from conversations with a large number of people who shared with me their experience, information, and ideas or helped me gain access to others who had the information I needed. I want to thank in particular Mort Abramowitz, Mahsood Ahmed, Fouad Ajami, Jean Jacques Albin, Eduardo Amadeo, Diego Arria, Anders Åslund, Ricardo Avila, Maureen Baginski, Daniel Bradlow, Clara Brillembourg, Matt Burrows, Nick Butler, Antonio Carlucci, Lucio Carraciolo, Miguel Angel Carranza, Maria Cristina Chirolla, Roberto Dañino, Kemal Dervis, Karen DeYoung, Thomas Fingar, Christo Gradev, Lou Goodman, Richard Haas, Victor Halberstadt, Husain Haqqani, Diego Hidalgo, Michael Hirsch, Rudolph Hommes, Robert Hutchings, Adnan Ibrahim, Stephen Jukes, Ellis Juan, Ray Kendall, Stephen Kobrin, Caio Koch-Weser, Michael Kortan, Paul Laudicina, Dimitri Lazarescu, Viktor Magunin, Doris Meissner, Jim Moody, Luis Alberto Moreno, Andres Ortega, Nelson Ortiz, Soli Ozel, Ana Palacio, Andres Pastranq, Guy Pfeffermann, Gianni Riotta, David Rothkopf, Gonzalo Sanchez de Lozada, Alberto Slezynger, Somchai Supakar, Peter Schwartz, Zhang Tai, Vito Tanzi, Dimitri Trenin, Ted Truman, Martin Wolf, and Daniel Yergin.

Thanks are also due to my agent Rafe Sagalyn and to my editors Gerry Howard and Rakesh Satyal at Doubleday in New York, Ravi Mirchandani at Wm. Heinemann in London, Gianni Ferrari at Mondadori in Milan, and Cristobal Pera at MondadoriRandomHouse in Barcelona. My brother Giuseppe Naím has always been a source of good humor and unconditional support, as have his wife Isabel and their family, Deborah, Daniel, Patricia, and Sofía.

Finally, this book is dedicated to those at the core of my own personal network, the group of people that makes so many things possible and valuable: my wife, Susana, and our children, Adriana, Claudia, and Andrés.

and Europol 192, 256
and hazardous waste 168–69
human trafficking in 103–4
new members 18, 52
shared Sovereignty in 256, 258, 270
Europol 192
establishment of 256

Farah, Doug 29, 150
FARC see Revolutionary Armed Forces of
Colombia
Federal Air Marshals 177
Federal Bureau of Investigation (FBI) 68,
88, 181, 189, 262
and challenge of combating illicit trade
26, 32, 179, 183, 247
and interagency conflict 177
Federal Express 19, 24, 149
Federal Protective Service (FPS) 177
Federales 67, 192, 194
FedEx see Federal Express
Feingold, David 105
Fie chen 149
Financial Action Task Force (FATF)
151–53, 195, 255, 256
Financial Crimes Enforcement Network
(FinCEN) 131
Financial Times 126, 147, 261
FinCEN see Financial Crimes Enforce-
ment Network
Flags of convenience 63, 142
Foreign Affairs 266
Foreign Policy Magazine 9, 11, 270
Fort Tilden 86
Foujita, Tsuguharu 172
Fox, Vicente 67
France
and arms trade 47, 59
counterfeiting in 120
law enforcement in 181, 189, 190,
237
and sex trade 3, 92
French, Howard 96
Friedman, Thomas 20
Fujian Province
and Golden Venture 86
and migration 86–87, 99
Fujimori, Alberto 55

G7 151–152
G8 195, 255
Garcia, Michael 176, 178
Garcia Marquez, Gabriel 1
Gates, Bill 49, 109
Geery manufacturing company 119
General Motors (GM) 33, 109, 119
Geneva, Switzerland 62, 206
Geopolitical Black Holes 261–65

Geopolitical Bright Spots 263–65
Germany 269
and arms trade 46, 51, 59
and environmental crimes 165
and human organ trade 157
and human trafficking 38, 87, 90–91
and money laundering 146, 156
and sex trade 3
Ghana
and arms trade 52, 63
and drug trade 73
and end–user certificates 29
GIIB 71
Glasser, Susan 178
Golden Venture 86–87
Gonaives, Haiti 167
Gongadze, Georgy 213
Goss, Porter 179
Goya, Francisco 172
Graduate Institute of International Studies,
Geneva 206
Great Wall Sing SUV 119
Greece 10
and flags of convenience 142
and human smuggling 97, 101
and sex trade 30
Greenpeace 203, 206, 226
Grenada
and money laundering 141
Gu Yanwu 1
Guangzhou 16, 164, 209
Guardian 273
Guatemala
and human trafficking 90, 98, 103
Gucci 2, 112
Guess 111
Guinea-Bissau 167
Guiyu, China 168
Gulf Cartel 66, 221
Guzmán, Joaquin "El Chapo" 67, 76, 84

Hadley, Steve 272, 273
Hainan Island, China 162
Haiti 63, 167, 262
and drug trade 29
fake cough syrup in 15, 123,124
and remittances 96
Hamas 142
Hamburg
and terrorism 35
Haqqani, Hussain 45
Harm Reduction 206–7, 252
Harry Potter 109, 122
Harvard University 30, 207, 270
Hawalas 134, 149, 227
Hazardous waste trade 158, 167–69,
174
Hebrides see Vanuatu

Russia 9, 35, 195, 258, 269
  arms trade in 47, 51
  and counterfeiting 113, 121, 122
  corruption in 30
  drug use in 72
  law enforcement in 84, 153, 178, 192,
    205, 206
  and Leonid Minin 46
  and money laundering 145, 146, 152
  organized crime in 79, 126, 183, 278
  sex trade in 91–92, 205
Rwanda 63
  and arms trade 48, 62
  genocide in 62

SAIC company 119
Saipan 95
Salt trade 223
Sampson, Anthony 56
San Diego 33
San Jose, California 193
Sanchez de Lozada, Gonzalo 83
Sao Paulo, Brazil 51, 61, 245
Sarajevo 92
SARS 167
Saudi Arabia 57
Sayaf, Abu 56
Schengen group 19
Scomi engineering firm 39
Securicor company 61
Security Council see United Nations Secu-
    rity Council
Sellier & Bellot weapons manufacturer
    52
Sengupta, Somini 96
Serbia
  and arms trade 52
  and counterfeiting 25
Sex trade 1, 25, 72, 91–93, 96–97, 197,
    215, 229
  and children 3, 93, 105, 162, 178, 184,
    200–201, 204, 207
  and human trafficking 3, 13–14, 24, 30,
    91–93, 95, 102–3, 105, 107, 162,
    205, 213, 224, 227
  and law enforcement/advocacy groups
    105, 178, 200–201, 203–4, 205,
    207–8, 233, 234, 241, 251, 253
Seychelles 141, 142
Shanghai, China 12, 200
  and counterfeiting 122
Sharjah, United Arab Emirates 49
Shenzhen, China 126
Shenzhen Evening News 123
Sheik, Tourab Ahmed 87
Sheriff Company 58
Sierra Leone
  and arms trade 29, 46, 63

civil war in 55
  and conflict diamonds 29, 56, 150,
    215
Silk Alley 2
Silk Road 26
Sinaloa, Mexico 67, 84
Singapore 167
  and counterfeiting 109, 117
  as a trafficking hub 164, 170, 200
Slovakia
  and arms trade 63
  and sex trade 30
Small arms
  effects of 60–61
  in Iraq 53
  production of 50, 51, 52
  regulation of 62–64, 205
  trade in 15, 48
  in the United States 33, 51, 52,
    58–59
Small Arms Survey 53, 60, 206
SMB Computer company 39
Smiling Wolf Consultative 209
Smirnov, Igor 28
Smirnov, Vladimir 58
Smith & Wesson gun manufacturer 51
Smurfs 78, 240
Snakeheads 97, 98, 101, 240
Snyder, Jack 270–72
Soderbergh, Stephen 214
Solidarity Center 205
Solnetsevo Brotherhood 183
Solomonyan, Artur 262
Somalia 63, 167, 262
Sonora Desert 102
Sony 33, 111, 125
  and PlayStation2 consoles 126
Soros, George 207
South Africa
  and arms trade 41, 48, 63
  and CFCs 170–71
  and drug trade 72, 73
  and environmental crimes 16, 165–66
  and human organ trade 16, 157, 160,
    161
  and money laundering 63, 146
Sovereignty 13, 44, 57, 142, 190, 192,
    195, 214, 256, 258, 274–76, 277
Spain 229, 261–62
  and counterfeiting 121, 122, 128
  and drug trade 121, 181
  and human trafficking 108, 220, 227
  law enforcement in 194
  and migrant workers 90, 275
  and terrorism 127, 138, 237–38
Spark see Chevrolet
Sri Lanka 55
  and drug trade 227